THE TROPOHOLIC'S GUIDE TO UNIVERSAL THRILLER TROPES

THE TROPOHOLIC'S GUIDES

CINDY DEES

CYNTHIA DEES PUBLISHING INC

CONTENTS

INTRODUCTION

Go ahead. Groan. Everyone does when they hear the word trope.

In recent decades, the word trope has come to stand for clichéd, trite, boring, predictable plots and plot devices. Writers have been encouraged to layer trope upon trope, overusing and abusing them until they've become a bad joke in the publishing industry and a thing to be assiduously avoided in the screenwriting industry.

Authors, editors, producers, readers, and viewers alike have turned their noses up at tropes, unfairly maligning them without understanding them at all. But in reality, tropes are absolutely funda-mental to the writing process and form the foundation of all stories. That's right. *All* stories.

They're big. They're powerful. They're archetypal. They're the stuff of myth and legend. They shape all the great epic love stories and give structure to all your favorite plots on the page and on the screen. In fact, they form the core of every great story ever told.

It's time to bring tropes out of the ridiculed corner and restore them to their proper and prominent place as essential tools for all writers. I plan to do this by:

-- properly defining what tropes are

-- demonstrating why they're the key to creating unforgettable stories that resonate powerfully with readers and viewers (which, ideally, will translate to you making a lot of money and becoming famous)

You might want to read that last bullet point again. I'll wait for you.

Now that I have your attention, let's proceed.

WHAT ARE TROPES AND WHY DO THEY MATTER?

Let's start at the beginning and talk about what a trope is.

The word trope originates from the ancient Greek work *trepein*, which means to turn, to direct, to alter, to change. *Trepein* evolved into the later Greek word *tropos*, which means turn, direction, way. Sometime in the 1530s, the Latin word *tropus* was first used to mean a turn of speech or figure of speech.

It is worth noting from these early definitions that the concept of a trope includes turns of direction and change. There's movement to tropes. They connote action. Travel from one point to another.

Which is to say:

Tropes are a roadmap of where a story must go. They're a way of marking certain scenes a story must contain, and they're a way of breaking down the plot of a story into its core elements.

To put it in the simplest possible terms, tropes are the basic structure that underpins every story—its beginning, middle, and end.

As it turns out, certain stories with specific beginnings, middles, and ends get told over and over again because audiences love them and can't get enough of them. Over time, these become classic stories, and we give them a name and label them a "trope."

Framed.

Blackmailed.

In Love With the Enemy.

Old Enemy Returns.

Victim Seeks Revenge.

These are the stuff of classic thriller tales. They've been around since the first thriller tale was ever told, and they'll be used in new thriller stories long after you and I are gone.

This is the classical definition of a trope and the one I use when I discuss tropes.

It's worth noting that a variation upon this classical definition of the word, trope, has come along in the past hundred years or so that's a source of great confusion among writers even to this day. So, let's clear that up before we go any further.

If you pop over to a modern dictionary to look up "trope," you'll find a second definition of the word, something along the lines of "a figurative or metaphorical use of a word or expression." The dictionary may add a line or two about tropes being "a common or overused theme, device, or cliché."

It's this definition that actually gets used most commonly when people talk about tropes in books.

Individual parts of a story that are *not* its core structure—character types, story elements, overused settings or themes, and yes, clichés—are often referred to as tropes or being "tropey." A few examples:

- An alcoholic P.I. down on his luck
- The P.I.'s secretary with a heart of gold who's in love with her boss
- The cigarette always hanging out the corner of the P.I.'s mouth
- The rumpled suit the P.I. wears and the stained tie that goes with it
- The mobsters who rough up the P.I. when he gets too close to the big boss

- The buddy on the police force who slips the P.I. some evidence or gives the P.I. a peek at a confidential file
- The big shootout at the end between the bad guys and the good guys

While these are all characters, character themes, story elements, or recognizable props, and most of them can be labeled cliché or overused—particularly when done poorly or not very creatively— none of them tell us anything about what's going to happen in the story.

They give us no hint as to the overarching structure of the story.

How does the story begin? Does a dame in a fancy fur walk into the P.I.'s office? Or does a murder happen, leaving a body on the street in a pool of blood?

What happens in the middle? Is the P.I. framed for the crime he didn't commit? Does the P.I. get caught in a mob turf war and have to investigate in spite of that? Does the P.I. discover a corrupt cop might have killed an informant?

How does it end? Does the P.I. get used as bait by the police to draw a criminal out of hiding? Does the P.I. prove the dame in the fancy fur did it and put her in handcuffs himself? Does the P.I. shoot it out with the bad guy and kill the murderer?

Granted, all thriller trope themes can be boiled down to the idea that good triumphs over evil; hence, we can assume the P.I. catches or kill the bad guy in the end.

But beyond that generality, we have no idea from looking at that list of characters, story elements, and props how the P.I. will get to the end result.

Okay, now we know what classically defined tropes are. But why do they matter?

They matter for three reasons:

First, every single member of your audience knows how tropes work.

And furthermore, they're all familiar with how classic tropes are supposed to go. If you start your story with the protagonist's identity being stolen and used to commit a crime, your audience members already know where this story has to go:

- They know the protagonist is going to get accused of committing the crime.
- He or she is going to have to prove he or she didn't do it while at the same time trying to find the person who stole his or her identity.
- The person who stole the protagonist's identity is going to hide, flee, and eventually be confronted by the protagonist.
- The protagonist catches the bad guy, turns said bad guy over to the authorities.
- The protagonist is finally cleared of all charges and his or her good name restored.

There are endless variations in how this basic story can proceed, but the core story will remain essentially the same. Every. Single. Time.

But...isn't this boring to readers and viewers?

Nope. Readers actually prefer to know where the story's going and feel smart for knowing where it's going to go.

Second, readers and viewers are trained to expect and look for tropes.

In fact, psychologists suggest that audiences crave the familiarity of tropes in their story-based entertainment.

Lisa Cron puts it brilliantly in her seminal book, Wired for Story, when she says, "We think in story. It's hardwired in our brain. It's how we make strategic sense of the otherwise overwhelming world around us."

I would take that one-step further and propose that not only do we think in story, but more specifically, we also think in tropes.

Tropes occur in an orderly fashion, and they show us the logical progression of events that must happen for a particular kind of story to reach a satisfying conclusion.

When you introduce any trope into a story, a specific set of problems is inevitably bound to occur as a result of that trope and require a specific resolution.

> **One of the great paradoxes of fiction reading and TV/film viewing is that audience members don't want to be surprised, at least not in the large-scale movements that form the core of the story.**

When readers pick up a thriller novel or viewers watch a thriller movie, they by golly expect the good guy to defeat the bad guy by the end of the story. If a reader picks up a mystery novel, he or she expects the mystery to be solved by the end of the story. Crime thriller? Justice had better be served before the final credits roll.

> **KEY POINT: If you, the writer, don't deliver on the reader's or viewer's expectations of how a trope will unfold and resolve in your story, the reader/viewer will be outraged. And outraged readers and viewers have an unpleasant tendency to leave terrible reviews, tell everyone they know how awful your story was, and never buy another book or watch another TV show or film you've created.**

Third, tropes are an incredibly powerful and useful tool for working writers.

- If you understand tropes thoroughly, your story's plot will unfold before you effortlessly (well, with somewhat less blood, sweat, and tears).
- Your characters will know what to do next when the sagging middle of your book is yawning before you like the Grand Canyon with the satisfying ending only a distant speck on the far side of the chasm.
- You'll know if you've delivered all the key scenes and story elements your audience expects from the trope(s) you promised them.
- Best of all, you will deliver a deeply satisfying story to your audience.

OBLIGATORY SCENES

One of the great beauties—and pitfalls—of tropes is that they all require certain major scenes to happen, usually in a specific order, to tell that particular story motif. If you're writing about a kidnapped child, he or she a) must be kidnapped, b) must be in danger of not being rescued, and c) be rescued.

Yes, I know that technically you can kill a child or fail to find the child, but killing children ranks right up there with killing dogs in fastest ways to tick off readers and viewers and is only tolerated in very rare cases by most audiences.

At any rate,

- **Every single trope has a logical starting point or inciting event.**
- **Every single trope has a logical middle that takes the form of an obstacle or conflict preventing its successful resolution.**

- **Every single trope has a specific black moment where all appears to be lost in a way unique to that particular trope.**
- **Every single trope has a logical and satisfying conclusion.**

When a writer creates a story, he or she enters into an unspoken contract with the reader or viewer. The writer agrees to deliver the story the reader/viewer expects. This contract also extends to the tropes the writer employs in the story.

If you break this contract with your reader/viewer, that consumer will not forgive you. Trust me. I've seen some of the hate mail and verbal attacks readers and viewers spew in fury at writers who break this contract.

KEY POINT: You must not fail to deliver the logical and satisfying conclusion your reader or viewer expects from the tropes in your story. Never, EVER, fail to deliver on the promise of the tropes you use.

Filmmaker, Stanley Kubrick said, "Everything has already been done, every story has been told, every scene has been shot. It's our job to do it one better."

Every trope has been used thousands or even millions of times. But they continue to exist because we love them. Why do we love them so much? They're universally recognizable and familiar to all of us.

They're old friends; we grew up with them. We've listened to and learned these classic tropes since we could understand speech or watch cartoons. They help us understand the world around us.

Your job as a writer is to put into action what Kubrick said. Find a way to take what is old and make it new. You must tell your story in your own voice, with your own perspective, while remaining true to the time-honored tropes you choose to use.

I can't tell you how many times I've asked editors, or heard other writers ask producers, or even heard writers ask their fans, "What book/show/movie are you looking for, right now?"

The answer is always some version of, "I want the same story that has always worked before and that I've loved in the past, but new and fresh. Different but the same."

I also can't tell you how many times I've gnashed my teeth over that answer or listened to other writers wail in frustration over it. Different but the same? What the heck does that mean?

Let me translate for you. Editors, producers, readers, and viewers want the classic tropes they've always loved and that have always appealed to them but told in a fresh, new way that makes them enjoy the trope all over again.

One last piece of advice about using tropes: it's easy to write mechanically when focused solely on trope, marching grimly through the obligatory scenes, never varying, never embellishing, never reaching for anything more. The most boring book or movie in the world is one that relies solely on tropes to define the story. However, the best book or movie in the world can also rely solely on tropes to define and tell a story.

Assuming all the requirements of a trope are met, quality of writing is not defined by using tropes or not using tropes, but rather how skillfully the writer uses them.

HOW TO USE THIS BOOK

This book covers tropes that are universal to all sub-genres of thrillers, be they psychological thrillers or crime thrillers, military or spy thrillers, sci-fi thrillers, legal thrillers, or some other kind of thriller altogether.

These thriller tropes are adaptable to *any* type of thriller story, or even to a thriller-based sub-plot in a book or screenplay that's not primarily a thriller.

Each trope description in this book includes:

- a definition of the trope
- adjacent, similar tropes
- why readers/viewers love this particular trope
- descriptions of the obligatory scenes that form the beginning, middle, black moment, and end of the trope's arc
- any additional scenes that are key to doing this trope justice
- a detailed list of questions to consider when writing this trope

- a detailed list of potential hazards and pitfalls of writing this trope
- examples of movies and books that use this trope

If you already have some idea of the trope or tropes you'd like to write about, you can go directly to those specific descriptions for inspiration and thought-provoking questions as you plan your story. Or you can browse this entire volume to explore possibilities you might like to write about.

This book is also a useful reference after you've drafted your story and are ready to start revising and refining it. You can check yourself against the lists and questions in this book to make sure you've delivered all the scenes your audience expects.

Last, this book can help define which readers will enjoy a certain trope and help you create marketing materials that will target the audience most likely to love the trope you're serving up.

One final note on the names I've given the tropes in this volume. When I started compiling lists of thriller tropes to write about, I couldn't find a single comprehensive list of them anywhere. I certainly couldn't find a list of thriller tropes that broke the 300+ major thriller tropes I'd identified into the major sub-genres of thriller fiction.

For what it's worth, I currently have eight volumes of thriller tropes planned to cover all three-hundred thriller tropes, divided into:

- Universal Thriller Tropes
- Psychological Thriller Tropes
- Crime & Legal Thrillers
- Spy & Political Thrillers
- Military & Action Thrillers
- Mystery & Paranormal Thrillers
- Sci-Fi Thrillers
- Fantasy Thrillers

Because no comprehensive list of thriller tropes already exists to my knowledge, I've had to come up with names for many of the tropes in this book. I did my best to signal clearly what each trope was about while not belaboring it with an overly long descriptive title.

Some of my original spreadsheet entries were laughably long. For example, "Special Operator, Former Law Enforcement Officer, Soldier, Spy, or other Operator Only Attacks, Punishes, Captures, or Kills People Who Violate His or Her Personal Moral Code". I ended up shortening that one to "By My Own Code".

Any ambiguity or clumsiness of titles is entirely my fault, and I'm happy to hear from you if you have better names for any of these tropes.

That said, let's dive into the tropes themselves...

ACCIDENTALLY FIND DANGEROUS OBJECT/INFORMATION

DEFINITION

This story typically begins with your main character finding something—as the title suggests, an object or perhaps some information—that he or she did not expect to find.

He or she may find it completely by chance or someone can put something into the main character's path to find. The protagonist may set out to look for one thing and find another or may not realize immediately exactly what he or she has found.

Indeed, it may be the reaction(s) of the person or persons around the main character who make the find's significance known to your main character and your audience.

The accidental object, information, file, or whatever thing is found may reveal everything your protagonist and audience need to know about a possible disaster happening. Or the found thing may be just the starting point for a larger investigation where your protagonist gradually uncovers the true nature of some other threat.

In either case, the means by which the protagonist comes into possession of the dangerous object or information will set the tone for your entire story.

Is it a comic moment of stumbling upon something? Is the discovery wrapped in mystery and fraught with danger? Is the moment taut with suspense as your protagonist starts the story in danger or is immediately endangered as a result of his or her find?

Of course, it's not enough for your protagonist simply to find something dangerous. The found object has to launch a series of events that will put your protagonist in danger—or even more danger —and suck him or her into dealing with the consequences of what he or she has found.

Typically, the goal is to stop the danger before it harms anyone... but your protagonist may or may not succeed entirely in achieving that.

The protagonist may try to hand off the dangerous object and wash his or her hands of the problem, but for some reason this isn't possible.

In response, he or she may volunteer to help deal with the danger of what they've found, or there may simply be nobody else to deal with it, forcing the protagonist to deal with it.

Which leads us to the protagonist's level of expertise in handling this particular type of problem. He or she may have no knowledge, training, or experience in handling the type of problem he or she now faces, and this may be a major element of your story.

The reason why your main character doesn't just hand off what he's found to someone else (or just throw out the dangerous object or information) and walk away from the whole situation will say a lot about your protagonist's character and personal motivations.

The danger suggested by the found object builds throughout the story. Meanwhile, the protagonist and any helpers he or she recruits will race to stop the unfolding crisis.

The nature of the harm promised by that initial found object will be determined by the tone of your story. Is the danger a painful revelation that might destroy a family? Or is the danger a catastrophe that will potentially destroy the human race?

As with all thrillers, you have the choice of managing at the last moment to stop the dangerous thing from happening, or you can unleash the disaster in all its awful glory.

In either case, by the end of your story, the protagonist must stop the absolute worst possible outcome from happening, or the main character manages to pull some sort of partial victory against evil from the jaws of defeat.

ADJACENT TROPES
-- Letter Sent Before Someone Died
-- Must Destroy Dangerous Object/Information/Weapon
-- Witness/Bystander Sucked Into Danger
-- Future Crime Predicted by Mundane Means
-- Dangerous Object/Information is Missing
-- Damaging Information Made Public
-- Something Found in Dead Loved One's Personal Effects
-- Cursed/Possessed Object

WHY READERS/VIEWERS LOVE THIS TROPE
-- any normal person could accidentally stumble across an object, information, or file, and find him- or herself in a similar situation...so this protagonist is particularly relatable

-- how fun would it be if a seemingly innocuous find led to something huge...and I got to be the one to pull on that thread, uncover something important, and save the day

-- my mundane, boring life or my mundane boring job/ knowledge, might lead to something exciting and important

--I could find something like that and get to be a hero

OBLIGATORY SCENES
THE BEGINNING:
Typically (and obviously) the opening of this story is usually the

moment your protagonist stumbles across something—an object, a letter, a file, a diary, perhaps some mysterious and unidentified thing —that pulls your main character into some sort of investigation, search, or race to save the day.

This is as close to a meet-cute opening as we'll find in the thriller genre. Hang with me here and hold off on rolling your eyes for a moment.

Borrowed from the comedy and romance genres, a meet-cute is defined as a scene in which two people meet for the first time, typically under unusual, humorous, charming, or cute circumstances, and go on to form a future romantic couple. This type of scene is a staple of romantic comedies, though it can also occur in sitcoms and soap operas.

In our case, the "meeting" is between your protagonist and the object or information that's going to start him or her down the road to an adventure. The two will be inseparably linked throughout the remainder of your story and together arrive at the inevitable conclusion of one having found the other.

This accidental find coming into your main character's life will irrevocably change him or her forever and send him or her on a perilous journey of self-discovery...which sounds an awful lot like the elements of a relationship and is something to consider when you write this story.

A well-developed protagonist, particularly one with no special expertise with regard to the found thing, is likely to have strong feelings about the mess it sucks him or her into.

In the beginning of your story, he or she may be excited, nervous, or intrigued by the found thing. But as the story progresses, these feelings are likely to become much more complicated until the danger eventually resolves for better or worse.

Your beginning (Act One) will typically end with the first crisis provoked by the discovery of the dangerous object or information. For the first time, the protagonist and your audience will see the *true* danger posed by the object or information.

. . .

THE MIDDLE:

The middle (Act Two) typically begins with the protagonist having to think long and hard about if and how he or she is going to continue forward with investigating or dealing with the dangerous object or information.

In Act One, the danger was largely hypothetical until that first demonstration of real danger. Now, in Act Two, the danger is both real and immediate.

Once your protagonist arrives at a decision to carry on, bigger and more dangerous action ensues. The protagonist's efforts to learn about the looming danger and stop it take on real risks that will endanger the main character's safety or life and may potentially endanger loved ones or many others.

If the protagonist hasn't recruited anyone to help him or her in the first part of the story, he or she may do so in the middle of your story. This decision to seek help or proceed alone may depend on his or her level of expertise in the problem he or she is dealing with. It may also depend on his or her psychology and personal motivations.

Government agencies might get involved. Research experts may come on board and provide information. Contacts, friends and allies —legitimate or otherwise—may help the protagonist.

This is also where the protagonist investigates the found object or information, learns more about it, and follows the trail of information to uncover more details about the threat posed.

Active investigation is the order of the day. Surveillance, stake-outs, research trips, thefts of information, covert meetings to collect illicit intelligence, and chase scenes that end with whoever's being chased getting away will populate the middle of your story.

In some cases, the initial danger that the protagonist understood to be the case turns out to be only the tip of the iceberg. New, more interesting, more shocking, more suspenseful information will be revealed through the middle of this type of story.

The danger itself should strike back at some point—putting your protagonist and/or loved ones in scary, possibly even mortal, danger. You may choose to have the danger ratchet up over a series of gradually increasing conflicts with the protagonist.

Alternatively, you may choose to wind up and release one big (surprise) attack upon the main character. In this case, you'll increase the suspense through the second act by showing your audience or hinting to your audience that something big and bad is building up and preparing to break loose or attack.

The worst of these attacks often marks the end of the middle and sends your story hurtling toward the black moment and final, climactic crisis.

BLACK MOMENT:

Two things need to happen in the black moment of this story:

First, the danger that was unleashed or provoked by the accidental find of the dangerous object or information has to come to fruition. The horrible thing promised or hinted at in the beginning of your story happens or very nearly happens in your black moment.

This is the moment of defeat for your protagonist. It isn't the ultimate defeat promised by the now unfolded danger, but it's darned close. We get a preview of the terrible outcome looming, and it's going to be devastating.

For example, if the destruction of a family is the ultimate danger, in the black moment we might see a terrible fight between two members of the family that estranges them and causes the other family members to choose sides in preparation for a final, climactic confrontation.

Another example: if a terrorist attack is the ultimate danger, the terrorists do a test run or smaller scale attack that's successful, or the thing they need to set up to make the larger attack work is successfully set up.

The second thing that needs to happen in the black moment is the protagonist needs to seriously question and doubt his or her ability to stop the ultimate bad thing from happening. Typically this happens after the preview attack I've just described. The protagonist has failed to stop the penultimate attack. What's to make the main character believe he or she can stop the even larger, climactic crisis?

THE END:

In the ending (Act Three), the ultimate crisis unfolds and occurs, or nearly occurs, in spite of the protagonist's best efforts to stop it.

All of this act is spent with the bad guy preparing and executing the ultimate plot and the main character planning and executing his or her absolute best effort to stop that plot from happening.

While the middle of the story is populated by action and events where both the bad guy and the main character get away, safe to try again another day, the ending of this story is not about running anymore.

This is where the big confrontation happens. Whoever has been running through your story (it can be the bad guy or the good guy) turns around to stand and fight.

All of the disparate elements of your story come together in the climax for one last, epic confrontation. The danger into which your protagonist accidentally stumbled is now ready to come to fruition, and it's up to your battered and bruised protagonist to make one last ditch, heroic effort to stop the danger from happening.

The danger, or the worst of the danger, is averted, evil is defeated, and your protagonist has prevented the looming catastrophe.

You may choose to include some sort of denouement where the protagonist rests, is rewarded, or celebrates the win with his or her companions and/or loved ones.

KEY SCENES

   -- the protagonist learns something not immediately obvious

about the found object or information that dramatically changes what he or she thinks about it and/or its risk

    -- the protagonist shows someone the found object or information and that person reacts with shock, fear, or some other extreme emotion

    -- the protagonist tries to hand off the problem to someone else

    -- the protagonist argues with someone regarding what do about the found thing and the danger it represents

    -- the protagonist and his or her ally/helper/sidekick/friend have a disagreement that threatens to or does separate them

    -- the danger is given a face (not necessarily human, but a face that the protagonist and your audience can attach human emotions to)

THINGS TO THINK ABOUT WHEN WRITING THIS TROPE

What danger do you plan to build your story around?

What object or information will start your protagonist down the path to discovering that danger?

Will the found thing lead your protagonist directly to the danger or will it obliquely start the main character down the path to discovering the danger?

Who and how many people will potentially be harmed by that danger? Why are these people personal to the protagonist to protect?

Does your protagonist know anything about the thing or information he or she finds?

Does your protagonist have the knowledge, training, and experience to deal with the danger(s) posed by the found thing? If so, where did he or she get it? If not, how will that lack of expertise handicap the protagonist in trying to deal with the danger?

Will the protagonist seek expert help? Who? What expertise does the person bring to the adventure?

Does your protagonist try to hand off the danger posed by the found object/information to someone else? If so, who? How? Why? If not, why not?

Why does your protagonist stay involved with the found thing and decide to see its possible danger through?

What will happen to show the characters in your story the real danger posed by the object or information? How do they react to it?

Is there a bad guy character trying to help along the danger posed by the object or information to take place? How? Why? Who is this person?

How is this bad guy character related to the found thing? Does he or she want to possess the found object or information? If so, why?

What larger danger does the found object or information ultimately lead the protagonist to? Who's at risk? How? Why?

Why was the object lost in the first place?

Who put the object where the protagonist found it? How? Why?

How does the backstory person who put or left the dangerous object or information where it is ultimately found relate to the current story as it unfolds? Is he or she dead or alive?

How does the danger get worse over the course of the story? How does it get much worse? How does it become truly terrible? What makes it nearly impossible to prevent?

At what point in the story does the protagonist seriously question what he or she is doing? What does he or she do about it?

At what point does the protagonist feel outmatched or over-matched by the danger he or she is facing? What does he or she do about it?

Who (or what) will do the dangerous act the found object or information is associated with? What is that dangerous act?

Will something devastating be revealed? Will something devastating happen? Will someone be harmed? Disappear? Die?

Is this potentially disastrous act worrisome enough to hold your audience's interest through the entire story?

Is this potentially disastrous act difficult enough to stop that the protagonist has a real possibility of failing to stop it?

How close will you come to the worst-case scenario happening in your story?

What would failure look like for the protagonist? How can you make that failure worse? Much worse? Completely devastating to the protagonist and to your audience were it to happen?

Do you actually want to have one of these devastating things happen in your story?

If the worst happens, how will your protagonist find some measure of success out of that defeat?

Is there a way to reverse that utter failure? If so, do you want to incorporate this failure and reversal into your story?

How far is your protagonist willing to go to stop the danger? Will you make him or her go that far or not? If so, how? If not, why not?

How will the protagonist and his or her allies overcome the danger in the end? Is it a clever solution? Original? Surprising? Plausible within the setting and rules of the world you've built?

Will you show the protagonist and companions' returns to the "normal" world after the danger has passed? NOTE: it's not strictly necessary to do so. If so, what will that look like? Will the protagonist be rewarded or recognized in some way? Is his or her safety, the safety of a loved one(s), or the safety of others reward enough?

TROPE TRAPS

Creating an object or information that immediately reveals the full extent of the danger, setting up a plot that has little development or little new information revealed over the course of the story.

There's nothing more than meets the eye to the found object or information. It doesn't lead to anything else.

Focusing too much on information gathering about the found thing in your story and failing to generate enough action, excitement, suspense, or danger commensurate with the type of story you're telling.

Creating a protagonist with no knowledge, training, or experience to handle the danger brought by the found thing...and yet who magically manages to act like an expert.

Creating an unlikable protagonist who is either so flawed or so perfect as to be unappealing and unsympathetic to your audience.

Your protagonist is such a lone wolf and so unwilling to trust or accept help from others as to appear unpleasantly anti-social and/or mean.

Failing to create in interesting backstory for the accidentally found object or information...a backstory that's integral to your plot.

Failing to increase the danger over the course of your story.

The danger posed by the found thing isn't worrisome enough to hold your audience's attention, concern, and worry.

A clichéd, predictable climax and resolution to your story that fails to surprise your audience in any way.

ACCIDENTALLY   FIND   DANGEROUS OBJECT/INFORMATION TROPE IN ACTION

Movies:

- Johnny Mnemonic
- The Creator
- The Gray Man
- Transformers
- The Maltese Falcon

Books:

- The Accidental Alchemist by Gigi Pandian
- Heart Shaped Box by Joe Hill

- Accidental Heroes by Danielle Steele
- The Quarry Girls by Jess Lourey
- The DaVinci Code by Dan Brown
- This Thing Between Us by Gus Moreno
- The Charm School by Nelson DeMille

2

BACK FROM THE DEAD

DEFINITION

In this story, a character is either declared dead, thought to be dead, or his/her death is faked for some reason. Then, as the name suggests, for some reason this character is "resurrected" or reappears very much not dead.

You may choose to have your protagonist be the person who returns from the dead. It works equally well for a secondary character —the client, partner, friend, or loved one of the protagonist—to come back from the dead. You can use a returned from the dead character as the target of an investigation or even as the villain in your story. Which is to say, you can play with many variations on this theme.

This story typically begins with the "dead" character already dead. Often, the inciting incident that launches your story's main plot is someone sighting the dead character and recognizing him or her. Again, this trope of many variations also allows for a person to fake his or her death to begin your story. It's also plausible to use the fake death and events leading up to it as backstory that's revealed in flashbacks throughout your story.

As soon as the dead person comes back from dead, complications ensue. The fact that this person is not dead may provoke an investigation into whether the person sighted is really the dead person, and if so, how he or she is still alive.

In the case where someone has been declared dead for their own safety, being spotted may trigger that danger. It's also possible this person is brought back from the dead when the danger has supposedly passed...but, of course, that turns out not to be the case.

Someone might fake their death or let someone fake it for them for a more complicated reason, which will be uncovered over the course of your story. A law enforcement agent or spy might need to go under deep cover and require the death of their official identity. A witness or informant might need to "die" before he or she assumes a new identity. Someone might want to "die" so they can pretend to be a ghost and haunt someone for revenge or to extract a confession of a crime. Feel free to use your imagination and have fun with why someone would fake their own death.

This complicated reason for faking one's death may be the premise for a story that goes in an entirely different direction from this initial set-up. Regardless of where else this thriller story goes, complications relating to the faked death still must be worked through over the course of the story. Be it the anger or hurt feelings of a relative, loved one, or friend who wasn't in on the ruse, or the loss of one's credit rating, there are bound to be consequences for the character who faked his or her death, and it's your job to show those somewhere in your story—to complete the trope, as it were.

You might show the characters in your story that the formerly dead character is definitely alive early on, or you may not conclusively prove that until the end of your story.

This is a flexible trope with tons of room for variations on the theme, but at its core, it's pretty simple. Someone comes back from being thought dead, complications ensue, and the fallout from the complications must be dealt with. Where and how you insert danger, suspense, and thrilling action is limited only by your creativity.

· · ·

ADJACENT TROPES
-- Secret/False Identity
-- Mistaken Identity
-- Old Enemy Returns
-- Missing Loved One Returns After Long Absence
-- Someone With No Identity Arrives
-- Secret Twin/Doppelganger

WHY READERS/VIEWERS LOVE THIS TROPE
-- getting a complete reset of my life, leaving everything that was before and starting completely fresh

-- the fantasy of a dead loved one returning to me

-- freedom to break the rules or the law because as a "dead" person, I live completely outside of the system. I'm beholden to no one

-- being completely invisible because I don't technically exist

OBLIGATORY SCENES
THE BEGINNING:
You may choose to begin your story well before someone fakes his or her death and lead your audience through the events that cause this person to make that decision and its consequences. Indeed, this could constitute the basis for an entire story.

Typically, however, you'll begin your story with someone already thought to be dead being spotted by someone who recognizes him or her. This witness, clearly not in on ruse, reacts by asking questions, making a fuss, or in some way blowing the cover of the supposedly dead person. In general, you'll want to show this series of events through the eyes of your protagonist, who may or may not be either the dead person or shocked witness.

In this part of your story, we'll typically see the dead person's reaction to being recognized and the witness excitedly telling others the news—which may meet with varying reactions from delight to rage to horror.

We also are likely to see the person(s) who represent(s) danger to the "dead" person finding out that the dead person is, in fact, alive. This person may or may not be the villain of your story depending on who the "dead" person is and who represents good and evil in your story.

The beginning usually ends with the first confrontation between the formerly dead person and whoever wants him or her dead for real. In the case where a person coming back from the dead sets off a whole separate chain of events, the beginning might end with the first confrontation between the forces of good and evil that will be in conflict over the course of your story.

THE MIDDLE:

If the person who came back from the dead is the main focus of your story, the complications to that person's life now that he or she is back may take up much of the middle of your story. All of his or her personal possessions have been sold or given away and they have no legal identity in the form of a driver's license, passport, bank account, or credit cards.

But more importantly, everyone who mourned the death is likely to have a strong opinion about having been put through that pain.

Old relationships, both personal and professional, must be resumed or resolved. Time has passed since the formerly dead person has interacted with anyone from his or her old life, and in the meantime those people have moved on, which is likely to cause complications for everyone involved. A spouse might have started dating or even have remarried. A child might not recognize or even fear a returned parent. An old boss might have loudly revealed how much he or she hated working with the dead person. A business partner might have taken ownership of the whole business. Your imagination is the only limit on the personal and professional complications a person back from the dead might have to deal with.

Lastly, anyone who wished to harm or kill the dead person is likely to come back to finish off the job. The middle of this story may revolve around the dead person running, hiding, and barely escaping danger, and/or trying to turn the tables and take out the person(s) trying to harm him or her.

If your story is *not* primarily about this character's return from the dead, the middle of your story is likely to be filled with the resurgent danger provoked by or set in motion by this person not being dead anymore.

This trope layers well with other tropes, so it's possible the main thriller action in the middle of your story will come from another trope—catching the terrorist the dead person was fleeing before, proving once and for all the criminal whom the "dead" witness testified against really is guilty, or stopping the technology the scientist faked his or her death to stop from being finished, for example.

In this case, the back from the dead character may act primarily as a source of starting information that launches some other investigation or mission that constitutes the primary plot of your story. But you still should consider weaving in the complications to the back from the dead character's life into the middle of your story, lest your audience wonder what ever happened to that character and feel dissatisfied that you left a major story thread hanging unfinished.

BLACK MOMENT:

In the case of the not-dead character being the main focus of your story, his or her black moment is typically when the thing catches up with them that they were running/hiding from in the first place when they faked their death.

The bad guy they were supposed to testify against captures or corners the not-dead person. The foreign government who wants the scientific secrets the not-dead character knows seizes the scientist and forces him or her to reveal secret information.

From a personal standpoint, the black moment for the not-dead character is probably their failure to receive forgiveness from loved ones and to resume previous relationships. The remarried former spouse chooses to stay with the new partner. The child decides not to have a relationship with the estranged parent.

In general, whatever plan the person had for faking his or her death has failed. They intended to remain hidden and unfound, but now everyone knows they're alive and where they are. They planned to stop a crime or terrorist attack, but now that crime or attack has happened or is about to happen. The information they wanted to "take to the grave" with them is now released.

THE END:

As hopeless as the situation might seem after the black moment, the not-dead person decides to give it one last try to sort out the mess he or she has made of both their life and death.

There is some sort of personal confrontation or reckoning to work out broken of failed relationships. This may involve the not-dead character making a grand apology and/or making some grand gesture of sacrifice or gift giving to gain the forgiveness of those whom he or she wronged by faking death.

There's also one last, climactic confrontation with the villain(s) of the story that's a life-or-death moment...death for real, this time. And now that the not-dead character knows exactly how large an effect his or her death had on everyone he or she loves, the personal stakes are even higher this time around.

And, of course, the external, good-versus evil, save-the-world stakes are also on the line in this final battle. This battle often has the feel of a David versus Goliath conflict. Your not-dead person is the little guy taking on the much bigger, much stronger, much scarier bad guy whom he or she was unable to defeat before and frightened enough of to fake his or her death—sacrificing his or her entire life—rather than confront.

This time around, the not-dead person would rather die for real and run and hide again, and that may be exactly what happens. In this trope, the odds should be stacked heavily against the not-dead person.

Your audience should strongly fear that this character might die as you lead your readers or viewers into this final confrontation. You may need to kill another major character earlier in the story to worry your audience about your willingness to kill the not-dead person. Or you may need to set up some ultra-compelling reason this character needs to live—they're the only surviving parent of a cute child who desperately needs them, for example.

If resolving personal issues needs to be a separate event from the final confrontation with the bad guy, you will need to choose what order you want to portray these scenes in. If your story is primarily a plot-driven thriller about stopping a great evil, you may choose to leave the big battle scene for last. But if your story is more of a psychological thriller or focuses mainly on the journey of the protagonist through danger, you might choose to leave the resolution of personal issues for last.

In either case, you can also consider adding a denouement where we see the not-dead character reunited at last with loved ones who've forgiven him or her and accepted his or her return from the dead.

KEY SCENES

-- the reveal to a loved one that the not-dead character is, in fact, alive. This may not be the same scene as the first meeting between the not-dead character and the loved one, which is also a key scene

-- the real reason for faking death is revealed for the first time

-- how the death was faked is revealed

--the not-dead character realizes the true cost (emotionally, professionally, or financially) to loved ones, friends, or coworkers of having faked his or her death

-- whoever helped the not-dead character (if there is someone) confronts the not-dead character about blowing it and being recognized

-- first face-to-face meeting between the not-dead character and the villain

THINGS TO THINK ABOUT WHEN WRITING THIS TROPE

Why did the character faking death choose to, or agree to, take this drastic step?

Why was "dying" necessary or the only, best option?

How did/will he or she pull it off? Was there a body or not? If there's a body, how was the medical examiner fooled...or was he/she in on the plan? How was this person legally declared dead? By whom? Was someone inside the legal system in on it?

What was the "dead" character's plan for staying dead? What new life was he or she planning to move on to?

How did the "dead" character get spotted? Did he or she go somewhere intentionally or subconsciously where he or she might get spotted, or was it purely coincidence or an accident to get spotted?

Who first spots the "dead" character and tells others he or she isn't dead?

What happens when loved ones hear the "dead" person might not be dead? What happens when enemies hear the "dead" person might not be dead?

Who goes looking for the "dead" person to find him or her and bring them back to their old life/home?

How does the "dead" character react when forced to return to his or her old life/home? Why?

Whose point of view will you tell your story from? The not-dead person? The person who spotted the not-dead person? A loved one? A colleague? A co-conspirator? Boss? Enemy?

How do family, friends, colleagues, and others feel when they find out the dead person is back from the dead? What do they do about it?

How does the now not-dead person feel when seeing family, friends, colleagues, and others from his or her old life? What does he or she say or do when meeting these people again for the first time?

Does the discovery of the not-dead person being alive lead to a larger plot? If so, what? What's the larger danger? Larger mission that now must be finished?

Is the mission that must be finished now the same mission that failed before or that the not-dead person ran from trying to finish when faking his or her death? If not, how *is* the danger that must be dealt with now tied to the not-dead character's fake death?

Does a person returning from the dead drive your story or is it a sub-plot? If it's primarily a premise to set up a larger story, how will you still deliver a satisfying middle, black moment, and ending for the back from the dead character's story arc?

Who's the villain in your story? How is he or she tied into the not-dead person's decision to fake death?

How does the not-dead person know the villain? Where they enemies before? Allies? Family?

How does the villain react to finding out he or she has been hood-winked by the fake death?

What is the villain going to do now that the dead person is back from the dead? Do the villain's plans change? Accelerate? Become more important than ever?

Why does your villain believe he or she is doing the right thing? Why does the villain think the ends he or she seeks justify the means he or she is using or planning to use?

Why does your not-dead character decide to confront the danger or villain whom he or she hid from before? Why now? Why not run again?

When in your story does your not-dead character seriously consider fleeing or hiding again...maybe not by faking death this time but just running or hiding?

What's different about the situation at the end of this story that makes it possible for the not-dead character to defeat the danger or villain this time around?

What does the not-dead character have to change about himself/herself or the situation before confronting the danger or villain this time?

Which element of your story is the most important—the personal fallout of having faked death or the professional, external stakes of stopping the villain? In what order will you resolve these two-story threads...or is there a way to resolve both story elements in a single climactic confrontation?

What does your story have to say about death? About grief and loss? About lies?

TROPE TRAPS

The "dead" person does something stupid, like watching their child play at school for example, that gets him or her spotted and your audience thinks they're TSTL—too stupid to live.

The decision to fake his or her death comes across as selfish and thoughtless because you failed to properly justify why there was No. Other. Choice.

Failing to portray the problems of being dead and having lost all possessions, identity, financial resources.

Failing to follow through on showing the personal relationship complications that the not-dead person will face with angry family members, friends, colleagues.

The way the person faked their death is implausible and unbelievable or so over-the-top as to be ridiculous.

Failing to do the forensic and/or legal research to come up with a believable way that someone might be declared dead.

Nobody's mad the not-dead character faked his or her death.

Your villain comes across as cartoonishly stupid for having fallen for the fake death.

The villain is not scary or dangerous enough to pose a big enough threat to have plausibly made the not-dead character fake death in the first place.

Nothing changes from when the character first faked his or her death until deciding to stand and fight the villain or confront the danger from before. Which is to say, failing to justify why he or she is willing to fight now when he or she ran before.

The danger that provoked the character to fake death in the first place is completely unrelated to the danger faced in the climax of the story.

Failing to resolve, for better or worse, personal relationship issues related to having faked death by the end of the story.

Failing to address any legal issues of having faked one's own death.

Failing to have the not-dead character learn anything from the experience of dying and seeing how it affected everyone who knew or loved him or her.

BACK FROM THE DEAD TROPE IN ACTION
Movies:

- Sleeping With the Enemy
- The Talented Mr. Ripley
- Gone Girl
- Pathaan
- Every Breath She Takes
- The Running Man
- 'Til Death Do Us Part

Books:

- Play Dead by Harlen Coben
- The Long Goodbye by Raymond Chandler
- Adam and Eve and Pinch Me by Ruth Rendell
- The Likeness by Tana French
- The Partner by John Grisham
- Gone Girl by Gillian Flynn
- In Cold Blood by Truman Capote

3

BIG SECRET

DEFINITION

In this story, someone has a big secret and has no interest in sharing it for some reason.

While this might seem like nothing more than a story element, it turns into an entire trope when there's a serious consequence to revealing the big secret and the secret keeper spends the whole story going to great lengths to keep it hidden, only to have it be revealed in the end, and the consequences happen...but worse after the secret's been hidden so aggressively.

The person keeping the secret may be your protagonist. In this case, you may spend much of the story in the protagonist's interior monologue as he or she agonizes about what will happen if the secret comes out and schemes to keep it hidden. You may or may not choose to have him or her reveal any or all of the details of the secret, even in interior monologue.

The protagonist may be someone who knows the secret keeper—a family member, loved one, close friend, coworker, boss, or law enforcement official. The arc of this person's story will revolve around figuring out the secret keeper is hiding something and then spending the remainder of the story trying to figure out what it is or trying to coerce the secret keeper into telling what it is he or she is trying so hard to hide.

However, if this protagonist loves the secret keeper or is committed to helping the secret keeper, the protagonist may not reveal the secret to others once he or she knows it. Or at least the loved one/friend/coworker may *intend* not to reveal it. However, once the protagonist knows the secret, it may be bad enough to put him or her into a sticky moral quandary over whether or not to reveal the secret to those who need to know—law enforcement, a spouse, a victim of the secret.

At the end of this protagonist's story, he or she almost always does the right thing and reveals the secret, or forces the secret keeper to reveal it, or drops hints to the right people so they can uncover the secret.

In either version of the trope, the secret comes out. It always does in this trope. Once revealed, the consequences the secret keeper feared inevitably come to pass.

The traditional moral of this story is that no secret stays secret forever and that, no matter how hard you try to dodge the consequences of your actions, you're always going to face the music eventually.

Of course, you're not required to tell a morally clear and upright story. Feel free to have the lesson of your story be something else entirely.

ADJACENT TROPES
-- Group Hides a Secret
-- Family Secret
-- Web of Lies
-- Secret Power(s)
-- One Crime Hides a Bigger One

. . .

WHY READERS/VIEWERS LOVE THIS TROPE

-- we all relate to the secret keeper: who doesn't have a secret that to us is "big" and could potentially hurt others if revealed

-- we love to be in on a big secret. We may not be able to keep it to ourselves, but we still want to be in the know

-- we've been harmed by others' secrets, don't like them, and want to see them revealed

-- we like feeling as if we're in the inner circle, the close-knit group who knows what's really going on

-- the trope appeals to our sense of conspiracies being out there that we could see if we only were in on the secret that others are keeping from us

OBLIGATORY SCENES
THE BEGINNING:

This story may begin innocuously, but something happens to bring attention to the secret keeper. He or she comes under suspicion in some sort of crime. He or she is caught being somewhere he or she shouldn't be. It may be as simple as the secret keeper witnesses an accident and has to give a statement to the police. Whatever you come up with, it puts a spotlight on the secret keeper, who would much rather not be the center of so much concentrated attention.

Someone sniffs that the secret keeper isn't being entirely honest. If your protagonist isn't the secret keeper, it's usually this protagonist that gets a whiff of not getting the whole story or the true story.

The beginning of this trope may conclude with the person who sniffs the deception or evasion directly confronting the secret keeper and asking him or her what they're not telling.

THE MIDDLE:

This confrontation sends the secret keeper into a frenzy of

distraction, evasion, deception, and in other ways dodging revealing their big secret.

The secret keeper may confess to a smaller crime in an effort to end a police investigation and keep authorities from discovering the much larger secret.

The secret keeper might employ an incredibly obvious bug or incredibly obvious tail to hide the second, more sophisticated bug or to distract from the professional and very sneaky tail following someone.

The secret keeper might in engage in a patently transparent cover-up of a fake secret or less damaging secret totally unrelated to the big secret, fully expecting the lesser secret to be revealed, but hoping it will satisfy the nosy people convinced there is a big secret.

The secret keeper might commit a smokescreen crime, admit to something embarrassing, or create some other totally unrelated distraction to get people to stop looking for the real, big secret.

In the middle of the story, your audience learns why the secret keeper is hiding the big secret. He or she may have had an affair and be terrified that revealing it will destroy their lover's marriage. The secret keeper may be the secret parent of a child to whom their parentage hasn't been revealed.

Have a field day with what the secret is and why the secret keeper is so determined to protect it from discovery. It's these machinations to hide the secret that will fill the middle of your story.

NOTE: Just make sure that revealing the big secret would cause sufficient harm to someone that the secret keeper has a compelling reason to keep the big secret to himself or herself.

Some or many details of the secret are typically revealed to your audience in the middle of the story. But those details may not be revealed to those trying to find out the secret nor to those who would be harmed by the secret.

The middle of this story is a true game of cat-and-mouse with the secret keeper and person(s) trying to discover the big secret dodging and weaving, tricking each other, following, bugging, and surveilling each other, break-ins in search of information, clandestine meetings and the like.

Regardless of whether your protagonist is the cat seeking the secret or the mouse hiding it, the action of the middle of the story will be the same—just told from the different point of view.

The middle of this story typically ends with the person pursuing the big secret cornering or trapping the secret keeper in a situation in which the secret keeper is going to be forced to reveal the secret. The secret keeper may be tricked, secretly recorded, or confronted by a loved one whom the secret keeper trusts...but who is wearing a wire.

This crisis is usually precipitated by the secret keeper's **refusal to reveal the big secret** and is made up of the worst possible consequence of his or her refusal to reveal the secret.

For example, the secret keeper may be arrested and thrown in jail, he or she may lose a job or a spouse may leave him or her or kick the secret keeper out of the house. The secret keeper may be forced to commit a crime or engage in a confrontation with someone instead of revealing the secret.

BLACK MOMENT:

The black moment may be a crisis caused by someone refusing to reveal the secret.

But the secret does come out. Despite all the secret keeper's best efforts to keep it hidden, the damaging big secret is revealed, and everyone who would be hurt by the revelation of the secret is, indeed, harmed. Marriages fall apart, kids feel betrayed, arrests are made, scandals explode...whatever you can think up that's appropriate in scale to your story.

The secret keeper has failed utterly, not only to keep the secret but to protect whoever or whatever he or she was protecting. Worse, the consequences he or she hoped to avoid happen, and they're probably even worse that the secret keeper anticipated because everyone's also mad that he or she either kept or revealed the secret.

. . .

THE END:

The climactic crisis of the story is caused by the **secret keeper revealing the big secret**.

As for the person pursuing the big secret, once it's revealed it may not be what he or she expected. Or it may be so much worse than even he or she expected.

The revelation of the big secret typically leads to one last problem that needs to be solved--to another conspirator, to a cache of something hidden that must be retrieved, to a need to arrest someone, or to some final confrontation.

The secret keeper may be recruited to help the person(s) who have pursued the big secret in the final confrontation.

OR

There's a big confrontation between the secret keeper, now secret revealer, and the person(s) harmed by the secret's revelation. The secret keeper may even be in life threatening danger when this confrontation occurs. He or she may need to find a way out of the confrontation or be rescued by those who put him or her into this jeopardy.

In either case, the secret revealer has paid the price for keeping the secret from those who wanted or needed to know it (this price usually comprises the black moment), and in the ending pays another price for revealing it.

By paying both of these prices—and having the prices themselves be steep enough—your audience should feel the secret keeper has paid sufficiently for having, keeping, and spilling a big secret. They are satisfied with the outcome of your story and feel as if all has ended as it should be.

. . .

KEY SCENES

-- the audience first gets a glimpse of what the big secret is

-- you identify to the audience someone innocent who will be hurt by the big secret if it's revealed

-- the person(s) who will ultimately go after the secret first realize there's a big secret being hidden

-- the protagonist, confronted by the person(s) hunting the big secret flatly refuses to tell, but in so doing reveals its existence

-- the protagonist pays a heavy price for one or more of the subterfuges he or she employs to dodge revealing the big secret or to distract everyone from its possible existence

--someone being protected by the secret keeper's silence thanks him or her, exhorts him or her to keep silent, or puts pressure on/coerces the secret keeper to stay silent

-- a loved one, family member, friend, coworker, or boss of the secret keeper exhorts him or her to tell the big secret and stop begin stupid or suffering needlessly over it

-- the second, deeper, and worst layer of the big secret is revealed to your audience. It's an ah-hah moment of just how truly awful the revelation of the secret would be. "We knew it would be bad, but we didn't know it would be *that* bad"

-- the person(s) most hurt by the reveal of the big secret confront the secret keeper after the secret has come out

-- the person pursuing the secret apologizes to the innocent(s) hurt by the secret he or she so doggedly worked to reveal

THINGS TO THINK ABOUT WHEN WRITING THIS TROPE

What's the big secret? What's the superficial layer of the big secret? What's the deep, super hidden core of the secret that's truly devastating? To whom is it devastating?

Who's keeping the secret that you're going to follow primarily in your story? Is this person the protagonist or ultimately the villain?

Whose point of view will you tell this story from—the secret keeper's or the person's who is trying to uncover the secret? Does one point of view or the other work better for the particular secret you've chosen?

Does anyone besides the secret keeper in your story know about the secret? If so, who? Why is he or she keeping it, too? Will they be dragged into your story or stay clear of it until the big secret is revealed?

What brings the secret keeper into a spotlight that makes him or her nervous about the secret possibly being discovered?

Who first suspects the secret keeper is keeping a secret? Why do they suspect this?

Does the suspicious person realize it could be a BIG secret? If so, how and why?

Who is the main person(s) digging to find out what the big secret is? What kind of investigation will he, she, or they launch? What resources will be used? What techniques? Who will help with the investigation and how?

Does the secret keeper require special skills, knowledge, or help to stay one step ahead of the person(s) trying to uncover the big secret? If so, what and who does he or she get help from?

How does the investigation get progressively closer to the truth, scarier, riskier, or more dangerous over the course of the story?

How does a game of cat-and-mouse spin out of control and become something bigger, personal, and obsessive to the secret keeper and the person determined to uncover the secret? How does that shift into a personal war show up in the story? How does it escalate and increase the danger, violence, tension, and stakes?

Will the secret keeper eventually reveal the superficial layer of the big secret in hopes of keeping the deeper, more devastating layer hidden? If so, when does he or she give up the superficial part of the big secret?

Will the secret keeper do something new, bigger, different, or desperate to divert attention away from the possibility of a deeper layer to the big secret once he or she has given up the superficial layer of it?

Does giving up the superficial layer lead to the black moment or result from the black moment?

At what point does the secret keeper refuse to give up the big secret or give up the rest of the big secret? What crisis does this provoke in your story? Is the crisis directed at the secret keeper? Does someone involved with the big secret try to silence the secret keeper? Does the person(s) trying to uncover the secret have a confrontation with the secret keeper?

What does his or her refusal to give up the big secret cost the secret keeper? Can you make that cost worse? Much worse? Totally devastating to him or her?

What makes the secret keeper finally give up the whole secret? Is this thing big enough to force him or her to change course and reveal the secret? Does this event, information, lesson, conversation, or threat need to be bigger, or much bigger, to convince your audience (and the secret keeper) that it's time for the secret keeper to give up and reveal the secret?

How does the reveal of the big secret precipitate one last, climactic crisis? What is that final crisis? Is it big enough to be in proper proportion to the size of the secret just revealed? Do you need to make that final crisis bigger? Much bigger? Catastrophic? How will you do that?

Who's at risk in the final crisis? The secret keeper? The person who forced the secret to be revealed? The victim(s) of the secret? Someone else?

How is the final crisis resolved? Who lives and dies? Who is arrested, fired, or ostracized?

What price does the secret keeper pay in the end for revealing the big secret? Who makes him or her pay it? Is your audience going to be satisfied that the secret keeper has paid sufficiently for first keeping and then revealing the big secret?

What lesson does the secret keeper learn?

What lesson does the person who dug so relentlessly to reveal the secret learn?

TROPE TRAPS

The secret is too simple. There's not a second (or third, or fourth) layer to the secret that makes it even worse than your audience will realize when the secret is first revealed.

The protagonist isn't sympathetic, particularly if he or she is a criminal.

The reason the secret keeper isn't revealing the secret isn't anywhere near scary enough to justify not telling the big secret, particularly when the stakes for not telling go sky high.

The big secret isn't big enough. The audience doesn't buy that someone doesn't just reveal it, let alone the secret keeper.

The build up to the grand reveal of the big secret makes the audience expect a much bigger and more impressive secret, and you fail to deliver a clever, creative, or devastating secret.

The audience roots for the bad guy—if you intend for the secret keeper to be the bad guy, the audience likes him or her better than the person trying to uncover the secret, or vice versa, the audience likes the person digging for the truth better than the secret keeper who's supposed to be your protagonist.

The cat-and-mouse game between the secret keeper and investigator is dull, uninteresting, predictable, or cliché.

The cat-and-mouse game between the secret keeper and secret seeker never becomes personal and never escalates beyond a professional disagreement.

No innocents will be hurt by revealing the secret, hence your audience has no reason at all to care if the secret comes out or not.

Failing to put the audience into a state of moral conflict over whether it's better to reveal secrets, or in the case of this one, it's better to keep it hidden.

The secret keeper doesn't bother to engage in any distractions, subterfuges, or efforts to pay a lesser price instead of revealing the big secret and relies only on refusing to talk, which is boring to your audience.

The secret keeper doesn't pay any real price for refusing to tell the secret, your audience thinks he or she has no reason to buckle and give up the secret, and your audience perceives the secret keeper as weak. Whether your secret keeper is the protagonist or the villain, it's a bad thing either way for your audience to think they're weak or dumb.

The audience isn't satisfied that the secret keeper has paid an appropriate price for keeping the big secret and ultimately revealing it and finishes your story deeply dissatisfied.

BIG SECRET TROPE IN ACTION

Movies:

- Gone Girl
- Shutter Island
- The Girl With the Dragon Tattoo
- The Sixth Sense
- Primal Fear
- The Crying Game
- The Usual Suspects

Books:

- The Silent Patient by Alex Michaelides
- The Thirteenth Tale by Diane Setterfield
- The Firm by John Grisham

- The Secret History by Donna Tartt
- Into the Woods by Tana French
- Presumed Innocent by Scott Turow
- The Woman in the Window by A. J. Finn
- The Ghostwriter by Robert Harris

4

BLACKMAILED/ EXTORTED

DEFINITION

Before we dive into this trope, let's first distinguish between blackmail and extortion. In the broadest legal terms, extortion is the act obtaining money, property, or services through coercion. In this context, blackmail is a specific form of coercion. But it's so common in the thriller genre that it is, in effect, its own class of crime.

Blackmail happens when someone threatens to reveal information about the target of the blackmail scheme (or family members or loved ones of the target). This information, if revealed publicly, will be embarrassing, socially damaging, or incriminating in some sort of wrongdoing. Of course, what makes it blackmail is a demand for money, property, an action, or services in return for not revealing the damaging information.

It's worth noting that, even if the damaging information is true, a person can still be charged with blackmail if he or she threatens to reveal it unless the victim meets his or her demand(s).

Extortion (excluding blackmail, obviously) doesn't rely on a threat to reveal information. Rather, extortion occurs when someone threatens violence, destruction of property, withholding testimony, or some other damaging action/inaction if the target doesn't cough up money, property, services, or some other form of payment.

For legal purposes, the distinction matters. But for the sake of discussing story structure, they're actually similar enough to combine into a single trope entry. Both rely on a villain saying, "Do this for me or else." In the case of blackmail the "or else" is release of damaging information. In the case of extortion, the "or else" is damage directly to the target, the targets' property, or the target's loved ones.

It's this threat that underpins the structure of this type of story.

The victim of the blackmail/extortion is often the protagonist of this type of story. In this case, the story begins with the blackmailer/extortionist approaching the victim, revealing that he or she has damaging information and demanding payment in whatever form he or she wants. The victim protagonist spends the middle of the story trying to gather the resources to pay off the blackmailer, seeking a way to wiggle out of paying the blackmail demand, or searching for a way to negate the blackmail threat for good.

Alternately, the protagonist may be someone whom the victim turns to for help in solving his or her blackmail/extortion problem. In this case, the problem solver-protagonist tends to take direct action against the blackmailer/extortionist. This protagonist may try to steal the information or get proof of the blackmail scheme. He or she may try to counter-extort or counter-blackmail the bad guy, or this fixer may try to kill the blackmailer/extortionist outright.

Although unusual, it's possible for the protagonist in this trope to be the blackmailer/extorter. In this case, you'll to want to create some compelling reason for your main character resorting to this illegal and dangerous tactic. This version of the story begins with your main character delivering the threat or demand to their target. The middle is taken up with the target doing his or her level best to find a way to stop the blackmail/extortion and your protagonist countering the victim's moves to stop the scheme.

In almost all blackmail/extortion stories, the black moment

revolves around the blackmail information being revealed or the threat the extortionist made coming to fruition.

The exception to this is when the blackmailer/extortionist is your protagonist. In this case, the bad guy-victim thwarts your protagonist from successfully releasing information, or the victim thwarts the protagonist from trying to do the damage he or she has been threatening.

In vast majority of stories employing these tropes, the victim of the blackmail/extortion overcomes their blackmailer or extorter in the end. The victim may stop the dissemination of the damaging information. The victim may find a way to silence or kill the blackmailer/extortionist. All the information may still come out, but the victim triumphs in some other way—maybe by circumventing potential damage in some way. Or the victim may simply take the hit from the fallout after the information comes out and survive it.

In the case of simple extortion, the victim typically stops the threatened damage or mitigates it enough that the victim and his or her loved ones survive. This stopping or mitigating often involves direct and violent confrontation with the extortionist in which the victim finally wins.

This trope ends with the blackmail/extortion scheme completely eliminated and the fallout from the revelations or damage successfully dealt with by the victim.

At its core, this is a cat-and mouse story, where the victim of the crime and the perpetrator engage in a personal and tightly connected interaction throughout the story...even if they're rarely or never in personal contact.

The target of the scheme and the perpetrator will engage in a delicate and possibly violent dance through your story as they test each other's nerve and play a dangerous game of chicken to see who will swerve first.

(For those of you unfamiliar with chicken, two drivers in vehicles drive toward each other on a collision course. The first person to swerve to avoid the imminent crash, to "chicken out" as it were, loses the game.)

ADJACENT TROPES
-- Framed
-- Past Catches Up
-- Damaging Information Revealed
-- Whistleblower

WHY READERS/VIEWERS LOVE THIS TROPE
-- we all have secrets we'd be horrified by if they were revealed

-- we all know someone we'd love to have something on, some way to limit their behavior, some way to get them to help us, some way to shut them up or shut them down

-- we all have people and/or things we love enough to be vulnerable over if they're threatened

-- this is a deeply personal threat, one that regular people who aren't special agents or spies can relate to intimately and intensely

OBLIGATORY SCENES
THE BEGINNING:
This trope begins at the moment when the threat is delivered. Do this, or else I'll expose X or destroy Y. It's worth to point out that your story may not actually start at the exact moment the ultimatum is delivered to the target of blackmail or extortion. You may choose to open with backstory events that set up the current-day blackmail or extortion.

Although I implore you to be extremely careful when starting a story with past events. They must be so riveting, so shocking, so compelling, that your reader will forgive you for not starting in the now with events happening at this very minute to the main characters.

No matter how scary the past crisis was, we already know the main character of the upcoming story survived. After all, the rest of the story wouldn't exist if he or she died or ended up incarcerated for life way back when. Which is to say, **there's little to no suspense to backstory as the opening of a story**.

The events in a backstory sequence happened in the past. The characters who died or were harmed are unknown to your audience in the opening moments of your story, and your reader or viewer simply doesn't have much empathy with them and isn't emotionally invested in what happened to them.

At any rate, you may also layer a blackmail/extortion story with some other thriller trope(s). In the case of multiple tropes appearing in the same story, they rarely all begin on page one of your manuscript or screenplay. Regardless of what order you introduce the various tropes you intend to explore, the actual blackmail/extortion trope commences at the moment the threat is delivered to the target of the scheme.

THE MIDDLE:

Most blackmail and extortion victims seek a way out of the pickle they find themselves in. They consider finding and stealing, or searching out and destroying, any information being held over their heads. The victim may try to neutralize the person who's blackmailing or extorting them, either by finding some creative way to counter-extort or counter-blackmail the person threatening them or by taking more drastic measures to harm or kill the blackmailer/extortionist.

It's also possible the target of this scheme may try to find a way to confess to something or reveal the information being held over his or her head to negate the blackmail. However, as the victim explores this option, the fallout would be too heinous to tolerate, and the victim inevitably backs away from this option.

Indeed, if the potential fallout isn't bad enough to dissuade the blackmail victim in your story from coming clean, you probably haven't created stakes big enough and bad enough to sustain your story.

This tension and conflict between the victim and blackmailer/extortionist may explode into violence and confrontation well before the black moment of your story. They may surveil each other, break into each other's homes or workplaces, follow, stalk, threaten, or terrorize each other, and otherwise play intimidation games to break the resolve of their opponent in this contest of wills.

The middle typically ends in a crisis where the victim snaps. He or she refuses to play ball anymore. The victim may refuse once and for all to pay up. He or she may stop payments or refuse to deliver dangerous or damaging information to the bad guy.

Whatever money, property, action, or service is being demanded is *not* delivered to the bad guy by the final deadline.

BLACK MOMENT:

The final failure to pay up by the victim is almost always the crisis that precipitates the black moment.

And, almost without exception in the blackmail trope, the information being held over the victim's head is revealed in the black moment. While it may not go fully public, someone whom the victim loves or values is typically given the damaging information, and the devastating fallout the victim has spent the whole story frantically trying to avoid happens despite his or her best efforts to prevent it.

Your victim may lose a marriage, lose a relationship with a loved one, lose a job and reputation, lose their home, business or wealth, Whatever will utterly devastate your victim happens in part or in full.

If the blackmail information would be catastrophic in a very broad way if made fully public, you may choose to do a limited release of the information in the black moment and save the potential full release for the climax of your story.

In this case, the victim will get his or her ultimate win by stopping the wider release of the information...pulling this off by the skin of his or her teeth, of course...saving the day and stopping evil from triumphing.

In the case of extortion, the victim once and for all refuses to do what is demanded of him or her...and the blackmailer/extortionist does not swerve. The bad guy pulls the trigger in part or in full and some or all of the threatened damage happens to the victim.

THE END:

The refusal of both the victim and the blackmailer/extortionist to back down in their game of chicken sets up the final confrontation. Bloodied and battered by the fallout from the black moment and the damage inflicted as a result of refusing to cooperate with the blackmail or extortion, the victim gathers himself or herself for one last go and stopping the coercion once and for all.

The victim may up the stakes by trying to kill the blackmailer/extortionist this time. He or she may spring some sort of blackmail or extortion of their own on the bad guy. Use your imagination in what a confrontation between these two adversaries might look like.

By the end of your story, these two hate each other's guts and have reached their absolute limits of rage. They may do extreme things that, under normal, rational circumstances, they would never consider doing. Indeed, the more extreme the conflict between these two, the better.

Your job, then is to cook up this intense confrontation and then make sure your story builds in such a way that you can plausibly take your main characters to this extreme confrontation.

Although the goal of any thriller is for good to triumph against evil, in this story, the good guy probably has taken some serious damage by the end of the story. Indeed, this trope lends itself to a fair bit of ambiguity in just how "good" your victim turns out to be.

The story inevitably ends with the blackmail or extortion scheme concluded. You may need to spend some time wrapping up the fallout from information revealed or damage done. It may also be necessary to show your audience what moving forward looks like for the victim.

KEY SCENES

-- the victim tries and fails to tell someone else about what's happening to him or her—either the other person won't listen, or the victim can't quite bring himself or herself to confess

-- the victim communicates a refusal to cooperate with the blackmailer/extortionist early on in your story, and the blackmailer/extortionist ratchets up the pressure or threat

-- the victim considers or explores extreme or violent responses that are wildly out of character for him or her

-- something happens to make the victim realize the fallout from the information release or threatened damage would be even worse than he or she already imagines it would be

-- a loved one or friend tries to find out why the victim is so upset and the victim shuts out him or her, causing personal conflict

-- someone actually finds out about the blackmail/extortion and tries to help the victim or to convince the victim to go to the authorities, causing more personal conflict

-- the blackmailer releases a little information or the extortionist threatens/does a small amount damage as a warning shot across the bow to the victim

THINGS TO THINK ABOUT WHEN WRITING THIS TROPE

What is the information that someone will be blackmailed over or the thing someone will be extorted over?

Who will be the victim and who will be the blackmailer/extortionist?

Who is your protagonist? Will you tell your story from the POV of the victim, the fixer recruited by the victim, or the blackmailer/extortionist?

Who's the underdog in your story? Is that the character you plan to identify to your audience as the protagonist?

If the bad guy in your story might be identified by your audience as the underdog, how will you ensure this character isn't more sympathetic than your good guy(s)?

What are the stakes to the victim if the threat leveled at him or her happens?

How can you make those stakes worse? Much worse? Absolutely awful?

Are these stakes high enough to plausibly prevent the victim from going to the authorities for help or from revealing blackmail information themselves?

Why is the blackmailer/extortionist engaging in this scheme? Is he or she just a bad person? Why does he or she believe they are in the right by doing this?

Does the blackmailer/extortionist think they're doing a bad thing but believe the ends justify the means? If so, what ends is he or she after?

Is there a way to put your blackmailer/extortionist under some sort of pressure of their own that makes success in their scheme a high-stakes proposition for him or her, as well?

What are the stakes to the blackmailer/extortionist? Can you make those bigger? Much bigger? Absolutely huge?

How does the victim react to the initial approach and threat by the blackmailer/extortionist? How does the blackmailer/extortionist react to that?

Can you plot this story as an ever-escalating series of actions and reactions between these two opposing characters? What would that look like?

Who escalates to violence first?

How will the blackmailer/extortionist terrorize the victim to keep him or her "in line" and cooperating with the scheme? What will the blackmailer/extortionist do to the victim or loved one/property/job/life of the victim?

Does the victim know the blackmailer or extortionist? If so, what's their past relationship? What's their backstory?

How did the blackmailer get ahold of the damaging information, or how did the extortionist choose this particular person as his or her target?

What past mistake has the victim made or past decision made/action taken by the victim that's now blackmailable or extortable? How does the victim feel about that mistake?

Who else knows about the past mistake or past decision/action that makes the victim vulnerable now?

Is there anyone the victim can talk to about the mistake? If so, who? Why does the victim trust this person? Is the victim right or wrong to trust this person? What would betrayal by this person look like? Is there a way to make this betrayal a real possibility or actually happen in your story?

If the victim seeks help in dealing with the blackmail/extortion, who does he or she turn to? What does that person do to help?

What is the cost to personal relationships between the victim and loved ones, friends, colleagues over the course of the story as the victim wrestles with this dangerous problem?

What tactic(s) will the victim try to stop the blackmail/extortion? What tactics don't work? Which ones make the situation worse and how?

What danger does the blackmailer/extortionist find himself or herself in over the course of the story from sources other than the victim? Who is the source of that danger?

Who are the colleagues/co-workers /boss/flunkies/gang/thugs

associated with the blackmailer/extortionist? What do they do over the course of the story? Are they just muscle or more?

Why does the victim shift from trying to stop the blackmail/extortion privately to flatly refusing to go along with the scheme anymore? What triggers this change of heart or crisis?

What will the victim do to put the blackmailer/extortionist in great personal jeopardy? How can you make this jeopardy worse? How can you make it so threatening that the blackmailer/extortionist must seriously consider backing down and ending the scheme?

Why doesn't the blackmailer/extortionist ultimately back down? What keeps him or her pressing ahead with their scheme? What's the blackmailer's/extortionist's mindset after it has become very risky for him or her, too?

Do you plan to have all the information ultimately revealed or to have the full extent of threatened damage happen to the victim? What's the full extent of the fallout from that?

How can you make that fallout both more personal and more hurtful to the victim and make it bigger, more public, and more humiliating or devastating to the victim?

How is the blackmail/extortion scheme going to end? Will there be nothing more to reveal and all the threatened damage has already happened? Does the victim find a way to stop the threat from happening? Does the victim find a way to neutralize (permanently) the blackmailer/extortionist?

Why does the victim ultimately refuse to swerve in the game of chicken but instead force a confrontation or final conflict?

Why does the blackmailer/extortionist ultimately refuse to swerve in the game of chicken but instead force a confrontation or final conflict?

What will the final conflict between these two characters look like?

How damaged will each of these characters be in their final confrontation?

What is the cost to both the victim and the blackmailer/extortionist at the end of the day of this series of events?

What or who does the victim lose in the end? What does the victim gain or learn in the end? Has the victim made peace with the cost? What does his or her life look like now?

TROPE TRAPS

The victim is flatly unlikable to some or all of your audience, possibly because of the scale and type of mistake he or she made in the past (that he or she is being blackmailed about or that set up the current extortion).

The blackmailer/extortionist is more sympathetic to some or all of your audience than the victim.

The thing the victim is being blackmailed over, or the threat being leveled in the case of extortion, isn't potentially devastating enough to elicit sympathy for the victim in your audience.

Your victim should logically go to law enforcement for help but you fail to give him or her a compelling reason not to.

The blackmailer doesn't have a compelling reason to engage in the blackmail or extortion but does it more or less randomly at this moment in time.

Your victim suddenly and out of nowhere develops violent or lethal skills to deal with the blackmailer/extortionist that the victim has never been trained in how to do.

The loved ones/friends/colleagues of the victim automatically are assumed and portrayed to be completely unwilling and unable to forgive a mistake made in the past or bad decision.

The victim's complete lack of trust in the people who love him or her and to stand beside him or her leads your audience to question just how big a jerk the victim is or just how bad his or her taste is in romantic partners, friends, and colleagues.

The violence of the victim's reaction to the threat leveled against him or her is out of all proportion. Which is to say, failing to match the severity of the threat to the level of danger and violence portrayed in your story.

Letting the victim get away scot-free and completely unscathed after hiding a past mistake or bad decision that put him or her into a position to be the target of extortion and having proof of this past mistake discovered, and ultimately revealed.

The victim implausibly is never physically or metaphorically bruised or bloodied by the conflict and confrontation with the blackmailer/extortionist.

The blackmailer/extortionist is so dangerous or so overmatches the victim that no victim in their right mind would stand up to this dangerous person.

The blackmailer/extortionist is too easy for the victim to identify, find, and endanger in some way.

The blackmailer/extortionist has no plan for if and when the victim balks at cooperating. The blackmailer/extortionist fails to actually up the stakes for the victim to force the victim to cooperate.

The final confrontation between the victim and blackmailer/extortionist isn't satisfying to the audience.

The outcome for the victim isn't satisfying to your audience or seems too harsh to your audience.

BLACKMAILED/EXTORTED TROPE IN ACTION
Movies:

- L.A. Confidential
- Strangers On a Train
- Goodfellas
- The Equalizer
- Derailed
- The Godfather, Part II
- Once Upon a Time in America

. . .

Books:

- The Stranger by Harlan Coben
- Five Survive by Holly Jackson
- The Associate by John Grisham
- Hostage by Clare Mackintosh
- The Big Sleep by Raymond Chandler
- Ace of Spades by Faridah Àbíké-Íyímídé
- The Quiet Game by Greg Iles
- The Perfect Family by Robyn Harding
- The Collective by Alison Gaylin

5

CONSPIRACY THEORIST IGNORED/PROTAGONIST DISBELIEVED

DEFINITION

This classic trope proves the old adage that what is old becomes new again. In ancient Greek mythology when Cassandra is given the gift of true prophecy, Apollo curses her prophecies to never be believed. To this day, her name is a rhetorical device for characters whose true prophecies are not believed.

In modern usage, this trope begins with the protagonist discovering a piece of information, stumbling upon a conspiracy, or putting together data, facts, or a series of puzzle pieces that point to some sort of looming danger or imminent disaster.

Small problem: the protagonist is someone who, for some reason, nobody in a position to stop the danger or disaster believes. The protagonist may be a conspiracy theorist who has espoused theories that are kooky or haven't panned out as real in the past. The protagonist may have no expertise whatsoever in the field in which the danger or impending disaster has been discovered, hence he or she isn't taken seriously. In most cases, the protagonist is some sort of amateur or hobbyist whom authorities don't have any real reason to listen to.

Perhaps the danger the protagonist has discovered is so outrageous or so implausible that no one in a position to do anything about it believes him or her. Perhaps the source of the information pointing at the danger is a crackpot website or some other unbelievable or seemingly unreliable source.

Regardless of why the protagonist is not believed or not listened to, that character is now presented with a problem. He or she is the only person who sees a danger or disaster incoming, which means he or she is the only person in a position to stop it.

This character, unable to hand off responsibility for stopping the potential disaster, decides to step up and take care of it himself or herself. This protagonist may recruit help, assemble a team, or go it alone. But success or failure rests squarely upon the shoulders of our plucky protagonist who has volunteered to stand up against the coming disaster.

At its core, this is a David versus Goliath story. The little guy—the unlistened-to, ignored, discounted guy—is the only one who sees the truth and can stop disaster.

You also might not be wrong to think of this as a "Boy Who Cried Wolf" story if your conspiracy theorist has tried to raise a red flag on other perceived dangers in the past that haven't turned out to be real.

ADJACENT TROPES
    -- Accidentally Find Dangerous Object/Information
    -- Witness/Bystander Sucked Into Danger
    -- Troubled Protagonist
    -- Amateur Sleuth
    -- Junior Spy Ignored
WHY READERS/VIEWERS LOVE THIS TROPE
    -- we all perceive ourselves as little guys...and love to imagine saving the world, becoming heroes, and reaping all the rewards of that
    -- most of us perceive ourselves as good guys. We believe ourselves to be noble, well-intentioned, and potentially heroic. If

faced with a crisis, we'd like to believe we would step up and do the right thing. (Indeed, many people who've never faced real danger are absolutely convinced they would do the heroic thing when faced with a life-threatening situation.)

-- we get enjoyment from watching the system, the "Man", get a black eye for missing something that some outsider amateur was able to spot and understand

-- most peoples' lives are pretty mundane from day to day. How exciting would it be to discover something so important that it could save the world

-- how cool would it be to be so smart and insightful that I spot something everybody else has missed, and furthermore, which is incredibly important

-- something unexpected could come along to completely shake up my boring life, reinventing both my life and me

-- the fantasy or actual realization that I have the potential and ability to change my life into something totally different than it is right now

OBLIGATORY SCENES
THE BEGINNING:

This story almost always begins with some sort of introduction to your reader or viewer of the protagonist living in his or her normal world—hello, Christopher Vogler and The Hero's Journey.

Many, I daresay the majority of, thrillers open by diving into the main problem of the story, or at least an action sequence, in the very first scene. We see the main character doing something dangerous or cool right away. Even if the main character is trying to do something perfectly mundane in the opening, in most thrillers, something happens to force him or her to do something dangerous, cool, or special.

Thriller openings need to grab your audience's attention and promise to hold that attention for the remainder of the story. They need to promise action, danger, and suspense, and they almost always give your audience a sneak preview of what kind of hero the main character of your story is going to be.

Big, exciting openings are one of the main story elements that pull your audience into a thriller story. While these make sense in most thriller tropes, the Conspiracy Theorist Ignored/Protagonist Disbelieved is unique in its need to establish the normalness, outsider-ness, amateur-ness, or possibly nut job-ness of your protagonist first.

The second scene (or series of scenes) almost always shows the protagonist discovering a huge problem. If the protagonist is right, this problem might lead to devastating consequences. It *must* be dealt with.

It is technically possible to reverse these two opening scenes or sequences. You can open with your protagonist discovering, piecing together, or in some other way discovering some terrible problem. But, for your audience to believe it when this character has a hard time getting anyone to listen to him or her, you're going to have to establish why that is...which means establish that your protagonist is a conspiracy theorist, amateur, outsider, or something else to explain why he or she isn't being listened to.

The rest of the beginning is usually taken up by your protagonist trying to convince someone, anyone, to listen to him or her.

Depending on how much or little help you plan to give your conspiracy theory protagonist over the rest of the story, you may choose to end Act One with him or her finally being believed, in which case, now the good guys are going to marshal their resources and head out to do battle with the huge problem the protagonist has discovered.

Alternately, you may choose to have your protagonist fail to get anyone to listen to or believe him or her. In this case, the protagonist may head out alone to stop the looming disaster, or the protagonist may assemble his or her own team of friends and allies to help deal with the problem only he or she sees.

Traditionally, the opening act of a thriller ends with a mini-crisis in the big plot problem that ups the danger and threat of the looming disaster.

However, this story arc not only revolves around stopping a disaster but also revolves around a personal story of trying to earn or redeem credibility. Hence, you have a choice to make. You may choose to end Act One by focusing on the external plot and giving your audience a glimpse of just how bad the looming disaster is going to be. Or you may choose to focus on your protagonist's personal struggle to be taken seriously and end Act One with him or her ultimately being believed or not being believed.

Both possible endings of Act One constitute a mini-crisis that will launch your story into the next act effectively.

THE MIDDLE:

If you didn't end the first act on a plot crisis that gives your audience a better idea of just how dangerous the problem is that your protagonist has uncovered, you'll undoubtedly do so in the middle of your story.

The middle is also where your protagonist is going to shift his or her attention away from trying to convince others that he or she is right and into taking direct action to deal with the problem he or she has spotted.

- The protagonist may join a law enforcement or government team that now takes the threat seriously and wants the protagonist's help.
- The protagonist, having failed to convince authorities of the authenticity of the threat, may assemble his or her own team of friends, allies, and experts to deal with the problem.
- Or the protagonist may head out into battle alone and start dealing with the problem alone.

In any of these cases, more information about the problem must be gathered. The person(s) causing the problem figure out somebody is trying to foil them and start taking direct action to stop your protagonist.

Conflict between the protagonist and the bad guy(s) commences and proceeds to grow more dangerous, more violent, and more intense.

As the villain's plan comes closer and closer to fruition, the stakes ratchet up higher and higher. You audience should grow more and more worried that the protagonist (and whoever he or she is teamed up with) might fail to stop the looming disaster—which is now on the verge of happening.

In the personal side of this story, the middle is where the protagonist is disbelieved by others. He or she may be ridiculed, ostracized, or even punished in some way for persisting in believing there's a problem and in taking action to solve it.

As the social, work, or relationship pressure on the protagonist builds higher and higher, the protagonist may experience doubt, second guess himself or herself, and even try to walk away from the quest to stop the big bad thing from happening.

The problem the protagonist first discovered has likely taken on a human face, and your hero is now locked in a human confrontation he or she neither asked for nor wanted, complete with all the fears, stressors, anger, and other negative emotions of human conflict. The potential personal cost to the protagonist of continuing on in this quest to stop something terrible builds until the protagonist must seriously question whether it's worth the price to carry on.

BLACK MOMENT:

The external plot problem of your story reaches the boiling point. It may spill over in part or in whole, depending on the type of problem you've chosen to write about. If there's a confrontation brewing between your protagonist and the forces of evil in your story, one happens now...and your protagonist loses. In fact, your protagonist loses badly enough that he or she believes there's no way to salvage the situation.

If your disaster centers around a single big, explosive event, for example, a nuclear weapon exploding, you will probably want to save that for the climax of your story. In this case, the plot black moment will need to revolve around some intermediate step along the way to the ultimate disaster.

For example, your protagonist may be racing to locate the weapon before it's moved to its final destination but fails to do so. Or the protagonist may try to stop the weapon from being armed, and fail. What's important in making the protagonist's failure to stop this piece of the puzzle is that he or she believes that this was his or her last realistic chance to stop the disaster. Having failed at this juncture, the catastrophe is now inevitable. The protagonist and your audience must think all is lost.

Obviously, audiences know that somehow you, the author, are going to come up with a brilliant way for your protagonist to save the day. But at this moment in the plot, you don't want your audience to see the path forward to success. For a black moment to be black, all must appear lost.

On the personal side of this story, whatever potential price the protagonist has been threatened with for pursuing this course of action comes due now and must be paid. He or she might lose a job, lose a relationship or friendship, lose a home, lose a family member, lose his or her reputation, or something else of great value.

The devastation is now complete. The protagonist has failed to stop the bad thing from happening, and on top of that, has paid a great personal price for being foolish enough to believe his or her own conspiracy theory and wrecks his or her life over it.

THE END:

If there's one last plot twist left that will make the disaster worse, this is when it happens. In the plot revolving around a single catastrophic event, that event now happens or threatens to happen.

It's now or never for the disaster to be halted. The protagonist comes up with a new plan, gathers his or her resources, and makes one last effort to stop the looming disaster.

Often, it's the protagonist's success at stopping a disaster that finally convinces skeptics around him or her to believe the threat has been real all along and the protagonist was right all along.

The ending is when the protagonist finally resolves the personal conflicts that have ended up entangled with his or her efforts to stop something terrible. The protagonist's loved one(s) might finally realize how much danger they're in and witness the protagonist's heroic efforts to save them. The government might quietly visit a skeptical boss to put in a good word for the protagonist—abruptly convincing the boss that the protagonist isn't a liar, after all. A spouse might see the protagonist on television, bloodied, battered, but heroic in the aftermath of a near disaster.

Or you might resolve the personal conflict more quietly. The protagonist might show proof to a loved one of what he or she has done. A friend might decide that it doesn't matter if the protagonist was right or wrong—they want to be friends anyway. The protagonist might promise a spouse that he or she will never try to save the world again.

You may choose to have your protagonist go back to her or her mundane, normal life—probably grateful for the boredom and normalcy of it now. You can end your story with the protagonist transformed and/or his or her life transformed in some way. And, of course, you can set up a sequel by showing your protagonist stumbling across some new and unbelievable problem in need of solving.

KEY SCENES

   -- the moment the protagonist first shows someone else what he or she has discovered

-- the *second* time the protagonist tries to convince someone in a position to fix the problem or that the problem is real

-- a loved one or friend doesn't believe the protagonist

-- a loved one or friend threatens the protagonist if they actively pursue their crazy idea (try to stop the looming disaster)

-- the protagonist walks out on a loved one or friend

-- the protagonist seriously doubts himself or herself

-- the protagonist tries to back out of fixing or helping fix the problem

-- first direct confrontation between the protagonist and the human expression of the looming disaster

THINGS TO THINK ABOUT WHEN WRITING THIS TROPE

What is the problem the protagonist is going to discover? Based on that, what's an interesting or unexpected way the protagonist can discover it?

Does the protagonist discover the looming disaster by accident? Does he or she put together seemingly unrelated pieces of information to arrive at a conclusion? Does he or she have some specialized knowledge or expertise that allows him or her to spot the problem?

Who is your protagonist? Is he or she a conspiracy theorist? Is he or she just some average person who discovered something wild that other people struggle to believe?

Why is your protagonist someone the authorities don't believe?

Why isn't your protagonist credible?

If he or she has espoused crackpot theories in the past, do they relate to the crackpot theory he or she has finally gotten right in this story? If so, how?

Is the protagonist an amateur, hobbyist, or civilian of some kind?

Does the protagonist have any special or specialized knowledge? If so, what?

Why hasn't anyone else found this problem? Why your protagonist?

Did the protagonist believe the evidence he or she found initially or not?

What convinced the protagonist the problem is real?

What will happen if this problem isn't fixed? What must happen to stop it?

How can you make the problem worse? Much worse? Much, MUCH worse?

How can you make the potential consequences unimaginably bad?

Having now cooked up a world-ending disaster, how can you make those huge, broad-brushed stakes deeply personal to the protagonist? How can you make those stakes even more personal and even more important to the protagonist?

Will the protagonist take the information he or she has found to authorities? If so, who? If not, why not?

Beyond not believing him or her, how do any authorities/experts respond to the protagonist's suggestion—or insistence—that there's a huge problem? What actions do they take in reaction to the protagonist?

Does the protagonist try to convince the same person again? Does the protagonist try to find some other expert or authority to convince?

When do the authorities finally believe the protagonist? NOTE: This can happen very early in your story, somewhere in the middle, or it may not happen until the very end.

What finally convinces the authorities that the protagonist is right?

If the protagonist becomes part of an official team put together by the proper authorities, what special expertise does he or she bring to the team to justify his or her presence on the team? Why doesn't the government, law enforcement agency, corporation, have anyone on staff who can do the same thing the protagonist can, or do it better?

Does the protagonist have trouble keeping up with (physically or metaphorically) the team he or she is asked to work with?

If the authorities do not ultimately invite the protagonist onto some sort of team to deal with the problem, is there still going to be a team fielded by the authorities to handle the crisis? If so, how will the protagonist and that team interact over the course of your story?

If nobody in authority buys the protagonist's theory, will the protagonist put together his or her own team to stop the looming disaster? If so, who are those people? What kind of expertise do they each bring? What are the internal politics, tensions, conflicts, and push-pulls between them?

If the protagonist decides to stop the big problem alone, why does he or she make that decision? Does he or she expect to die or not? Either way, how does that affect his or her actions over the course of the story?

How do loved ones or friends of the protagonist react to his or her "conspiracy" theory? How do they react to the protagonist after hearing his or her wild belief?

What is at stake personally for the protagonist if he or she doesn't give up this wild goose chase? Who or what will he or she lose by continuing to pursue this course of action?

How will complete information about the problem be uncovered?

How will you put a human face on the problem? Is there a bad guy plotting the whole disaster? Is there a conspiracy by multiple individuals to commit a crime of some kind? Did someone put the whole disaster into motion?

How will this human representative of the crisis interact with the protagonist? What sorts of confrontations, conflicts, and cat-and-mouse games will they play?

What information does the protagonist have to find or learn over the course of the story to stop the looming disaster? Where, when, and how will he or she find it?

What other conspiracy, theory, or guess does the protagonist get totally wrong somewhere in the story? What does that do to his or her confidence? His or her certainty of being right about the current problem? To his or her credibility? How do other characters around the protagonist react to his or her mistake?

How will the protagonist lose in the black moment? What specifically goes wrong? Does he or she screw it up? Get outsmarted? Not anticipate something the bad guy(s) did? Not move fast enough? Something else altogether?

On a personal level, who or what does the protagonist lose in the black moment? What can you do to make this loss even more devastating?

What changes between the black moment and the story climax that allows the protagonist to win the second time around?

How does the protagonist stop the looming disaster or defeat evil? Is it smart, plausible, or clever enough to make your audience read or watch your next project?

Is the way the protagonist wins believable even if it's not plausible?

Is the disaster stopped for now or stopped permanently?

How will those who've disbelieved the protagonist react when they find out he or she was right all along? How will skeptical loved ones and friends react?

How do the authorities react to the protagonist after the looming disaster is averted?

Will the protagonist get public credit for stopping the disaster or not? Either way, what does that look like?

How do the protagonist and loved ones/friends resolve their conflicts? Is it a happy outcome? A sad one? Has the power dynamic in the relationship changed? If so, how?

Does the protagonist go back to his or her original life, or does his or her life transform in some way? If so, how?

How does the protagonist change over the course of this story? How is he or she different by the end? How will you show these changes and differences?

If others try to pigeonhole the protagonist back into their former life, does he or she go willingly? Refuse to go back? Something else?

Has your protagonist proven his or her credibility and reliability by the end of the story? If so, how? If not, why not?

If your protagonist is widely believed by the authorities by the end of your story, why? How has he or she changed over the course of the story to make that possible?

TROPE TRAPS

The protagonist is a two-dimensional and clichéd conspiracy theorist, for example a gamer dude sitting at a computer in his or her mom's basement, or in a Faraday cage, or in the back of a dingy computer repair shop.

Not explaining how, if the protagonist is so smart, nobody believes him or her.

Having been right about this one crackpot theory or threat, the protagonist is suddenly right about everything.

Having spotted this one danger, the protagonist is suddenly an expert whom real experts listen to without any skepticism.

Not explaining why this "expert" protagonist is living as an amateur and devoid of any credibility or reputation with authorities who matter.

Not explaining why people in official positions with bona fide expertise in the same field haven't spotted the potential disaster that the protagonist has.

The authorities are too blindly skeptical and implausibly dismissive of the protagonist's theory/discovery.

The authorities are too blindly accepting of and implausibly willing to act upon the protagonist's theory/discovery too soon.

Painting all official people/authorities—government employees, law enforcement, scientists, analysts—as stupid, ignorant, biased, and unwilling to listen to reason.

The way the protagonist discovers the looming disaster is lame or many other people would also have already discovered it.

The stakes in the looming disaster aren't high enough to hold the interest of your audience.

Failing to create an antagonist character to frustrate, foil, and confound the efforts of the protagonist and relying solely on how bad the bad thing is going to be to sustain your plot.

If the protagonist stops the disaster alone, he or she magically develops a whole raft of specialized skills he or she uses to save the day...without any explanation of when, where, how, or why he or she abruptly knows these things.

By the end of your story, the Cheeto-chomping, couch-potato gamer is assigned to an elite government task force and runs around the world decked out like James Bond.

Failing to include or explore any of the protagonist's personal relationships in your story or how they affect his or her decisions.

Failing to make big stakes personal enough to the protagonist for your audience to relate to those stakes personally.

CONSPIRACY THEORIST IGNORED/PROTAGONIST DISBELIEVED TROPE IN ACTION

Movies:

- The Manchurian Candidate
- Edge of Tomorrow
- They Live
- Conspiracy Theory
- Blow Out
- Z
- The Parallax View

. . .

Books:

- The Camel Club by David Baldacci
- The Dante Club by Matthew Pearl
- The Girl With the Dragon Tattoo by Stieg Larsson
- Conspiracies by F. Paul Wilson
- Pattern Recognition by William Gibson
- The Pelican Brief by John Grisham
- Shutter Island by Dennis Lehane
- The Constant Gardener by John LeCarré

6

CORRUPT BOSS

DEFINITION

In this story, the protagonist realizes his or her boss is...wait for it...corrupt. What makes this an interesting story is the question of what the protagonist is going to do about it.

The answer to this question lies in the intersection of the protagonist's own ethics and moral standards and how important, powerful, and unassailable the boss is.

Which is to say, there are endless combinations of these two factors that will make your own version of this story fresh and unique.

Is the protagonist a low-level enforcer in the mob, while the mob boss has round-the-clock security (that can be bought off for the right price)?

It's a straightforward decision for the low-level enforcer until the Feds arrest him and tell him to inform on the boss or go to jail...and then the enforcer's mother is protected by the mob boss from an attack and saves her life...

You get the idea. This is a trope about a decision.

Does the protagonist turn on his or her corrupt boss or not? Your job is to make that decision as close to impossible to make as you can.

And, once the protagonist has decided to turn on his or her boss, you job is then to make acting upon that decision as risky as you possibly can.

This story is known for its twists and turns, divided loyalties, surprise developments and diabolical twists that keep your protagonist and your audience off balance and constantly scrambling to adapt as new information and new threats keep popping up.

This culminates in a confrontation between the protagonist and his or her boss where the corrupt boss is finally taken down and taken out.

ADJACENT TROPES

- -- Infiltrating a Group
- -- Insurmountable Villain
- -- Corrupt Corporation Exposed
- -- Reluctant Informant/Witness
- -- Own Government is Evil
- -- Corrupt High Official
- -- Incompetent Senior Officer

WHY READERS/VIEWERS LOVE THIS TROPE

-- most people are suspicious that some powerful organization or person they dislike is corrupt, and we love the idea of seeing that person exposed and removed from power

-- we derive great satisfaction from seeing people who think they're too powerful to face justice getting a good dose of it

-- we've all had a boss we can't stand and relate strongly to a story about taking down a horrible boss

-- we all love an underdog who overcomes his much more powerful adversary

-- we love to believe that the little guy has a lot more power to mess up the big dog's life than the big dog realizes

. . .

OBLIGATORY SCENES
THE BEGINNING:

We typically meet the protagonist of this tale going about his or her regular work life until he or she encounters their boss. The boss may be intensely charming or positively evil—that's up to you.

But then the protagonist witnesses the boss doing something, overhears him or her saying something, or finds some piece of information about the boss that seems to indicate he or she is up to no good.

The boss could be skimming money out of the group's bank, planning to oust another powerful member of the organization, secretly be in league with the enemy, or something else dastardly, immoral, or wrong.

Now the protagonist has a dilemma. Does he or she look the other way and ignore what he or she knows? Does the protagonist tell someone else?

OR

Does the protagonist investigate more on his or her own to try to find solid proof of what he or she now suspects?

The beginning introduces the other major characters in this story who will be critical to the protagonist's decisions and actions going forward.

The beginning ends with the point of no return for the protagonist. He or she does something or learns something that, if others find out he or she knows or has done this thing, will get him or her fired, harmed, or killed.

THE MIDDLE:

The protagonist working alone or with someone else, commences searching for more evidence against the boss.

Law enforcement may be involved. If so, they may be giving the protagonist a full support team, or they may be giving him or her no help at all, other than an offer of criminal immunity or something else equally nebulous.

The protagonist takes increasingly dangerous chances trying to get the evidence he or she needs to prove the boss is corrupt.

With each new piece of information gathered, the story changes courses, morphs into something else, or does something surprising.

All the while, the protagonist wrestles with big moral questions of loyalty, justice, and right and wrong. Should he or she stop this madness? Should he or she stop taking such huge chances in search of proof? Is he or she wrong about the boss? What if there's a plausible explanation for everything the protagonist has heard and seen so far?

The boss may realize somebody's investigating him or her but doesn't identify the protagonist as the mole. Indeed, the boss may trust the protagonist and ask the protagonist to find the disloyal employee and tell the boss...or the protagonist to kill the mole.

The protagonist's risk-taking and newfound courage may get noticed and rewarded within the organization before the boss realizes why the protagonist has suddenly had a change of personality.

This, too, creates a dilemma. The protagonist has unlocked the secret of how to succeed in this organization. If he or she abandons their secret investigation, he or she could rise straight to the top of this outfit and be a big, successful boss himself or herself.

Every stop of the way, the protagonist must ask himself or herself if this investigation is a mistake.

The middle may end with the protagonist finally finding the solid proof he or she needs to prove the boss is corrupt. Or it may end with the boss discovering that the protagonist has been snooping and disloyal to him or her.

The protagonist is thrown out of the organization, or worse, he or she is captured and questions about his or her activities. If your protagonist is a slick liar, he or she may avoid being killed, but the boss's trust of him or her is blown.

BLACK MOMENT:

The protagonist's ability to investigate the boss and prove the boss is corrupt has been ruined. His or her sneaky activities have been uncovered, and everyone else within the organization no longer trusts him or her.

Even if the protagonist isn't fired outright, he or she might as well have been. He or she is a pariah, outside the circle of trust.

If he or she has been kicked out of the organization, a friend may secretly contact the protagonist to express sympathy, but nobody will overtly acknowledge him or her.

The protagonist has well and truly failed to take down the corrupt boss. The protagonist's sense of right and wrong is outraged, but there's not a thing he or she can do about it.

The boss was too smart, too powerful, too protected by loyal flunkies to take down. The protagonist gave it his or her best shot but failed.

OR

The black moment can be purely a moment of emotional dilemma. The corrupt boss offers the protagonist the promotion he or she has always wanted into the job he or she has always dreamed of.

Does the protagonist reach for the brass ring he or she has always coveted, knowing that it means turning a blind eye to the boss's corruption, or does the protagonist throw away everything he or she has ever worked toward and wished for to be true to his or her sense of morals and doing the right thing?

If your story has been a series of dilemmas, this one is the mother of them all. The one thing the protagonist wants above all else is pitted against his or her moral code.

It's the sort of dilemma that will have your audience perched on the edge of its seats wondering what the protagonist is going to do.

THE END:

Something happens to help the protagonist make his or her final choice to do the right thing to try to expose or take down the corrupt boss.

Finally at peace with his or her decision, the protagonist turns his or her attention to planning how he or she is going to confront the boss and end him or her.

While the reality is that most underlings or informants are likely to turn over collected evidence to law enforcement officials and let them make a rather anti-climactic arrest, this boring ending isn't often used in thrillers. Instead, your audience wants to see the protagonist directly confront the dastardly boss who has led your protagonist on such a twisting chase.

Hence, this story almost inevitably leads to a direct confrontation between the protagonist and his or her corrupt boss. The protagonist has one shot (or one last shot) at taking down the boss. Get this wrong, and the protagonist will be destroyed, metaphorically or literally.

The protagonist must put everything on the line to have even a slim chance of defeating a much more powerful opponent with more resources, more experience...more everything.

It's a David against Goliath battle with your underdog protagonist having to pull out a miracle in the same way David did to kill Goliath.

For what it's worth, David used a sling to hit Goliath in the head with a stone, knocked the monster flat on his face, and then David rushed in and cut off Goliath's head. Feel free to symbolically have your protagonist knock down the boss, then jump in and destroy him or her when the boss goes down for the count.

At any rate, the protagonist prevails, the boss is defeated, and moral right is served.

The protagonist may still get kicked out of the organization or, at the other end of the spectrum, he or she might get put in charge of the organization.

It's up to you to consider the appropriate price the protagonist must pay for his or her disloyalty to the organization and what reward the protagonist deserves for his or her devotion to doing the right thing.

KEY SCENES

-- the protagonist tells someone he or she trusts that the boss might be corrupt, and that person tells him or her in no uncertain terms to leave it alone

-- the protagonist learns it's an open secret inside the organization that the boss is corrupt and that everyone looks the other direction from the corruption

-- the protagonist is pressured by someone outside the organization to expose suspected corruption in the boss

-- the boss does or says something nice or approving to the protagonist, notices an achievement of the protagonist's, or singles him or her out for attention and reward

-- The protagonist is nearly caught snooping

-- something happens that gives the protagonist a compelling need to keep his or her position inside the organization

-- someone else in the organization is caught being disloyal and the boss does something terrible to that person

-- the protagonist decides to stop trying to investigate the boss but then sees something that gives him or her no choice but to continue on

-- the protagonist's moral dilemma becomes impossible. He or she is paralyzed and can't make a choice. Either way, the consequences of the decision are unbearable

. . .

THINGS TO THINK ABOUT WHEN WRITING THIS TROPE

What organization does the protagonist work inside? Who's his or her boss?

What's the protagonist's position, power, and influence inside the organization?

Is the boss in a high enough position that being corrupt at that level has significant consequences for others?

What's the corrupt thing the boss is doing? Can you make it worse? Much worse?

Can the corruption evolve or grow over the course of the story into something with horrific consequences?

What does the protagonist see that first makes him or her suspicious that the boss may be corrupt?

Who does the protagonist tell about what he or she has seen or heard? Which is to say, who does the protagonist trust absolutely? Is the confidante a family member, friend, or coworker?

What does the confidante advise the protagonist to do or not do? What does the protagonist think of that?

Does anyone (particularly the authorities) try to coerce the protagonist into collecting evidence against the boss? If so, who? From what agency? How does this person approach the protagonist? What does the protagonist think of this development?

What reason does the protagonist have to be loyal to the organization?

What reason does the protagonist have to be loyal to the boss, specifically?

What are the consequences of disloyalty in this organization? How will we see these happen to someone else in the story?

What information does the protagonist need to find on the boss? How will he or she go about looking for it?

What new information does the protagonist find that confuses him or her or leads him or her to realize there's something else entirely going on, or something much bigger than he or she expected going on?

What are the twists and turns the investigation is going to take? What's surprising, unexpected, or shocking that the protagonist uncovers somewhere in the story?

How does the danger keep increasing in your story? What chances does the protagonist take, and how do they keep getting more risky?

When and how does the boss figure out somebody's snooping?

How much or how little support is the protagonist getting from someone else, either inside the organization as a co-conspirator or from outside the organization? Who's helping him or her?

What does the confidante think of the protagonist continuing this investigation and taking increasingly bigger risk?

What happens that keeps making the protagonist's moral dilemma worse? What are several more things that happen to deepen this dilemma?

At what point does the boss discover it's the protagonist betraying him or her? How does the boss react? What does the boss do?

What happens in the big confrontation between the protagonist and the boss? How does it get set up and by whom? Who else is involved with the final fight?

How does the protagonist ultimately prevail over the corrupt boss? Does the protagonist have help? If so, from whom and what does this person do?

What happens to the corrupt boss? Is he or she arrested? Does the boss flee? Does the protagonist kill the boss?

What happens to the protagonist? Is he or she penalized or rewarded in some way by the organization? Kicked out of it? Promoted?

Does the protagonist lose or gain friends out of this experience? If so, who? How?

Is the protagonist pleased about what he or she did or is he/she conflicted, regretful, afraid, or something else?

What lesson(s) has the protagonist learned? How is he or she changed? How does this affect the protagonist, his or her loved ones, and his or her life when the protagonist finally returns to his or her normal life?

TROPE TRAPS

The protagonist is too low level to plausibly see or hear the boss do corrupt things.

The protagonist doesn't have the knowledge or expertise to plausibly spot the boss's corruption.

The protagonist magically understands complex information well above his or her education level to spot the corruption.

The boss is a completely obvious villain and leaves the audience with no doubt whatsoever that he or she is a criminal in need of taking down.

The boss is really nice, supportive, and encouraging of the protagonist, and your audience feels bad that the protagonist goes after him or her.

The protagonist never faces moral dilemmas that are truly hard to navigate. Moral dilemmas aren't interesting if they're easy.

What's right and wrong for the protagonist to do in this story is never in any question. The correct path is totally obvious to everyone in your audience, and the protagonist seems too stupid to live for not seeing it immediately.

The protagonist has no personal stake in which way this story goes. Protagonists aren't interesting if all their decisions are bloodless, logical, and have no emotional component.

The protagonist magically develops breaking and entering or hacking skills to spy on the boss that the protagonist didn't have before.

The boss seems stupid for never suspecting the protagonist is informing on him or her.

The boss seems stupid for never noticing that the protagonist is spying, snooping, and surveilling him or her.

The consequences for getting caught being disloyal are sufficiently scary.

The boss never punishes anyone harshly in the story.

The danger never increases as the story progresses.

The protagonist is never in serious physical jeopardy.

The boss doesn't fight his own fights, and the protagonist never gets to confront him or her directly.

The protagonist pays no price nor receives any reward for exposing the boss to be corrupt.

CORRUPT BOSS TROPE IN ACTION
Movies:

- The Firm
- Michael Clayton
- Serpico
- The Insider
- Disclosure
- Silkwood
- Goodfellas
- The Irishman

Books:

- Layer Cake by J.J. Connolly
- Company Man by Joseph Finder

- Paranoia by Joseph Finder
- Company by Max Barry
- Disclosure by Michael Crichton
- The Circle by Dave Eggers
- The Insider by John Francome
- The Partner by John Grisham

7

DAMAGING INFORMATION REVEALED

DEFINITION

Unliked the blackmail trope where damaging information is withheld and used to extort someone, in this trope, the damaging information is revealed to open the story.

This means the main thrust of this type of story revolves almost entirely around managing and dealing with the fallout after the information comes out.

Of course, the degree of "public-ness" of the released of information is up to you. Damaging information may come out only to, say, one's spouse and wreck a marriage or it may be revealed on national news.

Likewise, the nature of the information itself that is released is open to many possibilities. It can be the stuff of traditional blackmail —damaging pictures of an affair, proof of a crime, emails plotting something nefarious, or embarrassing criticism of something or someone.

OR

The damaging information might reveal that a company knows

it's polluting the environment and killing innocents. It might reveal a plan to invade a neighboring country, or more sneakily, a secret plan to destabilize another government.

In general, the information being revealed to open your story is embarrassing or humiliating, is going to get someone in trouble, will cause a disaster, or will cause major conflict between the victim of the release and others.

The way the person(s) who are damaged by the information release react to this event is also open to many possibilities:

- The victim may choose to track down and exact revenge —or death—upon whoever released the information.
- The victim may spend the entire story proving the information false.
- The victim may spend the story attempting to rehabilitate his or her reputation, or repairing the damage caused by the information.

The release of highly damaging information may provoke a crisis of some kind—a lawsuit, a corporate takeover, or an international crisis between armies or nations. It may be this crisis that consumes the majority of your story.

The one thing that remains constant in this trope is your story arc:

- Damaging information is released in the beginning.
- The middle is taken up with the victim(s) of the information release reacting to it and trying to repair the damage.
- The black moment involves the victim(s)—your protagonist(s)—trying and failing to repair the damage.
- And the ending centers around the resolution of the problems caused by the release of the damaging information.

. . .

ADJACENT TROPES
-- Blackmailed/Extorted
-- Deathbed Confession
-- Diary/Old Letter/Old File Discovered
-- Posthumous Letter/Will
-- Whistleblower
-- Journalist Breaks Story

WHY READERS/VIEWERS LOVE THIS TROPE
-- we all know someone we'd just love to embarrass or stick it to... and revealing dirt on them is just the way to do it

-- we all have a secret or two that we dread anyone else finding out about and can totally empathize with the victim and any revenge he or she cares to take

-- becoming a hero for exposing corrupt, greedy, or evil people, corporations, or governments...getting to be David to an evil Goliath we hate

-- who doesn't love to watch someone, who was way too full of himself or herself, squirm

-- enjoy watching the great be brought low

OBLIGATORY SCENES
THE BEGINNING:
While it seems obvious that the story would open immediately with the release of the damaging information, which is the premise of or catalyst for the rest of the story, often your audience needs a little backstory or pertinent information first.

While it's not necessary for your audience to fully understand all the implications of the information's release, it is important that your audience recognize that the information is both really important and really damaging pretty quickly after it's released.

That said, you may choose to make the seriousness of the information's release clear initially through the horrified reactions of the characters who witness its release or find out about it soon afterward.

In this case, you will likely spend most of the rest of Act One showing your audience why the information is so damaging, particularly when the first fallout of its release occurs.

The beginning of the story is typically filled with reaction to the release of the information. Your characters will express dismay, shock, rage, and whatever other emotions are appropriate to your story. Friends, family, and co-workers may blame and shun the victim.

Act One often begins with the first crisis that results from the release of the information. An outraged spouse might demand a divorce. A lawsuit is filed against a major corporation. One country might launch a preemptive or retaliatory attack upon another.

In short, sh*t just got real.

THE MIDDLE:

The middle of your story is where the crisis deepens. The longer-term, potentially more damaging effects of the information release hit. The victim of the release might lose a job or get evicted from his or her home.

Your audience sees the results of being blamed or shunned—the victim misses a big event or opportunity that nobody told him or her about. Violence erupts. War breaks out.

This may be where the victim, fed up with being a victim, decides to strike back and takes action. He or she may go hunting for the source of the information's release to exact revenge. The victim, if wrongly accused or maligned, sets out to clear his or her name.

Whoever released the damaging information may have more attacks up his or her sleeve and launch them at the victim now.

Vice versa, the victim may commence attacking the person who released the information. A cat-and-mouse game may ensue as they both hunt each other.

Meanwhile, the consequences and fallout of the released information continue to build and harm the victim more and more. Reputations and lives are ruined. Infuriated or panicked victims make bad decisions and pile more mistakes on top of the original one(s).

If a net is closing in around the victim, he or she feels it coming and tries—to no avail—to evade it.

The entire middle of the story builds toward a crisis provoked by the released information that will destroy everything.

What exactly is that "everything"? That's up to you to define. Your job is to make sure your audience cares deeply about the thing or person about to be destroyed, though.

BLACK MOMENT:

Whatever awful outcome the victim was trying to avoid in the aftermath of the information release comes to pass, or the wheels are set in motion of it inevitably coming to pass.

The victim's best efforts to stop the disaster, to contain the damage, or to repair his or her life fails.

The worst thing the victim has been dreading happening comes to pass. His or her life is ruined. He or she fails to stop the awful thing he or she most fears from happening.

Personal relationships are destroyed, lives and reputations are ruined, and the war is lost. The worst possible outcome has occurred.

THE END:

Something or someone gives the battered and bruised victim a piece of information, a pep talk, a hint of some kind—some missing piece of information or help that the victim can use to turn the tide against the terrible things that have happened or are happening.

The victim, our protagonist, gathers himself or herself for one last herculean effort to stop the terrible thing that was provoked all the way back at the beginning of the story by that release of damaging information.

It's not uncommon in this trope that the initial release of damaging information sets in motion a chain of events that lead somewhere very far removed from the inciting event of released information.

While the black moment is the penultimate event in that chain of events, the end revolves around stopping the absolutely ultimate end point of that chain of events.

The monster, released from its cage in the black moment, must now be hunted, confronted, and killed. The terrible event that happened (or started) in the black moment must be stopped in its tracks or contained somehow to protect others.

The corrupt corporation, that won the lawsuit in the black moment and got away with murder, is finally exposed to all the world for the evil entity it is and destroyed.

This trope relies heavily on drawing victory from the jaws of defeat. Indeed, this trope opens with a defeat, and the entire story piles on more and more defeats until the protagonist finally manages to overcome all of it in the end.

KEY SCENES

-- the victim/protagonist finds out the damaging information has been released

-- someone whose opinion of him or her is valuable to the victim finds out about the damaging information and is hurt, disappointed, or furious at the victim

-- the victim feels alone, friendless, or abandoned

-- the moment the victim decides to fight back

-- whoever released the damaging information threatens to do even more harm to the victim if the protagonist doesn't stop coming for him or her

-- someone stands up for the victim or stands beside the victim, even if it's only moral support

-- the victim, having lost everything and everyone, decides to do whatever it takes to repair the situation, even if it means dying (literally or metaphorically)

-- the victim is forgiven for the transgression that was revealed in the damaging information

THINGS TO THINK ABOUT WHEN WRITING THIS TROPE

What is the information you'll release in the beginning of your story? What damage does its release cause? How is it damaging? Why is it damaging? To whom is it damaging?

What chain of events does the release of this information set in motion? How does it set that chain in motion?

Who is the protagonist (the primary victim) of your story?

Who will be the human face of what was damaged (the secondary victims)?

Who is your villain, which is to say, who is the human face of the chain of events that is set in motion?

Is there one villain who released the information and another villain who is triggered or activated by the chain of events that's set in motion? Are they working together or not? If so, how are they connected? If not, how will the information released by Villain #1 set Villain #2 into motion?

Why was the information released? What did the person(s) releasing the information hope to gain by doing so?

Why does the person(s) who released the information think it was the right thing to do? Was it actually the right thing to do? Do the ends justify the means?

Does the person(s) who released the information know how much damage it will cause? Do they care about the damage? Why or why not? Do they desire the damage? If so, why?

How can you make the fallout from this damaging information worse? How can you make it much worse? How can you make it absolutely catastrophic?

How can you make the fallout from the released information more personally damaging to your protagonist?

How will the fallout unfold in your story?

Is your story based primarily around managing fallout from the damaging information, or is it based around a chain of events that unwinds as a result of the damaging information being released? Or will you do both?

Is there more than one kind of fallout from the damaging information? Is at least one of these emotional, intimate, and personal to your protagonist? How about to your villain?

If there's only one main fallout from the damaging information, how will you show different takes on that fallout from various characters' points of view? How will it affect them each differently? For that matter, ask yourself this question for every different kind of fallout you're planning to explore in your story.

How will the damage and/or its consequences get worse and worse over the course of the story? What's the climactic damage or catastrophic event that your protagonist most dreads coming to pass? How will you make that come to pass?

Can you make this damage worse? Can you make it catastrophic on a larger scale? Can you make it catastrophic on a personal scale?

Once the worst consequence has happened, what resources does your protagonist have left to call upon to try one last time to contain or repair the damage?

What lesson will he or she learn from defeat (from the black moment) or what new information will he or she come across that makes success in containing the damage possible in the end? If the protagonist obtains new information, how will he or she get it?

How will the protagonist finally defeat the bad guy (if there is one), stop or contain the ultimate damage from the released information, and/or repair his or her reputation?

How will the protagonist and his or her loved ones, friends, and co-workers move on with life after this disastrous episode is resolved? Are they still connected? In contact?

Has forgiveness been granted to the victim/protagonist? If forgiveness is required, who asks for it? Who forgives whom? What does that moment of forgiveness look like?

TROPE TRAPS

Creating damaging information that doesn't seem all that damaging or dangerous and doesn't engage your audience's imagination right away.

Giving away all the important information right up front in the first dump of damaging information and leaving yourself nowhere to escalate the threat and the tension for your audience in the rest of the story.

The damaging information released has little or no personal impact on your protagonist...failing to plausibly engage your main character emotionally, and hence failing to engage your audience.

The damaging information doesn't lead to any other larger threat that must be contained, or it doesn't create a big enough mess for the main character to fix and that will sustain an entire story.

The chain of events unleashed by the damaging information's release is too obvious, too predictable, and boring.

The victim of the damaging information (typically your protagonist) doesn't suffer enough after the damaging information becomes public.

Conversely, the reaction to and fallout from the release of damaging information is way too big or overblown to be plausible in your story.

Whoever released the damaging information never suffers any consequences for having done so.

Whoever released the damaging information doesn't have any more means of causing havoc and fades out of your story and just disappears...never giving the victim of the damaging information a chance to get justice or retribution.

The protagonist has no allies, friends, or loved ones who stick with him or her through thick or thin...and comes across as a jerk for having nobody at all who believes in him or her.

Conversely, people who should plausibly abandon the victim of the release of damaging information remain inexplicably loyal.

The black moment isn't black enough. NOTE: This story already started with a defeat. You need to reach for very big defeats in your black moment to make that particular failure sufficiently devastating to your audience.

Failing to build to a big enough climax.

While your story may have traveled very far from the initial release of information, failing to wrap up the fallout from the damaging information.

Failing to show life after the release of the damaging information for anyone who was damaged by its release (failing to show confrontations, forgiveness, or reconciliations afterward).

DAMAGING INFORMATION REVEALED TROPE IN ACTION
Movies:

- Erin Brockovich
- The Post
- All the President's Men
- The Whistleblower
- The Insider
- Spotlight

Books:

- The DaVinci Code by Dan Brown
- The Pelican Brief by John Grisham
- The Winner by David Baldacci
- The Sigma Protocol by Robert Ludlum
- The Insider by Stephen Frey
- Paranoia by Joseph Finder

8

DEATHBED CONFESSION

DEFINITION

Somebody who is on the verge of dying confesses something and starts a chain of events that will become your story. Seems simple enough, doesn't it? Ahh, but there are so many possible variations on this theme that this is a fascinating trope to play with. It lends itself to many possible variations.

This story is often built with two parallel timelines, one told in the past (relating to the deathbed confession itself) and one told in the present (relating to the consequences or downstream effects of the confession). This dual timeline or dual storyline structure occurs when the information the dying person reveals has to do with some secret from the past that he or she chooses to reveal rather than take to the grave.

This story type often involves investigating some old crime, old secret, or old piece of information. It's possible or even likely that most of the players involved in this past event are already dead. Hence, this "old" event may lack tension or threat in the now. In this case, it's up to you to create some sort of current day threat that results from the confession of this old information.

In the Damaging Information Revealed trope, the person who releases the information is out to hurt someone—to overtly cause damage or chaos. In the case of a dying person making a confession, the motivation for his or her revelation is probably different. Perhaps it's guilt. Not wanting to take an important secret to the grave. Maybe a promise to wait until death to reveal something. It's even possible the dying person isn't aware what they're saying by the time they make their deathbed confession.

And of course, it's possible the person making a deathbed confession does so in order for some wrong to be righted, some threat he or she was too afraid to confront during his or her life to be eliminated, or some lurking danger of which he or she is aware to be dealt with.

Yet another variation on this trope is that the deathbed confession is an actual confession to a religious figure. It might get made in secret or it might not. It might be overheard, or the religious figure who received the confession may choose to share it with someone after the dying person expires.

Why the dying person waited until his or her deathbed to confess is up to you to explain. Or you may choose to let the dying person take his or her reasons for making the confession so late to the grave with him or her.

Typically, people surround themselves with family as death approaches. Perhaps the protagonist of your story is a relative or loved one who feels responsible for dealing with the fallout from their loved one's deathbed confession. Or the dying person may specifically set a quest for a loved one with their confession.

Alternately, family may choose to enlist an expert or professional to deal with the fallout from their loved one's deathbed confession. In this case, you'll need to find some way to make the chain of events personal and important to the outside expert who's brought in to deal with the fallout of the confession.

In yet another variation, the dying person may summon an expert, capable of handling the problem posed by their intended confession, to hear what they have to say before they die.

Once the confession has been made, the dying person typically dies or is fully incapacitated fairly immediately. If they were to survive deep into your story, they would be available to answer more questions and give additional information or support that would make the search for more information much less interesting to your audience.

Also, there's a reason the dying person waited until the last minute before death to 'fess up. It's very likely the dying person didn't want to be alive to deal with fallout from his or her confession and would be appalled to make the confession and then survive and recover. Although, this scenario poses another possible and unconventional variation on the deathbed confession trope.

At any rate, the remainder of the story consists of seeking and finding more information about the confession, seeking and finding the threat posed by this confession, and then neutralizing the threat.

As for why your protagonist embarks on this dangerous journey, that's up to you. Perhaps the protagonist made a promise to the dying person. Perhaps the protagonist feels familial loyalty to the dying person or wants to solve the problem uncovered by the deathbed confession as a tribute to the (dead) loved one. Perhaps the threat uncovered by the deathbed confession is so pressing the protagonist has no choice but to deal with it.

It's worth noting that the deathbed confession itself may introduce another trope—new information about a cold case crime is revealed, an unexplained disappearance is mentioned, a fugitive is revealed not to be dead after all. Sky's the limit on what the confession actually consists of.

Regardless of the new direction the deathbed confession sends your story, the requirements of this trope still must be met. There must still be a personal and/or pressing reason for the protagonist to pursue the fallout from the confession. The middle of this story must include investigation of the information revealed. The black moment and ending of this story must include dealing with some element that was suggested by the deathbed confession way back at the beginning of the story, and the request or demand of the deathbed confession must be met by the end of the story.

To be clear, a deathbed confession can simply be a reveal of previously unknown information before someone dies. In this case, it doesn't rise to the level of being a trope. A deathbed confession as trope must ask a question, make a request, or set some goal for the protagonist that your main character feels obligated to resolve.

While the confession itself may not be made in the form of a question, request, or demand, it nonetheless has that effect. The dying person passes on some responsibility to someone else who can deal with the thing they did not resolve.

One might reasonably argue that this trope is merely a variation upon a Dangerous Information Revealed Trope. However, it's such a common variation that it deserves its own entry in this volume. And I would argue that the motivation of the person revealing the information—be it to hurt someone/cause chaos or be it the last act of a dying person—is likely to make a significant difference in your story.

ADJACENT TROPES

--Accidentally Find Dangerous Object/Information
-- Dangerous Information Revealed
-- Diary/Old Letter/Old File Discovered
-- Posthumous Letter

WHY READERS/VIEWERS LOVE THIS TROPE

-- receiving a gift of great value in the form of valuable information

-- an exciting mystery drops into your otherwise mundane and boring life

-- you have one last chance to prove to a loved one how much you cared about them (and possibly to demonstrate your love for the dying person to the rest of your family)

-- getting a chance to live up to the expectations of a dying loved one, to do

something as big or heroic as they did in their lifetime, or to step into a family legacy

-- an otherwise tragic loss leads to triumphant victory against some evil or rights some great wrong

OBLIGATORY SCENES
THE BEGINNING:

This trope always includes a deathbed confession somewhere in the beginning, but it may not happen in the opening scene. It's possible the person who's going to make the deathbed confession isn't yet on his or her deathbed. In fact, he or she may start your story perfectly healthy, and some event may abruptly put that person on his or her deathbed.

Likewise, your protagonist may start the story nowhere near the dying person and may, instead, be called to the dying person's side.

Regardless of how you put someone on their deathbed and get someone close by to hear his or her dying confession, both must happen to set this trope in motion.

Almost without exception, the information revealed in the confession is incomplete and launches some sort of investigation, search, or mission, or the confession includes some sort of request or demand for action. Furthermore, this request carries the weight of being someone's final request.

The dying person typically dies before the end of Act One, leaving the protagonist fully on his or her own to pick up the gauntlet and complete the quest the dying person has set for them.

If you've set up some sort of dual timeline, somewhere in Act One you will want to give your audience the flashback scenes or backstory information that introduces the secondary story line. However, choose your spot(s) carefully and make sure your reader is fully invested in the main story line before you risk distracting them with a secondary timeline, flashback story, or parallel past events.

The beginning usually ends with some sort of event or crisis that proves the information shared in the deathbed confession is true/accurate. This event or crisis also is the first big plot twist that introduces real and immediate danger to the protagonist.

THE MIDDLE:

The middle of the story is where the major complications of the information revealed in the deathbed confession happen. If the confession launched the protagonist on an investigation, a search, or some sort of mission, that set of actions happen in Act Two.

The stakes must climb steadily through the story. You can accomplish this by revealing more and more details of the threat, by having the threat become more aggressive toward the protagonist, or you can throw your protagonist into mortal danger as he or she sets out to finish the task that was set for them by the dying person.

The personal stakes to the protagonist increase as the threat of failing increase. Whatever motivates him or her to pursue this quest becomes more challenging to stay true to. As the risks proliferate, the temptation to walk or run away from the mounting dangers also mounts. In most cases, the protagonist promised the dying person that he or she would see this thing through and fix it. In the middle, your protagonist will inevitably question their decision to make that promise.

If you've set up your story with some sort of dual story lines, you'll bounce back and forth between the two as needed in the middle of the story.

Consider ending you main story line's scene on a cliffhanger and jumping to the secondary story line, leaving your audience frantically wondering what's going to happen next in Story Line #1. They'll race through reading or viewing the next scene Story Line #2 to find out what happens in Story Line #1.

Meanwhile, end the next scene in Story Line #2 on a cliffhanger of its own that leaves your audience frantically wondering what happens next and racing through the next scene from Story Line #1 to find out what happens next in Story Line #2.

By bouncing from cliffhanger to cliffhanger, you can pull your audience forward through dual story lines at a breakneck pace that's both suspenseful and exciting.

As the cliffhangers unfold, the stakes, danger, and tension in your story builds toward a crisis, regardless of how many story lines you're running. The full threat posed by the dying person's request is revealed, and protagonist is probably feeling as if he or she is in way over their head. No wonder the dying person put off dealing with this thing for so long and ultimately passed it over to someone else to handle!

If you're using a dual story line structure, somewhere in Act Two, the two story lines should start to converge. They don't have to come together completely, but part of the suspense of your story will revolve around the two story lines starting to approach or entangle with each other (with the promise of a spectacular explosion when they finally collide).

BLACK MOMENT:

This is typically when the big threat or danger the protagonist has been racing to identify and stop blows up. The thing the dying person dreaded enough to wait until his or her deathbed to confess happens. Indeed, the worst thing the dying person feared happens. However, over the course of your story, the threat the dying person knew about has been revealed to be only the tip of a larger iceberg— one that your protagonist is now having to deal with.

It's worth noting that whatever the dying person feared is bad enough all by itself to defeat your protagonist in a fairly spectacular fashion. Often, the black moment and climax of this trope are delineated by the black moment being what the dying person feared and the climax being what your protagonist fears (and which is probably worse).

Keep in mind that the black moment has to feel like a big loss for your protagonist, big enough that the protagonist doesn't believe in that moment that he or she has any chance to win.

THE END:

This is when everything comes together into one big, final conflict. Whatever the dying person feared, the quest set by the dying person, and the crisis caused by the chain of events that have unfolded in your story all come together to make one gigantic mess that the protagonist must fix.

The pressure is unbearable as the protagonist's promise to see this crisis through collides with his or her desperate need to run far, far away from the danger he or she must now face.

Often, we see protagonists get one last piece of information or one last bit of help that makes them think they can win if they try again after the failure of the black moment. Often in this trope, it's one last nudge from beyond the grave, one memory of the dead person to whom they made a solemn promise, one reminder of their vow, that convinced the protagonist to give it one last try to resolve the crisis that has come to full and awful fruition.

After the climactic battle, it's common to see the protagonist visit the dead person's grave, perhaps visit a surviving family member, or in some way pay tribute to the dead person. Often the protagonist wants to tell the dead person the quest is resolved, tell the dead person they can rest in peace now, or just pay respects.

KEY SCENES

-- the moment when the protagonist realizes the request, demand, or mission the dead person asked of them is a lot more complicated, difficult, or dangerous than he or she was initially led to believe

-- the moment the protagonist realizes the dead person has gotten them in way over their head

-- something totally unexpected is revealed about the deathbed confession that goes well beyond what the dead person confessed to

-- the protagonist is angry with the dead person for getting them into this mess/danger

--the dead person (or a proxy) reaches out in some way to the protagonist to encourage him or her or to reinforce the importance of staying the course

THINGS TO THINK ABOUT WHEN WRITING THIS TROPE

Who is the dying person? How has he or she arrived at the point of death, which is to say, what are they dying from? How does that affect how the deathbed confession is delivered?

Who is the protagonist of your story? Why this person?

What is the information in the deathbed confession? What's the backstory surrounding that information?

To whom will the confession actually be delivered? Is this the protagonist? If not, who is it? How will that person convey what he or she heard in the confession to the protagonist?

Does the protagonist have a personal relationship with the dying person before your story starts? If so, what kind of relationship is it? How close are they? How long have they known each other? How well do they know each other?

Why does the dying person choose that particular person to hear his or her dying confession?

Is your dying person ultimately a good guy, a bad guy, or something in between? When in your story does the protagonist suspect this? When does your protagonist know this for sure?

Why is your protagonist the one person who steps up to deal with the dying person's final request? Why him or her? What's his or her motivation? Is that motivation strong enough to keep him or her going through the whole story? Can you beef up that motivation in some way?

What is the unresolved thing about the deathbed confession that still has to be dealt with now? What's the current and ongoing danger that must be resolved?

Why didn't the dying person deal with this thing before he or she died?

Why is the protagonist able to deal with this problem when the dying person was not? What skills or knowledge does the protagonist have (or acquire) that makes him or her more capable of handling the problem?

When and how does the dying person actually die?

What's the chain of events that's set in motion by the deathbed confession?

Is there other information that the protagonist can find that adds more understanding to the confession? Did the dying person know this additional information or not? If so, why didn't he or she reveal all of it? If not, why not?

What's the even larger problem the protagonist finds when he or she sets out to fulfill the dying person's last request? Can you make this problem bigger? Can you make it much bigger?

Does the protagonist get mad or resent the now dead person at some point in your story? When? Why?

Does your protagonist need help to deal with the problem? If so, who does he or she recruit to help? Why that person(s)?

What's the thing/event/outcome the dying person feared so much that he or she didn't reveal the information until the point of death? Or why was the information so critical to share before dying that the dying person went to great lengths to make a deathbed confession at all?

What makes the problem in your story even scarier than the dying person realized?

What's the thing/event/outcome your protagonist most fears? How is this even bigger and worse than the dying person had any inkling of?

After his or her defeat in the black moment, what's the lesson learned, information found, or reminder of promise made that will motivate your protagonist to give it one last try to prevail?

How does your protagonist (and friends) overcome the final obstacle and achieve victory in the final conflict?

When it's all said and done, the crisis solved, what does your protagonist do? How does he or she connect one last time with the dead person and bring your story full circle, back to the beginning, when the dying person made their confession and set this whole story in motion?

TROPE TRAPS

The deathbed confession is a complete and detailed information dump that a) leaves little to no room for new information reveals, and b) is wildly implausible for someone that near death to make.

The protagonist has no personal connection with the dying person and no reason to make a solemn promise to fulfill that dying person's final request and then go to a ton of trouble to keep that promise.

The protagonist doesn't have a powerful enough motivation to see the dangers through and it's implausible that, at some point, he or she wouldn't just give up and walk away.

The deathbed confession doesn't start a chain of events that cascade through your story.

The deathbed confession doesn't come across as a big enough secret to have been kept until the last second before death.

The dying person hangs around long enough to have shared a lot more critical information, and yet never tells the protagonist things that would be incredibly useful or important.

The dying person is a big, ole' drama queen, and his or her final request is overdramatic or even melodramatic and sends the protagonist on a dumb or wild goose chase.

While real people may be assholes right up to when they die, your audience may not buy your dying person acting that way by withholding vital information or setting up your protagonist to fail or die. (Unless, of course, your dying person is the villain or associated with your story's villain.)

The protagonist gets sidelined by some other crisis in your story and never fulfills the final request of the dying person.

The protagonist breaks his or her promise to the dying person and doesn't do what he or she promised to do.

When the protagonist finally gets to the big confrontations at the end of the story, the dead person's biggest fear was lame or not worth having gone to so much trouble over.

After the black moment, there's no even bigger crisis to deal with or the situation hasn't gotten even worse.

You fail to give your audience a moment of closure where the protagonist acknowledges or sits with having fulfilled his or her promise to the dead person.

DEATHBED CONFESSION TROPE IN ACTION
Movies:

- Citizen Kane
- The Legend of Bagger Vance
- Diamonds
- The Fountain
- The Giver
- Wanted
- The Kite Runner

Books:

- Atonement by Ian McEwan
- The Confessor by Daniel Silva
- The Tenth Justice by Brad Meltzer

- The Last Confession by Solomon James
- The Keeper of Lost Causes by Jussi Adler Olsen
- The Confession by John Grisham
- The Silent Patient by Alex Michaelides
- The Dying Hour by Rick Mofina
- The Confession by Jo Spain

9

DIARY/OLD LETTER/OLD FILE DISCOVERED

DEFINITION

In this trope, someone, typically the protagonist, discovers a diary, an old letter, or an old file that leads to some sort of mystery or crime in need of solving. Again, this trope technically falls under the Accidentally Find Dangerous Information trope. But it's such a common story type that, like Deathbed Confessions, it deserves its own entry in a volume of thriller tropes.

In this story, someone has recorded dangerous information but then never shared it with anyone else. Perhaps keeping the information private was intentional or perhaps it was accidental. But in either case, the information has remained hidden for a long time.

You can go as old as you'd like with your found information—potentially thousands of years if you want to do a lot of historical research! Regardless of how recent or old the information is inside the diary, letter, or file, it leads your protagonist on some sort of hunt, chase, or mission.

The information may or may not be complete, and filling in the blanks may be a major part of your story. As your protagonist learns more, the danger increases. He or she may uncover a plot, a crime, or something else with people alive today who have no interest in seeing it exposed.

Like the deathbed confession, this trope often employs a secondary timeline in the past. You may choose to tell this story of past events in flashback, real time with headers to indicate a jump into the past, through other found documents, or in the imagination of your main character.

Regardless of whether you make it a complete story line or not, the events of the past detailed in your found document(s) will ultimately intersect with current events to cause a crisis of some kind that the protagonist must handle.

It's worth noting that someone discovering an old, written document (usually) isn't particularly exciting or dangerous, which can make for a very dull opening to a thriller novel. Likewise, sitting around reading old documents also doesn't make for interesting or compelling action. Your challenge, then, in writing this trope is to find a way to make your audience care about your protagonist, feel anxious about him or her, and be desperate to know what happens next to him or her.

Unlike the deathbed confession, your protagonist must find some compelling personal motivation for seeing through the mess that he or she has uncovered. In this trope there's no promise made to a dying person to guilt the main character into pressing onward in his or her mission; hence, the mystery, crime, or crisis revealed in the old diary, letter, or file must do the heavy lifting of motivating your main character to stick with it to the end.

This means your diary, letter, or file must lead (quickly if you don't want to lose your audience's interest) to a problem big enough or dangerous enough that the protagonist feels compelled to solve it. Ideally, the protagonist has personal skin in the game that helps make the crisis feel absolutely necessary to him or her to resolve.

ADJACENT TROPES

-- Posthumous Letter
-- Accidentally Find Dangerous Object/Information
-- Mystery in Personal Effects
--Deathbed Confession

WHY READERS/VIEWERS LOVE THIS TROPE

-- the personal connection of reading someone's private thoughts or correspondence

-- the voyeurism of reading someone's private thoughts or correspondence

-- who doesn't love a good puzzle to solve

-- enjoying the historical context of old writings—a glimpse into a distant or disappeared past, culture, or time

-- the past—our past or our family's past—can reach out to affect our present in unexpected ways that shake up our mundane lives

-- I found something cool that everybody else overlooked

OBLIGATORY SCENES
THE BEGINNING:

This trope begins with the discovery of a diary, an old letter or letters, an old file—some sort of written document that has been hidden, forgotten, or packed away until now. Somebody, often the protagonist, stumbles across or in some way unearths these written documents and reads them.

The document(s) reveal some sort of mystery, crime, crisis, or shocking information that sends the main character on some sort of quest or investigation.

Because reading an old diary isn't necessarily the most exciting action sequence to open a thriller novel with, it's not uncommon for this trope to be paired with some other, more action-oriented trope. In that case, the discovery of the diary, letter, or file often happens a few scenes into your story while the more exciting beginning of the other trope sucks in your audience.

The protagonist typically does some initial investigation to learn more about the document(s) he or she has found and the information revealed in the writings. There's often a second inciting incident in the beginning of this trope where the act of doing an internet search or asking questions of relatives, friends, or someone associated with the document(s) provokes a reaction that actually launches the main action of your story.

The beginning ends with some sort of mini-crisis provoked by the protagonist revealing to others that the diary, letter, or file has been found. A criminal revealed in the old writings may try to silence or kill the person who found the diary, letter, or file. A law enforcement or government official may warn off the protagonist. Someone may threaten the protagonist. An attempt may be made to steal the diary, letter, or file. You get the idea. Have fun with this crisis and come up with something exciting and surprising to your audience.

THE MIDDLE:

The chain of events set in motion by the information in the diary, letter, or file unfolds. In most cases, the information in the writings is incomplete. At a minimum, it's only told from one point of view. There is usually more information for the protagonist to search for and find. With each additional bit of information, the danger and the unfolding crisis must ratchet up.

If people are still alive who were involved with the original events described in the writings, they surface and have strong opinions about continuing or stopping any ongoing investigation. If the writings are old enough that no contemporaries of the events described are alive, then you will need to create someone with a vested interest in stopping the protagonist from finishing his or her investigation or mission to reveal the whole story or stop the problem the writings have revealed.

As the forces trying to stop the protagonist line up against him or her and the protagonist's efforts to learn the full story and stop the bad thing from happening gather steam, more clashes ensue. Violence may threaten break out, and the danger rises exponentially as your middle rises toward a crisis.

BLACK MOMENT:

Typically, the black moment in this story involves the crisis that the protagonist expects to happen as a result of reading the diary, letter, or file and his or her subsequent investigations. This is the obvious crisis, even though it's still a crisis. And it's still a major defeat for the protagonist. He or she might not have been fully prepared going into the conflict, or he or she might lack a vital piece of information that would have been helpful.

This failure may send the protagonist back to the drawing board to figure out what he or she missed...or this failure may be the moment when the protagonist realizes he or she is in way over his or her head.

This is also the moment that tests the protagonist's resolve to see this crisis through to a successful conclusion. This failure is big enough, scary enough, and dangerous enough that he or she seriously contemplates bailing out and fleeing the quest, mission, or crisis they now find themselves engaged in. Doubt and fear overwhelm the protagonist in this dark moment.

THE END:

In this trope, the protagonist often learns one last, key bit of information or finds one last document that helps him or her realize how to go about defeating the bad guy or stopping the crisis that's unfolding. Because this trope revolves around knowledge—finding out something from an old diary, letter, or file—it's very common for one last piece of written information to be the mechanism by which the protagonist ultimately figures out how to defeat the evil forces arrayed against him or her.

That said, it's not necessary for the final push, the final burst of motivation or confidence, to come from a written document. It can come from an ally, friend, or loved one, or even from within the protagonist himself or herself.

Armed with the knowledge, skill, or weapon that will turn the tide, the protagonist goes into battle one last time and engages in a climactic confrontation with the forces of evil or the danger that was laid out way back in the beginning in that dusty, forgotten diary, old letter, or old file. And this time, the protagonist succeeds.

Often, the wrap-up of this story includes what happens to the diary, letter, or file. Sometimes, it's donated to a museum. Perhaps it's hidden away again. You can even choose to have your protagonist burn it. But, in most cases, the writings are relegated to history. They've been laid to rest as it were.

KEY SCENES

-- the reading of the diary, letter, or file and the realization that this is something big

-- the first discovery that the problem, quest, or crisis laid out in the writings remains unresolved today

-- introduction of the current day bad guy associated with the story the writings tell

-- the first direct conflict between the protagonist and the bad guy

-- someone tries to steal, destroy, or suppress the writings (who may or may not be the bad guy)

-- the protagonist tries to walk away from the investigation...but gets sucked back in (against his or her will)

-- the protagonist discovers the problem is so much worse than was described in the writings

-- some threat from the past combines with a present-day threat to make the situation even worse

. . .

THINGS TO THINK ABOUT WHEN WRITING THIS TROPE

What is the written thing that will be discovered in your story? Where will it be discovered? How will it be discovered? Who discovers it?

Is the person who discovers the writings your protagonist? If so, how is he or she related to the writings found? If not, why this protagonist? Who brings him or her in to deal with the mystery in the writings? Why does someone bring him or her in to help or take over the investigation?

How will whatever is in the writings be or become personal to the protagonist? What motivates him or her to see this investigation through, no matter what?

Is the protagonist personally connected in some way to the writer of the found writings? If so, how? If not, how can you make that connection?

How old are the writings? What information is in the writings that sets off the initial investigation?

What information is left out of the found writings? When will you reveal this information in your story? How will you reveal it?

How is the left-out information more dangerous than the information that's included?

What sort of mystery, crime, quest, or mission is revealed in the writings?

How dangerous does the protagonist believe his or her investigation is going to be initially?

How will you make the finding of some old, forgotten, or hidden writings suspenseful enough to interest and hold the attention of your audience?

How will the protagonist pursue learning more about the situation described in the writings?

What makes the investigation dangerous? How can you make it

more dangerous? How can you make it much more dangerous? How can you make it downright deadly?

Does the protagonist have the expertise he or she needs to deal with the crisis that unfolds, or does the protagonist need to learn something to be able to deal with what's unfolding?

Does the protagonist recruit expert help? If so, who? What kind of expertise does the person(s) bring to the story?

Who will become the human face of the threat in the writings? Is it a killer? Someone with a secret he or she wants to remain hidden? A conspirator? A terrorist? Someone else?

How will the antagonist try to scare off the protagonist? How will the antagonist try directly to stop the protagonist?

What kind of conflict will the protagonist and antagonist engage in? Is it a game of cat-and-mouse? Does one terrorize the other? Do they hunt each other? How can you make this more fraught? More dangerous? More tense for your audience?

What did the person who wrote the diary, letter, or file most fear would happen? What does that look like when it really does happen?

How and why does the protagonist initially fail to stop the bad guy or bad thing from happening?

What does the protagonist learn that makes him or her able to defeat the bad guy or bad thing in the climactic confrontation?

What does the protagonist do with the actual diary, letter(s), or file(s) when the whole story is over and the crisis resolved?

TROPE TRAPS

Your story opening is boring and you lose your audience before you ever engage them.

The information in the diary, letter, or file is too complete and leaves nothing for the protagonist to discover and leaves no questions in your audience's minds.

The diary, letter, or file is written in too modern language or uses anachronisms for the time in which it was written.

The protagonist is magically an expert in all the things he or she needs to know how to do to investigate the writings and solve the subsequent crisis.

The protagonist has no vested, personal interest in solving the unfolding crisis and extremely implausibly decides it's worth dying over to solve.

The writer of the diary, letter, or file was omniscient and always exactly right.

The threat from the past and the threat from the present never intersect and have nothing to do with each other.

There's never a human face put to the problem, mystery, crime, or crisis the writings describe. (Man against the System or the Machine isn't nearly as riveting as Man against Man.)

The writings are overquoted or underquoted, and in either case, they're hard to read, hard to understand, or just dull.

The protagonist doesn't have a plausible motivation to pursue this dangerous investigation.

The protagonist never questions his or her devotion to solving this mystery, crime, or crisis.

The black moment isn't black enough and the big climax isn't big enough to overcome the rather dry and unexciting way this trope started.

The audience never finds out what happened to the diary, letter, or file that started this whole mess.

DIARY/OLD LETTER/OLD FILE DISCOVERED TROPE IN ACTION

Movies:

- National Treasure
- The Ninth Gate

- Possesion
- The Goonies
- The Thomas Crown Affair

Books:

- The Thirteenth Tale by Diane Setterfield
- The Lake House by Kate Morton
- The Secret History by Donna Tartt
- The Book of Air and Shadows by Michael Gruber
- The Ghostwriter by Allessandra Torre
- The Shadow of the Wind by Carlos Ruiz Zafon
- The Historian by Elizabeth Kostova

10

ENEMIES ALLIED IN DANGER

DEFINITION

In this trope, two people who are enemies or who come from enemy nations or enemy groups of some kind must work together to stop some evil.

They may be assigned to work together by their superiors, or they may be thrown together by circumstances or events. They may remain enemies throughout your story or they may become friends along the way.

It's worth taking a moment to clarify the difference between rivals and enemies.

Rivals both want the same thing and are competing to have it. One of them will get it or get it first. It's not a destructive competition, however. While the one who doesn't get it will be disappointed, the good thing he or she wanted still exists and can be tried for another day, or possibly shared.

Enemies on the other hand, want opposite things. Only one of them can get the outcome they want, and the other person irrevocably loses or fails. Enemies operate in a win-lose situation. It's fully a destructive competition with the highest possible stakes.

Enemies will actively work to make the other person lose,

whereas rivals simply race to get to a prize first. Enemies will destroy something rather than let their enemy have it whereas rivals both want the same prize and won't destroy it to prevent their rival from getting it.

A common arc for this type of story is:

- A problem occurs that requires the combined expertise of two enemies to solve it.
- Forced together, they want nothing to do with each other. As they work together on the problem.
- They reluctantly find common ground and possibly form a friendship.
- One of them betrays the other.
- They break apart to deal with the problem solo in hopes of getting the outcome he or she wants.
- But, when the big crisis hits, the enemies must work together one last time, like it or not, to stop the great evil or terrible event.

ADJACENT TROPES
-- In Love With the Enemy
-- Pitted Against Each Other
-- Criminal Helps Cop
-- Partnered with a Civilian
--Defending Despicable Client

WHY READERS/VIEWERS LOVE THIS TROPE
-- the friction of partners sniping at each other adds humor and delicious tension

-- the conflict that is sky-high between these characters adds even more doubt over whether these two enemies will manage to save the world or not

-- we like the idea of our enemies finally being able to see our character strengths and good attributes

-- if we had a chance for our enemies to get to know us, we might gain forgiveness from them

--we'd like to believe our enemies can overcomes their hatred and mistrust of us

OBLIGATORY SCENES
THE BEGINNING:

This story may begin with something bad happening on screen or on the page, or this bad thing may have already happened and is discovered to start your story.

This bad thing (the inciting event) affects two different people, groups, or nations who happen to be enemies.

Indeed, a smart bad guy might plan intentionally to attack two opposing people/groups/nations, knowing that they're wildly unlikely to be able to work together to defeat him or her.

Individually, the people/groups/nations realize they're not capable of defeating the bad guy on their own, or perhaps they don't have all the expertise or knowledge necessary to defeat the bad guy.

Individually, they also realize (to their chagrin) that the only person/group/nation with the expertise or knowledge they lack to defeat the bad guy is their enemy. And the more mortal they are as enemies, the higher the stakes in your story.

An offer is made by one side or the other to join forces—just for now—to defeat their common foe.

It's only at this point that the actual protagonists are ordered or assigned to work together.

As you can see, a fair bit of set-up must happen before your main characters come together. Typically, it's ideal to compress all of the background set-up as much as possible so you can get your main characters together and sniping at each other as quickly as possible.

Act One is usually marked by friction, arguments, and highlighting all the differences between your main characters. They are, in fact, enemies, and that must be made abundantly clear in the beginning of this type of story.

These two characters usually set hard boundaries between themselves—things they refuse to discuss or things they don't want the other one to do or say. They may even demark spaces, literal or metaphorical, that they don't want to share.

While they may be polite at first, their interactions rapidly devolve into bickering, outright fighting, working against each other, pulling against each other, and actual sabotage.

This inability to work together is usually what gets them into the first crisis of your story. The pair's reaction to the first crisis is often uncoordinated or at odds, and they fail to handle the crisis successfully.

THE MIDDLE:

The middle frequently begins with the fallout of the pair knowing they screwed up and possibly getting into trouble over it.

After that, two main plot threads will dominate the middle of your story.

First, the problem your protagonist pair is dealing with is getting worse, potentially exponentially so after the pair's big screw-up at the end of Act One.

The second main plot thread is the evolving relationship between your enemy protagonists. Fighting isn't working, so it's time to try something else. Perhaps grudgingly, your protagonists must now begin to work on becoming real partners.

Because it's danger that brought these two together, you should think in terms of ratcheting up the danger dramatically through the middle of your story. Whatever the initial problem was, it should become much, much worse by the end of the middle.

Likewise, what starts out as a grudging effort to set aside differences and work together grows into a real friendship or possibly even more.

Your protagonists must let down their guards, find common ground, and discover all the ways they're more alive than different. What specific things they bond over are up to you, but they connect on a personal and emotional level as they combine their skills and expertise to combat the growing threat.

As the middle of your story builds toward a crisis, your protagonists who have now become a team, a well-oiled machine as it were, have more success in their efforts. Working together is, in fact, better than working against each other.

BLACK MOMENT:

Lest your audience become complacent in how wonderfully your former enemies are now getting along, in the black moment one or both of your protagonists betrays the other.

They may do it unwillingly or because they were ordered to, or they may eventually remember their first loyalty to their own group/nation and revert to their traditional and expected behavior by sabotaging the other enemy protagonist.

Meanwhile, the problem the enemy-partners have been scrambling to stop blows up in their faces. The thing they were hoping wouldn't happen, does. Not only has their relationship imploded, but so has their mission. Indeed, you'll find that their relationship and the mission will tend to parallel each other in developing and devolving throughout your story.

All appears lost.

THE END:

It's in this moment of complete failure that, if they're to defeat the bad guy and stop the terrible crisis, one or both of the protagonists must give up the one secret/piece of information/hidden skill that they each have been holding back from their partner.

One of their groups or governments might also share something it has been holding back to turn the tide and give the protagonists one last shot at stopping the bad guy or crisis.

In spite of the betrayal(s) of the black moment, these enemies-friends-enemies must set aside their differences and work together if they're to prevail over evil. Getting to a place where they can do this may require forgiveness before the climactic battle. Or it may be in the aftermath of the climactic battle that these two finally make peace with each other.

Your protagonists may end the story as friends, or they may go their separate ways and return to being enemies, albeit respectful of each other now.

KEY SCENES

-- the moment the two enemies first meet. It's usually a catastrophe of some kind

-- the first big fight between them

-- finding something they have in common with each other (may happen more than once)

-- their superiors warn them against becoming too chummy/comfortable with each other

-- they each disobey orders so they can help their partner or advance the mission in some way

-- they question what they've always been told or have believed about their enemy

-- they're individually upset or hurt by their partner's betrayal

-- they each put themselves in harm's way to save their partner

. . .

THINGS TO THINK ABOUT WHEN WRITING THIS TROPE

Who are your two enemy-protagonists? Why are they enemies? What differs in their beliefs, morals, values because they're enemies?

Are they personal enemies or are they institutional enemies, meaning they come from enemy organizations, governments, cultures, nations?

Are they assigned to work together, do they find each other by accident or by coincidence, or do they join up as a pair in some other way?

What's the problem they're going to have to work together to solve?

Why can't they each solve the problem individually? Why is it bigger than each of them?

What do each of them (and their respective organizations, nations) bring to the equation that will make them, as a pair, capable of defeating the big evil?

Are there more people working with this pair to assist them in their mission? If so, who? In what capacity?

Have they met before? If so, when, where, how, and why? If not, why not?

Do they know anything about each other before they meet? If so, what? How do they find this out? If not, what are their first impressions of each other?

Why do they hate each other? What about the other partner drives each of them absolutely nuts (in a bad way)?

What do they initially argue or fight over?

What are some more important or significant things they disagree, argue, or fight over?

How does their bickering get in the way of them getting on with their mission? How does it cause a problem or even a failure within their mission objectives?

What's the first thing they discover they have in common? How do they figure this out? What are other things they eventually discover they have in common?

What's something they each like about the other one?

How does the development of their friendship parallel the progress of their mission?

How is the danger getting worse, and worse yet, as the story progresses?

Are they working on their own, or do they have some sort of support, team, or allies who help them? If so, how do their respective allies/friends/colleagues get along? Do they mirror the budding friendship, or are they still stuck in the initial hatred/enmity stage?

What do their superiors think of these two working together? Were the superiors forced into this uncomfortable alliance by *their* bosses? Do the opposing superiors get along or are they mortal enemies?

At what point in the story do your protagonists' superiors start to get worried that they're becoming too close or are becoming good friends? Why do their superiors worry about this?

Are your protagonists under orders to keep certain secrets from their partner? If so, what secret(s)? Why?

What does the mission/evil/bad guy turning into a crisis look like? How can you make it worse? How can you make it much worse?

In what way does each of your protagonists destroy the friendship? Why? Are they ordered to do so? Does something happen to make them distrust their partner again? Do they learn something disturbing about their partner? Do they eventually remember why they're loyal to their own "side" and regret becoming friends with the enemy?

How does each protagonist find out what the other one has done that constitutes a betrayal of their friendship? How does each one react in private? How does each protagonist react directly to the other one?

How bad is their separation/break-up/return to refusal to work together?

How does this return to enmity allow the bad guy/evil/crisis to explode? What does this explosion look like?

How devastating is this failure to each of your protagonists? How can you make the stakes even higher and the failure even more devastating?

How does the big plot failure in the black moment mirror the failure in the partners' friendship and vice versa?

What secret/withheld skill, information, knowledge does each partner bring to the table after the failure of the black moment that will help the pair finally defeat the big evil? Do their superiors know they're sharing this secret? If so, why wasn't this shared before now? If not, how will the superiors react if and when they find out the protagonist has unilaterally decided to share this secret?

How do these shared secrets ultimately allow the protagonists to win against the big evil in the end?

Do the protagonists make up and forgive their mutual betrayals of each other before they go into the climactic confrontation against the big evil? If not, how will they manage to work together to complete their mission in spite of the friction between them? If so, what does that reconciliation look like?

Who needs to forgive whom for what? How completely can and do they forgive each other?

If the protagonists make up after the big victory in the final confrontation, why do they bother to make up when they can just as easily go their own ways and never deal with each other again? What's the motivation for working out their differences?

How will you leave the status of their friendship? Will the story end with them being good buddies? Will they go back to their respective homes, jobs, countries, liking each other but not staying in touch? Will they end the story respecting but not liking each other? Will they go back to being enemies?

How about their respective organizations/nations? Will they end old enmities or will they remain enemies?

What have each of the protagonists learned about their enemy that they didn't know when the story started? Are they changed by that knowledge? If so, how and why? If not, why not?

TROPE TRAPS

Creating clichéd enemies. Typically, one character is well drawn, plausible, and has life breathed into him or her while the other character ends up being a cliché version of that main character's enemy or worst nightmare.

The big evil isn't big enough or bad enough for these enemies to plausibly come together to defeat it in spite of their enmity.

The protagonists are so opposite that, in the eyes of your audience, they would never plausibly find anything to respect or like about the other one let alone work well together in a high-threat situation.

The bickering, arguing, and fighting between your protagonists is *pro forma*--fighting for the sake of fighting. They don't have any real or serious differences in beliefs, opinions, values, or morals that cause believable friction.

The thing(s) they have in common are not significant enough to overcome their general hatred of each other.

Failing to answer this question for your audience: If these two people are truly enemies, how did they become friends so quickly?

The protagonists act so unprofessionally relative to what's expected of them based on their career, training, education, training that your audience doesn't buy their bad behavior (or their friendly behavior) as plausible.

One of the protagonists is way more skilled/knowledgeable/dangerous than the other one causing a power imbalance that makes the relationship wildly lopsided...where one of them should totally be in charge and the other one should clearly be subordinate, hence doing away with the plausibility of any real friendship between them.

The big evil they're supposed to be working to defeat gets lost in your story in the midst of all their relationship drama.

The secrets they withhold or the betrayals they perpetrate upon each other don't make sense to do—they're clearly only a device to cause conflict in your story but aren't logical things for either character to withhold or do.

The protagonists become friends too easily. They become enemies again too easily. They never do act like adults.

The pair's big failure in the black moment shouldn't have been a failure. They're too skilled, too smart, or too good at what they do to have failed together. Which is to say, you haven't made the threat big enough to defeat them both when they're working together.

The last secret or information that's revealed so the protagonists can win in the end isn't significant enough to plausibly turn the tide in favor of the protagonists and against the big evil.

Failing to resolve the relationship in a satisfying way for your audience.

Failing to resolve the relationship in a plausible way for your audience.

This one friendship is so amazing that it's sufficient to change the attitude of entire organizations or nations...in a highly implausible rapprochement of enemies.

ENEMIES ALLIED IN DANGER TROPE IN ACTION
Movies:

- The Man from U.N.C.L.E.
- Lethal Weapon
- Training Day
- Gorky Park
- The Fate of the Furious
- Rush Hour
- Mr. & Mrs. Smith
- The Hitman's Bodyguard
- Face/Off

• • •

Books:

- The Lion's Game by Nelson DeMille
- The Passage by Justin Cronin
- The Empress File by John Sandford
- Spy Camp by Stuart Gibbs
- The Gray Man by Mark Greaney
- The Faithful Spy by Alex Berenson
- The Athena Project by Brad Thor

11

FRAMED

DEFINITION

Criminal law defines a frame-up as the act of falsely implicating a person or person(s) in a crime by providing false evidence or testimony.

In this trope, someone is framed for doing something that will get him or her in trouble. While it's not necessarily a crime the victim is set up to appear as if he or she did, in almost all cases, there are serious negative repercussions for being believed to have done something bad.

In the framed trope, it's not merely being set up to look guilty for a crime that creates a full story arc. Rather it's the effort for the framed person to clear his or her name and prove his or her innocence that provides the main movement of the story.

The framed person spends most or all of the story trying to prove he or she didn't do what they've been accused of doing. The basic arc of this story is typically, framed for doing something, fighting the accusation/blame/consequences, and eventually clearing one's name.

It's worth noting this isn't a simple case of law enforcement mistakenly getting it wrong and wrongly accusing someone of committing a crime. This is a malicious and deliberate attempt by the framer to set-up the framed victim to take blame for a crime they didn't commit.

Even if this is a secondary trope and your story's primary trope follows the person trying to solve the crime or even the person who did the frame-up, the arc of the victim will remain the same. The victim will doggedly pursue clearing his or her name throughout your story, and for this arc to be completed, he or she must successfully prove by the end of the story that he or she has been framed.

There are several potential variations on this basic story:

- An innocent person might frame himself or herself to save someone else from taking the blame for something the second person did (or appears to have done). For example, a parent might take the blame for a crime their child committed.
- The protagonist might spend the story trying to clear someone else's name—a loved one, friend, colleague, or client who's been framed.
- A guilty person might frame himself or herself for committing a crime. He or she might do it to throw off an investigation by setting up "too obvious" evidence that will break down under closer examination.
- Someone might frame a guilty person for a crime in lieu of real proof being available. In this case, the framer is attempting to see justice done to someone who will otherwise get away with their misdeed.
- A dead person might be framed for a crime they didn't commit by the person who did the crime (or by someone protecting the real criminal) so the dead person, who can't fight back, takes the fall for committing the crime.
- An entire nation or government entity can be framed for a crime, and in this case, it's called a false flag operation. But the principle remains the same.

. . .

As for why one person frames another, it's usually a way of diverting blame away from the guilty party. In some stories, the framer might frame someone to harm the victim or ruin the victim's reputation, family, or business.

ADJACENT TROPES
-- Wrongly Accused
-- Clear My Name
-- Inadmissible Evidence
-- Wrongly Convicted
-- Supernatural Being Causes Crime
-- Possessed/Controlled

WHY READERS/VIEWERS LOVE THIS TROPE
-- it appeals to the terror in all of us of how fragile our freedom is. I could be taken down at any time for something I didn't do

-- we all know someone terrible who we know needs to be taken down...even if it's not specifically for the awful things they've actually done

-- loathing of bad people getting away with things because they're too rich or too powerful to suffer consequences

-- visceral fear of not being believed when we're telling the truth

OBLIGATORY SCENES
THE BEGINNING:
This story typically begins with the framed person finding out he or she has been framed. This victim may not even be aware of the crime they've been accused of having happened.

(For the purposes of this entry, I'll refer to the thing the victim is accused of as a crime with the understanding that it can be some other kind of misdeed a person is wrongly accused of having done.)

We may learn about the crime at the same time the victim does.

OR

You may open your story by showing the crime happening, staged or described so your audience doesn't know who did it. You may also choose to show some initial evidence being found at the scene of the crime that implicates your frame-up's victim, if that's how he or she is going to be framed.

You might even follow the official investigation for a few scenes before the evidence framing your victim is solid enough for the victim to be accused.

This opening is more typical when a frame-up is a secondary trope in your story and the primary trope follows the investigation and solving of the crime itself. In this case, the frame-up is a red herring or distraction the investigator must see through mid-story enroute to finding the real killer (who may or may not be the person who framed the victim).

If you choose to open with the crime and a bit of investigation, and the frame-up victim is, in fact, your main character, you may encounter audience confusion. You can fix this by starting the story in the frame-up victim's point of view and showing your audience—in a series of scenes that bounce between your victim's point of view, the crime, and the finding of false evidence—what the victim is doing at the same time the crime unfolds and the false evidence against him or her comes to light. This method keeps your victim front and center as the protagonist.

You can end Act One of this story in a variety of ways:

- The framed person is accused of or perhaps arrested for the crime they're loudly proclaiming they didn't do.
- With the first confrontation between the framed victim and the person whom the victim believes is framing him or her.
- With a major twist in the string of evidence being uncovered about the crime and who did it. This twist typically will further implicate the framed person for having committed the crime.
- If you're doing a variation on the Framed trope, the end of Act One may be where that variation is introduced. You might reveal that the person being framed is dead. You might reveal to the audience that the person being framed for the crime might actually have done it. You might reveal that the person being framed is guilty of doing other bad things for which he or she has never been punished.

THE MIDDLE:

If you're not lost in all the possible variations of this trope already, congratulations! The middle is where you're going to take this already very messy trope and make it even messier. This is where you'll reveal bits and pieces of the investigation into the crime that lead investigators ever more firmly toward believing the framed person's guilt. But the middle is also where you'll reveal bits and pieces of information to your audience that make them ever more doubtful of your framed character's guilt.

Your goal is to put your audience in direct conflict with the investigators in your story who are diligently, if wrongly, trying to solve a crime. By the end of the middle, you want your audience mentally screaming at the police or other investigators that they're wrong, they're not seeing the real evidence, that they're making wrong assumptions, or believing the wrong people.

As the investigation continues and draws toward conclusion at the end of Act Two, the net should close ever tighter and more inescapably around the framed victim. The victim should be ever more frantic, panicked even, that the frame-up is working and that nobody will believe him or her when they swear they didn't do the crime.

The entire "wrong" investigation typically concludes by the end of Act Two, when there's an arrest of the victim, or even a conviction of the victim about to happen.

BLACK MOMENT:

The black moment is obvious in this story. It's the moment when the framed person is held responsible for the crime they did not commit. They're arrested or convicted if a trial has been ongoing throughout the middle of your story. The investigators are certain they've got the perpetrator and they're finished investigating, satisfied they've got the right person.

The victim has not been believed. And now the consequences of failing to convince the authorities of his or her innocence are landing upon them in all their awful, unjust, horrifying reality.

For your audience, this should be a really uncomfortable emotional story beat. If you've done your job as a writer, your audience is appalled that an innocent person has been successfully framed and is now going to suffer wholly undeserved and unjust consequences of this gigantic mistake.

The victim of the frame up loses everything. Family, friends, coworkers—everyone turns their back on the victim, leaving him or her alone, abandoned, and unable to prove he or she is innocent.

THE END:

To everyone but the victim, the story is over. The police or lawyers, jury, and judge move on to their next case. The investigation is closed. The victim has lost job, family, money, and home. Or the victim is languishing in jail awaiting trial or being remanded to prison to serve a sentence.

Into this "ending" must drop something new. A piece of information. A lab result that got lost until now. A snitch overhears someone say something about the crime. The victim, or maybe someone working on the victim's behalf, puts together seemingly unrelated bits of information that have been staring him or her in the face the whole time and suddenly understands something new.

This eleventh hour information must get put in front of the right people, typically the police investigator or maybe in front of a lawyer or judge. It may not be easy to get these people to question their own certainty that they correctly solved the crime. Indeed, it may be necessary to find information that proves who actually did commit the crime before the authorities will consider reversing their wrong decision(s) about the framed victim.

The frame-up is finally revealed, and it becomes clear the victim didn't commit the crime, after all, particularly if the real criminal is ultimately revealed.

While it's possible to end a Framed trope simply by the framed victim proving he or she didn't do the crime they were accused of, your audience will howl if you don't reveal who actually did the crime. This detail isn't required by the trope, but it is required by basic good story telling not to leave such a gigantic plot thread hanging, unresolved.

KEY SCENES

-- the first time someone in law enforcement or investigating the crime speaks with the framed victim

-- the first time the framed victim has to admit that a piece of evidence seeming to link him or her to the crime is legitimate or real

-- the person investigating the crime has a moment of doubt over whether he or she has identified the correct perpetrator. (You can skip this step if you want your investigator to be incompetent or deeply hated by your audience for his or her blind certainty.)

-- the framed victim tries to convince a loved one that he or she didn't do the crime, and the loved one doesn't believe the victim

-- the framed victim passionately defends himself or herself to the authorities and isn't believed

-- the person who framed the victim and the victim have an encounter. The framer may or may not reveal who they are and what they did, and the victim may or may not realize they're talking to the framer...but the audience likely will

-- apology by the investigator(s) to the victim after he or she is cleared

-- meeting, and maybe reconciliation, between cleared victim and loved ones who have shunned him or her. Some big apologies are owed and may or may not be offered or accepted. Trust may or may not be restored

THINGS TO THINK ABOUT WHEN WRITING THIS TROPE

Who's getting framed? For what? By whom? Why? How?

What are the details of the crime for which your victim is going to be framed? How exactly did the crime really happen? Now, how will the framer convince the authorities that the crime happened differently? Will the framer disguise the true events of the crime? Or will the framer leave those factual events alone and merely ascribe some or all of the events to the framed victim?

How do the framer and framed victim know each other? What's their past history?

If the framer doesn't know the victim, what's the super compelling reason the framer has for choosing that particular victim?

Who's investigating the crime? How smart is he/she? Will the investigator bring in help? If so, who? What kinds of resources does the investigator have access to? Although the villain is the person framing the victim, the investigator trying to prove the victim is guilty is the main antagonist—the main source of conflict—with the framed victim throughout your story.

Who's the protagonist of your story? Why is his or her viewpoint of this story the best one to tell it from?

Will you use more than one point of view in this story? Will you tell any of the story from the framer's point of view? The victim's? The investigator's? Other people's?

Do you plan to portray the actual crime at all in your story? If so, when does it make sense to show the crime itself to your audience? First? After introducing important characters or events before the crime? [Beware of belaboring your opening with backstory, however. It's death to many an otherwise terrific thriller.]

Will you show the whole crime in one scene? Will you show bits and pieces of it in flashback throughout the story? In hypothetical imaginings of the investigator as he or she pieces together what happened? In memory flashbacks by the actual perpetrator?

Will you let the audience know up front who committed the crime, or will you let them guess along with the investigator(s)?

If you answered why the framer is framing the victim already, look at your answer. Is there a deeper reason you can also use? Is there a more selfish reason? An unconscious reason? Is there something about the framed person that triggers some deeply repressed thing inside the framer? How will you reveal these deeper reasons throughout your story?

How does the framed person go about proving he or she didn't do the crime? What investigation(s) of his or her own will be undertaken? Are they legal? If not, how illegal are they? Who will the victim get help from?

Who believes the victim of the frame-up when he or she says they're not guilty? Who doesn't believe the victim? Is there friction in your story between the believers and non-believers?

What thing(s) did the framed victim do for real that make him or her look guilty?

Why doesn't the victim have an alibi or why is the alibi unbelievable, flimsy, or unrevealable to the investigating authorities?

Will the victim lie or manufacture fake evidence to prove his or her very real innocence? Does this get him or her into trouble? If so, what kind of trouble?

Does the victim try to get ahold of or see the evidence against him or her? If so, does the victim do this legally or illegally? Does someone show the victim the evidence against him or her? Is it an investigator? An attorney? A friend? An enemy? The framer?

What's the worst thing that could happen to the victim if he or she can't convince the authorities that he or she is innocent? Can you make that worse? Can you make it much worse? Can you make the consequences absolutely devastating? Are these consequences plausible in your story? What do you have to tweak in your story to make the devastating consequence plausible?

What's the final piece of framing evidence that "proves" the victim's guilt to the investigators?

What happens to the victim when the investigators decide he or she is the perpetrator? Is the victim arrested? Charged? Tried? Convicted?

What happens to the victim's life and loved ones when investigators decide the victim is the perpetrator? Can you make these events worse? Can you make them much worse? Horrific?

What new information comes to light at the end of the story that will change the outcome of the investigation? Who finds it? How?

Does the victim take an active part in finding the exonerating piece of information or not? If not, does this sudden new information feel plausible to your audience, or does it feel like the author waved a magic wand to pull their story out of the toilet?

Who has to be convinced to look at the new information?

How does the new information convince the investigators that they made a mistake?

Keeping in mind that people hate to admit they're wrong, how is the new information solid enough to convince the investigators?

Who reopens the case or investigation?

How will you reveal who really committed the crime, if you plan to do so in this story?

What lesson(s) does your framed victim learned over the course of this story? What does he or she learn about himself or herself?

What does the victim learn over the course of the story about loved ones? Friends? Coworkers? The justice system? The investigator? The framer? How do these lessons change the relationships with each of them by the end of the story?

Who owes the framed victim an apology once he or she is cleared? Will you show all these apologies in your story? None of them? A few key ones?

Will the now cleared victim accept some or all of the apologies? If so, which one(s)? Why? Why not?

How much of the damage to the now-cleared victim's life is resolved by the end of your story? How much of the damage remains?

Will you repair any of the damage by the end of your story, or will you leave it for a sequel or to your audience's imagination to fix?

TROPE TRAPS

The person being framed is incapable of doing the thing he or she is being accused of (maybe for lack of skill, strength, knowledge, or intelligence).

The framer doesn't have a compelling reason to set up the victim other than just being mean or selfish, or it's not explained in ways your audience finds plausible.

The previous relationship between the framer and framed victim isn't developed or explored in the story.

The framer isn't knowledgeable or skilled enough to plausibly stay ahead of modern investigators/law enforcement professionals and modern technology.

The way the victim is framed would be easily spotted by the latest investigative tools or technology.

The victim is so perfect and pure that the audience doesn't have any reason AT ALL to wonder if the victim might have actually done the crime.

The victim never panics and does anything stupid over the course of your story to make the situation worse...coming across as implausible to your audience.

The victim does so many stupid things to make the situation worse that your audience loses all sympathy for him or her.

The real perpetrator of the crime and/or the reason they did it is lame, uninteresting, or not big enough for your story when finally revealed to the audience.

The real perpetrator of the crime is so obvious to your audience that audience members can't believe the police don't see it.

The authorities are way too fast to believe the new information at the end that clears the victim. They don't push back against the veracity of the miraculous new evidence that appear all of a sudden and don't push back at all against being proven wrong.

Everything goes right back to normal after the victim is cleared of the crime. There's no damage at all to their life, relationships, or job.

You fail to address the destroyed trust between the victim and everyone who didn't believe him or her when they said they were innocent.

The victim too easily forgives the people who abandoned him or her during your story.

You fail to show the framer getting what he or she deserves, even if it's as simple as police knocking at his or her front door.

FRAMED TROPE IN ACTION
Movies:

- The Fugitive

- North by Northwest
- Gone Girl
- Double Jeopardy
- Primal Fear
- Minority Report
- The Lincoln Lawyer

Books:

- The Firm by John Grisham
- If I Die Tonight by Alison Gaylin
- The Innocent Client by Scott Pratt
- Presumed Innocent by Scott Turow
- The Devotion of Suspect X by Keigo Higashino
- The Girl Before by J.P. Delaney
- Assumed Identity by David Morrell
- Tell No One by Harlan Coben

12

GROUP/FAMILY/TOWN HIDES A SECRET

DEFINITION

In this trope, a group of people have a secret. They all know it, but they're all participating in a pact to hide the secret from anyone outside the group. Somebody arrives—a newcomer to town, a new employee, a cousin, or perhaps a child who has grown old enough to realize a family secret swirls around him or her.

This outsider may not initially realize a big secret is being kept around him or her. In almost all cases, this outsider will be the protagonist of your story. It's through his or her eyes that your audience will gradually begin to sense that something is not right, or all is not as it seems.

Often the family or town with a secret appears idyllic at first. A pleasant, safe, even sweet surface disguises the dark secret roiling beneath. As the outsider learns more about the people in the group and the facades of people in the group begin to slip, it gradually becomes clear to your protagonist and your audience that everyone is keeping a secret.

Often, the secret everyone is hiding leads to a secondary story trope. Someone in the family has a supernatural power that needs to be hidden. A (sympathetic) fugitive is hiding in town. A mysterious benefactor has arrived and, in return for gifts, the group remains silent and asks no questions. Someone is terrorizing the family or town into silence. A possessed or demonic child is being hidden.

It's worth pointing out that humans in general stink at keeping secrets. However, the fact that a group of people are keeping a secret together takes some of the pressure off individuals within this group not to spill the secret. Group members can talk about the secret among themselves whenever a need to tell someone about it arises.

It's this tendency to talk about the secret with others in the know that may provide the first opening for your protagonist to catch a hint of what's really going on.

For a reason you'll need to invent, the protagonist has a burning curiosity about the secret everyone around him or her seems to be in on. And yes, human curiosity is probably enough to start the protagonist down the path of investigation.

Poking into the big secret inevitably gets pushback from the secret keepers, and that pushback becomes progressively more dangerous or even violent as the secret keepers get more worried that the secret might be revealed.

Eventually, the protagonist uncovers the big secret...and then something climactic happens as a result. Possibilities include an old crime being revealed, a murderer(s) caught, or a tragedy uncovered. In more thrilling possibilities, a monster could be let loose, new crimes may be committed in an effort to hide an old crime, or a family could be torn apart.

ADJACENT TROPES

-- Loved One/Friend/Coworker has a BIG secret

-- Only One Willing to Solve a Crime

-- Secret Cabal/Deep State

-- Mess With My Family and Find Out

. . .

WHY READERS/VIEWERS LOVE THIS TROPE

-- we all like to think of ourselves as perceptive and smart. We'd be a great amateur sleuth if a secret was being kept around us

-- the omnipresent certainty that people around us know things we don't, and furthermore are keeping those things from us

-- we've all been excluded from cliques or groups in our lives and relish the fantasy of the loner, the outsider, taking down the whole "in" group

-- David against Goliath. The little guy/gal singlehandedly takes down the whole rotten Goliath

--our sneaking suspicion that certain types of groups are corrupt is proven correct

OBLIGATORY SCENES
THE BEGINNING:

This story typically begins with the protagonist arriving for the first time in the town, entering the group for the first time, meeting a family, or coming home to his or her own family after a long absence.

The family/group/town is almost always portrayed as strangely, excessively, shockingly idyllic. Everyone gets along, everyone seems abnormally happy, everything seems calm, peaceful, even perfect. This very perfection should cause both your protagonist and your audience to be somewhat disturbed, or at least question how anyplace is this wonderful.

Even if you choose not to create disturbing perfection at the outset of your story, at a minimum, there is never an initial indication that there's a dark secret lurking beneath the surface--at least, not in the opening scene, where Joseph Campbell's "hero's normal world" is more normal than normal has ever normaled.

It's possible to have your protagonist be part of a family/group/town and never have left. In this case, the protagonist has never sensed anything wrong or off until your story begins. In this case, the inciting incident that starts your story will be some unusual event that, for the first time, causes your protagonist to have questions about his or her family/group/town.

Once you've established the external face that your family/group/town shows the outside world, you can then commence dropping hints into all this normalcy that all is not as it seems. Your protagonist and your audience learn at the same time that more is going on than meets the eye.

By the end of Act One, the protagonist finds solid evidence that there's a big secret and everyone but the protagonist is in on it.

Act One often climaxes with the first backlash against the protagonist's curiosity. It's more than a stern warning to leave it alone. It's typically a veiled threat or possibly an intentional scare of the protagonist.

THE MIDDLE:

Whereas plain old curiosity might have propelled your protagonist in Act One, after the big scare at the end of Act One, the protagonist has a decision to make. Does he or she leave the secret alone as he or she has been clearly ordered to do, or does he or she continue to poke around and find out more?

At this point, you will have to come up with a stronger motivation for your protagonist to continue investigating than mere curiosity. The stakes have risen high enough that it will take more than being nosy to keep your protagonist looking for more information.

Through the middle your protagonist continues to uncover bits and pieces of information. But, with each new clue, the danger rises. There will be more warning shots fired across the protagonist's bow, warning him or her off of the investigation. There may be surveillance, threats, vandalism, and eventually direct violence against the protagonist. The closer he or she gets to uncovering the secret, the more danger swirls around him or her.

The protagonist may call in help. The protagonist may find someone who knows part of the secret and befriends him or her. A false friend may emerge who tries to guide the protagonist away from poking any more.

People in on the secret are willing to lie, intimidate, bully, and terrorize the protagonist to keep their secret.

But no matter how hard they try to foil the protagonist, he or she gets closer and closer to the heart of the secret.

As Act Two ends, the protagonist learns something really big about the secret or may discover most or all of the big secret. Learning this provokes a gigantic reaction from those trying to keep the secret. The protagonist poses an unacceptable threat to reveal the secret to the world and must be stopped. And in the climax of Act Two, the keepers of the secret make a big move to silence the protagonist.

BLACK MOMENT:

The protagonist may know the big secret now, but he or she is silenced. The protagonist may be imprisoned. He or she may be blackmailed. Loved ones of the protagonist may be threatened with violence or death.

After all of this work to find out the secret, the protagonist has succeeded. But, in succeeding, he or she has failed in his or her goal of revealing the secret with those who need to know it. If the protagonist discovered a murder, he or she cannot tell the police. If the protagonist discovered a huge conspiracy, he or she can't stop it. If the protagonist uncovered a devastating family secret, revealing it to the rest of the family will destroy it and devastate everyone the protagonist loves.

OR

The protagonist is at a dead end. He or she can go no further with figuring out what the secret is because the only people who know are flatly refusing to tell.

The protagonist has risked everything to find out the secret and now has lost family, friends, job, home and still doesn't know what the big secret is. His or her quest to learn the truth has utterly failed and cost him or her everything.

THE END:

The protagonist may discover the last and most explosive piece of the secret in the final act of your story, which provokes the final and most dangerous violence of reaction from those whose secret the protagonist has discovered.

This is often where someone who knows the secret and privately wants it to come out may give the protagonist a key piece of the puzzle or a hint about where to look for the truth. Done clumsily, this can feel like a deus ex machina moment where the author has magically brought in an outsider to break the logjam the protagonist is stuck in. Be careful if you use this device to introduce the person who helps the protagonist out of the black moment well before now. Give that person a plausible reason for helping the protagonist in his or her darkest hour.

OR

The protagonist gathers himself or herself for one last confrontation with those keeping the secret. The protagonist may escape from imprisonment and flee the town with the secret keepers on his or her heels. The protagonist may confront the secret keepers with a tape recorder or video camera. The protagonist may arrange for law enforcement to secretly surveil a confrontation between the protagonist and those who know the big secret.

The protagonist may think he or she knows the whole secret, but in the final confrontation, one last, shocking piece of the secret is typically revealed. The protagonist, staggered by this revelation, may lose focus for a moment. It's in that moment that the secret keepers strike, attacking and nearly defeating the protagonist.

Of course, the protagonist rallies one last time, fights off the secret keepers, and gets away, revealing the entire ugly truth in dramatic fashion.

After winning that final fight, the protagonist rips away the veil of secrecy and reveals the secret to everyone. Police or journalists arrive. Everyone in the family knows the ugly secret, now.

The consequences of the secret's reveal finally occur. Justice is served. Truth conquers lies, and good conquers evil.

The protagonist typically walks away from the family/group/town at the end of this story. His or her work is done. The truth has come out. But, the family, group, or town has usually imploded, and the protagonist is usually not welcome or invited to stick around.

The protagonist walks off into the sunset.

KEY SCENES

-- the first crack in the perfect façade of the family/group/town

-- the protagonist's moment of realizing for sure that there's a secret—a big one—and that everyone else knows it but him or her

-- someone tells the protagonist to leave it alone. The tone of this approach might be pleading, afraid, warning, or downright threatening

-- the protagonist seriously considers abandoning the investigation

-- the protagonist is at a dead end and stuck...and someone surreptitiously gives him or her a hint that helps the investigation get moving again

-- someone in a position of authority orders the protagonist to quit poking around

-- the protagonist finds the first information that reveals how big, unsavory, dangerous, or deadly the secret is

-- the protagonist goes from hunting to hunted

--the protagonist goes from hunted to hunting

-- the protagonist's last interaction with the family/group/town after the secret has been fully revealed. Often there's blame and recrimination against the protagonist and the protagonist can only take away the satisfaction of having uncovered the truth as he or she leaves

THINGS TO THINK ABOUT WHEN WRITING THIS TROPE

What kind of grouping is keeping a secret in your story? Is this a type of group that many of your audience members might be suspicious of and share your protagonist's suspicions? For example, an exclusive country club, a secretive fraternity/sorority, an ultra-extreme church group.

What's the secret? What are the various layers of the secret that your protagonist will peel back (and in what order) over the course of your story?

Who is your protagonist? What brings him or her to this family, back to his or her family, to this group, or to this town?

What's the protagonist's compelling reason to stay long enough to solve the mystery of the big secret? Why doesn't he or she just leave when things start to get weird?

What's the protagonist's initial motivation for digging into what the secret might be? What's his or her deeper, more compelling, ultimately irresistible motive for sticking around to discover the full secret? Does this motive stand up to violence and possible death? If not, make the motivation strong enough to explain why your protagonist is willing to risk death to get his or her answers.

Who helps the protagonist with his or her search from outside the family/group/town?

Who helps the protagonist with his or her search from inside the family/group/town?

Who actively hinders the protagonist's investigation? How? Why?

What do the secret keepers fear will happen if the secret if revealed? Are they right? How can you make the stakes even higher if the secret comes out? Higher still?

Why is the protagonist determined to reveal the truth? What does he or she personally have to gain by succeeding and to lose by failing?

Who pretends to help the protagonist but actually misleads him or her, lies to him or her, or surreptitiously hinders him or her? How? Why?

Who does the protagonist trust? Is he or she right to do so? Why?

Who does the protagonist distrust? Is he or she right to do so? Why?

How will the secret keepers react to the protagonist's curiosity? Make a list of gradually increasing responses. How violent will the secret keepers become to keep their secret hidden?

Will the secret keepers work individually to foil the protagonist or will they work together to stop him or her? What does each of those look like?

What will the secret keepers do to stop the protagonist from revealing the secret when he or she has most of it figured out—enough to do a lot of damage?

What's your black moment? What does the protagonist learn that's bad enough to cause the secret keepers to attack him or her (but that's not yet the full story)? What do the secret keepers do to stop the protagonist from revealing what he or she already knows?

How will the protagonist get the last, climactic piece of the secret? How explosive is it? Can you make that final piece of the puzzle more explosive? A lot more explosive?

How dangerous/violent is it for the protagonist to get the last piece of the secret? Can you make it more so?

How is the reveal of the last piece of the secret personally devastating to the protagonist?

What kind of outside response occurs when the protagonist tells everyone (who needs to know) about the secret?

What happens to the family/group/town once the secret is out? Does it implode? Pull together? Fall apart? Do people flee? Move away?

What does the final interaction between the protagonist and the family/group/town look like? Do they reconcile, is the protagonist rejected, or does he or she walk away?

What lesson(s) has the protagonist learned?

What lesson(s) has the family/group/town learned...or not learned?

Does your story ultimately say that revealing secrets is a good thing or a bad thing? Why? How do you convey this?

TROPE TRAPS

The secret isn't big enough for a whole bunch of people to be willing to keep it hidden.

The secret isn't big enough for the protagonist to risk everything to uncover it.

The protagonist has no good reason for digging up the secret other than simple curiosity.

The protagonist would not plausibly continue on with his or her investigation after it gets dangerous (hence the need for a compelling motive).

The protagonist never feels any doubt or misgivings about what he or she is potentially doing to peoples' lives, no matter how bad the secret might be.

The family/group/town waxes implausibly dangerous or violent too fast as the protagonist starts learning about the secret.

The secret is too simple and lacks enough layers and twists to keep your audience riveted to what will be revealed next.

If someone gives the protagonist a key piece of information or a critical hint to get to the full revelation of the secret, that person appears out of nowhere or with no apparent motivation to save the hero, and it feels contrived and awkward to your audience.

The final piece of the puzzle isn't dramatic enough. It's the core of the whole secret and falls flat when the protagonist and audience finally reach it.

The family/group/town members are too willing to forgive the protagonist for tearing their world apart.

The protagonist is hailed as a hero even though he or she has destroyed a bunch of peoples' lives.

Failing to acknowledge that destruction by the end of your story.

The protagonist pays no price at all for the damage he or she has wrought...even if it was the right thing to do. Even who was keeping the secret disagrees that it was the right thing to do.

Failing to have any confrontation with the secret keepers and protagonist over morality, ethics, or the right and wrong of keeping secrets.

GROUP/FAMILY/TOWN HIDES A SECRET TROPE IN ACTION
Movies:

- Murder on the Orient Express
- Hot Fuzz
- The Stepford Wives
- The Wicker Man
- The Village
- Get Out
- The Invitation
- Midsommar

Books:

- Sharp Objects by Gillian Flynn

- The Girl on the Train by Paula Hawkins
- The Couple Next Door by Shari Lapena
- The Woman in Cabin 10 by Ruth Ware
- The Secret History by Donna Tartt
- The Ritual by Adam Nevill
- The Shadow over Innsmouth by H.P. Lovecraft
- Harvest Home by Thomas Tryon
- The Lonely by Andrew Michael Hurley
- Salem's Lot by Stephen King

13

HEROIC SACRIFICE

DEFINITION

In this story, things go so badly that the hero or heroine ultimately must die to save others. This heroic sacrifice can happen at the beginning of a story and set the tone for the rest of the story and for the actions of the surviving characters. It can happen in the middle of the story, particularly in the black moment, and propel the surviving characters to prevail in the climactic conflict at the end of the story, or it can happen at the end of the story as the culmination of the final conflict and guarantee victory for the good guys.

A common variant on this heroic sacrifice is that character who is simply "too cool to live" or so good and so pure, "too good for this world" that we normal people can't ever live up to either of these heroes. They inevitably have to die because they're not suited for living mundane lives in the normal world.

Another variant on this hero type is a character who's not afraid to die. Perhaps he or she is a person of intense faith. Or he or she has suffered greatly, is emotionally exhausted, and is ready to die. The terminal patient with nothing to lose and who decides to go out a hero falls into this category.

And then there's the character who simply sees it as an honor to die for his or her loved ones, comrades, or friends. In the service of a great good. He or she knows what must be done and steps up to take one for the team. This is perhaps the most heroic character of all—a regular guy or gal who's willing to lay down his or her life for loved ones or for his or her beliefs.

In this trope, some sort of problem is set up in the opening. War breaks out. A terrorist must be stopped. A gunman takes a group of hostages. The problem almost always involves a mortal threat to a group of people. Usually, they're innocent victims or civilians, but it can also be a group of soldiers who are sent into danger, for example.

The hero/heroine may be part of that group or may be sent in to rescue the imperiled group.

The problem gets worse and worse and all other attempted solutions fail, until only someone sacrificing his or her life will solve it. Into this "me or everyone else" dilemma, a hero/heroine steps forward and offers to sacrifice himself or herself.

The hero/heroine typically dies, although not always. Regardless, the hero/heroine's willingness to die, and the actions of being willing to die make it possible, save the day. The innocents/others are safe and the hero/heroine's sacrifice has not been in vain.

ADJACENT TROPES
-- Pitted Against Each Other
-- Isolated Together and Dying
-- Insurmountable Villain
-- Dying Cop/Detective
-- Outnumbered/Outgunned
-- The Deadly Game (one of us must die)

WHY READERS/VIEWERS LOVE THIS TROPE
-- we'd all like to believe we'd step up and be heroic if we found ourselves in that situation

-- we love to imagine ourselves as so cool or so good that we're too good for this world

-- we love to imagine ourselves as Joe or Jane Regular but ending up being a revered hero by everyone

-- we desperately hope that if we're ever in danger, a hero/heroine will step up and save us (and we desperately fear that no one will)

OBLIGATORY SCENES
THE BEGINNING:

A problem occurs. This needs to be a big problem that needs to grow exponentially worse over the course of the story and it needs to pose mortal danger to everyone involved with it. Frequently, a large group of innocents or civilians are put in harm's way.

We may see innocents living their normal lives until they're sucked into this crisis.

We may also see our eventual hero/heroine living a normal life until sucked into this crisis. The hero/heroine's very deep regularness is often emphasized. This is no one special.

Once the problem has occurred, we see initial reactions to it that fail to resolve it. We learn along with the protagonist that the situation is only getting worse and more dangerous.

Act One often involves a civilian or innocent dying to emphasize just how dangerous a problem this is.

THE MIDDLE:

The problem only gets worse.

The appropriate response agencies form a plan for dealing with this crisis. The plan is put into motion and various snags, glitches, and obstacles must be overcome. We realize the plan isn't perfect and the people putting it into effect must adapt, make changes, and discard portions of the plan that would ensure its success because of operational constraints.

Meanwhile, we see the situation getting worse for the inno-cents/civilians. They may be panicking, having health crises, men and women or women and children might be separated. Threats by the bad guys escalate. The war isn't going well for the good guys.

The good guys scramble to get their people into place to respond to the crisis but are always one step behind the bad guys.

The situation goes from bad to worse and worse to terrible.

One by one, the various options the good guys are considering fail or become impossible to use. The clock is ticking and time is running out for the good guys to save everyone who is in jeopardy.

Act Two ends with the last, best option for stopping the crisis being put into action...

BLACK MOMENT:

...and it fails. The good guys have failed to stop the bad guy(s). The innocents, and indeed everyone in jeopardy, are not only in much more serious jeopardy but are inevitably going to die, now.

The protagonist has failed. The people he or she works with have failed. The agencies in charge of affecting a rescue have failed.

Moreover, the people working with the protagonist are likely going to die, too.

The attempt at rescue or stopping the crisis has gone as badly as it's possible for it to go, short of everyone dying.

It's into this the hero/heroine must face the harsh truth that someone must die to turn the tide of this disaster.

THE END:

Your hero announces his or her plan to sacrifice themselves to whoever needs to know. Superiors or colleagues may try to talk him or her out of the decision, but they fail to change the hero/heroine's mind.

The climactic conflict happens as the hero/heroine jumps into the breach and sacrifices himself or herself at the critical moment.

The tide is turned, and the good guys are able to prevail at last.

The innocents or colleagues are saved, the bad guys are stopped, and good triumphs over evil.

If the hero/heroine lives, he or she is rescued after the battle is won and whisked away to get medical help.

Live or die, the hero/heroine is recognized after the fact for his or her heroism. Do not skip this element in your story. Heroes and heroines deserve this after the magnitude of their sacrifice, and you're likely to offend your audience if you don't properly acknowledge someone who gave his or her life to save others. Personally, I'm *still* mad that the Black Widow didn't get full honors and a big funeral scene after she sacrificed herself in *Avengers Endgame*.

Loved ones grieve but are proud of the hero/heroine's sacrifice. The hero/heroine is honored (alive or posthumously), and the larger public acknowledges the heroism and will theoretically remember and celebrate the hero/heroine's sacrifice forever.

KEY SCENES

-- the problem first endangers innocents or the hero/heroine's teammates

-- the authorities try the obvious fix to the problem but it doesn't work. At all

-- the hero/heroine realizes that the authorities need help

-- the hero/heroine has a good reason to live, which is to say, their sacrifice is real and their life has value that makes the decision to die hard

-- other people have the same opportunity to step up and do the heroic sacrifice but don't

-- the hero/heroine's superiors may try to talk the hero/heroine out of their sacrifice...but also, they need someone to turn the tide

-- the hero/heroine's goodbye to loved ones before he/she goes forth to die

THINGS TO THINK ABOUT WHEN WRITING THIS TROPE

What's the crisis that's ultimately going to require your hero/heroine's great sacrifice? This forms the plot spine of your book, so go big, go creative, go high-concept.

How can you start the crisis smaller and build it into one where there's no choice left but for someone to die to fix it?

Are there innocents or civilians in mortal danger? If so, who? How are they endangered?

If the hero/heroine is going to sacrifice his or her life to save comrades, who are those comrades and how are they put into mortal, unsavable danger?

Who's the hero/heroine? Are they already a heroic person or are they regular and rather average when your story begins?

How will you introduce your hero/heroine to your audience? How will your hero/heroine be relatable? How will he or she be likable?

What about the hero/heroine's regular life is going to make the decision later to die a difficult one with meaningful sacrifice?

Who are the hero/heroine's loved ones? What do they think of the hero/heroine at the beginning? Do they know he or she is capable of such heroism?

How do the authorities try to fix the problem but fail? How do their attempts to fix the problem only make it worse?

What do the bad guys want? Why do they believe they're in the right to be doing what they're doing? Why do these means justify their ends?

How will the bad guys escalate the crisis over the course of the story?

Will the bad guys kill innocents or the hero/heroine's comrades in the middle of the story to escalate the tension? If so, who? How? Why?

Why does the big plan the authorities have put in place to solve the crisis fail? How does it fail? What goes wrong? Who is hurt or dies? Can you make the failure bigger? More catastrophic?

How has this failed plan just completely screwed the good guys who are still trying to fix the problem and completely screwed any innocents caught in the middle?

What's the likely consequence of the big, failed rescue/solution attempt going to be? Can the bad guys partially or wholly implement that before the end of the story?

What specific event makes it clear someone's going to have to die to fix this mess?

What prompts the hero/heroine to decide to sacrifice himself or herself?

What does the hero/heroine's thought process look like as he or she contemplates making this momentous decision? What goes through his or her mind? Does he or she talk it over with anyone? If so, who?

Who does the hero/heroine tell about the decision before acting upon it, if anyone?

Does the hero/heroine say goodbye to anyone before leaving to go die? If so, who? What's said?

How does the hero/heroine sacrifice himself or herself? How does it turn the tide of the final conflict? Does it surprise the bad guys? Does it surprise the good guys?

What's the outcome of the climactic battle? Who is rescued? Who dies besides the hero/heroine?

Does the hero/heroine live or die?

If the hero/heroine lives, who rescues them? How hurt are they? Where are they taken for medical care?

What kind of recognition is given to the hero/heroine after the fact?

Who grieves for them?

. . .

TROPE TRAPS

The crisis you set up isn't severe enough to warrant someone sacrificing his or her life.

Nobody we care about deeply is put in mortal danger to warrant someone dying for them.

The bad guys are evil for the sake of evil and have no motivation to act the way they do, hence they look like cardboard villains.

The bad guys aren't smart enough and dastardly enough to plausibly outwit all the forces arrayed against them by the good guys.

The good guys aren't compelling enough and engaging enough for us to care deeply about whether they live or die.

The hero is so cool or so perfect from the very beginning that we don't find him or her relatable.

All the other options for solving the crisis are not explored and exhausted by the time the hero/heroine decides to die for others.

You fail to make your audience understand why this character is willing to die at all.

Failing to give the hero/heroine anything to live for; hence, the sacrifice isn't as big a deal as it would otherwise be.

The hero/heroine is so unheroic to begin the story that we don't believe this person would step up and willingly choose to die.

The hero/heroine is manipulated into making the decision to die for others.

The hero/heroine's death fails to save everyone or almost everyone they hoped to save.

Your audience spots some other way the day could've been saved without your hero/heroine having to die.

The hero/heroine is not properly celebrated for his or her great sacrifice and your audience is mortally offended by that.

HEROIC SACRIFICE TROPE IN ACTION

Movies:

- Saving Private Ryan
- The Terminator
- Armageddon
- The Bodyguard
- The Dark Knight
- Valkyrie
- X-Men: The Last Stand

Books:

- The Hunger Games by Suzanne Collins
- The Stand by Stephen King
- The DaVinci Code by Dan Brown
- The Passage by Justin Cronin
- The Spy Who Came In From the Cold by John Le Carré
- The Chamber by John Grisham
- The Prometheus Deception by Robert Ludlum
- The Last Oracle by James Rollins
- The Poet by Michael Connelly

14

IMPOSTOR IN OUR MIDST

DEFINITION

In this trope, the protagonist is not the impostor. Rather, the protagonist is the person who goes about finding and exposing the impostor in your story. That said, much of your story may revolve around the impostor as a primary character whose life, motivations, or POV you may also spend a fair bit of your story exploring.

As for your impostor, his or her scheme is two-fold.

First, he or she must successfully impersonate someone else and convince everyone around him or her that the impostor is really who he or she says she is. He or she may pretend to be someone who left long ago and whom nobody recognizes now. He or she may make up a persona and insert himself/herself and a fake identity into a workspace, group, close-knit community, town, or even a family.

It's not enough for the impostor simply to decide he or she wants to pretend to be someone else. It's boring and not the source of much or any conflict, particularly if they get away with the ruse. The impostor has to have a larger goal.

Second, once everyone is convinced he or she is real, the impostor must then do whatever it is he or she has set out to do in this elaborate, dangerous, and time-consuming scheme. This dastardly plan may end up being an entire trope of its own—revenge murder, steal national secrets, destroy some group from within.

The scale of the thing the impostor is trying to do will set the tone for your entire story. Does the impostor want to start killing off the senior executives of a company? Steal national security secrets? Abscond with a giant inheritance? Become famous?

Of course it's possible to go small scale and personal with this type of story as well. Does the impostor want a family of his or her own, even if he or she has to trick a family into believing he/she is part of it? Perhaps revenge is the goal? Embarrassing someone who once embarrassed him or her? Getting away pretending to be someone else simply because he or she can?

The conflict between the protagonist and impostor always becomes personal. It will be emotional, intense, and fraught all on its own. And, if their conflict *really* blows up in your story, it can be the source of a whole lot of tension, suspense, danger, and even violence.

That said, the impostor's end goal is probably the source of some of the larger-than-life, good against evil, save-the-world (or at least save-the-day) feel of your story that makes it a thriller.

Whatever overarching plan the impostor has, beyond just pretending to be someone else, the protagonist should be harmed in some way by the impostor's plan. Otherwise, why would your protagonist go to all the trouble and risk of trying to expose the impostor?

The protagonist may feel supplanted by the impostor and that may be sufficient to arouse the protagonist to take a closer look at the impostor. Perhaps the protagonist catches a hint of what the impostor is ultimately planning to do. Perhaps the protagonist will lose a job, lose money, or lose a loved one if the impostor succeeds at implementing his or her plan.

Once the protagonist becomes suspicious of the impostor, then the game is on. The impostor dodges the protagonist's efforts to expose him or her as a fake, and the protagonist maneuvers to trick, trap, or in some way expose the impostor for what he or she really is.

At some point, the tables may turn and the impostor may

commence searching for ways to discredit or destroy the protagonist, who's threatening the impostor's scheme. The protagonist may become the hunted and have to go on the defensive to protect self, reputation, job, family, life, or more from the impostor. This is a perfect reversal for a midpoint reversal in your story, by the way.

Eventually, the protagonist confronts the impostor. It's possible the impostor wiggles off the hook one last time. But eventually, the impostor does something radical or desperate to silence the protagonist who knows the truth and is attempting to expose the impostor. There's a final confrontation where the protagonist finally proves he or she is correct and the impostor is exposed.

Whatever consequences you have planned for your impostor happen and the protagonist is finally vindicated. The consequences to the impostor should be commensurate with the harm his or her scheme would have caused should it have succeeded.

This can be a straightforward trope of a good guy trying to thwart a bad guy. Or this can be a deeply nuanced trope of flawed people with gray motives acting at cross-purposes where both or neither is "good" or "bad".

NOTE: Take a look at the Infiltrating a Group trope to get a sense of what the impostor may be thinking and doing, from his or her point of view, while he or she is worming their way into the group.

ADJACENT TROPES
-- Infiltrating a Group
-- Secret Twin/ Doppelganger
-- Back From the Dead
-- Stealing Your Life
-- Missing Child/Spouse Returns After Long Absence
-- Only Survivor
-- Loved One Possessed

. . .

WHY READERS/VIEWERS LOVE THIS TROPE

-- how fun/cool/interesting would it be to shed our own lives and become someone else, particularly someone rich, powerful, or successful

-- leaving behind our boring dull lives and stepping into a glamorous or adventurous world

-- being the only one who sees through a subterfuge that fools everyone else

-- being more observant, more clever, than everyone else

-- saving everyone around you from an insidious threat

OBLIGATORY SCENES
THE BEGINNING:

We usually meet the protagonist first in this story lest the audience not be certain who they're supposed to be cheering for. Soon thereafter, into the protagonist's normal world, a newcomer arrives.

The "newcomer" may actually be someone allegedly returning after a very long absence—long enough that people who knew this person before might not recognize him or her now.

This newcomer is, of course, the impostor. You may choose to let your audience in on this secret right away. In this case, your audience knows something your protagonist does not and will watch with interest to see how the protagonist figures it out.

You may choose to let your audience figure out the secret of the impostor along with your protagonist. In this case, the audience has suspicions and doubts right along with your protagonist and may even question your protagonist's judgment as the story unfolds.

You can play the opening so your audience doesn't know who to believe. Is the protagonist correct in being suspicious of the impostor, or is the impostor telling the truth and the protagonist ultimately an untrustworthy narrator?

The impostor typically spends most of Act One establishing his or her identity and convincing everyone he or she is who he/she says they are.

By the end of Act One, you may be ready to have the impostor embark on his or her main scheme. Indeed, his or her first act toward that ultimate goal may be the mini-crisis that ends this section of your story.

Act One also may end with the first serious challenge by the protagonist to the impostor's identity. It may be triggered by the impostor making his or her first big move toward getting what he or she wants. This mini-crisis marks the beginning of the open conflict between the protagonist and impostor.

THE MIDDLE:

If the protagonist didn't challenge the impostor's identity to end Act One, the protagonist will probably do this to start Act Two. This may cause consternation in the secondary characters who are involved with both the impostor and protagonist in your story. The protagonist's suspicions trigger conflict between him/her and the other characters, and trigger conflict with the impostor.

We get to know both the protagonist and the impostor better in the middle of the story. We learn about their pasts, their motivations, their goals, their wants and needs—because these are probably all in conflict between the protagonist and the impostor.

The protagonist starts testing the impostor and trying to trick the impostor into slipping up. If the impostor is faking being a professional in some career field, the protagonist challenges that expertise. If the impostor is posing as a long-lost family member, the protagonist challenges his or her memories of the past and knowledge of the family.

Other characters in your story may take the impostor's side and defend him or her from the protagonist's suspicions. The more the protagonist presses his or her investigation, the more risk there is to him or her of losing friends, reputation, job, or even family.

Meanwhile, the impostor is moving ahead with his or her plan to achieve whatever he or she wants. The impostor may try to take over a company, kill someone, get an inheritance, collect a reward of some kind, sell off valuable property and keep the proceeds, steal family heirlooms, manipulate a government agency into doing or not doing something he or she will benefit from, infiltrating an agency that handles classified information, or anything else sneaky and dastardly you can think up.

Part of the protagonist's effort to expose the impostor includes trying to figure out what the impostor wants and what the impostor's end plan is. Once the protagonist figures this out, he or she will also go to work trying to foil the impostor's plan. This effort may get the protagonist in trouble as he or she interferes with things he or she wouldn't normally have the right or power to mess with.

At some point in the middle, the impostor spots the protagonist's efforts to unmask him or her and may go on the offensive to discredit or ruin the protagonist. This is a perfect moment to act as the midpoint reversal in your story. The hunter becomes the hunted as the impostor commences stalking the protagonist, now.

The conflict between the protagonist and impostor may stay under the table and secretive for a while, but at some point, it explodes into open conflict, which will suck in the other characters of your story and force them to take sides—Team Protagonist or Team Impostor.

This conflict builds to a crisis where these two foes face off directly against each other and the protagonist calls out the impostor publicly. This crisis also involves the protagonist doing something to try to stop the impostor's dastardly plan.

BLACK MOMENT:

In the black moment, nobody believes the protagonist when he or she attempts to expose the impostor. The impostor has gotten away with his or her ruse, and worse, the impostor's ultimate plan is about to come to fruition.

The impostor launches the finale of his or her evil plan...and gets away with it. If the impostor's plan was to murder an executive, he or she succeeds. If the plan was to steal national security secrets, the impostor walks out of CIA Headquarters with a flash drive full of files. If the plan was to steal an inheritance, the will is read and everything is given to the impostor.

The protagonist has lost credibility, reputation, friends, family, job, or all of the above. His or her ability to stop the impostor seems completely gone. The protagonist has fired his or her best shot at the impostor and missed.

All is lost for the protagonist and the victory for the impostor appears complete.

THE END:

Some piece of information comes to light that changes the tide and puts the protagonist on the path to finding final, irrefutable proof that the impostor is a fake.

OR

The protagonist manages to find a way to give the impostor some sort of identity test that the impostor finally fails.

OR

The impostor gets cocky and slips up.

Regardless of how it comes to pass, the protagonist finally finds a way to challenge the impostor's identity and prove, once and for all, that the impostor is a fake. The protagonist pulls this off in the nick of time before the impostor's final, dastardly plan comes to fruition.

The people who've previously disbelieved the protagonist finally see the truth and accept that the impostor is a fake. The impostor may be arrested, run out of town, or flee. Whether or not you choose to let the impostor get away will depend on how criminal/not criminal his or her behavior and plan have been.

Pretending to be a long-lost child who comes home and joins a family is far less criminal in nature than posing as a businessman, taking over a company, selling it, and putting all the proceeds into one's personal bank account. That said, the person posing as a lost child may do far more emotional and psychological damage in the long run than the fake businessman.

At any rate, the protagonist rejoins the family, friend group, job that he or she was kicked out of. His or her reputation is restored, and people who previously distrusted and disbelieved the protagonist may apologize but will definitely believe him or her, now.

Everything is put back the way it should be. The evil interloper has been removed and order is restored.

That said, there may be lingering damage, emotional or psychological, that is going to take time to heal. You don't have to show the entire healing process, but you may consider give your audience a glimpse of the people most hurt by the attempted con doing something to start down the road to healing.

KEY SCENES

-- the protagonist meets the impostor and is initially taken in by the ruse

-- the impostor does the first thing that jars or startles the protagonist...and the protagonist ignores or dismisses it

-- the protagonist expresses his or her nascent suspicions to someone else, who dismisses the protagonist's concerns

-- someone the protagonist deeply cares about expresses to him or her a need for the impostor to be who he/she says they are

-- the protagonist becomes certain the impostor is a fake and decides to prove it

-- the impostor passes an identity test the protagonist was sure would trip up him or her

-- the impostor embarrasses or humiliates the protagonist when a plan to expose the impostor backfires...or when the impostor sets up the protagonist to embarrass or humiliate himself or herself

-- the impostor not quite confesses to the protagonist that he or she is an impostor and dares the protagonist to prove it

-- the protagonist considers the possibility that he or she is wrong and should maybe give up on this costly obsession of his or hers

--after losing everything, the protagonist feels a spark of hope when the new information, new identity test, or slip up by the impostor appears. Does the protagonist dare give it one more try to convince everyone of the truth

THINGS TO THINK ABOUT WHEN WRITING THIS TROPE

Who is the impostor posing as? Why pretend to be that person? What does the impostor have to gain by becoming that person?

Who is the impostor really? Does his or her backstory have any bearing on your story? If so, flesh it out. If not, pick a few important details from the impostor's past to show that will answer your audience's questions about why this person is a con artist.

What's the impostor's larger, evil plan? What does he or she want to do, get, learn? How does he or she plan to go about getting it? Why?

What does the impostor do to establish his or her bona fides and "prove" he or she is the person he/she says he/she is?

Who is your protagonist? What's his or her role in the group the impostor is infiltrating? What's the protagonist's alleged relationship to the impostor when the impostor shows up? Coworker? Neighbor? Sibling? Something else?

What's the impostor's story as he or she explains a long absence or explains coming to this place at this time? Why now?

What knowledge would the impostor have about the role he or she is playing if he or she really was that person? Expertise in a profession? Knowledge of family members? Memories about the town?

What does the protagonist think of the impostor when they first meet? Is the protagonist skeptical from the moment he or she lays eyes on the impostor, or do the protagonist's suspicions develop later?

What's something the impostor screws up shortly after arriving? How does he or she explain it away?

Does the protagonist ignore or excuse the first mistake the impostor makes in his or her role? If so, why? If not, how does the protagonist react?

What happens that first makes the protagonist suspicious of the impostor? Does anyone else see the same thing and respond with suspicion also? What do others think about it if they hear about it secondhand?

Who around the protagonist buys the impostor's act completely? When and how does this person(s) defend the impostor to the protagonist?

Who are the impostor's ardent supporters, willing to go after the protagonist on behalf of the impostor? How does the impostor cultivate these true believers?

Who around the protagonist doesn't entirely believe the impostor's act? Is this person willing to go out on a limb and agree with or help the protagonist even when it makes other people angry? If so, why? If not, why not?

How does the protagonist's belief that the impostor is a fake cause friction, tension, and arguments with those around him/her and the impostor?

In what ways does the protagonist try to trick the impostor into making a mistake or to test the impostor?

How does the impostor know the right answers to the protagonist's questions?

At what point does the impostor realize the protagonist isn't buying his or her charade? How does he or she feel about that? How does he or she react to that?

What does the impostor do to interfere with the protagonist's poking around into the impostor's identity and bona fides?

When do the protagonist and impostor enter into direct conflict with each other? Is it subtle? Overt? Polite but tense? Nasty? How does it escalate? Can you make the escalation worse? Can you make their conflict much worse? Can you make it into outright warfare?

What specifically does the protagonist do to escalate matters between himself/herself and the impostor?

What specifically does the protagonist do to escalate matters between himself/herself and the protagonist?

How can you make the impostor's evil plan worse, more damaging, more deadly? How can you make it much worse? How can you make it disastrous or even apocalyptic?

What are the consequences to the protagonist, his or her loved ones/friends/coworkers, and to the world if the protagonist fails to stop the impostor either by exposing him/her as a fake or stopping the impostor's evil plan?

When, why, and how does the protagonist publicly confront the impostor and accuse him or her of being a fake? How does the impostor wiggle out of it?

What consequences land upon the protagonist for his or her grand declaration about the impostor being believed by everyone else to be wrong? Does he/she lose friends? Lose a job? Lose family? Lose something else?

What piece of information does the protagonist get that helps him or her prove the impostor is a fake in the end? Does the protagonist finally find an identity test the impostor fails? Or does the impostor slip up and out himself/herself?

Is it more important in your story for the protagonist to stop the impostor's evil plan or to expose the impostor? For plotting purposes, always solve the biggest problem last if you can't solve both problems at the same time. The most elegant ending would generally be to stop the evil plan and expose the impostor to everyone as a fake simultaneously.

What happens to the impostor once he or she is exposed and his/her evil plan thwarted? Is the impostor killed? Arrested? Allowed to flee?

Who owes the protagonist an apology after the impostor is exposed and the protagonist is proven correct? How are those apologies delivered? Does the protagonist accept them?

How do the losses the protagonist has suffered get reversed at the end of your story? Is his/her job restored? Friends and family return? Something else?

What long-term emotional and psychological damage has the impostor done to the people he or she hoodwinked? Will you show a glimpse of these characters beginning down the road to healing at the end of your story or not? If so, how?

What has the protagonist learned from this whole experience?

TROPE TRAPS

The impostor could never plausibly pull off the role he or she is faking because it would take too much technical knowledge. It's very hard to fake being a surgeon when you're handed a scalpel and asked to perform a complicated procedure.

The person the impostor is supposed to be would have been old enough to remember and have had enough detailed knowledge of the people, places, and events he or she left behind years ago that the impostor can't possibly memorize or find out enough detail to fake out the people he or she used to know.

The impostor is SO good at pretending to be someone that absolutely nobody suspects anything or asks any questions.

Failing to have anyone ask any hard questions of the impostor. Even the most happy person to see a long-lost person is going to have questions about where someone has been, what they've done all this time, and why they've been gone so long.

The protagonist is so suspicious so quickly that he or she comes across as unlikable to your audience.

The protagonist is a jerk to the impostor well before the protagonist is certain the impostor is a fake and is unlikable to your audience.

The impostor is so charming and so likable that your audience ultimately wants him or her to succeed at the ruse.

The impostor has no compelling reason to pretend to be someone else. Just for kicks is a really lame reason to most audiences.

The impostor's evil plan—the whole reason he or she is engaging in this lengthy, difficult, risky ruse—is lame or not going to get the impostor something big enough to justify the time, effort, and risk.

The impostor's evil plan isn't evil enough to keep your audience's interest through the whole story. It's not big enough, dangerous enough, damaging enough, ambitious enough, or audacious enough.

The impostor fails to get everyone to believe his or her identity before starting to execute his or her evil plan...and logically would cause the plan to fail.

There's some obvious question or test your audience can think of to prove whether or not the impostor is who he or she says he/she is... and your protagonist doesn't do it. I mean, DNA tests are easy and fast these days. Get a cigarette butt, coffee cup, or hair follicle (or some spit if the protagonist is clever) and find out if the protagonist is related to anyone who ought to be his or her blood relative. Side note: fingerprint identification takes weeks or months in most cases.

You fail to have anyone take the impostor's side when the protagonist starts attacking him or her and accusing the impostor of being a fake. A good con artist is going to cultivate some ardent supporters.

Absolutely nobody will listen to the protagonist let alone entertain his or her accusations, which signals your audience that the protagonist isn't honest, reliable, or believable...and hence isn't heroic or worth rooting for through your story.

The suspense lags and the action bogs down as you let your protagonist get mired in arguments, futile identity tests, and family/personal drama.

The stakes of failing to stop the impostor's evil plan don't keep rising through the story and there's no rising tension, danger, or suspense for your audience as the story progresses.

You fail to let the impostor succeed or come very close to succeeding and shy away from letting bad things happen in your story.

The protagonist doesn't lose enough or suffer enough consequences for his or her stubborn refusal to let go of this obsession with proving the impostor is a fake.

The punishment to the impostor is not commensurate with his or her attempted evil plan nor commensurate with the harm he or she caused everyone around him or her.

You fail to have any lingering emotional, psychological, or relationship damage after the impostor is exposed. Everyone goes back to normal as if nothing happened and there are no hard feelings for awful things said or done to the protagonist.

IMPOSTOR IN OUR MIDST TROPE IN ACTION
Movies:

- The Talented Mr. Ripley
- Catch Me If You Can
- Taking Lives
- Shattered
- The Guest
- Unlawful Entry
- The Hand That Rocks the Cradle

. . .

Books:

- The Likeness by Tana French
- Six Days of the Condor by James Grady
- The Passenger by Lisa Lutz
- The Last Flight by Julie Clark
- The New Husband by D.J. Palmer
- The Amateurs by Marcus Sakey
- The Half-Sister by Sandie Jones
- The Charm School by Nelson DeMille
- The Imposter by Elaine Dundy

15

INFILTRATING A GROUP

DEFINITION

In this trope, your protagonist goes undercover to get inside a gang, cult, group, organization, agency, or government. It can be an overtly criminal or immoral group the protagonist is seeking to gather evidence or take apart from the inside. Or it can be an overtly good, or at least legal, group that the protagonist is infiltrating to search for corruption, corrupt members, or illegal activity.

The protagonist assumes a false identity or may use his or her own identity but disguise his or her true purpose. He or she may know exactly what he or she is looking for when entering the group, or the protagonist may have to poke around, learn the lay of the land, watch the group's activities for a while, and sniff out who the bad people are and where the bad things are happening.

In most cases, the protagonist has outside help. At a minimum, he or she usually has a boss who has sent them on this infiltration mission.

It is possible for someone to take the initiative to infiltrate a group on their own—their child joined a cult and a parent wants to get close to the child to rescue him or her, someone might infiltrate a gang with the intent to get close to the person(s) who murdered their brother and to kill the killer, a spy takes the initiative to get recruited by a foreign government while in deep cover and can't break cover to let his or her superiors know what he or she is doing.

In these cases, the protagonist is in extreme danger and has no safety net. There's no van full of cops or FBI agents across the street waiting to pull him or her out if the infiltration is uncovered.

Even when someone infiltrating a group does have official support, he or she is still in real danger. If discovered, very bad things could happen to him or her and happen too quickly for anyone to rescue him or her.

In this story, there's a group with secrets. The protagonist joins the group under false pretenses and commences investigating the group and looking for secrets. The danger mounts the more risks the protagonist takes and the more dangerous the information he or she learns.

Eventually, the protagonist is discovered and must find a way to get out alive with his or her incriminating information.

OR

The protagonist's information is used to raid the group or take down the bad actors the protagonist has identified. In that battle, the protagonist must find a way to get out alive...with both sides shooting at him or her.

In the end, the protagonist accomplishes his or her mission. The group's secrets or corrupt members are exposed, and action is taken to neutralize the threats they pose.

At its core, this is a straightforward good versus evil story. The intense tension comes from the constant, unrelenting threat of being caught and the awful consequences to the protagonist if that were to happen.

NOTE: Take a look at the Impostor in Our Midst trope to get a better idea of what the bad guys or other members of the infiltrated group may be thinking, suspecting, and doing to expose this protagonist who is, in fact, an impostor within their group.

ADJACENT TROPES
   -- Impostor In Our Midst
   -- Sucked Into/Escaping a Cult
   -- Escaping a Dangerous Group
   -- Insider Discovers a Conspiracy
   -- Off-the-Books Op
   -- Ticking Time Bomb

WHY READERS/VIEWERS LOVE THIS TROPE
   -- the tension in this trope is unrelenting and truly thrilling

   -- it's a David versus Goliath tale, the lone operative taking on an entire corrupt organization, one that anyone who considers himself or herself to be a little guy or gal relates to

   -- many of us work in organizations we suspect of having nefarious motives. How cool would it be to prove it and take down our office, employer, club, family, or other organization that bugs us

   -- going undercover takes no special skills other than nerve...so every audience member can readily picture himself or herself doing what your protagonist does

OBLIGATORY SCENES
THE BEGINNING:
To begin this story, the protagonist is often introduced in his or her normal world, giving your audience a sense of what the protagonist is leaving behind and risking losing to go undercover. Doing this also grounds your audience in who the protagonist is, what his or her values are, and why he or she is about to embark on this dangerous mission.

Also, very early on, we may meet the protagonist's superiors or back-up crew who will be standing by to attempt a rescue of the protagonist if the mission goes badly.

And, of course, we see the group the protagonist is infiltrating. You may show your audience the group from the outside first, establishing who its members are and how powerful they are. Or you may choose simply to throw your protagonist into the group and let your audience learn about the group along with the protagonist.

In reality, your protagonist is highly unlikely to go into the group without doing extensive research first and without having a very, very good idea of who the major players are, who's dangerous, who or what the target of the investigation is, and how the protagonist is going to secretly communicate with people outside the group while under cover. You can establish any or all of this before he or she goes undercover, but doing so may reduce the stress level of your audience more than you'd like to.

Act One may involve big information dumps as the protagonist learns a great deal about the group once he or she is inside it. To counteract this, you may want to introduce some sort of danger or risk to the protagonist right away.

Act One usually ends with the protagonist getting into trouble for doing something he or she wasn't supposed to, or getting caught snooping, or arousing the suspicions of someone inside the group and possibly having a confrontation with that person.

THE MIDDLE:

The protagonist works his or her way deeper inside the organization, learning more about its inner workings, exposing conflicts, secrets, and activities that may be suspicious but not yet enough to convict someone of a crime.

The more the protagonist snoops, goes places he or she isn't allowed, eavesdrops, and sneaks around, the more danger he or she is in.

At the same time, suspicions may be mounting about who the protagonist really is. Typically, the protagonist has a nemesis inside the group who isn't buying the protagonist's act for a minute and is a source of ongoing trouble. This nemesis may follow the protagonist, snitch on the protagonist, or watch the protagonist so closely that the protagonist can't do the important investigation work he or she really needs to do.

In the meantime, it's common to have some sort of problem occur in the protagonist's real life outside of the undercover assignment. A family member gets sick. A spouse is sick and tired of waiting at home while the protagonist is gone so much and causes marital problems. Another case the protagonist worked on in the past is going to trial and needs his or her testimony...or the case takes a turn that requires the protagonist's personal attention.

This outside problem pulls at the protagonist's attention and time and causes additional problems that add to his or her stress. The distracted protagonist may make a mistake that nearly gets him or her caught or killed.

The protagonist may be asked to commit a crime on behalf of the group, which is another source of potential crisis. While (law enforcement) undercover operatives may have permission to gamble, beat up someone, or steal something, they likely don't have permission to commit murder. Because of this, it's very common to see criminal groups demand that the protagonist kill someone on behalf of the group. Indeed, this test has become cliché in infiltration stories.

Act Two builds toward a crisis as the protagonist closes in on finding out what he or she has come to find.

Another common stressor for your protagonist in this trope is if his or her undercover persona/world intersects with his or her real life—someone outside the group recognizes him or her in a bar or restaurant, he or she is caught communicating with someone outside the group, or someone from his or her real life comes looking for him or her intentionally.

If you've been building a personal or outside crisis for the protagonist beyond the current infiltration, it comes to a head as Act Two ends. The protagonist is put in an impossible position of choosing between his or her vital work undercover and the crisis in his or her real life. The more personal that crisis is, the more difficult this dilemma will feel to your protagonist and to your audience. The protagonist inevitably chooses the undercover assignment, believing he or she can wrap it up quickly and still make it back to the real world to deal with the outside or personal crisis.

This haste may actually lead your protagonist to push too hard, to try too soon to end the investigation or to take the one risk he or she knows better than to take under normal circumstances.

The protagonist takes one last, gigantic (possibly ill-advised) risk to get the final piece of information, evidence, or proof of a crime, and the final moment of Act Two is often that moment.

BLACK MOMENT:

This is the moment in your story when everything falls apart.

Your protagonist is exposed, his or her cover blown, and gets caught...or gets caught in the crossfire. He or she fails to get the last piece of evidence or gets the evidence but is caught red-handed with it.

The personal or outside crisis has also blown up, and because of the protagonist's choice to stick with the undercover assignment at the end of Act Two, it goes as badly as it's possible to go. The protagonist's presence, attention, and action were required, and he or she failed to give any of them to the personal or outside crisis.

The protagonist's rash actions at the end of Act Two may separate him or her from the ability to communicate a need for rescue or may physically separate him or her from the team that's supposed to be nearby to rescue him or her.

The protagonist is alone, in terrible trouble, and has failed all the people in his or her real life who were depending on him or her.

. . .

THE END:

The forces assigned to rescue the protagonist may rally, antici-pating what the protagonist would do when in trouble and find a way to locate him or her. The protagonist may be beat up, tortured, exhausted, and with no resources except his or her own ingenuity and will to live or will to return to loved ones.

Into this moment of utter failure, the protagonist gathers himself or herself one last time and makes one last herculean effort to survive, escape, and get back to his or her real life.

He or she may have help—a member of the group may trade helping the protagonist for a rescue with him or her. Someone may pass the protagonist a key to a door or to handcuffs, my cut restraints, distract a guard, or in some other way give the protagonist a tiny opening that he or she can exploit to escape.

The protagonist's rescue team may attack, creating a diversion that draws away guards, would-be killers, or the big bad guy long enough for the protagonist to grab the evidence and flee.

Regardless of how you plan for it to happen, the protagonist finds a way to extract himself or herself from the group and gets out. He or she may take down or kill a bunch of the bad guys on the way out, as well.

The climactic battle concludes with the good guys winning. This may involve only the protagonist being a one-person wrecking or killing machine and singlehandedly taking out most of the group. Or the protagonist's support team may help the protagonist take down everyone in the group.

The bloodied, battered protagonist walks out of the carnage with his or her evidence or having destroyed the group utterly. He or she returns to loved ones, family, or colleagues and gratefully (and possibly apologetically) reunites with them.

There may be a clean-up operation of arrests, criminal charges, and the protagonist making a report, testifying, or handing over the evidence he or she has gathered that takes down the entire organization permanently.

Last of all, you may choose to end with some sort of denouement where the protagonist is shown reunited with his or her loved ones and resuming his or her real life, back in his or her normal world. The protagonist has come full circle.

KEY SCENES

-- the moment the protagonist enters the group. The emotional and sensory impressions should come thick and fast

-- the protagonist makes a friend in the group

-- the protagonist slips up or makes a mistake and earns himself or herself a suspicious group member who will become a nemesis

-- the protagonist meets the big boss of the group for the first time

-- the protagonist nearly gets caught snooping, investigating, eavesdropping, or breaking a rule but gets away in the nick of time

-- the protagonist's friend saves him or her from getting in trouble but may get in trouble himself or may take punishment for the protagonist

-- the protagonist's family, personal life loved ones/friends, or outside boss contact them at an awkward moment and cause the protagonist big problems with the group

-- the protagonist is distracted by personal, real-world problems and makes a big mistake

-- the protagonist confronts the big boss of the group. This may not happen until as late as the final battle is already over

-- the protagonist apologizes to family, friends, coworkers, bosses for letting them down and receives forgiveness

THINGS TO THINK ABOUT WHEN WRITING THIS TROPE

What is the group the protagonist is going to infiltrate? Why is the protagonist going inside the group? What specifically is he or she hoping to find?

Who is the protagonist in his or her real life? What's their job, who's their family, what responsibilities does he or she have? Hobbies, interests, pets, other passions?

Does the protagonist have a support team of some kind? What kind of team? Who's on it? What resources does this team have? What are they doing while the protagonist is inside the group?

Who are the people in the group? What beliefs, values, and morals do they hold as a group? Are any or all of these flawed, twisted, or destructive in some way?

Who leads the group? In what way(s) is this person scary, charismatic, brilliant, and/or dangerous? In what way is this leader twisted, manipulative, harmful, dangerous, or something else extreme?

Is the protagonist there to take down the leader of the group, or is the protagonist's plan to avoid the leader entirely and do something else? How can you foil the protagonist's plan...either to get close to the leader or to stay far, far away from the leader, and make the opposite happen in your story?

Who within the group befriends the protagonist? What's that person's role in the group? Does that person want to escape or not? How loyal is that person to the group and to the group's leader? When faced with a choice of saving his/her friend (the protagonist) or betraying the group, which will this person choose? Does that answer change over the course of the story? If so, why?

Who in the group becomes suspicious of the protagonist first? Why? Does the protagonist make some mistake that causes this person to be suspicious, or is this person just naturally suspicious?

How will the suspicious group member turn into a nemesis for the protagonist? How does this person interfere with the protagonist's plan and goals?

What does the protagonist's contact with the group's leader or senior members look like? Does it go well or poorly?

Does the protagonist have to do something the leader asks for to prove his or her loyalty? If so, what? Does the protagonist do it? If so, how? If not, how does he or she dodge doing the thing?

Who are the protagonist's family, loved ones, friends, and coworkers? What do they think of what the protagonist is doing?

Does the protagonist stay in touch with his/her real-life friends during the infiltration mission? If so, how? If not, why not?

What happens in the protagonist's real life that demands he or she sneak away from the group to deal with it? Can you make this problem worse? Much worse? A crisis?

How will the protagonist deal with this real-life problem in the midst of his or her undercover operation? What does he or she do? How? When? Does he or she get caught?

In what ways will the protagonist's identity be tested by the group? By the group's membership gatekeeper? By the protagonist's friend inside the group? By the suspicious nemesis? How will the protagonist pass each of these tests?

What does the protagonist have to do to find whatever he or she is looking for inside the group? How do the steps of finding this thing get progressively more difficult and dangerous?

Does anyone outside the group from his or her real life recognize the protagonist at some point and nearly blow the mission? If so, who, how, and when? How does the protagonist cover up for the slip up?

Does someone from the protagonist's real life interfere with the infiltration operation in some way? Does a family member call a phone they're not supposed to? A coworker not realize the protagonist is undercover and contact him or her? Something else?

What will the consequences be if the protagonist is caught by the group and exposed as an infiltrator? Can you make those worse? Much worse? Truly terrifying?

Will the group take retribution on loved ones, friends, or coworkers of the protagonist if he or she gets caught? If so, how?

How does the problem in the protagonist's real-world life blow up into a crisis? Does this provoke the protagonist to hurry, take too big a chance, or do something else that ends up with him or her getting caught?

Why does the protagonist feel pressure to hurry up his or her investigation and try to go for the big, final piece of evidence, information, or thing he/she is looking for? Which is to say, why is the protagonist running out of time? Is there a reason related to the group in addition to whatever's going on in the protagonist's personal life? If so, what reason?

What does the protagonist do or not do that gets him or her caught?

Where is the protagonist's support team outside of the group (if he or she has one) when he or she is caught? Why can't they barge in and pull out the protagonist right away?

What happens to the protagonist after he or she is caught?

Will someone come to rescue him or her? If so, who, how, and when? If not, will someone help the protagonist from inside the group so he or she has a chance at escape? If so, who, how, and when?

Will there be some sort of distraction that helps the protagonist escape? If so, what? Who causes it and how?

What does the final battle look like? Does the protagonist fight alone and take out everyone who gets in his or her way? Does the support team fight its way in while the protagonist fights his/her way out?

Who is killed, injured, or apprehended in the final battle? Who does it?

How does the protagonist get out alive?

Does the protagonist find whatever he or she is looking for and bring it out with him or her? What is the thing?

What does the clean-up after the battle look like? Who's arrested, hauled away, hospitalized?

What does the protagonist's reunion with loved ones, friends, or coworkers look like?

Who apologizes to whom? Does the protagonist apologize for not helping with the real-world crisis? Do the loved ones, friends, and coworkers apologize for interfering with the protagonist's infiltration mission?

Will you show your audience a slice of the protagonist's return to his or her real life or not? If so, what will that look like?

TROPE TRAPS

The group that the protagonist is infiltrating is not sufficiently dangerous or risky to hold your audience's attention and make them nervous.

The reason the protagonist is infiltrating the group could be better handled some other way, like by a court order, search warrant, or technological surveillance.

The protagonist doesn't make sense to be the person who infiltrates the group. Someone with different or more appropriate expertise makes more sense.

Nobody is suspicious of the protagonist when he or she shows up to enter the group.

The protagonist is never tested by group members to see if the protagonist is who he or she says they are.

The group itself is wildly cliché and bores the audience. Zombie cult members walking around drugged and vague in white clothing, or government agents in suits who all operate like mindless robots, is really dull.

The leader of the group is ridiculously cliché as well. He or she is all seeing and all knowing, or a total, charismatic creep.

The members of the group have no free will at all.

The members of the group have no legitimate reason(s) for staying within the group, which is obviously corrupt and awful to all the group's members.

The protagonist fails to do sufficient preparation before going undercover and knows little to nothing about the group, which makes the protagonist look stupid and impulsive.

The protagonist doesn't bother to or take time to set up some sort of rescue team or support team outside the group, which makes the protagonist look stupid and impulsive.

There's no way for the protagonist to contact anyone on the outside or anyone on the outside to contact him or her...even if it's a basic signal like a plastic bag stuck in a tree or a chalk mark on something.

Your protagonist has no life whatsoever outside the group and doesn't seem like a real human being.

Your protagonist has no other problems or distractions the whole time he or she is undercover and doesn't seem like a real human being.

The group's corrupt member(s) are cartoonishly bad and one-dimensional—all bad all the time.

Nobody befriends the protagonist...just how unlikable is the main character, anyway?

You don't find ways to continue ratcheting up the danger, tension, and threats to the protagonist as they get deeper and deeper inside the organization.

You don't throw every stressor you can at the protagonist to up his or her own tension, suspense, and risk.

The protagonist never makes a mistake. Everyone makes mistakes sometimes, so your perfect protagonist doesn't seem like a real person.

The loved ones, friends, and coworkers of the protagonist come across as selfish jerks for not understanding the importance of the mission he or she is doing and bothering him or her mid-mission.

The audience doesn't buy the group, once it has caught the protagonist, not killing him or her immediately.

The group's leader monologues at the protagonist in cartoonish bad guy fashion.

The protagonist remains functional after beating or torture that would kill anyone else. That's not how either of those work.

The protagonist transforms magically into a one-person wrecking machine or killing machine when it's time to make his or her big escape. This comes across as implausible if you haven't established his or her extreme fighting skills earlier in the story. Side note: even excellent fighters struggle solo against two opponents, let alone many.

The group has no emergency plan at all for a scenario like the protagonist finding out the big secret and fleeing with it. How dumb is this group and its leaders?

Failing to show the protagonist reuniting with loved ones, friends, or coworkers after the big fight.

No apologies are offered to the protagonist by people from his or her real life who almost got him or her killed and they come across as selfish jerks that make the audience mad.

The protagonist doesn't apologize for not being there for loved ones when he or she was needed at home and comes across as a selfish jerk.

Failing to maintain an unrelenting sense of danger and tension on every page and in every scene of this story.

Failing to create a protagonist your audience can deeply identify with. Infiltrating a corrupt group is a type of cool, thrilling, behavior average people can readily imagine themselves doing. But if you create a character who's so badass or tough that he or she isn't relatable, you'll pull your audience out of enjoying the story personally and emotionally.

INFILTRATING A GROUP TROPE IN ACTION

Movies:

- The Departed
- Point Break
- Donnie Brasco
- Reservoir Dogs
- Miss Sloane
- The Infiltrator

- Eastern Promises

Books:

- The Spy Who Came In From the Cold by John Le Carré
- The Odessa File by Frederick Forsyth
- The Brotherhood by Jerry B. Jenkins
- The Banker by Dick Francis
- The Follower by Jason Starr
- The Informationist by Taylor Stevens
- The Insider by Stephen Frey
- The Survivor by Gregg Hurwitz

16

IN LOVE WITH THE ENEMY

DEFINITION

In this trope, two people—who are enemies and remain enemies through the story—come into close contact, typically through conflict, and fall in love over the course of the story.

The essential tension is this story is between their duty to their country, organization, family, or other group and the strong emotions they feel for their enemy-lover.

By the end of the story, each of them must make an impossible choice between their loyalty to their respective group and their personal feelings of love.

To be true enemies, their end goals must preclude each other, meaning if one of them wins in the conflict they're engaged in, the other must lose.

There are no outcomes where both can get what they want at the same time. (If this were the case, they would merely be rivals competing to get to the same, similar, or compatible outcomes first.)

The groups each of your lovers work for, are members of, or are loyal to are enemy groups. They can be a pair of nations, armies, government agencies, corporations, mob organizations, gangs, clans, families, you name it.

Each of the enemy groups has goals that, if achieved, mean the other group will fail, lose, or cannot achieve what it wants at the same time.

Into this win-lose scenario of fighting groups, the two main protagonists come into direct conflict.

> NOTE: I'll call them the hero and heroine to minimize
> confusion, but the genders can be any combination of hims,
> hers, theys, or something else that you'd like.

As the conflict between their groups grows into a crisis, the lovers are put under more and more pressure to choose their own side in the conflict over the person they love.

This dilemma of loyalty or love grows into a crisis right alongside the plot crisis between their competing groups. The moment of decision comes, one or both of the lovers chooses their group over love, and they are torn apart.

Into this utter emotional devastation, there's one last, climactic battle between their opposing groups. The outcome can go any way you'd like, but after the dust has settled, the lovers realize they cannot live without each other. They would rather leave their respective groups and be together than remain loyal to their groups and be apart.

The lovers finally get together, whether or not their respective groups approve of the union. They often leave—or flee—and go somewhere far away from the conflict so they can be together, safe and in love.

NOTE: In the Enemies Allied by Danger trope, the enemies set aside their enmity just long enough to defeat the big danger, and then they go back to being enemies (or at most, friends). In this trope, instead of remaining enemies, the enemies instead fall in love.

. . .

ADJACENT TROPES
-- Enemies Allied in Danger
-- Turning the Enemy
-- Help the Target Instead
-- Loved Ones on Opposite Sides of the Law
-- Conscience vs. Country

WHY READERS/VIEWERS LOVE THIS TROPE
-- he/she/they love me enough to give up everything they've ever believed in

-- he/she/ they will sacrifice their honor, their oaths, everything they stand for to be with me

-- an enemy is the epitome of a dangerous lover—you can't get much more dangerous than someone who's out to destroy you

-- breaking out of my dull, boring life to be with someone exotic, different, foreign, and exciting

--how thrilling is it to break all the rules and be with someone totally forbidden

OBLIGATORY SCENES
THE BEGINNING:
A conflict exists between two opposing groups. Someone from each of those groups encounters someone from the opposing group... and sparks fly. The options for what kind of conflict, how it's being acted out, and how the hero and heroine first meet is only limited by your imagination. There's no one formula for this.

The hero and heroine can meet in direct combat on the field of battle or in a violent fight of some kind.

They can both be pursuing the same object or information. Perhaps both trying to steal it or to find it before the other side does.

The hero and heroine's groups may be trying to control the same territory, buy out the same company, or any other form of conflict you can think of,

The future lovers can first meet in a boardroom, courtroom, bar, or anywhere else they might bump into each other while pursuing their side's goal(s).

The point is, they meet when they clash face-to-face in some way. Conflict is baked into their relationship from the very moment they meet. Indeed, these two have been in conflict with each other since *before* they ever met.

In this case, you'll need to come up with some compelling plot reason that they keep running into each other over and over—enough times for romantic sparks to start flying between them. The challenge with this approach is they may feel both love and hate for each other in the early going of this story. While audiences love it, this complicated set of feelings can be challenging to portray believably and well to your audience.

In this scenario, the external plot problem between the opposing groups gets worse and worse until an initial crisis between the groups may throw the hero and heroine (back) into direct conflict against each other. They may even have orders to kill each other. This first crisis between their growing feelings for each other and the conflict between their groups is likely to form the climax of Act One of your story.

OR

What I call the West Side Story opening:

The hero and heroine meet on neutral ground in an environment where they don't know the other one to be their enemy. They can bump into each other in a store or museum, meet in a coffee shop or on a deserted road, or even at the home of a mutual friend.

Again, the sky's the limit on imagining how these two encounter each other away from their sphere of conflict. In this scenario, they meet, sparks fly, and they're strongly attracted to each other long before they ever find out they're actually enemies. Only after they've met and started to form a romantic attachment do they meet again as enemies.

In this scenario, they may see each other multiple times without ever realizing they're enemies. You may let them be well on the way to in love before they figure out who the other one is, in fact. And you may let the exterior plot conflict between their opposing groups really start to develop and move toward an initial crisis before the two of them figure it out.

If, in the first-plot mini-crisis they finally see each other working for the other side, imagine their shock when they realized the person they have a huge crush on is none other than their mortal enemy. What a terrific climax to the first act this makes.

OR

For some reason, the two enemy groups must work together to solve a larger problem. They don't like each other but are willing to set aside their enmity long enough to work together to defeat a larger evil that they both have in common and have a shared interest in defeating.

Neither side has all the skill, knowledge, or expertise to defeat the big evil alone, hence the two sides must pool their skills and resources to bring down this serious threat.

In this scenario, the hero and heroine are assigned to work together for as long as it takes to defeat the big bad guy. They may snarl and snipe at each other for much of Act One...but are those sparks of irritation or attraction, or some of each?

At the end of Act One when the first mini-crisis between the enemy-partners and bad guy occurs, those sparks of irritation may abruptly shift to sparks of attraction and concern for each other.

. . .

THE MIDDLE:

Two things happen in the middle of this story. First, the external plot conflict either between the hero and heroine's enemy groups or between their temporarily allied groups and a big external bad guy gets worse. The danger rises, the stakes rise, the threat to the hero and heroine gets exponentially worse, and the action gets more and more tense.

Second, the relationship between the hero and heroine heats up... a LOT. For example, they may go from hating each other to irritating each other, to reluctantly attracted to each other, to overtly attracted, to falling in love. (This progression is merely an example of possible developing feelings. Feel free to build your own progression.)

Superiors of the hero and heroine may tell them to cut out the fooling around with the enemy.

Friends and allies of the pair may aid and abet their relationship.

The hero and heroine seek opportunities to be together alone in a relatively safe situation so they can explore their romance.

Meanwhile, the two of them may work together to investigate, surveil, follow, reconnoiter, or attempt to attack the external big bad guy, if there is one.

If they're still expected to work against each other, they may half-heartedly send reports back to their superiors on each other. They may continue to collect information on the other one's group and report that which is likely a source of serious friction between them. The pair struggles with ethical dilemmas of whether or not to warn their lover in advance of impending actions or attacks by his or her own side in the conflict.

Their superiors question their loyalty to the cause, and both lovers find themselves on thin ice within their group. Other group members question their loyalty and trustworthiness, and rightly so.

Act Two rises toward two simultaneous crises: first, there's a big fight between the enemy groups the hero and heroine belong to. Or there's a big fight between their two temporarily allied groups and the big bad guy.

Second, in either scenario the hero and heroine are both put into a position of having to choose to do something to save or protect their lover or to do the best thing to advance the cause of their own group to the detriment of their lover's group.

This terrible choice may arise during the climactic crisis of Act Two, or it may arise at the very end of the act as the big crisis concludes.

BLACK MOMENT:

Both the hero and heroine are devastated when their lover chooses duty and loyalty to his or her own group over love. Worse, because one or both of them hesitated to make the choice or first attempted to protect their lover before choosing group over love, the big fight went badly for their group.

They suffer professional repercussions for their hesitation or mistake, which may be real or may only be perceived to have happened by their superiors. Either way, one or both of them is(are) blamed for their group's failure in the conflict at the end of Act Two.

Not only have they each lost the person they love, but they've also betrayed their group, not to mention their oaths, duty, and loyalty to that group. Their careers are destroyed, their lives are probably destroyed, and worst of all, their hearts are destroyed.

THE END:

Devastated by the black moment's events, the hero and heroine individually realize they are miserable without each other and cannot live without their true love. Honor, duty, country, and oaths be damned, they're going to search for a way to get back together.

They feel guilty for betraying each other in the black moment and probably find a way to communicate across enemy lines to express their remorse and regret for their wrong decision. They each want a second chance to get it right.

Into this attempt at reconciliation, the climactic battle typically winds up and gets ready to commence.

If the lovers' groups are temporarily allied to defeat a big bad guy, the lovers usually work together desperately and find a way to turn the tide in their groups' favor. They find new information, discover a heretofore unseen weakness in the big bad guy, or they come up with a creative plan to defeat the big bad guy.

In this scenario, they implement the plan together and lead their respective groups through the climactic battle to victory against the big bad guy

OR

If the lovers' groups are about to engage in a climactic battle against each other, the lovers will each find a way to come together to survive the battle. They may not participate in the battle other than to search out their lover and mutually protect each other. It's not uncommon that they simply take cover and ride out the battle, their only goal to keep each other safe. They may flee the battlefield immediately after the fact and go in search of a safe, anonymous place to hide from retribution from both of their groups and to be together.

Alternately, the lovers may each do something dramatic and heroic on behalf of their own side in the climactic battle that doesn't involve harming or killing each other, but that restores their honor.

From their own side of the conflict, they may each do something to protect the other from afar.

Regardless of the outcome of this battle between their groups, whose outcome they may not care about at all anymore, the lovers will join each other in the aftermath. They each resign from their groups or just desert their groups and leave. Again, the lovers are likely to go far away from the conflict and find a place where they can be safely together.

The lover may or may not reconcile with their respective groups before they come together forever, and they may not care if they reconcile or not as long as they can be with the person they love.

As for their groups, each may choose to leave the lovers alone, or they may only choose to leave the lovers alone for now.

If you end your story with both groups looking for or pursuing the lovers, your audience will remain worried about the pair's safety and not feel as if the story is truly over, yet.

KEY SCENES

-- the hero and heroine meet for the first time and sparks of some kind fly

-- the hero and heroine bicker and expose their prejudices about each other's groups

-- the hero and heroine find something they have in common

-- the hero and heroine have their first date or somewhat romantic moment when it occurs to both of them that they have a big, big problem...they're falling for their enemy

-- superiors get wind of the romance and forbid it from continuing

-- the hero and heroine defy their orders to break off the budding romance

-- they each protect or save each other from harm by their respective group. (Hero saves heroine from his group, heroine save hero from her group.)

-- the hero and heroine declare their love for each other. (May not happen at the same time)

-- the hero and heroine each keep a big secret from the other...and the moment when they each discover it

-- the moment they each realize the other has betrayed them in some way

-- the moment they each realize the other has chosen loyalty to his or her group over them

-- they save each other's lives

-- they apologize to each other

THINGS TO THINK ABOUT WHEN WRITING THIS TROPE

Who are your hero and heroine? What do they do? What characteristics do they have in common? What's different about them? What beliefs do they not share?

What groups do they each belong to? Why are those two groups enemies? Can you make the groups' hatred of the other group worse? Much worse? Absolutely mortal enemies?

What conflict or crisis or big bad guy must be stopped in your story? Will the hero and heroine's respective groups work against each other in this story or together?

How, when, and where do the hero and heroine meet?

Do the hero and heroine know they're enemies when they meet? If not, when do they find that out and how?

How do they get along and not get along when they first meet? How much friction is there between them?

What skills, knowledge, and/or expertise do the hero and heroine each have? Why is this important to the conflict they're engaged in?

What do their superiors think of the budding romance when they find out about it? What do they say to the hero and heroine about it? Do they order the pair to stop the romance?

How do the lovers defy any orders to stay apart or keep things professional?

What do the hero and heroine fight about?

What secret(s) do the hero and heroine each keep from the other?

How do their friends, family, coworkers, allies feel about the budding romance? Who tries to break up the hero and heroine? Who helps them spend time together?

How will the hero and heroine periodically arrange to spend time together alone so the romance can develop?

How do the hero and heroine each betray each other in some way? When?

Do the hero and heroine warn each other of something their own group is doing that could be harmful to the other one's group? How much trouble would they get into if their own group found out about the shared information/intel?

How does their duty—their oaths, jobs, loyalty to the group— come into direct conflict with their romantic feelings for each other? What dilemmas or tough decisions do the hero and heroine have to face as their loyalty to their own group and their feelings come more and more into conflict?

How does the big conflict in the book get worse through the middle of the story? How does it get much worse? How does it become absolutely awful?

What are the potential consequences if the hero and heroine don't beat the big bad guy together or if their two groups come into direct and catastrophic conflict? How bad could it get? How can the outcome get worse? Much worse? Truly terrible?

Why do the hero and heroine each choose their group over their lover in the black moment? What's each of their motivations?

How does each lover find out about the other one's betrayal? How do they feel and react?

How devastated are each of them? How do they display this to your audience?

How do the hero and heroine each come to the realization that they're miserable apart, that they can't live without each other, and that they've each made a terrible mistake by choosing loyalty to their group over love?

How do the lovers communicate to each other that they've made a mistake? By what means do they talk, text, email, see each other?

Do the lovers come together to plan or find a way to beat the big bad guy? If so, have they made up already, or does making up happen while or after they build their clever plan for victory?

If their two groups enter into direct conflict, do they make up before, during, or after this big conflict? What do they each do going into the big conflict? Do they warn the other one of their own group's plans? Do they trade promises to stay out of the fray? Do they promise to find each other?

What provokes the start of the final, climactic battle? Does time run out to stop the bad guy or keep the two enemy groups apart? Are all the remaining options for stopping the bad guy short of battle or stopping the confrontation between the two enemy groups exhausted?

What do the hero and heroine do during the final conflict?

How does each of them protect the other one in some way or save the other one's life?

How does the battle end? Who wins? What harm is done or who dies? How do the hero and heroine individually feel about the outcome? Do they care who won or lost?

At what point do the hero and heroine decide to walk away from the enmity between their two groups so the two of them can be together forever? Do they leave the group formally? Do they have permission to leave? Do they desert? Flee?

Where do they go to be together forever? Are they safe? Are they at peace? Will their two groups leave them alone?

TROPE TRAPS

The hero and heroine are so different or believe such different things they would never plausibly like or respect each other, let alone fall in love.

The hero and heroine have nothing in common that might draw them together.

The chemistry between the hero and heroine doesn't work. The friction between them doesn't transition logically into attraction.

The couple fights constantly and you rely on all the bickering and arguing to convince your audience that these two like each other, which it won't do.

The pair's superiors don't freak out sufficiently when they find out about the budding romance, or they freak out too much (depending on the situation and type of groups the hero and heroine belong to).

The hero and heroine's friends, family, and coworkers don't freak out enough at the budding romance or freak out too much. None of them help and none of them try to sabotage the relationship. Which is implausible. Humans are nosy and like to interfere.

The crisis in the story isn't big enough to put the hero and heroine into an impossible, insurmountable dilemma.

The hero and heroine aren't loyal enough to their respective groups to feel as if they're in an impossible situation. The groups the hero and heroine belong do don't require or inspire enough loyalty to put the hero and heroine into an impossible situation as they start falling in love.

The consequences aren't bad enough for the hero and heroine if they were caught consorting romantically with the enemy, and your audience feels no great worry about them getting caught.

The audience doesn't like the hero and heroine enough to care if they end up happy.

The audience doesn't feel invested enough emotionally in the hero and heroine as a couple to worry greatly if the pair doesn't find a way to be together.

The couple never betrays each other, never keeps any secrets, and never warns the other one in advance of harmful things about to happen. C'mon. They're in love. They're not thinking straight and are going to make mistakes, slip up, and encounter moral quandaries with no right answer.

The climactic confrontation/battle at the end of the story isn't dangerous or harmful enough to push the hero and heroine to the very edge of disaster, losing the other, complete ruin for both of them or death.

The hero and heroine aren't devastated enough to have lost the person they love and don't feel guilty enough for choosing their group over love, making your audience think the pair don't deserve each other or happiness.

The hero and heroine never apologize to each other for not choosing the other one over love.

The hero and heroine are casually allowed to keep their jobs, membership in the group, and be together forever with the enemy, and your audience doesn't buy it for a second.

There's no price for the hero and heroine choosing each other over their groups, and your audience doesn't feel they've earned their happily ever after.

Failing to resolve how the groups respond to the couple choosing love and ending your story with the groups still searching for or pursuing the couple, making for a worrying and unsatisfying ending... unless of course you're planning a sequel sooner rather than later.

IN LOVE WITH THE ENEMY TROPE IN ACTION
Movies:

- Mr. & Mrs. Smith
- Allied
- The Spy Who Loved Me
- Knight and Day
- Mission Impossible II
- Notorious
- The Thomas Crown Affair
- Valkyrie

Books:

- The Night Manager by John Le Carré
- The Black Widow by Daniel Silva

- The Chemist by Stephanie Meyer
- Red Sparrow by Jason Matthews
- The Bronze Horseman by Paullina Simons
- The Spy by Paul Coelho
- The Sympathizer by Viet Thanh Nguyen
- The Book Thief by Markus Zusak

17

KIDNAPPED

DEFINITION

In this trope, the protagonist is the victim of a kidnapping. (In the volume on Crime & Legal Thrillers, there's a separate trope revolving around the protagonist solving a kidnapping.) The suspense and tension of this trope come from the kidnapped person's desperate efforts to escape, to communicate his or her plight to someone, and/or to catch the attention of someone, anyone who will tell the authorities where they are and to send help.

This is a trope of psychological and emotional warfare between the kidnapped protagonist and his or her kidnapper, and it's a trope of the emotional journey of the protagonist—his or her will to survive and determination to hang on to his or her identity versus helplessness, despair, and depression.

Kidnapping is a deeply personal crime. One evil, bad person kidnaps an innocent person who's just going about his or her normal life. The scale of this crime is deeply relatable to all members of your audience. They can all easily envision themselves being snatched out of their regular, boring, mundane existence and thrust into this situation.

It's much harder for most people to envision living through a nuclear apocalypse, for example. It's so big, so farfetched, so out of our individual control, that we struggle to imagine what it would be like. The scale alone—thousands or millions of injured, sick, and dying people makes it incomprehensible to us. But one guy snatching one person—me—off the street and doing something bad to us? That we can all imagine vividly.

It's common for this trope to be layered with its matching trope—the story of the person(s) trying to find and rescue the kidnapped protagonist. That story will have its own protagonist, of course—the person who's the driving force behind the effort to rescue this protagonist. In this combination of tropes, you'll undoubtedly tell your story from both the kidnapped protagonist's point of view and the protagonist trying to solve the kidnapping's point of view, also.

This story usually begins with the kidnapping itself. The middle is consumed by the protagonist's struggles, both physical and emotional to stay alive and stay sane while seeking ways to get help or escape. The black moment is often when the protagonist's big escape attempt fails and he or she loses all hope of getting away or living. The ending, of course, revolves around the protagonist finding a way to escape, finding a way to communicate with an outsider and ask for help, or for the people trying to find and rescue the protagonist finally succeeding in doing so.

In reality, 97% of all juvenile kidnapping victims are recovered alive. For adult victims, 22% are found dead. In 2022, the U.S. had NCIC entries for 359,094 missing children, and 115 of those were stereotypical kidnappings, which include:

- Keeping the child overnight or at least one hour
- Kidnapper intends to keep the child permanently
- Kidnapper transports the child 50 miles or more
- Kidnapper demands a ransom
- Kidnapper kills the child

Which is to say, stereotypical kidnappings are quite rare in the

U.S. In other parts of the world that are more dangerous, kidnapping is much more common; however, trafficking for sexual exploitation, forced labor, and forced marriage are much more common reasons for kidnapping people than ransoms and terror attacks. 81% of all kidnapping victims are teenagers, which makes sense in light of their probable use in trafficking and enslavement.

92% of sex trafficker/kidnappers are men, while most digital kidnappers are female. 49% of all child kidnappings happen by a family member while abductions by a stranger account for only 0.35% of missing child cases.

I could on at length about kidnapping statistics around the world —just do your research before you choose a setting for your story to get an idea of what kinds of kidnappings are most common, who the typical kidnappers in that area are, and what kind of kidnapping predominates in that area.

In my volume on Backstory Romance Tropes, I wrote at length about Stockholm Syndrome and Enslavement and how the psychology of those work, so I won't repeat it here. But be aware that Stockholm Syndrome is real and a very common way the human mind protects its person from the horrors of what's happening to him or her.

Also of note, people who suffer enslavement of any kind often experience psychological trauma highly akin to Stockholm Syndrome as a means of surviving the horror of their experience.

At any rate, this trope usually ends with the kidnapped protagonist escaping on his or her own, the protagonist successfully asking for help and that help arriving, or the person(s) searching for him or her finding him or her and affecting a rescue, either by paying a ransom and making an exchange or by raiding the place where the protagonist is being held captive.

ADJACENT TROPES
-- Missing Child

-- Solving a Kidnapping
-- Rescue Mission for Prisoner/Hostage
-- Brainwashed
-- Frightened into Mental Breakdown
-- Escaping a Dangerous Group
-- Fleeing Enslavement

WHY READERS/VIEWERS LOVE THIS TROPE

-- one of our greatest fears is the loss of our freedom and this trope vicariously walks us through how we would survive it and regain our freedom

-- this story teaches us survival lessons we really don't want to experience for real to learn those lessons

-- outsmarting someone who thinks they're smarter, stronger, or meaner than we are

-- we all like to think we would find an indomitable will to survive in a situation like this

-- perhaps parents' greatest fear is getting distracted for just a second and their child being kidnapped. Parents *need* to believe that, if their child was kidnapped, he or she would find a way to survive and gain his or her freedom and come back home

OBLIGATORY SCENES
THE BEGINNING:

The kidnapping happens. It's very easy to research online the various ways that people are kidnapped. It varies by age, place, and type of kidnapper, so do your homework...and then be creative.

The more subtle, insidious, or dastardly the approach by the kidnapper to the victim, the smarter a villain the kidnapper will appear to be, and the more your audience will fear for the kidnapped protagonist.

The mental shock of being kidnapped is severe. Your protagonist may freeze, panic, have no idea what to do, or react in some other way that doesn't initially include fighting back. Particularly if he or she is drugged, injured, or immobilized, the protagonist may not have a chance to fight back.

However, as the protagonist adapts to his or her new reality, he or she is very likely to test the boundaries of his or her imprisonment. The protagonist will try to escape, physically fight for his or her freedom, defy the kidnapper, and cause trouble. Unfortunately, any decent kidnapper is prepared for this and bribes, bullies, terrorizes, or physically subdues the protagonist, ending any ideas of quick escape and return home.

This revolt and its subsequent quashing often forms the mini-crisis at the end of Act One.

THE MIDDLE:

The middle of this story is where the big emotional ups and down will happen. As time passes, despair and depression set in. As torture or abuse happen, the breakdown of identity and will to survive happen. As the protagonist becomes solely dependent upon the kidnapper for food, water, and the means to simply stay alive, Stockholm Syndrome may set in.

If you're running another trope that involves someone trying to rescue this protagonist, most of the middle of your story will probably be taken up with that, and you'll only give your audience snippets of this trope in the form of check-in scenes showing how the kidnapped protagonist is doing and how dire his or her situation is becoming.

Act Two builds to a crisis of will the kidnapped protagonist survive long enough to be rescued? It's a race against the protagonist's declining physical and mental health, the mental breakdown of the kidnapper, and how fast the person(s) trying to free the protagonist can find him or her and arrange a rescue.

Act Two may end with a crisis where the kidnapper experiences a mental break and decides to or tries to kill the kidnapped protagonist. Some event may happen that pushes the kidnapper into deciding it's time to cut his or her risks and dispose of the protagonist.

OR

The kidnapped protagonist has been biding his or her time, planning and preparing to attempt an escape. In this case, Act Two ends with the protagonist launching his or her escape attempt.

The choice of one of these endings will depend on how much resiliency, will, cleverness, and agency your kidnapped protagonist is capable of and whether or not his or her conditions of captivity allow for any chance at all for an escape.

BLACK MOMENT:

The kidnapped protagonist's big escape attempt fails. He or she is caught by the kidnapper, or something goes wrong in the plan— perhaps the person to whom the protagonist passed a message is in cahoots with the kidnapper or didn't understand what the protagonist was trying to tell him or her.

Now, the kidnapper is enraged and the protagonist is punished, immobilized, or heavily locked up/restrained such that no more escape attempts are remotely possible. Moreover, the kidnapper loses all sympathy, all mercy (assuming he or she had any to begin with) and is angry enough to kill the protagonist now. The kidnapper starts the process of working himself or herself up into an angry enough state to kill the protagonist. It's only a matter of time, now, before the protagonist dies.

By trying to escape, the protagonist has sealed his or her fate and is going to die, now. All is lost. There's no more chance at freedom, and now there's no more chance to even live.

THE END:

This story ends with the protagonist freed and the kidnapper arrested, dead, or long gone, never to be seen again, hopefully. There are, however, many paths to this ending for this trope.

- The person(s) searching for the protagonist find him or her, raid the place where he or she is imprisoned, defeat the kidnapper, and free the protagonist.
- The protagonist manages to get some sort of message to an outsider asking for help, and the authorities come, catch or kill the kidnapper, and free the protagonist.
- The protagonist, with nothing to lose, does something extreme to free himself or herself and manages to escape on their own.
- The protagonist gets loose, the kidnapper slips up, and the protagonist takes his or her shot at attacking and possibly killing the kidnapper. Once the kidnapper is incapacitated, the protagonist runs or calls for help and is rescued.
- Someone who knows the kidnapper realizes what he or she has done and intervenes to help the protagonist escape.
- A random stranger recognizes the protagonist from TV, posters, milk cartons and calls the authorities, alerting them to the protagonist's whereabouts. The authorities arrive and rescue the protagonist.

I could go on and on with possible endings, but I'll leave you to cook up your own smart, exciting, dangerous ending that's tailored to both your story, your protagonist, your kidnapper, the amount of time that has passed, where your story is set, and all the other elements that will affect how your protagonist finally escapes or is rescued.

The very end of your story typically involves the protagonist returning home to loved ones, safe at last. Don't skip this step. Your audience has been put through an emotional ringer and this trope explores one of the most frightening possible events to all humans. They need the closure of seeing the protagonist safe, home, and back among loved ones.

KEY SCENES

-- the protagonist wakes up for the first time and realizes he or she is captive

-- the protagonist demands to know why he or she has been kidnapped. (He or she may or may not get an answer. If not, there's an additional key scene where the protagonist figures out why he or she has been kidnapped)

-- the protagonist figures out what the kidnapper has planned for him or her

-- the protagonist tries to make friends with the kidnapper, to suck up, to get better treatment, promises to behave in return for being unchained or for getting more food, for example

-- the protagonist spots a weakness, a habit, a mistake the kidnapper has or does that might be exploited to escape and starts planning

-- the protagonist has a moment of utter despair and gives up

--something happens or the protagonist thinks of/remembers something that makes him or her determined to live

THINGS TO THINK ABOUT WHEN WRITING THIS TROPE

Who's the kidnapper? What's his or her state of mental health? What's his or her mindset regarding violence? How did that come to be?

Does the kidnapper work for someone? If so, who? What does that person want? What orders does the kidnapper receive? What's the kidnapper's job? How did he or she get into this kind of work? What does the kidnapper think of his or her work?

Who is the protagonist? Why is he or she targeted for kidnapping?

What about the protagonist does the kidnapper want to exploit? How does the kidnapper plan to exploit it?

How does the kidnapping happen? Is the protagonist just snatched or is he or she lured into a situation that makes kidnapping him or her easier?

At what point does the protagonist realize he or she is being kidnapped? How does he or she react? What does he or she do?

How does the kidnapper keep the protagonist captive? Restraints? Cage? Drugs? Hostile place? Something else?

Does the kidnapper have help? Is there more than one kidnapper?

Where is the protagonist taken? Why there?

Does the kidnapper want a ransom or does the kidnapper simply want to exploit or sell the protagonist?

How does the protagonist revolt initially to his or her captivity? What form does it take? How does that go? How does the kidnapper subdue the revolt?

What's the protagonist's emotional journey through the story? (And yes, I realize that's basically asking you to describe the whole book. Sorry.) What thoughts and emotions does the protagonist experience and in what order? How does his or her mindset change in response to the things the kidnapper does to him or her?

When does the protagonist despair?

When does the protagonist give up hope of ever being rescued?

When does the protagonist feel totally and permanently abandoned by his or her loved ones? Is he or she right or wrong? How will you let your audience know if the protagonist is right or wrong, or will you leave that unanswered for your audience?

Does your protagonist experience Stockholm Syndrome? If so, what does that look like?

Does your protagonist try to bargain with the kidnapper? If so, for what? How well or poorly does it go?

Does your protagonist grieve his or her situation?

How does your protagonist try to stay strong physically and mentally? Does it work or not?

What touchstone does your protagonist cling to in order to give him or her hope and a continued will to live?

What efforts are going on, out of sight of your protagonist, to rescue him or her? Will you show these in your story? Will the protagonist get wind of them, perhaps on a radio or news broadcast, or maybe the kidnapper tells the protagonist?

How does the kidnapper hide the protagonist?

Does someone associated with the kidnapper realize or know the kidnapper is keeping a captive? What does that person think about it? Does that person have any contact with the protagonist? If so, how does that interaction go?

What does the protagonist have to do—for now—to stay alive, maybe to lull the kidnapper into a false sense of security?

How does the protagonist plan to escape? What's the plan? What's the weakness he or she plans to exploit? Does the protagonist recruit someone else to help him or her escape?

How does the big escape plan fail? Why does it fail?

What does the kidnapper do to the protagonist after he or she attempts to escape?

How will the protagonist ultimately get away from the kidnapper or be rescued? What are the steps to that plan? How can it almost fail? How close to failure can it come but still be pulled out at the last second?

What happens to the kidnapper in the end? Is that satisfying to your audience? Can you do something more satisfying for your audience?

Who are the loved ones the protagonist returns home to in the end? What does that reunion look like?

What lessons has the protagonist learned about himself or herself throughout this whole experience?

TROPE TRAPS

The kidnapper is cliché, cartoonish or predictable.

The protagonist is so stupid about getting into a situation where he or she can be kidnapped that your audience doesn't like him or her and isn't sympathetic to the trouble he or she has gotten themselves into.

The kidnapping itself would have logically been stopped, witnessed, or interfered with by a bystander.

The kidnapper does things that would give any person with some gumption and initiative plenty of opportunity to escape, and the audience is mad the protagonist doesn't take those opportunities.

Failing to explain why the protagonist doesn't try harder to escape.

The protagonist spends so much time feeling sorry for himself or herself, despairing and wallowing in misery, that the audience dislikes him or her.

Showing so much torture, suffering, or gross things being done to the protagonist that your audience stops reading or watching your story because it's too overwhelming emotionally.

Failing to show or at least allude to enough bad stuff happening to the protagonist that the audience is sufficiently worried about their safety and that your audience buys the level of terror your protagonist is experiencing.

All the bystanders are too dumb to perceive that the protagonist is obviously in distress and in need of help. This will infuriate your audience. If your audience members can see it, surely other people should be able to spot it, too.

The kidnapper is dumb and doesn't move, properly hide, or properly restrain the protagonist. Then, when your protagonist fails to escape this dummy, the protagonist himself or herself comes across as too stupid to live.

The way the protagonist finally escapes is lame, obvious, or could have been done much sooner.

The protagonist never takes any initiative to help himself or herself but merely waits passively for someone to come get him or her, and your audience dislikes him or her.

The way the rescue is done would get the protagonist killed and the audience doesn't find it smart or plausible.

The fate of the kidnapped in the end isn't satisfying to your audience.

Failing to show the protagonist safely returned to home, family, and loved ones.

KIDNAPPED TROPE IN ACTION
Movies:

- Room
- Cardinal (Season 1)
- 10 Cloverfield Lane
- Split
- Captivity
- The Disappearance of Alice Creed

Books:

- Still Missing by Chevy Stevens
- The Never List by Koethi Zan
- The Collector by John Fowles
- The Marsh King's Daughter by Karen Dionne

- Comfort Food by Kitty Thomas
- Living Dead Girl by Elizabeth Scott

18

KILL LOVED ONE TO SAVE OTHERS

DEFINITION

This trope revolves around perhaps the most difficult decision any human being ever has to make—the decision to let a loved one die (or kill a loved one outright) to save the lives of many others. Which is to say, this entire trope is about the worst possible black moment any character could ever face.

This whole story arc is a set-up whose sole goal is to arrive at a black moment so wrenching, so heartbreaking, that it will nearly kill your character.

In this story, some crisis occurs that the protagonist is recruited to stop. The crisis is going to kill a lot of people. Because you're asking your protagonist to let a loved one die, it's typical that the sacrifice will save a LOT of people. Thousands. Millions. All of humanity.

The only way for your protagonist to stop the crisis and save the masses of innocent people at risk is to let a loved one die or to kill them outright. Ultimately, the protagonist makes the decision, the great sacrifice happens, the crisis is stopped, and many, many peoples' lives are saved...but at great, great cost.

A variation on this trope is the villain who forces the protagonist to let loved ones die or kill them outright. For example, your protagonist knows something classified that, if revealed to the bad guy, will allow the bad guy to kill a whole lot of people. The villain gets a hold of the protagonist's loved one and commences torturing the loved one to force the protagonist to talk. If the protagonist holds out, the villain will eventually kill the loved one.

It probably still qualifies as a thriller if your protagonist is forced to be the one to actually kill a loved one, although to me personally, that feels more akin to a horror story.

At any rate, this is a highly emotionally charged trope. Your job is to let your protagonist and your audience see the horrific dilemma coming early in the story and build the anticipation all the way through until the moment where the impossible, devastating choice must be made.

ADJACENT TROPES
-- Loved One in Jeopardy
-- Pitted Against Each Other
-- Lethal Lottery/Life Auction
-- Family Threatened During Trial
-- Loved One Possessed

WHY READERS/VIEWERS LOVE THIS TROPE
-- we all think of ourselves as heroes who will do the right thing... this is the ultimate test of our (vicarious) heroism. Could we do *this* and be an ultimate hero

-- if we were among the thousands or millions of innocents in jeopardy, we'd *really* like the person making this decision to choose us over their one or few loved ones

-- we find the journey to this impossible decision both harrowing and uplifting, terrifying and gratifying, to take in our own minds

--this is a decision we *never* want to face, but we wonder what it would be like to face a dilemma of this scale, so we want to experience it fictitiously as a mental exercise of "what if"

OBLIGATORY SCENES
THE BEGINNING:

Some sort of problem begins. It may start small at first. Nobody may realize just how bad it's going to get before the end. But it's definitely a problem and it definitely needs to be dealt with. Enter our protagonist who is assigned to stop the problem. He or she may be part of a team or a group assigned to stop the problem, or he or she may be working solo.

An asteroid might be heading for Earth. A nuclear reactor is having a problem. A power outage is affecting a classified military laboratory.

The problem may seem large but be far away or in the distant future, or it may seem like a small problem at first but with hints of potential to spiral into something much bigger.

OR

A protagonist may be assigned to investigate, pursue, or arrest a bad guy. It's a routine assignment, part of his or her job. There's no reason to expect it to be anything other than just another day at the office.

The protagonist needs to serve a warrant to a mobster. An undercover cop who's been embedded with a group about to rob a bank is told to make the arrests now before anyone gets hurt. A U.S. marshal is collecting the family of a criminal and moving them into protective custody today. A military unit is sent out to investigate intel that a terrorist may be in a certain location.

Again, it's a problem with a certain amount of implied risk, but it's nothing out of the ordinary for your protagonist to handle.

Whatever inciting incident you choose, as Act One unfolds,

things do not go according to plan. The problem isn't fixed using the regular containment techniques. What normally works, doesn't. The problem gets worse, and the beginnings of alarm start to build.

Act One ends with a mini-crisis in which the problem not only is getting worse, but we get our first look at the potential for it to get really bad.

THE MIDDLE:

The middle of this story is a scramble to contain the damage from the mini-crisis at the end of Act One and to stop the problem from getting any worse...and failing to do both.

The problem continues to grow, spiraling out of control and turning into a full-blown crisis. The protagonist, on the ground and nose-to-nose with the growing crisis, knows full well just how bad this could get and is very alarmed. He or she may be the first person to really send out serious warnings and demand a full crisis response.

Typically, there's a bureaucrat, politician, or boss who fails to listen to the protagonist's urgent warnings. The boss doesn't believe the reports from the protagonist, whom the boss doesn't like much. The bureaucrat has an agenda of his or her own that makes him or her slow to respond or is incompetent and responds incorrectly. The politician is covering his or her own behind and doesn't want to escalate the response and draw media attention or cause public alarm.

But the protagonist prevails over the bad boss, goes around the bad boss, or makes such a stink that the boss's superiors get wind of the problem.

More experts, more resources, and/or more government agencies are brought in to help deal with the crisis as it spins up.

OR

If your story is more of a single protagonist versus single villain or small group of villains tale, the middle is where they engage in direct conflict. The protagonist tries to stop the villain and the villain tries to stop the protagonist. There may be surveillance, chase scenes, break-ins, fights, and other conflicts as the protagonist tries to catch the villain or foil the villain's plan.

The conflict becomes more and more personal as these evenly matched foes try to best each other but can't get the upper hand. They both grow frustrated and eventually enraged. It's even possible the protagonist kills a loved one of the villain somewhere in the middle of the story.

The villain either loses patience or decides to go for the jugular and target the protagonist's lover(s). Act Two climaxes with the villain setting up the ultimate crisis for the protagonist where the protagonist must give the villain what he or she wants or else the villain will kill the protagonist's loved one. Alternately, the villain may set up a scenario where the villain personally must let a loved one die or kill a loved one to save a whole bunch of innocents the villain is about to kill.

BLACK MOMENT:

The protagonist must choose between the life of a loved one and saving the lives of a lot of innocents or possibly between a sacred oath or duty. Your protagonist (and your audience) should have seen this moment coming, dreaded it, done everything in his or her power to avoid it, and agonize over it now that the moment of decision is here.

Black moments don't get much blacker than this, and your audience will expect you to lean into the pathos and tragedy of it.

While letting a loved one die may be a decision the protagonist has no choice but to make, and it may, in fact, be an obvious choice with only one right answer, that won't make the moment of actually making the decision any easier.

Your black moment may be more protracted than most in this trope as you draw out the protagonist's last frantic efforts to avoid having to make this choice. This is not a black moment to rush. After all, getting to this moment is the whole point of your story.

THE END:

Once the decision is made, events accelerate rapidly toward the big climax. The sacrifice of the loved one(s) is made, or at a minimum, the loved one's fate is sealed and there's no turning back.

The protagonist now can do what he or she must to stop the crisis once and for all. There's one last push to do the nearly impossible thing required to halt the crisis at the last moment before catastrophe. Stopping the crisis pushes the protagonist and anyone with him or her to their very limits, but they manage, by the skin of their teeth, to pull it off. The innocent masses are saved.

OR

With nothing left to lose and not in a great mental or emotional state, your protagonist is probably willing to sacrifice himself or herself pretty freely at this point to kill the villain.

After the death of the loved one, one, last, climactic battle between the protagonist and the villain still remains. The protagonist, energized by grief, rage, and loss, finally has the strength of will to overcome the previously unbeatable villain. They clash, they fight, and ultimately, the protagonist defeats the great evil.

In either version of the ending, the protagonist emerges, bloodied, battered, and devastated, from the hell he or she has just gone through. He or she may be alive and hailed as a hero, but this protagonist almost always walks away from all the glory to grieve in private.

It's a victory, but a sad one that has come at a very high price. While the relieved masses celebrate, the heavy-hearted protagonist disappears. Maybe he or she will emerge one day to save the world again, but for now, this hero wants nothing more to do with heroics.

. . .

KEY SCENES

-- the moment when it first becomes clear that a routine problem isn't going to be routine after all

-- the protagonist first warns a loved one that there's a problem and they should take action to avoid it (lock the doors, get out of the house, leave town, arm themselves)

-- the protagonist's co-worker or boss doesn't initially believe the problem is getting as bad as it is

-- the moment when the large group of innocents at risk realize how much danger they're in

-- the moment when the protagonist realizes his or her loved one is in mortal danger

-- the protagonist tries to get his or her loved one out of danger but fails—he or she is too late, the loved one refuses to leave, the protagonist can't warn the loved one for some reason

-- the villain informs the protagonist he or she has the protagonist's loved one(s) and the protagonist panics

-- the moment in which the protagonist chooses the loved one over the innocent many or over his/her sacred oath/duty. It may last for only an instant, but the protagonist revolts against what he or she must do

-- the moment when the protagonist discovers his or her loved one is dead

THINGS TO THINK ABOUT WHEN WRITING THIS TROPE

What's the crisis your story is built around? How does it unfold and grow bigger step by step?

Does your crisis start out huge and dangerous or does it start small and apparently innocuous?

Who is your protagonist? What's his or her expertise, training, knowledge, or skill that makes him or her the right person to deal with the unfolding crisis?

What about your protagonist makes him or her relatable and human?

At what point does it become clear to the protagonist that the small problem or regular crisis is becoming something much worse? What happens regarding the crisis? What changes in the situation? What does the protagonist see or learn?

Who does the protagonist tell that the situation is getting worse? Does that person believe him or her? What does that person do about it?

Who does your protagonist love who is going to die? Spouse? Child? Sibling? Parent?

Or is the loved one who's going to die intentional family? Teammate? Brother- or sister-in-arms? Best friend? Lover?

What's the backstory between the protagonist and the loved one(s)? How long have they known each other? How close are they? What conflicts cause friction between them?

What do the protagonist's and loved one's normal lives look like right up until the story begins? How do their normal lives break down and eventually fall apart over the course of the story?

What conflicts between the protagonist and loved one play out during the story, only to become meaningless or to be solved as the black moment approaches?

Does your protagonist have to choose between the life of one person he/she loves and another person he/she loves? (I'll kill your wife or I'll kill your kid. Choose.)

Does your protagonist have a sworn or sacred oath or duty that he or she must break to save the life of a loved one? Will he/she break that oath or try to break it to save the person he/she loves?

Who tries to talk the protagonist into making the decision to let the loved one die? (The loved one himself/herself? A superior? A friend? Someone else whose loved one will die if the protagonist doesn't let their own loved one die?)

Who tries to talk the protagonist out of making the decision to let the loved one die?

How early in your story does it become clear that the protagonist is headed toward having to make this impossible decision? Can you at least hint at the possibility of a terrible, looming dilemma fairly early on?

What does the protagonist try to do to stop the unfolding crisis that fails? Make a list of all the options and try to anticipate anything your audience might come up with that are possible ways to solve the crisis short of letting the protagonist's loved one(s) die. How will you rule out every single one of the options on your list that your protagonist doesn't actually try and fail at.

If there's a villain:

- What does the villain do to try to foil the protagonist?
- Which of the villain's tactics succeed and which tactics fail?
- Why is the villain doing this terrible thing?
- Why does the villain believe these extreme means justify the end?
- What's the relationship between the protagonist and villain prior to this story?
- Why is the conflict personal between them?
- What has the protagonist done to the villain in the past and what does the protagonist do during the story that arouses such hatred and rage in the villain?
- Why does the villain choose to make the conflict even more personal by going after the protagonist's loved one(s)?

Who are the (many) innocents in danger from the crisis or from the villain? How many of them are there? Are there enough potential victims to make the protagonist's decision to sacrifice a loved one obvious and necessary?

How will you personalize and make relatable the stories of a whole bunch of people to your audience? Will you choose a few potential victims and tell their stories? If so, who? What are their stories? How did they end up in this mortal danger?

How will the protagonist be offered the choice by the villain or by the crisis itself? Who will put the decision in front of the protagonist?

How will the protagonist relay his or her decision to the villain or to the appropriate authority?

Does the protagonist get a chance to say goodbye to the loved one(s)? If so, what is said? If not, how does the protagonist feel about that? Does he or she say a personal goodbye? If so, what is it?

How does the loved one(s) die? Does the protagonist witness or hear it?

Will you show the loved one's death, or is it merely understood in your story that the loved one dies? (When the asteroid hits or the explosion happens, for example.)

How does the protagonist react when he/she knows the loved one has died?

What does the protagonist still have do to stop the crisis or to kill the villain?

What's the protagonist's mental and emotional state as he/she enters into the final battle or climactic fight to stop the great evil?

How does the protagonist's devastating loss, grief, and/or rage help him or her overcome the great evil or catastrophic crisis and stop it?

How can you make it a very close thing that the protagonist almost doesn't stop the great evil or stop the great crisis? Can you make it an even closer call? Closer still to complete disaster?

What does the protagonist's hero's recognition look like? Cheering crowds? A parade? A meeting with an important official?

Does the protagonist embrace being a hero or reject it? Why?

Does the protagonist go back home to where the loved one would normally be, or does he/she choose not to?

Where does the protagonist ultimately go to escape the cheering crowds and privately grieve? Will you show this in your story? Will you show the protagonist walking off into the sunset and leave where they go to your audience's imagination?

TROPE TRAPS

The protagonist is too perfect to begin the story. (A perfect hero/heroine might not struggle with the decision he or she must make in the black moment.)

The protagonist isn't deeply relatable. Your audience doesn't get invested enough in this person to care much when the character gets to the black moment.

The crisis starts out earth shattering and you give yourself no room to build tension.

The crisis never gets terrible enough to require such a gigantic sacrifice from your protagonist.

You fail to explain why other obvious solutions that don't include sacrificing a loved one weren't tried.

The way the protagonist and company go about handling the crisis isn't technically correct or at least plausible.

The protagonist doesn't have the right training, skills, or knowledge to handle the crisis that he or she is suddenly the point person for dealing with. Someone else should have taken over.

The protagonist magically develops special operations skills, detailed scientific knowledge, or martial arts/fighting skills mid-story with no training, education, or practice.

The protagonist fails to ask for help that's actually available—from friends, coworkers, law enforcement, the military, the academic community.

The loved one(s) of the protagonist walk right into the bad guy's hands and come across as too stupid to live.

The loved one(s) have chances to save themselves and fail to take them...and your audience thinks they deserve to die.

The loved one(s) try to talk the protagonist out of killing them and come across as selfish (particularly if the loved one resorts to guilt tactics).

The crisis is so extreme that it's not plausibly solvable at all or the villain is so much more skilled, powerful, and well-positioned than the protagonist that the good guys have no plausible chance of winning.

[**NOTE**: I realize the remainder of this list may be annoying, but stay with me, here. There is going to be an appropriate tone to strike with a story of this type for whatever audience you're aiming your story at. It's up to you to know your target audience and what that group will consider an acceptable reaction by your protagonist to the events of the story.]

- The protagonist makes the decision to let a loved one die (or to kill the loved one outright) too quickly or too easily to be likable.
- The protagonist hesitates or waffles too long over the decision to let a loved one die and comes across as weak.
- The protagonist isn't sad enough, mad enough, or just emotional enough at the death of the loved one (s).
- The protagonist is too sad, too mad, or too emotional at the death of the loved one(s) to be plausible, relatable, or likable.
- The protagonist sets aside his or her grief/rage too easily or too completely before heading into the final confrontation or into the final push to end the crisis and is unlikable for it.
- The protagonist is too happy at being hailed as a hero at the end.
- The protagonist isn't sad enough over the loss of the loved one(s) at the end.
- The protagonist returns to his or her normal life or goes on with his or her new life too quickly, easily, readily, at

the end of your story.

KILL LOVED ONE TO SAVE OTHERS TROPE IN ACTION

Movies:

- Arrival
- The Box
- Avengers: Infinity War
- Knowing
- The Forgotten
- The Seventh Sign

Books:

- The Spy Who Came In From the Cold by John Le Carré
- The Winner by David Baldacci
- The Maze Runner by James Dashner
- The Mistborn Trilogy by Brandon Sanderson
- The Dark Tower VII by Stephen King
- The Traveler by John Twelve Hawks

19

LOVED ONE IN DANGER

DEFINITION

In this story, the protagonist is engaged in some sort of conflict with a bad guy. Not only does the bad guy come after the protagonist to hurt him or her directly, but being a very smart bad guy, the villain also goes after the people the protagonist loves.

While this love interest is typically the spouse, girlfriend, or boyfriend of your hero, in reality, it could also be a best friend, family member, beloved boss, or neighbor—anyone to whom the protagonist feels deep loyalty and responsibility for their safety.

Once the loved one is put into jeopardy by the bad guy, the protagonist has a limited number of choices:

- He or she can deny knowing the endangered love interest and pretend the love interest is just some random person who means nothing to the protagonist.
- The protagonist can honorably sacrifice his or her own love and happiness to break up with the love interest for his or her safety. (Of course, this gambit usually fails because the bad guy is smart enough to see that the protagonist is still fully in love with the ex-love interest,

and hurting the love interest will still hurt the protagonist.)
- The protagonist can attempt a rescue that may or may not get the love interest killed.
- The protagonist can give the bad guy what he or she wants and lose both the conflict and his or her good reputation.
- The protagonist can choose honor over love and sacrifice the love interest.

These last two are the stuff of legendary heroes, but they are, nonetheless, viable options for your protagonist.

This trope, while not specifically about love, does typically revolve around a protagonist who loves someone or is in love with someone.

The love interest or loved one may or may not be aware that the protagonist has these feelings about him or her, but the bad guy(s) most certainly know...and are happy to exploit the protagonist's feelings.

Since bad guys tend not to be super picky about who they harm en route to harming the bad guy, it stands to reason that the love interest/loved one is going to find himself or herself in mortal danger at some point over the course of being loved by the protagonist.

This core of this trope is the moral dilemma and personally terrible choice of love or duty, love or honor, love or failure. None of these are simple choices, and they're all painful.

ADJACENT TROPES
-- Pitted Against Each Other
-- Family Threatened During Trial
-- Special Operator Avenges Loved One

-- Mess With My Family and Find Out

-- Loved One Controlled by Alien

WHY READERS/VIEWERS LOVE THIS TROPE

-- who doesn't want to be under the protection of a heroic protagonist

-- he or she loves me enough to sacrifice everything—including his or her own happiness—to keep me safe

-- the honor, goodness, and purity of purpose of the protagonist makes him or her incredibly attractive to most of us...and we all love the fantasy of being loved by someone like that

-- we all can imagine how we would feel if someone we loved was put into mortal danger, and we love to imagine we would take heroic action to rescue our loved one

OBLIGATORY SCENES
THE BEGINNING:

The protagonist's love for the love interest of loved one is established. Meanwhile, the loved one or love interest may not realize the protagonist feels that way.

However, the protagonist's long looks when the love interest isn't looking, the tender concern the protagonist shows to a family member, or the warmth and depth of friendship the protagonist shares with a close friend are all clear for anyone else to see, including the bad guy(s).

The story may start with the protagonist and bad guy already in open conflict. Or that conflict may develop soon after the story starts.

The bad guy may make a few attacks aimed directly at the protagonist but fail to land a punch that hurts the protagonist in a significant way.

At that point, the frustrated bad guy decides to take the fight to the protagonist's loved one/love interest. This is when the stakes leap exponentially.

Now the protagonist's personal feelings are involved, an innocent is in danger through no fault of their own other than being kind to the protagonist or loving the protagonist, and the bad guy has crossed a red line in the protagonist's moral code.

This escalation by way of attacking, kidnapping, threatening, intimidating, or in some way putting the love interest/loved one in danger is often the climax of the beginning that launches the rest of the story's action.

THE MIDDLE:

The middle is where the protagonist tries various tactics to protect the love interest/loved one and the bad guy tries various tactics to terrorize, capture, or harm the love interest/loved one in a way most painful to the protagonist.

While the bad guy may show some restraint initially in what he or she is willing to do to the love interest/loved one, as the protagonist continues not to give in, back down, or give the bad guy what he or she wants, the gloves come off and the bad guy escalates the harm he or she does to the love interest/loved one.

As the loved interest/loved one's suffering increases, so does the stress upon the protagonist.

It's in this heightened state of tension that he or she may resort to breaking up with their love interest, telling a loved one never to contact or speak with them again, physically moving away or going away from a loved one, or declaring publicly that he or she has never had any feelings for the love interest/loved one.

The irony is that it doesn't really matter to the bad guy whether or not the protagonist is passionately in love with the love interest or deeply cares about the loved one in jeopardy.

At the end of the day, whoever the bad guy terrorizes or harms is still an innocent person and the protagonist is likely to feel a moral obligation to save that person and to feel guilt that any person is suffering because of him or her.

As the bad guy ratchets up his or her terror campaign, the protagonist reaches the breaking point. It's into this extreme tension that a confrontation erupts between the protagonist and bad guy(s) to end Act Two.

BLACK MOMENT:

Perhaps because of his or her extreme state of emotion, the protagonist loses when he or she confronts the bad guy(s). The protagonist fails to rescue the love interest/loved one or at a minimum fails to stop the terror campaign against the love interest/loved one.

Not only has the protagonist failed to defeat evil, but he or she has let down someone he or she loves. It's the worst possible sort of failure. The protagonist probably cares less about failing at his or her job, duty, mission, or assignment than he or she does about failing to protect the person he loves.

If the protagonist had a good reputation prior to this huge failure, it's ruined now. He or she has truly lost everything and disappointed everyone who matters to him or her.

THE END:

The devastated protagonist gathers himself or herself for one last try at saving the love interest/loved one.

By now, the protagonist probably doesn't have any expectation of surviving the final battle, but the protagonist is ready to sacrifice his or her life at this point. The only thing that matters now is the safety of the love interest/loved one.

The climactic battle takes place. Spurred on by his or her determination to save the love interest/loved one and by his or her total willingness to die in the process, the protagonist finally prevails over the bad guy(s).

This is often staged as a one-man army (the protagonist) taking on all the bad guys and their evil minions, where the protagonist lays waste to everyone and everything that gets in his or her way.

The protagonist rescues the love interest/loved one or stops the evil thing or person threatening the love interest/loved one.

The bad guy is defeated, the person he or she loves is safe, and the protagonist has defeated evil, putting the world order back the way it's supposed to be where good triumphs over evil.

KEY SCENES

-- the protagonist is with the love interest/loved one and his or her feelings of love are very clear to your audience

-- the bad guy spots the love interest/loved one and gets an evil idea to use that person to hurt the protagonist

-- the protagonist first realizes something bad has happened to the love interest/loved one and it's probably the protagonist's fault

--the protagonist demands to know if the bad guy is behind the harm to his or her love interest/loved one, or the bad guy delights in announcing to the protagonist that he or she is behind the harm to the love interest/loved one

-- the love interest/loved one tells the protagonist not to worry about him or her and go get the bad guy(s)

-- the love interest begs for a rescue by the protagonist

-- the protagonist is emotionally broken by his or her guilt that the love interest/loved one is in such jeopardy because of him or her

-- someone gives the protagonist a pep talk and tells him or her to do what he or she knows is right

--the bad guy lords it over the protagonist that the protagonist has failed to protect the person he or she loves

--the protagonist shifts from despair to righteous anger and girds himself or herself for the final battle

--the protagonist apologizes to the love interest/loved one, and the love interest/loved one wants no part of an apology. He or she only wants the bad guy crushed.

THINGS TO THINK ABOUT WHEN WRITING THIS TROPE

Who's your protagonist? What does he or she do? Who are his or her friends, family, coworkers, and love interest?

Does the love interest know how the protagonist feels about him or her? If so, how does the protagonist demonstrate those feelings?

If the love interest doesn't know how the protagonist feels, how does the protagonist hide those feelings from the love interest/loved one...but not hide their feelings from the audience?

How does the love interest/loved one feel about the protagonist? Does the protagonist know or not? How does the love interest/loved one demonstrate his or her feelings to the protagonist? Does the protagonist see the love interest/loved one's feelings?

Who's the bad guy(s)? What's his or her relationship to the protagonist? What's their past history if they have any?

What does the bad guy want? Why and how does harming the protagonist help the bad guy get what he or she wants?

Does the bad guy enjoy harming the love interest/loved one of the protagonist? What does the bad guy do to him or her? Can you make it worse? Can you make it much worse?

Will the bad guy show some restraint at first with the love interest/loved one that devolves into craven harm? If so, what does that look like?

How does the love interest/loved one feel about being used as a pawn to harm the protagonist?

Does the protagonist deny having any feelings for the love interest/loved one?

Does the protagonist break up with the love interest, try to end contact with the loved one, or physically remove himself or herself from proximity to the love interest/loved one? If so, how does that go over with the love interest/loved one? How do they react?

What things does the bad guy do to the love interest/loved one? How do these get worse over the course of the story? Can you make them worse? Much worse?

When does it become really personal for the protagonist? How does he or she escalate the conflict between himself or herself and the bad guy(s)?

Does the bad guy taunt the protagonist? If so, what does that look like? Does he or she use the terrified love interest/loved one to mentally torture the protagonist?

How does the conflict between the protagonist and bad guy(s) blow up and spin completely out of control to end the middle of the story?

What does failure look like to the protagonist? Is he or she accustomed to losing like this? How does losing affect him or her?

Does the love interest/loved one get harmed (or even killed) in the protagonist's failed rescue/attempt to defeat the bad guy/emotional confrontation with the bad guy? How does the protagonist feel about this?

What changes to make the protagonist think he or she can beat the bad guy after having just suffered a crushing defeat?

What changes about the final battle from the end of the Act Two battle that turns the tide in the protagonist's favor this time?

Does the protagonist rescue the love interest/loved one, or does the love interest/loved one rescue himself or herself while the protagonist is occupied battling the bad guy(s)?

What happens to the bad guy(s)? Is everyone who threatened the love interest/loved one dead? Have they all fled never to return? Or is there a distant threat that the bad guy(s) might come back one day to finish off the love interest/loved one?

If the love interest/loved one lives, what does their reunion look like? Does the protagonist apologize or express guilt for the harm that has befallen the love interest/loved one? Does the love interest/loved one accept the apology or brush it off as not necessary?

What lesson has the protagonist learned from this experience?

Do the protagonist and love interest/loved one continue their close relationship at the end of this story or not?

TROPE TRAPS

The protagonist is naïve or thoughtless not to realize that his or her affection could put a love interest/loved one in danger and not to have taken precautions already, and this makes him or her unlikable to your audience.

The protagonist is so clueless he or she doesn't realize he or she is telegraphing his or her true feelings to everyone around him or her, and this makes him or her unlikable to your audience.

The love interest isn't worthy of the protagonist and the audience doesn't want him or her rescued.

The bad guy isn't scary enough to hold your audience's attention or make audience members tense, nervous, or worried.

The bad guy has no motivation to torture anyone but does it simply because he or she enjoys doing it and comes across as lame or dumb.

The bad guy has no coherent plan for how harming the love interest/loved one of the protagonist is going to force the protagonist to do or not do what the bad guy(s) wants and comes across as lame or dumb.

The love interest/loved one doesn't fight back when the protagonist tries to break off a relationship with him or her and seems weak and unworthy of the protagonist.

The love interest/loved one doesn't fight for himself or herself against the bad guy(s) but is helpless and just depends on the protagonist to save him or her, which ticks off your audience.

The protagonist never gets emotional as the stakes rise and doesn't feel like a real or relatable person to your audience.

The protagonist, out of his or her mind with worry, magically never makes a mistake.

You telegraph a happy ending where the protagonist will successfully rescue the love interest/loved one so loudly that your audience never feels any tension or worry over the outcome and is bored by your story.

You chicken out on killing the love interest/loved one when it's really what your story calls for.

There's no fallout between the protagonist and love interest/loved one as a result of this terrifying experience for both of them, and this seems deeply implausible to your audience.

LOVED ONE IN DANGER TROPE IN ACTION
Movies:

- Taken
- Die Hard
- Deadpool
- Inception
- The Dark Knight
- Ransom
- Mission: Impossible III
- Man on Fire
- Spider-Man

Books:

- The Couple Next Door by Shari Lapena
- Along Came A Spider by James Patterson

- Hostage by Robert Crais
- The Husband by Dean Koontz
- The Survivor by Gregg Hurwitz
- The Silence of the Lambs by Thomas Harris
- Sharp Objects by Gillian Flynn

20

LOVED ONE IS A CRIMINAL

DEFINITION

In this trope, the protagonist falls in love with someone or loves a family member, close friend, or coworker and discovers that the beloved person is actually a criminal. This thrusts the protagonist into a moral dilemma of asking himself or herself if he or she can love a criminal, should love a criminal, and loves a criminal in spite of this person being a criminal.

At its core, this is a conflict between the logic of the mind and the feelings of the heart. While there's a tendency to assume that the heart will always win, ideally, you'll keep your audience guessing until the very last minute whether the protagonist is ultimately going to choose to follow head or heart.

This story establishes a loving bond between the protagonist and someone whom we see commit a crime early in the story or whom the protagonist finds out has committed a crime early in the story. Don't be shy—swing for the fences and feel free to make it a big, messy crime, the sort that really tests the protagonist's love and loyalty.

The protagonist has an agonizing choice to make. He or she can stand by the person they love, perhaps help conceal the crime, not turn in the loved one to authorities, and possibly become an accessory of some sort to the crime and subject to criminal penalties as well. Or, the protagonist can do the right thing legally, turn in the love interest/loved one to the law, watch the love interest/loved one suffer the consequences of his or her crime (which are likely to be severe if you're doing your job as a writer), and potentially lose the love of the love interest/loved one because of the protagonist's betrayal.

This trope may lead to a happy ending where the criminal accepts the consequences of his or her actions, the protagonist and love interest/loved one stay close, and the protagonist is forgiven for going to the authorities.

This trope may just as easily lead to an unhappy ending where the protagonist gets in trouble as well, the protagonist and love interest/loved one suffer terrible consequences for their crimes, and any affection between the pair is utterly destroyed.

ADJACENT TROPES
-- Witness/Bystander Sucked Into Danger
-- Family Secret
-- Loved Ones on Opposite Sides of the Law
-- Insider Discovers Conspiracy
-- Loved One Isn't Human

WHY READERS/VIEWERS LOVE THIS TROPE
-- many of us fear betrayal by a loved one and this trope taps into our common anxieties
-- we've all discovered unpleasant truths about a loved one...and at least it's not as bad as this
-- we vicariously learn from how these characters find their way through to love on the other side of a devastating revelation about a loved one or mess it up so badly they lose the love they have
-- we want to believe that the people who love us do so unconditionally

-- we're prompted to ask ourselves what we're overlooking about the people we love

--we would all like to think those who love us would forgive us if we screwed up in a really big way

OBLIGATORY SCENES
THE BEGINNING:

The loving relationship between the protagonist and the love interest/loved one is established. The true depth of this love is important to establish as well if the coming dilemma is going to feel real to your audience.

Also in the beginning, we see the love interest/loved one commit a crime. Or we see the protagonist learn about a crime that has been committed by the love interest/loved one. It's not uncommon to start the story with the crime itself. That way, your audience is already cringing when the protagonist warmly and lovingly greets the love interest/loved one. The risk to opening in this fashion is confusing to your audience as to who your protagonist is.

The protagonist is immediately thrown into a moral crisis. If he or she knows about a crime, he or she has a moral and legal responsibility to let the authorities know. But this is someone the protagonist loves deeply. Can he or she bring himself or herself to turn in someone they love? The protagonist hesitates, caught on the horns of this dilemma and does nothing for now while he or she wrestles with the decision.

The beginning usually ends with the first challenge to the protagonist. A police officer shows up asking questions about the love interest/loved one. News reporting shows a victim of the crime and portrays the devastation of the victim or the victim's family, putting the emotional and guilt screws to the protagonist.

Will the protagonist continue to stand by and do nothing or will the protagonist take action? And if so, what action will he or she take?

Will he or she help the love interest/loved one conceal the crime, or will the protagonist turn in the love interest/loved one?

THE MIDDLE:

Into this quagmire of indecision, the middle launches with new and bigger complications. The terrible consequences to the loved one should he or she be turned in are spelled out for the protagonist. Corruption within the law enforcement agency the protagonist would be turning the love interest/loved one over to become apparent.

The repercussions of the crime itself become more complicated. Someone comes after the love interest/loved one for revenge. Someone wants back something that was taken. Accomplices in the crime put pressure on the love interest/loved one to keep their mouth shut, or they put pressure on the protagonist to keep silent. This pressure can take many forms—pleading, bullying, threats, or violence.

Law enforcement investigates the crime and circles around the love interest/loved one and possibly around the protagonist, putting pressure on both parties to tell what happened. More and more evidence stacks up pointing at the love interest/loved one.

Legal authorities may cajole, coerce, or threaten the protagonist with legal consequences of their own if the protagonist doesn't tell the authorities everything he or she knows.

Meanwhile, the guilt continues to build in the protagonist's gut.

Fear builds in the protagonist that he or she will lose the love of the love interest/loved one if they crack and talk. Likewise, the longer the protagonist stays silent, the more fear builds over what will happen to him or her if he or she talks.

The investigation by authorities, the cover-up by the love interest/loved one, and the pressure upon the protagonist to talk and not to talk grow to a crisis. Act Two often ends with some sort of major confrontation between law enforcement and the love interest/loved one, which the protagonist may or may not get in the middle of.

. . .

BLACK MOMENT:

The love interest/loved one's crime is exposed. The protagonist may be tricked or terrified into doing it, or someone else may finally expose the crime and who did it. The love interest/loved one blames the protagonist for talking, or law enforcement blames the protagonist for not talking.

Either way, the protagonist is hit with the consequences of his or her action or inaction. It's a no-win scenario, and he or she has lost both the love and trust of the love interest/loved one and is paying a price form the authorities for not speaking up sooner.

There are a few variations on this black moment that involve non-legal consequences for the protagonist having not told law enforcement earlier about the crime. Other criminal parties injured by the love interest/loved one's crime may take retribution upon the love interest/loved one or upon the protagonist. It's not unheard of that the love interest/loved one is actually killed in this revenge event.

The non-criminal victim(s) of the love interest/loved one's crime may come looking for retribution. Again, both the love interest/loved one and protagonist may be targeted and harmed. In this scenario also, the love interest/loved one may actually be killed.

In every case, however, the protagonist pays a heavy price for his or her indecision and more importantly, loses the love interest/loved one literally or metaphorically.

The love interest/loved one, instead of sticking around to face arrest may flee and become a fugitive, leaving the protagonist to face the authorities and take some or all of the blame for him or her. This betrayal is devastating to the protagonist, who has still lost the love interest/loved one and is now in huge trouble with the law.

THE END:

The love interest may return to turn himself or herself in, confess to the crime, and clear the protagonist of charges. Or the love interest/loved one may have a climactic confrontation with law enforcement officials and end up arrested or dead. Or the protagonist may talk the love interest/loved one into turning himself or herself in...but it doesn't go well and there's some sort of nearly catastrophic confrontation.

There may be a climactic fight between the love interest/loved one and enemies, other criminal elements, his or her accomplices, or even between the love interest/loved one and the victim(s) of the original crime. Law enforcement may show up to this fight to break it up. The protagonist may have called the authorities in the first place to send them to this fight in a last-ditch attempt to save the love interest/loved one's life.

In all these scenarios, there's a big confrontation, the truth comes out about the crime, the protagonist does something to get back on the right side of the law, which may or may not involve turning in the love interest/loved one, and the love interest/loved one faces the music for his or her crime.

This reckoning may involve getting arrested, confessing to the crime for a reduced punishment, heading off to jail to do the time for the crime, being seriously injured saving someone innocent and earning clemency for his or her original crime, or, of course, dying.

Perhaps the protagonist makes peace with his or her ultimate decision to talk or not to talk. Or perhaps, he or she ends the story bearing a large burden of guilt for what he or she chose.

Maybe the love interest/loved one forgives the protagonist for talking, maybe not.

Maybe the authorities forgive the protagonist for not talking, maybe not.

Whatever outcome you choose, it's up to you to know your specific audience and deliver a satisfying ending to your readers or viewers.

. . .

KEY SCENES

-- the protagonist first confronts the love interest/loved one about the crime

-- the love interest/loved one begs the protagonist not to go to the authorities

-- the protagonist seriously questions his or her indecision

-- the protagonist encounters a victim of the love interest/loved one's crime

-- the authorities threaten, intimidate, or in some way pressure the protagonist

-- the protagonist gets really angry with the love interest/loved one

-- the protagonist is put in danger by the secret he or she is keeping

-- the protagonist can't live with himself or herself and his or her life falls apart in some major way

-- the protagonist has to face whether or not his or her love for the love interest/loved one is unconditional or not

-- the love interest/loved one has to face the protagonist after the protagonist is paying a heavy price for staying silent

--the protagonist accepts responsibility for the harm down, his or her guilt, and the consequences of his or her talking or not talking

THINGS TO THINK ABOUT WHEN WRITING THIS TROPE

Who's the protagonist? Who's the love interest/loved one who commits a crime? What's their relationship like? How will you demonstrate its strength?

What crime is committed? Will you show it to your audience in real time? In flashback? In snippets? From the viewpoint of the love interest/loved one? From the viewpoint of the victim(s)?

Will you show the crime accurately or will you obfuscate what really happened for part of your story? If so, what parts? How? Why?

How does the protagonist find out about the crime the love interest/loved one has committed? What's his or her initial reaction? Does he or she share it with the love interest/loved one or not?

Does the love interest/loved one know the protagonist knows about the crime? If not, why not? When and how does the love interest/loved one find out the protagonist knows?

Who else knows about the crime? Are any of these people likely to tell the authorities about the crime? Why or why not? What's done to silence them?

Does the love interest/loved one try to talk the protagonist out of telling what he or she knows?

What investigation does law enforcement do? What do the authorities know about the crime? What do they suspect about the crime?

Do the authorities have any initial reason to believe the protagonist might know something about the crime?

At what point do the authorities begin to suspect the protagonist might know something about the crime? Why? How?

How do the authorities approach the protagonist to get information? How does that initial conversation go? Does the protagonist lie outright or just not tell the truth?

How do the authorities ratchet up the pressure on the protagonist to talk?

How do the authorities ratchet up the pressure on the love interest/loved one to confess?

Who are the victims of the crime? Are they bad guys? Sympathetic to your audience?

Does the protagonist have reason to feel sympathetic to the victims of the crime? How can you make his or her sympathy bigger? Deeper? Even more intense?

What are others saying about the crime? Do any of these comments put pressure on the protagonist to tell the authorities or to keep his or her silence?

Does the protagonist talk to anyone about his or her dilemma either directly or indirectly? If so, who? Why does the protagonist trust this person so much? Is his or her trust misplaced or not?

When do the protagonist and love interest/loved one first talk specifically about the crime? Who says what? How does this talk go?

If there are more talks, how do they change in tone and increase the tension and pressure on both parties?

Who comes looking for the love interest/loved one for retribution or answers? How does this build into a crisis?

Are there accomplices to the crime? Who are they? What are they doing through the story? What do they say to the protagonist and to the love interest/loved one?

What crisis will the middle of your story build up to? Which people end up confronting one another? How does that go? Is the protagonist willingly or unwillingly involved? What happens to him or her?

How does the whole thing fall down around the protagonist's head? How does he or she lose the love interest/loved one? Is it a literal or metaphorical death?

Does the love interest/loved one break off the relationship heading into the black moment or does the protagonist?

At what point do the authorities figure out the protagonist knows about the crime and demand answers and threaten to or press charges against the protagonist?

What's the climactic confrontation at the end of your story? Who confronts whom? Who wins and loses? Who lives and dies?

What's the protagonist's role in the final confrontation? Does he or she call the authorities to warn them of the fight? Is the protagonist present at the confrontation? Does the protagonist try to save or protect the love interest/loved one? Does the protagonist participate in the confrontation?

What happens to the love interest/loved one in the end?

What happens to the protagonist by the end of the story?

Do the protagonist and love interest/loved one reconcile by the end of the story or not? Why? How?

What lesson has each of them learned through this experience? (It can be a good or bad lesson.)

What is life like for the protagonist when the story ends? How has it changed from the beginning of the story?

TROPE TRAPS

The protagonist comes across as weak, wimpy, and waffling for not making a decision about what to do?

The love interest/loved one doesn't come across to your audience as lovable enough to engender the protagonist's loyalty.

The decision to turn in the love interest/loved one seems right and obvious to your audience and they disapprove of the protagonist's hesitation.

The protagonist comes across as someone who would never turn in the love interest/loved one, and your audience doesn't buy his or her dilemma being real.

The love between the protagonist and love interest/loved one doesn't come across as unconditional enough to turn this scenario into a dilemma for the protagonist.

The protagonist hesitates on what to do for so long the audience gets tired of waiting for him or her to get off the fence and do something.

There's no repercussion outside the law pointed at the love interest/loved one for their crime.

The victim of the crime is unlikable and your audience fully wants your love interest/loved one to get away with it...which makes your audience resent the protagonist for considering turning in the love interest/loved one.

Your audience doesn't buy that there are no accomplices whatsoever, even if that simply means someone else knowing about the crime. Practically nobody can keep a secret entirely to himself or herself.

Law enforcement authorities are too smart or too stupid to be plausible.

Law enforcements bully the protagonist completely unrealistically.

The confrontations between the love interest/loved one and whoever they tangle with seem contrived or crated just to provide action for your story and not real conflicts.

The protagonist gets caught in the middle of events that he or she should logically have nothing to do with and would logically stay away from, and your audience doesn't buy your plot points.

The love interest/loved one doesn't get the consequences he or she deserves or that are logical based on the crime he or she committed.

The loved interest/loved one easily and fully forgives the protagonist for turning him or her in.

The authorities easily and fully forgive the protagonist for not telling them about the crime or not doing it sooner.

Everything goes back to normal at the end of your story and nothing and nobody has changed.

LOVED ONE IS A CRIMINAL TROPE IN ACTION Movies:

- The Godfather
- Goodfellas
- The Departed
- Donnie Brasco
- Mystic River
- Blow
- Eastern Promises

Books:

- Gone Girl by Gillian Flynn
- Before I Go to Sleep by S.J. Watson
- The Suspect by Michael Robotham
- A Simple Plan by Scott Smith
- The Firm by John Grisham
- The Midnight Line by Lee Child
- The Secret History by Donna Tartt

21

MEMORY LOSS/FILLING IN THE BLANKS

DEFINITION

Before we start this trope, please bear with me for a moment while I talk a tiny bit about amnesia. True, permanent memory loss is typically the result of serious physical trauma to the brain. It is not selective, although that's the way it's often portrayed in fiction. If you forget your own name or don't recognize your spouse, you've also forgotten how to talk, how to walk, how to cook, drive, or any other skill beyond infancy.

I wrote a more detailed description of the actual science of amnesia in my Tropoholic's Guide to Internal Romance Tropes, so I won't repeat the whole thing here. Read that or consider doing proper research if you plan to write a true amnesia story.

That said, it is possible for people to repress memories, particularly as a result of emotional or psychological trauma, and that's what this trope relies on.

Someone wakes up covered in blood and it's not theirs, but they have no idea where it came from. Someone is dragged out of the ocean with no idea how they got there. Or, of course, someone is the victim of a dastardly experiment to wipe out their memories but retain all of their other memories of life skills (and usually, killing skills).

This trope can also involve your protagonist realizing that he or she has a missing piece of memory from sometime in the past. A chunk of his or her childhood is gone. He or she can't remember the summer before college when a sibling or parent disappeared. Any piece of a character's life that a person was reasonably old enough at the time to remember is fair game to be lost.

This trope begins with your protagonist waking up or gaining consciousness in some strange place or situation, and he or she has no idea how he or she got here. Or the story begins with some inciting event making the protagonist realize that he or she has no memory of a specific period of time.

The story then, is the protagonist's effort to regain his or her lost memories, find out what happened that caused him or her to forget a period of time, and then to deal with the fallout of whatever he or she discovers about their own past.

This is one of those tropes that can go in as many directions as there are writers in the world. What happened, why it traumatized the protagonist, why he or she blocked the memory, and what the consequences of those events will be now that they've been dredged up again is possible in this trope.

While this trope carries an entire story beautifully on its own, it also can be paired easily with other tropes that deal with what happened in the past, secrets being kept and then revealed, or the consequences of past events causing new problems in the present.

ADJACENT TROPES
-- Haunted by Visions of a Crime
-- Don't Remember Committing a Crime
-- Brainwashed
-- False Memory Planted

-- Troubled Protagonist
-- Solving Night Terrors/Sleepwalking
-- Brain/Identity Erased

WHY READERS/VIEWERS LOVE THIS TROPE

-- losing our memory is a highly relatable fear. With diseases like Alzheimer's on the rise, many of us know how devastating losing one's memory is and how tied our identity is to our memories

-- a possible bad boy/bad girl vibe clings to this character that makes him or her super appealing

-- we'd secretly love to start over with a clean slate, or at least a different slate in life. While this protagonist may have a very bad slate to deal with, it's still new and different

-- how cool would it be if I had hidden skills or talents waiting to be uncovered? Or what if I'm secretly rich or important

-- I can finally see people around me as they really are

-- how cool would it be if I'm at the center of a big, exciting plot and I get to step up and be a hero

OBLIGATORY SCENES
THE BEGINNING:

This story almost without exception beings at the moment the protagonist realizes he or she is missing a memory or missing a block of time. He or she is confused, perhaps frightened, worried about what he or she might have done, and intensely curious about why he or she can't remember. Because most people know that repression of a memory is usually the result of trauma, this character has good reason to be concerned about why he or she can't remember a chunk of time.

Soon after the character becomes aware of the memory loss, strange or inexplicable things start happening. Perhaps he or she starts getting brief visions or snippets of memory that are alarming or make no sense:

- They don't seem connected to his or her life.
- He or she has no memory of ever being in such a place or that place.
- The memories involve someone the protagonist doesn't recognize.
- He or she is behaving in a way he or she never would.
- The snippets don't seem related to one another.
- The snippets are bizarre or wildly confusing.
- He or she can't do the things he or she remembers doing.
- They're disturbing or violent.

In response to these tidbits or visions, the protagonist may not know if they're real and may sincerely wish they would stop. Initially he or she may ignore the images.

But then things start happening to or around him or her. These odd events, strangers talking to the protagonist as if they know him or her, objects discovered in his or her possession he or she has no memory of obtaining, start popping up. Any number of possibilities exist for hinting at the events the protagonist doesn't remember yet.

The protagonist remembers encounters of something or someone that forces him or her to seriously consider investigating the lost time or lost memory(ies). This may constitute the mini-crisis that ends Act One.

Or something happens to scare or endanger the protagonist so badly to end Act One that he or she has no choice but to find out what happened in that block of lost time.

.   .   .

THE MIDDLE:

The protagonist investigates his or her past actions. This may involve talking to family, friends, or people who knew the protagonist in the past block of missing time. It may involve trying to retrace his or her steps through a period of time.

In almost every case, the protagonist initially can't understand why he or she might have gone somewhere atypical, interacted with someone unusual, or in some way deviated radically from his or her usual patterns of behavior.

If the repressed memory is in the distant past, the investigation may be one of interviewing people from his or her past, going back to visit places from that part of his or her life in an effort to trigger more memories, or even therapies like hypnosis to try to recover memories.

Regardless of how the protagonist investigates the missing time, the investigation triggers a response from someone. That response is an additional source of suspense, tension, and danger for your story.

Keep in mind, nobody represses good memories. They suppress terrible, violent, disturbing, or traumatic memories.

As the protagonist gets closer and closer to learning the truth, the people or forces that benefit from the protagonist not remembering anything take direct action to stop him or her from learning anything more. They may try to scare off the protagonist, re-traumatize the protagonist to trigger a new suppression of memories, or to harm or kill the protagonist.

Meanwhile, the protagonist has become so obsessed with learning the truth, so focused on stopping the disturbing snippets of memory from upsetting him or her that he or she is absolutely determined to uncover what happened in that missing time.

As these two forces clash, their conflict explodes into a crisis that ends the middle of your story.

OR

The midpoint reversal of your story, which usually happens halfway through the middle of your story and halfway through Act Two, may be the moment when your protagonist remembers a vital chunk of the missing time. He or she may not recall everything yet, but he or she remembers enough to know that he or she was the victim of or committed a crime or a disturbing/violent act.

And he or she may remember enough that it provokes a big reaction from other people who were involved with the event(s) in the lost piece of time.

The protagonist may abruptly go from hunter of information to hunted. Instead of searching for the past, he or she may suddenly find himself or herself running from it, possibly running for his or her life.

As the hornet's nest the protagonist has unknowingly kicked stirs to agitated life, people from his or her past, or total strangers if he or she has yet to recover the entire block of lost memory, come after him or her. They no doubt want to silence the protagonist and stop any further investigation to the partially remembered past events.

Like the other version of this middle, people who stand to lose everything by the protagonist fully regaining his or her memory may try to scare off the protagonist so he or she will stop poking into the past. They may try to re-traumatize the protagonist to trigger a new suppression of memories, or they may even try to harm or kill the protagonist.

Instead of the protagonist chasing down people from his or her past and provoking a crisis, in this version the people trying to silence the protagonist chase him or her down and provoke a crisis wherein they hope to silence the protagonist and stop his or her recalling of past events for good.

In either version of the middle of this story, it's a common device that your protagonist abruptly remembers skills, talents, or information that prove useful in the investigation but that he or she has no memory of learning or knowing.

The learning of this ability is also buried in that block of missing time. Because of this, the special ability inevitably proves useful to the protagonist when it comes time to deal with the fallout from the missing block of time.

Given how rotten a time this person is having in general while excavating past trauma, it's a nice perk to give a cool hidden ability to this protagonist. It's not required, but audiences do get a kick out of it, and it plays into a fantasy we all have of how cool it would be to suddenly, magically develop some super cool skill or talent. What constitutes super cool will, of course, depend fully on your target audience and should be chosen with your audience in mind.

BLACK MOMENT:

Often, the black moment is the *full* recovery of all the utterly terrible memory(ies) that devastate the protagonist. He or she may realize someone he or she trusts and loves actually betrayed him or her in some horrible way, or may finally realize the full extent of the betrayal. He or she may have been blamed for some terrible event that wasn't really his or her fault.

The protagonist may actually have committed some terrible act of violence or some major crime during the lost piece of time. He or she may not recall why, yet, but he or she still has to grapple with the truth of what he or she did and it devastates him or her.

Knowing the truth may destroy a family relationship for the protagonist. It may force him or her to go to law enforcement and confess to a crime. It may cause the protagonist to leave a job, leave a home, or lose his or her entire friendship/support group.

The protagonist wishes he or she had never decided to fill in the blanks of his or her memory, but it's too late. The truth is out and it has ruined the protagonist's life.

For what it's worth, this moment can happen relatively earlier in the story than most black moments, Particularly in the case where there's significant fallout to unravel after the protagonist regains his or her memory (at least in part), or where there's significant negative reaction to the protagonist regaining his or her memory, Act Three may be significantly longer than usual.

THE END:

This is the reckoning. The protagonist confronts the people who wronged him or her, where the people whom the protagonist wronged confront him or her. The consequences of the truth being uncovered come to full fruition:

- These consequences may involve running from law enforcement and eventually getting caught.
- The protagonist may turn himself or herself into law enforcement.
- The protagonist may tell law enforcement about others who've committed a crime.
- People harmed by the protagonist may come after him or her to confront or harm him or her.
- The protagonist may engage in kangaroo justice and personally go after the people who harmed him or her.
- Someone may try to silence the protagonist once and for all by killing him or her.
- Someone may want something back that the protagonist took and come for it, prepared to do violence to get it.

You get the idea. There are many possible kinds of consequences that will be tailored to whatever events you've created that took place in your protagonist's missing block of time. The key in your story is that these consequences should be dramatic, larger than life, dangerous enough that the protagonist has a real chance of not surviving them, and appropriate to the events the protagonist has finally remembered in full.

In the ending, the protagonist confronts the people who did bad things to him or her. The protagonist also confronts those who've known all along what really happened to the protagonist during the missing block of time and kept it secret. (Which is why this trope is often paired with a Family Secrets trope.)

The protagonist breaks off relationships with family, friends, coworkers, or other associates who knew what happened and didn't tell the protagonist, didn't help him or her learn the truth, or actively interfered with him or her learning the truth.

The protagonist deals with the past events, may make peace with them, or starts down the road to making peace with them, perhaps through therapy, going to a new place and making a fresh start, or something else appropriate to your protagonist.

KEY SCENES

-- the first snippet or flash of memory and the protagonist's reaction to it

-- the protagonist is terrified by something he or she remembers or gets a vision of

-- the protagonist feels as if he or she is losing their mind...and maybe a loved one helps that sensation along.

-- someone random and scary approaches the protagonist and acts as if he or she knows the protagonist (and maybe hints at something bad the protagonist did)

-- the protagonist learns or remembers something frightening enough that he or she considers stopping the investigation, but then something happens to compel him or her to continue

-- someone from the past threatens the protagonist and he or she has no idea why

-- the person(s) who the protagonist will later find out perpetrated bad things against him or her is very loving, friendly, supportive, kind, helpful, nice, or pleasant to the protagonist

--the protagonist is so horrified by or immobilized by the memories flooding back that he or she nearly dies as someone tries to harm him or her or he or she is in danger

THINGS TO THINK ABOUT WHEN WRITING THIS TROPE

Who's the protagonist? What is his or her normal life like? How will you portray that to your audience?

Is this character someone your audience would not expect to be harboring a repressed memory as a result of some horrific trauma? Can you make the contrast more striking or shocking between how normal this person is now and how deeply abnormal the events in the lost time are going to turn out to be?

What happened in the block of time he or she has lost? How recently or long ago did it take place? How old was the protagonist when it happened? How does how long ago it happened affect what the protagonist remembers and how he or she recalls it as his or her memory starts to return?

Does the lost event(s) have layers that the protagonist can uncover gradually? If not, can you build in layers to the event(s)? Are the layers gradually more horrifying and traumatic? Can you make them more so?

What's a shocking twist that, once recalled, puts a whole new spin on what the protagonist has remembered up until that point?

Can you build in multiple shocking twists that will keep your audience guessing at what really happened? That will keep your audience unsure if the protagonist is a good guy or bad guy? That change that other characters are possible villains or add possible villains to the lost events? What are all these twists?

In what order will you unpeel the layers of the event(s) and their various twists to keep your audience off balance and guessing?

Are the lost events enough unlike what your audience would expect of the protagonist that they'll be shocking, thrilling, and unexpected to your audience? If not, how can you make those events shocking, thrilling, and unexpected? How can you make them more shocking, thrilling, and unexpected? Much more?

Who are the other people involved in the lost events? Does the protagonist know some or all of them now in his or her normal life? If so, in what capacity? How well does the protagonist know them? How close is the protagonist to them? How much or little does the protagonist trust them and why?

Are any of the people from those lost events total strangers to the protagonist now? How did that happen?

Are any of the people from those lost events keeping an eye on the protagonist in some way? If so, how? Are they watching or surveilling the protagonist? Do they have an informant in the protagonist's life who reports back to them?

What event triggers the protagonist to realize he or she is missing memory of a block of time? Is this event creative? Exciting? Does it capture your audience's attention and imagination? Can you make it more shocking? More terrifying? More relatable?

How does the protagonist react to this triggering event? Does he or she think they're crazy? Had a terrible dream? Pretend it didn't happen? Try to forget it?

What second thing happens that forces the protagonist to acknowledge that he or she is missing a block of time or memory?

Why does the protagonist decide to investigate what happened? What's his or her motivation? Can you make it more compelling? More impossible for him or her to walk away from?

What does the protagonist fear has happened? Is he or she ultimately right or wrong?

How is what really happened *so much worse* than the protagonist initially feared?

Who does not want the protagonist to remember the lost event(s) and why? Who wants to stop the protagonist bad enough to harm him or her and why?

Why is the protagonist recovering his or her memory dangerous to him or her? To others? How does that danger increase with every new layer of information/memory the protagonist recovers? (Plotting geek that I am, I often build a spread sheet of each piece of memory in the order that they're recovered, who reacts to it, and what that person does. This way I can easily track the danger and tension levels to make sure they're always rising.)

What lengths will the people trying to stop the protagonist from regaining the lost memories go to in order to stop him or her?

Is the protagonist going to be in legal trouble once the full truth comes out? What does he or she do about that? At what point do the authorities get involved and how?

When does the protagonist shift from being the hunter seeking information to the hunted being silenced? Who's hunting the protagonist, how, and why?

What crisis provokes a vital, important, key memory to break loose and come flooding back? Why is this piece of the memory devastating to the protagonist?

What triggers the full memory(ies) to come back? What last, awful bit of the events does the protagonist recall that take it from bad to absolutely terrible?

What's the fallout from the protagonist finally remembering everything? Does someone come after him? Does he or she go after someone? Does law enforcement get involved? Do victims come looking for retribution or to recover some physical object? (The answers to these questions may actually take up a fair chunk of the back end of your story, so I apologize for how deceptively simple these few questions sound.)

What's the emotional and psychological fallout the protagonist has to grapple with after remembering everything? How does he or she go about dealing with or starting to deal with this fallout?

Does this fallout impair him or her in some way? If so, how? How does it interfere with what he or she must do to fix or finish dealing with the past trauma and lost events? If so, how?

What does the final confrontation between the protagonist and your ultimate villain look like?

How does the protagonist prevail in the end? Does he or she have help from someone? If so, who?

When the climactic confrontation is finished, how does the protagonist feel about the people who were involved in the past traumatic event(s)? Does he or she confront those people? Why or why not? If so, how does that go?

How does the protagonist carry on with life at the end of the story? Does he or she forgive the people who traumatized him or her? Enter into therapy? Walk away? Start a new life? Something else?

TROPE TRAPS

The protagonist doesn't come across as normal enough in the beginning for the audience to relate to him or her.

The event that makes the protagonist realize he or she has a repressed memory isn't interesting or shocking enough to grab your audience's attention and hold it.

The repressed memory isn't traumatic enough for your audience to buy that the protagonist suppressed it.

The repressed memory is only one big secret. Once revealed, there's nothing more to surprise the audience.

There are no twists, shocks, or revelations that keep the audience guessing or off balance.

There are no current bad guys associated with the repressed memory and no current day consequences if the memory is revealed. It's just a bad memory and lies there like a sad, stinking, dead fish once revealed.

The person(s) trying to silence the protagonist doesn't have a compelling enough reason to keep him or her quiet and doesn't have a plausible enough reason for becoming violent or dangerous toward the protagonist.

The danger the protagonist finds himself or herself in is too little or too much to be commensurate with the events he or she is recovering.

The bad guy in the memory and in current day isn't bad enough, not scary enough, not smart or devious enough to set your audience on edge.

The protagonist forgives the people who knew about the past events and didn't tell him or her too easily.

The people who knew but didn't tell don't suffer appropriate consequences and your audience is mad about that.

You fail to show the protagonist taking any steps toward making peace with the uncovered events by the end of the story.

MEMORY LOSS/FILLING IN THE BLANKS TROPE IN ACTION

Movies:

- The Bourne Identity
- Total Recall
- Shutter Island
- Before I Go To Sleep
- The Long Kiss Goodnight
- The Machinist
- Mulholland Drive

Books:

- The Girl on the Train by Paula Hawkins
- What Alice Forgot by Liane Moriarty
- The Mase of Bones by Rick Riordan
- Memento Mori by Jonathan Nolan
- The Man Who Forgot His Wife by John O'Farrell
- The Rook by Daniel O'Malley
- Turn of Mind by Alice LaPlante
- The Memory Box by Eva Lesko Nateillo

22

MISSING CHILD/LOVED ONE/FRIEND

DEFINITION

I almost didn't combine the Missing Child trope with the Missing Loved One/Friend trope because of how huge the public reaction to a missing child is in comparison to attention and worry garnered by a missing adult.

The sympathy and public concern garnered by an innocent child in danger are so great and so visceral, especially to parents, that they engender extremely widespread attention and effort to help find the missing child.

However, at their core, they're the same trope. Your protagonist's child, loved one, or close friend is missing, and he or she is panicked and will move heaven and earth to find them and bring them home.

NOTE: For simplicity in this trope, I'm going to refer to the missing person as a "loved one", but this includes a child, spouse, close friend, teammate, coworker, or other person whom the protagonist loves deeply and would do anything to find and rescue.

While the missing child is more likely to get the public heavily involved, the mechanics of the protagonist pushing the authorities relentlessly to find their missing loved one and bring him or her home, or the protagonist engaging in his or her own frantic search for the missing loved one is the same.

This story begins with the loved one disappearing, and the story revolves around the efforts to find him or her. The protagonist may or may not involve the authorities, may do his or her own search for the missing loved one, or a combination of the two may happen in your story.

While the reality is that the authorities would prefer the frantic loved one stay home and stay out of the way while they conduct the search, this usually doesn't make for a very exciting thriller. Hence, your protagonist is likely to become involved in the official investigation, do his or her own investigation in secret or in defiance of the authorities, or not involve law enforcement in the first place.

Ultimately, the missing loved one is found. He or she may or may not be alive, depending on how dark a story you're writing.

This trope is often combined with the Kidnapped trope where the missing loved one's experience of being held captive is interwoven with his or her loved one's (and/or the authorities') efforts to find him or her. In this combination, the story bounces back and forth in simultaneous time showing what's happening to the missing loved one at the same time the investigation in progressing.

If the missing loved one was kidnapped, the kidnapper is almost always caught or killed by the end of the story—again it depends on how dark a story you're telling. You may choose to have the kidnapper disappear, only to strike again in a later story or sequel, or just leave him or her out there, a danger to us all.

If the loved one initially went missing for a reason as simple as a child wandering off into the woods, a family member going silent because a cell phone died, or a friend getting lost in the back country while on a hike, something sinister must happen to the missing loved one next to make this story rise to the level of being a thriller.

A variant on this trope is the loved one intentionally disappears.

He or she is in some sort of danger that compels him or her to flee and not want to be found. The protagonist may or may not be aware of why the missing loved one fled. Even if the protagonist knows why the loved one has chosen to disappear, the protagonist is determined to find the missing loved one anyway.

Typically the protagonist wants to help the missing loved one in some way. The protagonist believes the missing loved one should face the consequences the loved one is running from. Or the protagonist has some special skill or knowledge that will help the protagonist fix the situation he or she is running from. Or the protagonist wants to catch up with the missing loved one and disappear with him or her.

You can probably think up other reasons why the loved one has chosen to disappear and why the protagonist would be determined to find him or her.

ADJACENT TROPES
-- Kidnapped
-- Solving a Kidnapping
-- Client Goes Missing
-- Dangerous Information/Weapon/Person Missing
-- Mess With My Family and Find Out
-- People Are Disappearing

WHY READERS/VIEWERS LOVE THIS TROPE
-- this story taps into one of our greatest fears—losing a loved one—and we fantasize that if it happened to us, we would find a way to bring the loved one home safe and sound

-- we need to believe our loved one would persevere and survive while we would persevere and never give up until we find him or her

-- we would like to believe we would step up and be a hero if one of our loved ones disappeared

-- in a chaotic and terrifying situation, we would find a way to be in control and make a rescue happen

-- we like to believe we would see to it that the bad guys are brought to justice or retribution

OBLIGATORY SCENES
THE BEGINNING:

The loved one disappears. This may not initially be cause for alarm, but very rapidly it becomes a panicked crisis for the protagonist.

When the protagonist goes to the authorities for help, he or she may not initially get the response he or she expects and wants. The protagonist knows the missing loved one well enough to know something is very wrong but may struggle to get anyone official to believe him or her initially.

It's worth noting that a missing (young) child gets a faster response from law enforcement than a missing adult. Children (not including teens) are less likely to run away or disappear for personal reasons than adults.

The missing loved one may leave some message or clue behind that's alarming to the protagonist. The protagonist may realize the missing loved one didn't leave the message, or a clue may hint at foul play. Or the protagonist may realize the information left behind is a lie meant to mislead someone or hide the fact that the loved one has fled.

With or without the involvement of law enforcement, the protagonist starts frantically searching for the missing loved one.

The beginning typically ends with the mini-crisis that indicates foul play is involved, now. A piece of clothing is found, a ransom note or call is received, signs of struggle or blood is discovered. The missing loved one is not only missing but is also in grave danger.

If the loved one disappeared intentionally, the end of Act One crisis often reveals the reason why the loved one fled and just how much danger he or she is in.

THE MIDDLE:

The search for the missing loved one gets going in earnest. The protagonist and the authorities pursue every lead and every clue. There may be a trail of breadcrumbs left by the missing loved one that the protagonist follows.

You may employ false leads, dead ends, and setbacks to keep your audience worried about whether or not the missing loved one will be found.

The protagonist's panic and fear should compromise his or her decision-making and actions to at least some extent. He or she may rely on another loved one, trusted friend, or professional to keep him or her focused or stop foolish decisions.

If the protagonist partners with someone else (official or unofficial) to search for the missing loved one, friction develops as the protagonist wants to press harder, work faster, or take excessive risks, while the partner argues for caution, rest, and a methodical approach.

The middle of this story often culminates in the protagonist (and partner) almost catching up with the missing loved one but barely missing him or her. There may be a direct confrontation with the bad guy or kidnapper who's holding the missing loved one captive.

If the loved one has gone missing of his or her own volition, this crisis is usually a chase, pursuit, or ambush by the protagonist (and partner) to attempt to catch the missing loved one. At the last second, the missing loved one slips away and is in the wind again.

Alternatively, this crisis may involve the bad guy(s) pursuing the loved one and the protagonist simultaneously catching up with the loved one. One interferes with the other catching the loved one, who slips away in the confusion or fight.

. . .

BLACK MOMENT:

The protagonist has failed to find the missing loved one. This time, when the loved one disappeared, there are no clues left to follow, no way to pick up the trail of the missing loved one again.

The protagonist's interference in the investigation or refusal to involve the authorities has ruined the investigation and it's his or her fault the loved one may never be found, now.

Even worse, the protagonist's misguided effort to rescue the loved one may have made his or her situation exponentially worse. The kidnapper is now enraged. The bad guy(s) pursuing the loved one are now determined to kill him or her when they catch up with the loved one.

The protagonist has no way to continue his or her search. The loved one is well and truly lost.

THE END:

Some new piece of information emerges. A new clue is found. Someone reports seeing the loved one. An informant calls in a tip.

The protagonist (and partner) race to follow up on the clue or tip before the missing loved one slips away again. This is the protagonist's last chance to find the loved one and rescue him or her before something terrible happens to the loved one.

The protagonist (and partner) have a climactic confrontation with the kidnapper or bad guy(s) pursuing the missing loved one. This time the loved one doesn't get whisked away or flee.

The protagonist may break off from the fight to rescue the loved one while a partner or law enforcement engages with the bad guy. The protagonist and loved one may join the fight and turn the tide or may kill the big bad guy. Or they may have all the challenge they can handle merely getting out of the fight alive.

When the dust settles and the fight is over, the bad guy(s) are dead, the missing loved one is found, and the danger to the loved one is over. He or she is now able to return home safely with the protagonist.

KEY SCENES

-- the moment of panic when it dawns on the protagonist that the loved one is *missing*

-- the protagonist argues with another loved one who says they're overreacting

-- the authorities lecture or threaten the protagonist to stop his or her independent efforts to find the missing loved one

-- the protagonist is fooled or taken in by a fake clue, fake tip, or fake helper

-- the protagonist rashly does something that sets back the search

-- the bad guy threatens to do something terrible to the missing loved one or sends proof of having done something terrible to the missing loved one

-- the missing loved one leaves behind a clue for the protagonist to find that only he or she understands

-- the moment of reunion between the loved one and the protagonist

THINGS TO THINK ABOUT WHEN WRITING THIS TROPE

Who's the person who goes missing? What's his or her relationship with the protagonist? Can you make this relationship closer? More tightly linked?

How will you show your audience how much the protagonist cares about the missing loved one?

How does the missing person disappear? What happens to him or her? Does it start out innocent and turn ominous or does it start out ominous?

Is the missing person kidnapped or does the missing person intentionally disappear?

If kidnapped, why is the missing person kidnapped? Why him or her specifically? Is it random or is there some reason he or she is targeted?

If the missing person chooses to disappear, why does he or she make this choice? What's the backstory that leads him or her to flee? What danger is he or she in? Can you make that danger worse? Much worse?

Who's the bad guy in your story? Is it a kidnapper or someone out to find and harm the missing person?

What's the bad guy's motivation? What does he or she want? Why? How does he or she plan to get what he or she wants?

Does the protagonist involve law enforcement or not? Why or why not?

If the authorities are involved with the search, how will the protagonist work with them? How will he or she work behind the back of the authorities?

Who is partnered to work with the protagonist if the authorities are involved? What's the relationship between the protagonist and the partner initially? How does that relationship unfold? What do the protagonist and partner have in common? How do they drive each other crazy, not in a good way?

NOTE: You might take a look at the Enemies Allied In Danger trope for information on unlikely or hostile partners being forced to work together.

How does the protagonist (and partner) get very close to catching up with the missing loved one but then not quite reach him or her? What does that event look like? What or who prevents the protagonist (and partner) from reaching the missing person in this crisis?

What new clue, tip, or piece of information revives the dead-ended search for the missing loved one? How does the protagonist find it? Who provides it to the protagonist?

What does the climactic confrontation with the bad guy(s) look like? Can you make it bigger, more dramatic, more dangerous, more violent, more thrilling?

What does the protagonist do during the climactic battle? Does he or she fight the bad guy or break off to go looking for the missing loved one?

Do the protagonist and newly rescued loved one join the climactic fight or do they run away together?

Who captures or kills the bad guy(s)? Does the loved one want to personally capture, harm, or kill the bad guy(s)? Does that happen or not?

How does the way the climactic battle ends mean the loved one is safe, now? How are all the risks to him or her eliminated?

TROPE TRAPS

The missing person does something so stupid (that results in his or her kidnapping) and that he or she should have known better than to do that the audience has no sympathy for him or her.

A missing child acts much smarter or much dumber/more naive than his or her age reasonably suggests and your audience doesn't buy the child as plausible.

If an adult person chooses to disappear, why is the protagonist so freaked out? Which is to say, failing to justify his or her panic.

The protagonist doesn't have a sufficiently compelling reason to go after a missing adult loved one and his or her relentless determination to find the missing loved one isn't plausible.

The bad guy's reason for wanting to hold captive or harm the missing person is lame or nonexistent. Evil for evil's sake is boring to audiences.

The missing person never tries to escape, negotiate with the bad guy, or in any way save himself or herself or make his or her situation better.

NOTE: Read the Kidnapped trope for plausible ways a victim of kidnapping might react to being held captive.

The clues your protagonist (and partner) follow to find the missing person are boring, straightforward, linear, and don't include any red herrings, twists, or surprises.

The way the protagonist (and partner) must miss catching up with the missing person is cliché and annoys the heck out of your audience.

The climactic confrontation isn't big enough.

The bad guy(s) aren't smart enough, dangerous enough, or evil enough to make your audience deeply worried about the survival of the missing person or about the outcome of the climactic confrontation.

The big battle at the end fails to tie up all the loose ends of potential danger to the now-recovered loved one.

MISSING CHILD/LOVED ONE/FRIEND TROPE IN ACTION

Movies:

- Taken
- Flightplan
- Prisoners
- Ransom
- The Vanishing
- Searching
- Frantic

Books:

- The Child Finder by Rene Denfield

- One by One by Ruth Ware
- Long Lost by Harlan Coben
- Then She Was Gone by Lisa Jewell
- The Last Thing He Told Me by Laura Dave
- The Girl With the Dragon Tattoo by Stieg Larsson
- The Couple Next Door by Shari Lapena

23

MISTAKEN IDENTITY

DEFINITION

In this trope, the protagonist is mistaken for someone else, which causes a Problem (capital P). That problem's complications and dangers form the action of your story and are eventually resolved, culminating in the mistaken identity being sorted out. But before that happens, the protagonist may be chased, kidnapped, arrested, the target of an attempted murder, or any other mayhem you choose to cook up.

A case of mistaken identity is often used as the basis of a comic story, so feel free to add a humorous element or humorous moments to this otherwise tense, taut thriller.

A common variant on this trope is to tell the exact same story, but from the point of view of the person who did the mistaken identifying. In this version, it's the protagonist who misidentifies someone else and a Problem ensues. For example, the protagonist-assassin kills the wrong person. Now, he or she's got the family of the wrongly killed person coming for him or her, he or she still has to find the correct person to kill, and his or her employer is furious the paid-for hit hasn't happened and is threatening him or her.

This trope is frequently paired with another trope that explains why a mistake has been made in identifying the misidentified character. Secret twins, doppelgangers, clones, robots—they're all seen alongside this trope.

In and of itself, being mistaken for someone else does not make for an entire story arc. This rises to the level of a thriller trope only when being mistaken for someone else leads to a big problem and a series of dangerous events while the misidentification gets sorted out.

Solving the big problem may suffice to prove that the misidentified person isn't who others think he or she is. Or the misidentified person may have to undertake some task, investigation, or mission of his or her own to prove he or she isn't who others think he or she is...while at the same time doing what's necessary to stay alive.

ADJACENT TROPES

-- Secret Twin/Doppelganger
-- Secret/False Identity
-- Stolen Identity
-- Stealing Your Life
-- Doppelganger Commits Crime
-- Shape-shifter/Skinwalker
-- Cloned

WHY READERS/VIEWERS LOVE THIS TROPE

-- we enjoy the fantasy of becoming invisible, moving through the world with nobody knowing who we are and what we're doing

-- we get to reinvent ourselves

-- we love the idea of stepping into someone else's life that looks more interesting, more comfortable, more cool than our own

-- we get to leave our own boring life and temporarily live a life of excitement and danger

-- all of a sudden, I'm yanked out of my mundane life and thrust into a life where I get to be a hero, be more powerful or important, discover talents I didn't know I had, and save the day

OBLIGATORY SCENES
THE BEGINNING:

This story typically begins with the protagonist going about his or her everyday life. All of a sudden, someone he or she has never met or seen before says or does something shocking to them, says or does something that makes no sense, and clearly seems to recognize him or her. This story is a great candidate for a big, action opening with a stunned protagonist abruptly having to run or fight for his or her life.

The protagonist may or may not figure out immediately that the other person has confused him or her with someone else. The shocked protagonist is probably more interested in staying alive initially than stopping and trying to explain to someone trying to kidnap or kill him or her that they have the wrong person.

Additionally, this person misidentifying the protagonist usually doesn't know the protagonist very well or at all. This person may be working off a photograph to identify the person he or she thinks the protagonist is, or someone else may have pointed out the protagonist to the bad guy.

The misidentifier legitimately believes the protagonist is his or her target. Even if the protagonist swears up and down that he or she isn't who the bad guy thinks he or she is—and may produce a driver's license, passport, or other identification to prove it—the bad guy isn't about to listen. The bad guy believes the protagonist is hiding his or her true identity, anyway.

What began as a simple case of mistaken identity balloons into a dangerous situation for the misidentified protagonist. The beginning ends with a mini-crisis that makes it clear to the protagonist (and your audience) that he or she is in real and serious trouble. This crisis often forces the protagonist to step away completely from his or her regular life, perhaps for the safety of loved ones, and temporarily assume the life of the person for whom he or she has been mistaken. It's only by becoming the person he or she has been mistaken for that the protagonist can unravel this mess and return to his or her own identity.

THE MIDDLE:

Whatever mess the protagonist has landed in just keeps getting worse. The protagonist shifts from confused to afraid to determined to figure out what's going on, to solve the problem, and to get back to his or her regular life.

The protagonist learns about the life of the person he or she has been mistaken for and steps more and more into that person's identity. The protagonist may even move into the other person's house, wear his or her clothes, attend meetings as the other person, and most importantly, enter into direct conflict with whoever misidentified him or her.

Whatever danger or excitement the protagonist's look-alike was in before the mix-up, the protagonist lands squarely in the middle of it. Whatever special skills, knowledge, and expertise the look-alike might have are not skills the protagonist probably has. He or she has to improvise, learn on the fly, and scramble to survive the lookalike's world, which becomes a primary source of tension for your audience. Will this poor person find a way to stay alive long enough to convince anyone that he or she is not who they think he or she is?

It's possible in the middle of the story that the protagonist might briefly encounter the person for whom he or she has been mistaken. If this happens this early in the story, the look-alike takes off, leaving the protagonist to sort out the mess from which the look-alike is fleeing.

It's possible the protagonist commences tracking his or her look-alike, intent on dragging him or her back to deal with his or her own mess. If you do this, it's ideally placed as a midpoint reversal where the hunted protagonist turns into the hunter on the trail of his or her look-alike.

The protagonist may also decide he or she has had enough hiding and fleeing and turns the tables on the bad guy, commencing hunting him or her down with the intent to expose, stop, or harm him or her.

The protagonist may turn for help to people from his or her original life. Or the protagonist may turn to friends and allies of the person for whom he or she has been mistaken. The protagonist may not be able to go to the authorities for help, particularly if the authorities have gotten wind of the bad guy chasing him or her, leading the authorities to believe that the protagonist is a bad guy, also.

At some point, the original friends and family of the protagonist are likely to tell him or her to stop pretending to be this other person and to return to his or her regular life and they ultimately grow impatient with the protagonist. Or they may be afraid of how violent the protagonist's new world is and flee from it when they see how over their own heads they are in that world.

The first bad guy to mistake the protagonist's identity may lead to a bigger bad guy and a bigger bad guy, still, during the middle of the story.

Regardless of who is chasing whom, by the end of the middle, events have come to a head and a crisis erupts. The bad guy catches up with the protagonist or vice versa, and they're prepared to have it out.

What may precipitate the big crisis is the protagonist finally confronting the bad guy and declaring once and for that he or she is not the person the bad guy thinks he or she is. The bad guy, who still doesn't believe the protagonist, attacks.

BLACK MOMENT:

The protagonist barely gets away alive from the confrontation with the bad guy. He or she can't do this anymore. He or she doesn't have the skills, knowledge, or expertise it takes to stay alive in this other person's world. The protagonist is in over his or her head and is going to die if this mess doesn't get sorted out and fast.

Small problem: nobody believes the protagonist when he or she swears not to be the person for whom he or she has been mistaken.

Worse, the friends and family from the protagonist's previous (real) life have abandoned him or her. The protagonist has lost his or her real life, and now he or she has messed up his or her alternate life.

Worst of all, the protagonist's best effort to confront the bad guy went terribly. He or she has no shot at surviving this mess that he or she has gotten into.

THE END:

The protagonist has no choice but to gather himself or herself for one last, herculean effort to end this mess by confronting the ultimate bad guy(s). This may be the big boss or the big gun who's been brought in to deal with the pesky protagonist.

NOTE: The crisis leading into the black moment was provoked by the bad guy(s). The final confrontation to end the story may, in fact, be provoked by the protagonist.

Before the protagonist goes into this fight, he or she may seek an edge. The protagonist may search the look-alike's belongings, may seek advice or information from a friend or ally of his or her own or of the look-alike's. The protagonist may go to some other source for something to give him or her an edge...or at least a chance to win.

In the absence of finding something that will give the protagonist an edge, it's not uncommon that just before the fight, or during the fight when things are going badly for the protagonist, the look-alike shows up to help him or her. It not uncommon that the pair use their striking physical resemblance to trick the bad guy in some way during the final fight. Side by side, the look-alikes fight the bad guy and finally defeat him or her.

With the protagonist and the look-alike in the same place at the same time, it's finally possible to unravel the case of mistaken identity. The look-alike resumes his or her life, safely now that the protagonist and he or she have gotten rid of the bad guy.

The protagonist finally returns to his or her real life. However, he or she is profoundly changed by the experience of living the look-alike's life. The protagonist brings new skills, new confidence, new friends to his or her life and you may choose to show him or her applying these things to it.

KEY SCENES

-- the protagonist gets a look at an image of the person whom he or she has been mistaken for and realizes there really is a major resemblance

-- the protagonist pretends to be the look-alike for the first time

-- the protagonist returns to his or her real life temporarily but is forced to leave it either because of the risk to loved ones or because of some development in the look-alike's life that he or she must deal with

-- the protagonist's family and friends tell him or her to stop this madness and stop pretending to be the look-alike

-- the protagonist tries to tell the bad guy(s) they've got the wrong person and it goes very badly

-- the protagonist realizes he or she is in way over his or her head and is probably going to die. For the first time, the protagonist yearns for his or her boring, dull, safe life back

-- the protagonist and look like meet face-to-face

-- the protagonist uses his or her new skills and new confidence for the first time in his or her old life and it's clear things are going to be different going forward

THINGS TO THINK ABOUT WHEN WRITING THIS TROPE

Who's the protagonist? Who's the look-alike? What are each of their lives like and how are they as unlike as possible? Can you make their lives more unlike? Even more?

What's the event in which the protagonist is first misidentified? Is it scary to the protagonist? Dangerous? Exciting?

Who misidentifies the protagonist? How does this person get it wrong? Why is the bad guy convinced he or she has identified the right person?

What does the bad guy do to the protagonist once he or she has made the misidentification? Does the bad guy try to kidnap the protagonist? Kill him or her? Take something from him or her? Demand information? Something else? How can you make this approach scarier to the protagonist?

When does the protagonist realize that he or she has been mistaken for someone else? Does he or she know the person for whom he or she has been mistaken? If so, how? For how long? How well?

When and how does the protagonist figure out what the bad guy(s) wants? Does the protagonist have it? Does the protagonist need to find the thing the bad guy(s) wants, figure out where the look-alike hid it, and then hand it over to the bad guy(s)? Does the protagonist have to find out some information the bad guy(s) wants that the protagonist needs to protect or get to good guys?

Does one bad guy pursue the protagonist through the whole story, or do progressively bigger, badder, and scarier bad guys come after him or her?

At what point does the protagonist step into the life of the look-alike? How? Why?

What do the real-life friends and family of the protagonist think of him or her assuming the life of this stranger for whom he or she has been mistaken? Do they try to help or sabotage it? How does that go?

Does the protagonist go to the authorities for help? If so, why do the authorities want the protagonist to continue the ruse of being the look-alike? Why does he or she agree to do it?

If the protagonist doesn't go to the authorities for help, why not? Why can't he or she? Is it a compelling enough reason that your audience will buy it?

What skills does the protagonist have to learn to pass for the look like? What things from the look-alike's life does the protagonist have to do? How do these go? Does he or she flub or get it right?

What does the protagonist like about the look-alike's life that he or she has stepped into? What does he or she hate or fear about it?

If progressively bigger bad guys come after the protagonist, who are they? How does each one of them get more menacing, more lethal, and more scary?

At what point does the protagonist realize he or she is completely outmatched by the bag guy(s)? What does he or she do about that?

At what point do the protagonist's old friends and family and/or new friends abandon him or her and refuse to go along with the ruse any longer? Why? How does the protagonist feel about this?

What provokes the bad guy(s) to launch a direct attack against the protagonist? How does the protagonist both survive and lose in that confrontation?

What piece of information, weapon, hint, secret, or something else will the protagonist discover that makes him or her think it's possible to defeat the bad guy(s) and to provoke a final confrontation?

When does the look-alike show up? Before the final fight? During it? After it's almost over? After it?

Do the protagonist and look-alike work together to win the final fight against the bad guy(s)? If so, how? What do they do? Do they use their similar physical appearances to their advantage in some way?

Who survives the fight and who doesn't?

Once the bad guy(s) are defeated, who has to be shown the protagonist and look-alike side-by-side to convince them that the protagonist has been misidentified all along?

Is the look-alike safe now or not? Does he or she leave to go into hiding or some kind of protection?

What does the reunion between the protagonist and his or her family and friends look like?

What lessons learned or new skills and confidence does the

protagonist take back to his or her real life? How are things different and better now in his or her life?

TROPE TRAPS

The way the protagonist mistaken for someone else isn't exciting, interesting, or engaging and doesn't suck in your audience.

The protagonist doesn't look enough like the look-alike for people to mistake him or her for the look-alike upon close examination or for an entire story.

The protagonist should logically just go to the police and ask for protection and help sorting out the mistake but doesn't.

The protagonist doesn't try to prove he or she isn't the look-alike but just goes along with the mistaken identity for no compelling reason.

The look-alike has no compelling reason to flee from his or her life or to hide.

The look-alike comes across as a jerk for abandoning the protagonist with the mess of his or her life to sort out.

The bad guy(s) don't continue to get scarier and more dangerous as the story progresses.

The thing the bad guy(s) want from the protagonist is silly, lame, dumb, or not appropriate to a story of this scale.

The reason the bad guy(s) want something from the protagonist—or want to capture/kill the protagonist—isn't compelling enough to justify how relentlessly they pursue the protagonist.

The protagonist's initial fascination with the look-alike's life seems creepy.

The way the protagonist takes over the look-alike's life is pathetic, selfish, or weird and makes him or her seem unheroic.

The protagonist magically develops the special skills, knowledge, and expertise he or she needs to impersonate the look-alike, survive, and actually fight the bad guys, and your audience doesn't buy it.

The protagonist is too willing to go into dangerous situations he or she is wildly unqualified for and then handles them with skill and expertise he or she absolutely doesn't have.

The protagonist never messes up and makes mistakes or gets in over his or her head.

Failing to explain why and how the bad guy(s) continue to misidentify the protagonist as the look-alike. How dumb *are* these people?

Failing to give the protagonist a compelling reason to confront the bad guy(s)?

Failing to give the protagonist even the ghost of a chance in a fight against the bad guy(s)? Why would the protagonist commit suicide by going into a fight he or she knows for sure he or she is going to die in?

Failing to have the look-alike show up in the story.

Failing to have the look-alike help the protagonist in any way after all the protagonist has done for him or her or gone through for him or her.

Nothing changes from the end of the Act Two crisis where the bad guy(s) defeat the protagonist until the climactic fight to explain why the protagonist magically wins this time.

When the protagonist goes back to his or her real, mundane life, he or she is unchanged and goes back to being average, boring, dull, and mundane.

MISTAKEN IDENTITY TROPE IN ACTION

Movies:

- North by Northwest
- Desperately Seeking Susan
- The Wrong Man
- Knight and Day
- The Man Who Knew Too Much

.   .   .

Books:

- The 39 Steps by John Buchan
- Mistaken Identity by Lisa Scottoline
- The Talented Mr. Ripley by Patricia Highsmith
- The Likeness by Tana French
- The Third Twin by Ken Follett
- The Spy Who Came In From the Cold by John le Carré

24

MUST DESTROY DANGEROUS OBJECT/INFORMATION

DEFINITION

The protagonist in this story is responsible for finding and destroying a dangerous object or information. The object can be anything from a homicidal doll to a nuclear weapon—your imagination is the only limit on what it might be. The challenge is typically to find and get possession of the object or information or simply to find it and destroy it wherever it is and no matter whose possession it is in.

This is as simple a trope as you'll ever find in a thriller, and yet it's one of the most popular and enduring story arcs across all subgenres of thriller fiction. It's very frequently layered with other tropes involving a second save-the-world threat, or with tropes pertaining to the protagonist, his or her past, and the villain and his or her goals.

The protagonist in this story is typically an expert in his or her field with cool skills, special training and expertise, courage, and significant support from the organization he or she works for.

Less typical, but not unheard of, in this trope is the lone wolf operator—or even a civilian—who encounters something deadly or finds dangerous information and realizes it must be destroyed as soon as possible. Rather than wait for support or handing it off to official authorities, for some compelling reason, this protagonist feels a need to go ahead and destroy the object or information now.

Standing in the protagonist's way is a bad guy(s) who wants the object or information, wants to use the object or information to harm others, or who already possesses the object and must create it, hide it, move it, and finally use it. The bad guy(s) may also have a team, allies, or entire organization behind him or her to help them use the dangerous object or information.

In the end, the protagonist and his or her allies find and destroy the dangerous object or information, defeat the bad guy(s), and keep the world safe.

ADJACENT TROPES
-- Accidentally Find Dangerous Object/Information
-- Ticking Time Bomb
-- Stealing Important Object/Information
-- Dangerous Missing Person/Object/Information
-- Sentient Object Does Crime
-- Stop Weapon of Mass Destruction

WHY READERS/VIEWERS LOVE THIS TROPE
-- we fantasize about being as cool, skilled, heroic, and unambiguously good as the protagonist in this story

-- we may fantasize about being friends with the protagonist of this tale, of working with him or her, or even of being romantically involved with him or her

--we wonder if we could become like the protagonist. What would it take for us to become that strong and fit, that smart, that good a fighter and shooter, and do the sorts of things he or she does

-- we would love to be an insider to a cool agency or organization like the protagonist's and know big secrets the public doesn't have any idea of

--we would love to leave behind our boring, mundane life and live on the edge, having adventures, excitement, and seeing exotic locations

OBLIGATORY SCENES
THE BEGINNING:

A dangerous object or information comes to light. The protagonist personally may discover it and its danger, or the organization the protagonist works for may assign him or her to find or obtain a dangerous object or information. Because the opening of this story is more about discovery than exciting action, it's important to establish right away the stakes attached to the dangerous object or information and establish an atmosphere of heavy tension even if there's not instant danger.

You may accomplish this with a mission in-brief in a cool, classified facility shrouded in secrecy, or when the protagonist receives a disguised message, an encrypted email, or the "special" phone rings, for example.

The protagonist commences learning about the object or information and commences looking for it or planning how to obtain it so he or she can destroy it.

A bad guy(s) also commences hunting for the dangerous information or object if this is going to be a race to find the dangerous MacGuffin. Alternatively, the bad guy(s) may start your story in the middle of or perhaps just finishing creating the dangerous object or compiling the dangerous information.

The beginning often ends with the first confrontation between the protagonist and the bad guy(s). It may be as direct as a skirmish, or it may be more subtle—they spot each other, surveil each other, or make some sort of opening move against the other.

THE MIDDLE:

The race is on between the protagonist and his or her allies and the bad guy(s). The good guys need to figure out what the bad guy(s) is planning, find/hide the dangerous object or information, and the bad guy(s) is racing to deploy it before the protagonist and pals stop him or her.

This tends to be a heavy action story, and the middle is stacked with surveillance, chase scenes, infiltrations, ambushes, and other excitement. Because of how linear a story this ends up being, the middle is where you may choose to break up this trope with events relating to any other tropes you may have layered into your story. Instead of introducing an entire other trope and all its obligatory scenes, you may choose to introduce some personal problem the protagonist is wrestling with—a family dispute, a relationship problem, a psychological or emotional problem.

If the protagonist wasn't initially sure exactly what the object or information was, in the middle of the story the protagonist peels that onion, first getting hints at what it might be and eventually finding out fully what it is.

The actual danger of the object of information is always even worse than initially understood or briefed to the protagonist. The stakes go up with every new piece of information the protagonist uncovers.

In this trope, it's especially important to keep in mind that the goodness of your good guy is determined by the badness of your bad guy. The bad guy(s) needs to be smart enough, devious enough, and diabolical enough that your audience is seriously worried the bad guy(s) will succeed in his or her dastardly plot for the dangerous object or information.

You can lean into the protagonist working largely in the dark to begin with, armed with little information and having to figure out what he or she is up against on the fly. Another way to build audience worry is to create a bad guy or bad guy group that is significantly larger, stronger, better armed, and more informed than the protagonist and his or her resources.

This trope tends to move to or through multiple (exotic and exciting) geographic locations as the protagonist and bad guy(s) race to reach the dangerous object or information first or as the protagonist chases the bad guy(s) and the dangerous object or information.

The ever-building conflict between the protagonist and his or her allies and the bad guy(s) finally comes to a head at the end of Act Two when they clash in direct, open conflict.

BLACK MOMENT:

Although the protagonist may almost win, the bad guy(s) manages to get a hold of or keep hold of the dangerous object or information, and the bad guy(s) gets away with it.

The dangerous object or information has slipped through the protagonist's fingers, which is a disaster. Now the bad guy(s) is going to use it to cause disastrous harm. Indeed, the failed attempt to grab the dangerous MacGuffin to end Act Two may have just sped up the bad guy(s) timetable to do the terrible thing...by a lot.

The protagonist loses track of the bad guy(s) and/or dangerous object or information after this defeat. Now he or she may not know where, when, or how it's going to be used to harm many people.

The protagonist was so close to success...but now he or she is back to square one. Worse, the protagonist knows the bad guy(s) is almost ready to do something terrible and the protagonist isn't in the correct place or position to stop it. The disaster appears total.

THE END:

The protagonist and allies get a piece of intelligence, some information, a hint, a lead of some kind—something that lets them get back on the trail of the bad guy(s). However, time is running out to stop the terrible thing the bad guy(s) has planned, so it's a frantic race to get there in time.

All the searching, following, and planning of the middle is

repeated but greatly compressed into a frantic race to get to where the bad guy(s) and the dangerous object or information are and stop them from harming a bunch of people.

At the last minute before disaster, the protagonist finds the bad guy(s), who is on the verge of executing their dastardly plan using the dangerous object or information or may have already started the attack.

There's typically a big fight between the protagonist and his or her allies and the bad guy(s). Often the bad guy(s) launches hie or her plan in the midst of the fight and the protagonist has to break off from the main fight to stop the plan...in the nick of time, of course.

Some of the bad guy(s) may get away to come back in a later story, madder and badder than before, or they may all be captured or killed in this climactic conflict.

Usually, the protagonist and his or her allies don't get away from the final fight completely unscathed. One or more of the good guys are injured or killed, but their deaths are heroic sacrifices that contribute significantly to the overall victory and help save all the innocents who would've been harmed.

The protagonist secures the dangerous object or information and returns home to mourn the dead and to be hailed as a hero. The recognition and reward may be very public or very private. Afterward, the protagonist looks forward to resting and recuperating...or moves on to the next mission to save the world.

KEY SCENES

-- the protagonist gets pushback from a loved one about having to be the one to do this mission. Why can't the organization get someone else

-- the protagonist deals with something handicapping him or her in tracking down the dangerous MacGuffin—a rookie teammate, an injury, a terrible boss. This scene may recur at various key moments where the thing or person hampers the protagonist

-- the protagonist's first encounter with the bad guy(s) and the protagonist realizes how outgunned or outmanned he or she is

-- the protagonist learns something about this mission his or her superiors didn't tell him or her about that reveals it's much more dangerous than the bosses revealed (and the bosses usually knew it)

-- the protagonist takes out a lower-level bad guy, but now a higher level and more skilled bad guy is going to come for him or her

-- the protagonist realizes he or she may have to die to stop the bad guy(s) this time

-- the protagonist and his or her allies have a chance to stop the dangerous object or information but fail

-- someone betrays the protagonist. This may be a personal or a professional betrayal, or both

-- the protagonist's personal problem almost causes him or her to blow it in the climactic confrontation

THINGS TO THINK ABOUT WHEN WRITING THIS TROPE

What's the dangerous object or information, who are the bad guys who plan to use it, and what do they plan to do with it?

Who's the protagonist? What agency or organization does he or she work for? If he or she doesn't work for anyone, what does he or she do with his or her life?

Why is this particular protagonist the person called upon to deal with the dangerous object or information? Why not someone else? What are this protagonist's special skills that make him or her the right person for the job?

How does the protagonist find out about the dangerous object or information? Is he or she told about the bad guy(s) who plan to use it and what they plan to do with it, or is that not known in the beginning?

Who are the family members and friends of the protagonist? Are they even necessary to introduce to your audience? If so, what role do they play in your story? Are they part of the crowd of innocents who will be harmed if the protagonist fails? Or are they a source of personal conflict and/or distraction to the protagonist through the story?

What personal problem does the protagonist have that interferes with his or her ability to do this mission? Does he have beef with his or her boss or with a team member, a pressing family problem, an injury, or an emotional or psychological demon he or she is wrestling with, for example?

Will the protagonist work alone or will the protagonist work with a team? If there's a team, who are the members? Can you pare down the number of team members by having each character perform multiple roles in your story?

What's the technical skill each team member brings to the mission? What's the personality type each team member brings to the mission? What problem does each team member cause or pose to the protagonist and to the mission?

What resources do the bad guy or bad guy group bring to the table? In what way(s) do the bad guys outgun and out man the protagonist and team? What advantages do the protagonists have over the bad guys?

Can you make the balance of power more lopsided in favor of the bad guys? Much more?

Are the bad guy(s) creating the dangerous object/compiling dangerous information, or are they searching for it the same way the protagonist is?

What specifically do the bad guys plan to do with the dangerous object or information once it's in their possession and ready to use? Who are they targeting? Where will they use it? When? How do they plan to get the dangerous MacGuffin into place to use?

In what order will you reveal the pieces of the bad guy(s) plan so the stakes rise throughout your story and the tension continues to rise? Which is to say, can you rank order the information about the plan and reveal it from least to most scary?

How does the protagonist's personal problem interfere with the mission? Can you make that interference worse? Much worse? Bad enough to potentially tank the whole mission and /or get the protagonist killed? How does this interference happen? When? Why?

Do the bad guys provoke the conflict at the end of Act Two, or does the protagonist initiate that confrontation? Or is the moment when both the good guys and bad guys simultaneously reach the dangerous object or information and fight over who's going to take possession of it?

How do the bad guys win and get away with the dangerous object or information? What goes wrong for the protagonist and his or her team? Can you make the loss worse? Much worse? Devastating?

Has this failed attempt to get a hold of the dangerous object or information sped up the bad guy(s)' timetable for the attack? If so, how soon is it planned for now? Can you shorten that timeframe so the protagonist has almost no chance to get there in time to stop it and is going to have to do something extraordinary to race to it?

What shocking piece of information can you reveal about just how dangerous the MacGuffin is that makes it absolutely necessary that the protagonist try one more time to stop the bad guy(s), even if he or she and the whole team have to die trying?

What hint, intelligence, or information does the protagonist receives that lets him or her know where to go to find the bad guy(s) and the dangerous object or information?

What does the protagonist change up about the final confrontation in an effort to win this time?

Is the climactic confrontation exciting enough, big enough, action-filled enough, deadly enough to be appropriate to your story? Can you make it bigger? More dangerous?

Does the bad guy's(s') evil plan launch before or during the climactic confrontation, or does the protagonist get there in time to stop it from happening? (The type of event the bad guys are planning will determine whether any or all of the evil plan can start or not. A bomb can't partially explode, for example, but a poison gas cannister can partially release.)

How specifically does the protagonist stop the evil plan?

Who lives and dies in the final fight?

When the mission is over, does the protagonist receive any kind of reward or recognition? If so, from whom? Is it public or private? Official or unofficial? From whom would the protagonist find a heart-felt thanks most meaningful?

What does the protagonist do when the mission and its aftermath are completely over? Is there a plot thread your audience wants to see the ending for (a kiss between the protagonist and another character, a hospital visit with a character who ultimately lived and is going to recover, the protagonist being greeted by a pet)? Or will you forego showing your audience what comes next and just end the story?

TROPE TRAPS

The protagonist is so badass, such a one-person wrecking machine, that the audience never feels any sense of doubt over whether he or she will succeed and crush the bad guy(s).

The protagonist has no personal life and no personality, and never develops either.

The protagonist's superiors withhold vital information during the in-brief that no reasonable person would withhold.

The bad guy(s) make his or her plan ridiculously more complicated than it has to be and your audience finds it stupid or implausible.

The bad guy(s) is bad for the sake of being bad and has no compelling motivation for doing what he or she is planning to do.

The dangerous object or information is wildly cliché and has nothing about it to make it unique, interesting, or surprising to your audience.

The bad guy(s) isn't smart enough, devious enough, or diabolical enough to pose a real threat to the protagonist.

The protagonist's support team is so competent that the protagonist isn't necessary and/or team members steal the show and are much more appealing and likable than the protagonist.

The protagonist's support team is so incompetent and bumbling that the audience hopes they all die and that the protagonist ditches them all.

There are no layers to the dangerous object or information and the plan to use it. There's one reveal and then the protagonist and audience know everything.

The stakes never go up in the story.

The danger never goes up as new information is revealed.

The stakes of failing to stop the evil plan never become personal for the protagonist.

The protagonist and his or her team never suffer any serious losses. They never pay any price for their mistakes and failures.

The protagonist and/or the protagonist's team never make any heroic sacrifices to save teammates or save the targeted innocents.

The climactic battle isn't climactic enough.

The good guys simply brute force their way through the bad guy(s). They never have to outwit, outsmart, or outmaneuver the bad guy(s).

There's never a moment in the final battle where the audience believes the protagonist might fail.

Not setting up a belief in your audience that you might actually kill the protagonist, by failing to create stakes big enough that the protagonist might need to die to save everyone.

Not being willing to kill a character earlier in the story so your audience is nervous that you might kill an important good guy in the final battle.

The good guys don't pay a high price for victory.

The bad guys don't pay a very high price for failure.

Any reward or recognition the protagonist receives after the dust has settled is too public for a person in his or her profession, or it comes from someone the protagonist wouldn't care about receiving thanks from.

Failing to wrap up secondary or minor plot threads your audience nonetheless gets heavily invested in and wants to see how they end.

MUST DESTROY OBJECT/WEAPON/INFORMATION DANGEROUS TROPE IN ACTION

Movies:

- Raiders of the Lost Ark
- National Treasure
- Mission: Impossible 2
- Sneakers
- The Sum of All Fears
- Inception
- The Rock
- Minority Report
- The Peacemaker
- Three Days of the Condor

Books:

- The Hunt for Red October by Tom Clancy
- The Third Coincidence by David Bishop
- Orphan X by Gregg Hurwitz
- Collision Course by Hans Holzer
- Digital Fortress by Dan Brown

- The Moscow Vector by Robert Ludlum
- The Eight by Katherine Neville
- Ice Station by Matthew Reilly
- The Templar Legacy by Steve Berry

25

NEIGHBOR/COWORKER FROM HELL

DEFINITION

For your sake, I hope you've never had a neighbor or coworker from hell. But if you have, this is the trope for you to work out all your trauma, fear, and rage at them.

In this story, the protagonist has a terrible, horrible, no-good neighbor or coworker who openly delights in making everyone around him or her miserable. Or worse, the protagonist has a quiet, pleasant enough seeming neighbor or coworker who's surreptitiously doing horrendous things and burying the evidence out back.

Personally, I find the latter significantly scarier to imagine.

In the openly obnoxious neighbor/coworker version of this trope, the story usually starts with a minor dispute over something trivial but annoying and escalates over the course of the story in a cycle of retaliation until the protagonist and neighbor/coworker are engaging in open warfare.

It usually ends when the neighbor or coworker finally commits a serious crime and the authorities or the boss finally take action to punish or get rid the neighbor/coworker. This version of the trope is often paired with other thriller tropes, while the neighbor or coworker from hell acts more as a distraction than the main attraction in the story.

In the quiet but scary neighbor or coworker version of this trope, the protagonist is typically observant, more so than everyone else living or working with the neighbor/coworker and spots something concerning—a pattern of odd behavior, visitors who come and never seem to leave, late night visits to the closed office, or odd smells coming from that house or cubicle. Use your imagination and have fun with what your protagonist spots.

The protagonist goes to the authorities or boss and usually gets no help or worse, the police/boss do a cursory investigation and find nothing wrong with the neighbor or coworker's behavior. It then falls solely to the protagonist to figure out what the heck the neighbor or coworker is up to. This may grow increasingly dangerous as it becomes clear to the protagonist that the neighbor/coworker is up to something very, very bad.

What that very, very bad behavior is can take the form of anything awful thing you care to imagine. One characteristic it should have, though, is the act of the protagonist knowing about it should put the protagonist's life in grave danger.

If and when the scary neighbor/coworker finds out the protagonist knows about his or her activities, the neighbor/coworker comes for the protagonist to silence him or her for good.

ADJACENT TROPES
-- Conspiracy Theorist Ignored/No One Believes You
-- Voyeur/Being Watched
-- Witness/Bystander Sucked Into Danger
-- Killer's Right In Front Of You
-- Cops Won't Listen
-- Haunted House/Building

. . .

WHY READERS/VIEWERS LOVE THIS TROPE

-- we all can relate to having that one neighbor or coworker we fantasize about catching committing a crime so we can report them and get them hauled away or fired.

-- we'd love to have our own frustrations with neighbors or coworkers seen, validated, sympathized with, and believed

-- we love the catharsis of Schadenfreude (the pleasure of seeing someone face comeuppance), and it's even better if we're the one who makes it happen

-- we'd all like to be bold and brave enough to confront the obnoxious neighbor or coworker who we're secretly a little afraid of

OBLIGATORY SCENES
THE BEGINNING:

We may meet the protagonist going about his or her daily life before noticing or being bothered by a neighbor or coworker. You might choose to do this particularly if you're going to push your protagonist to the edge of irrational violence and need to establish that he or she is usually a perfectly rational, calm, and non-violent person.

The neighbor or coworker does something outside the bounds of normal behavior that catches the protagonist's attention. This is usually a minor irritant. The neighbor shovels their snow onto your sidewalk or the coworker takes your lunch out of the communal refrigerator and eats it.

The more the protagonist observes this person, however, the odder the neighbor or coworker's behavior appears. The protagonist becomes suspicious and watches the neighbor/coworker in earnest, now.

The beginning usually ends in one of two ways: the protagonist either witnesses the protagonist do something mildly criminal or that breaks the rules but doesn't catch video of it so people will believe him or her. Or the protagonist goes to the police or the boss to report the neighbor or coworker's behavior and isn't taken seriously or believed.

When this rises to the level of a mini-crisis to end this act, however, is the neighbor or coworker now become aware of the protagonist's interest in him or her and probably knows the protagonist reported him or her to the police/boss.

THE MIDDLE:

The now angry neighbor or coworker may commence a harassment campaign against the protagonist that ratchets up through the middle of the story. At some point, this protagonist gets angry enough to retaliate, and then this escalates into war. The pair will antagonize each other and commit increasingly mean acts against each other. The protagonist may try to de-escalate the situation, but to no avail.

In the case of the quietly criminal neighbor or coworker, the police might drive by a few times to check on the neighbor, or the boss might come by the workspace a few times, but the neighbor or coworker is always on his or her best behavior, and the protagonist comes off looking delusional. The protagonist is fully on his or her own to collect evidence to prove he or she isn't making it all up.

In this scenario, the middle is occupied by surveillance, following the neighbor or coworker, setting up cameras, traps, or other gadgets. The neighbor or coworker is no dummy and figures out he or she is being watched and takes steps to foil the protagonist's efforts to collect evidence.

Moreover, in a classic midpoint reversal, the neighbor or coworker may commence stalking, hunting, or intimidating the protagonist. This is when things get really dangerous for the protagonist. Now, the protagonist has drawn the attention of a dangerous and possibly deranged criminal and ticked off him or her. From hunter to hunted, the threat to the protagonist skyrockets.

The middle of the story ends with a major, direct confrontation between the protagonist and neighbor/coworker, usually engineered by the protagonist with an eye to getting proof for the police or the boss. But it goes badly. The protagonist gets the worst of the confrontation and doesn't get the evidence he or she needs. When he or she goes to the police or boss to warn them or beg for help, the protagonist *still* isn't believed, and furthermore, the protagonist may be told to seek mental health help and leave the neighbor or coworker alone.

BLACK MOMENT:

The protagonist has failed to get anyone to listen or take him or her seriously. The neighbor or coworker has the upper hand and has successfully tricked the authorities or boss. The protagonist is completely unprotected and the neighbor or coworker can take revenge on him or her any time he or she would like.

Friends, family, and coworkers think the protagonist has lost his or her sanity and abandon him or her and this obsession over a neighbor or coworker.

The protagonist is evicted, loses his or her job, may be fined or even arrested, and may be charged with a crime of his or her own. The protagonist's life is ruined. He or she has no one to blame but himself or herself. The neighbor or coworker helped ruin him or her, but it was his or her own obsession with proving himself or herself correct that really got him or her into trouble.

THE END:

The final confrontation between the protagonist and the neighbor or coworker from hell may be initiated by either one of them. The neighbor or coworker may initiate a confrontation by coming to harm or kill the protagonist. Conversely, the terrified protagonist may snap and decide it's me or him or her. The protagonist goes forth to take out the neighbor or coworker on his or her own and ambushes or attacks outright.

In either case, there's a direct fight where only one of the participants is going to walk away. This fight is to the death (literal or metaphorical) and they both know it. Ultimately, the protagonist wins, and he or she finally has his or her proof that the neighbor or coworker is fully as terrible, criminal, or deranged as the protagonist has been saying all along.

The evidence the protagonist needs to make the police or the boss believe him or her is finally exposed. The neighbor or coworker is arrested, fired, or once and for all removed from the protagonist's life.

The protagonist has proven himself or herself right. Others finally believe him or her. The neighbor or coworker from hell is gone, and life can, at long last, go back to normal.

KEY SCENES

-- while with someone else, the protagonist sees the neighbor or coworker do something

really alarming. When the protagonist asks the person he or she is with if they saw it, the

person with them sees nothing wrong with it

-- the neighbor or coworker catches the protagonist snooping or watching him or her

-- the police tell the protagonist gently or not so gently that he or she is delusional and

needs to stop the snooping or watching

--the protagonist wonders if he or she is delusional or if he/she is losing his/her mind

-- someone gives the protagonist an ultimatum to stop with this obsession and leave the neighbor or coworker alone

-- the neighbor or coworker sets up the protagonist to look like a bad guy, and comes

across in the same encounter looking perfectly innocent

-- the neighbor or coworker does something that really scares the protagonist and makes him or her realize the neighbor/coworker has no boundaries on how badly they'll

behave

-- the neighbor or coworker threatens the protagonist's family, friends, or loved ones

-- the protagonist realizes that what the neighbor or coworker is secretly doing is SO much

worse than he or she first realized

THINGS TO THINK ABOUT WHEN WRITING THIS TROPE

Who's your protagonist? What's his or her normal life or job like?

Who's the neighbor or coworker from hell? What is this person overtly or secretly doing that's illegal or breaks the rules?

How and how often do the protagonist's and neighbor/coworker's paths cross?

What does the neighbor or coworker first do that annoys the protagonist?

What's the second thing the neighbor or coworker does that really captures the protagonist's attention or ire?

Does the protagonist initially brush off what they saw that looks vaguely or definitely criminal, meaning the protagonist thinks, "Surely not," and discounts what he or she witnessed?

What are your protagonist's personality, temperament, morals, values, and beliefs that make him or her upset that the neighbor or coworker is breaking the rules or possibly doing something criminal?

What about your protagonist makes him or her determined to prove the neighbor or coworker is doing something wrong and to bring it to the attention of the proper authorities?

Why doesn't the protagonist just give this whole thing up at some point and decide it's none of his or her business? Why does the protagonist refuse to let go of this bone?

How do family, friends, other neighbors, and other coworkers react to the protagonist's stubborn insistence on pursuing this thing? What do they expect of the protagonist based on what they know of him or her? Agree with it. Disagree with it?

At what point does the protagonist realize he or she may be witnessing crime(s)? How does the protagonist react to that?

At what point does the protagonist go to the police, homeowner's association, a supervisor, or the boss to share what he or she has seen and is worried about? How does that authority figure react to the information?

Does the authority figure check out the protagonist or neighbor? If so, what does the authority figure do? If nothing, why not?

Does the neighbor or coworker spot the authority figure checking out him or her? If so, how does the neighbor/coworker behave and react? If not, what does the authority figure see in this brief snapshot looking at the neighbor/coworker?

What do friends, family, and other coworkers think of the protagonist's suspicions? Do they support the protagonist or think the protagonist is being irrational, unreasonable, and overreacting?

What happens to escalate the tension between the protagonist and the neighbor/coworker?

If you're writing the openly awful neighbor or coworker who does increasingly nasty things to your protagonist, how will you justify the retaliation(s) the protagonist does in a way that doesn't make him or her seem petty, vengeful, and mean? For example, is everything the protagonist does an attempt to catch the neighbor or coworker doing something bad and get proof?

If you're writing the quiet but dangerous neighbor or coworker who's doing something criminal, violent, and/or psychotic, how will the neighbor/coworker's behavior escalate and how will the danger to the protagonist escalate as the protagonist's efforts to figure out what's going on and get proof of it get more risky?

What are the growing layers of harassment behaviors between the protagonist and openly awful neighbor/coworker? You might want to make a list of actions and reactions that get ever more outrageous.

If the neighbor or coworker is secretly engaging in criminal activity, what's the activity? How does it get more violent, more dangerous, more harmful, closer to doing something horrendous, over the course of your story? Why does it escalate? What does that escalation look like?

Who will potentially be harmed if this neighbor or coworker isn't stopped? Can you put more people at risk? Can you make the risk much worse?

What are the stakes if the protagonist doesn't stop the neighbor or coworker from doing what he or she is doing? Can you make these stakes higher? Much higher? Even higher still?

How good is the neighbor/coworker at hiding his or her nefarious activities? How does he or she hide the criminal activity? How do these nefarious activities grow in scale and danger over the course of the story?

How much danger is the protagonist in for becoming aware of the neighbor/coworker's nefarious activities? Who will the neighbor/coworker get in trouble from if he or she is caught?

Does the neighbor/coworker try to buy the protagonist's silence or in some way coerce the protagonist into saying nothing to anyone? Perhaps the neighbor/coworker threatens the protagonist's loved one, for example? How does that attempt go? How does the protagonist respond?

When, how, and why does the protagonist go back to the police or boss to try again to convince the authorities that the neighbor/coworker is up to no good? How does that go?

What happens to the protagonist's state of mental health? Does he or she descend toward irrational behavior? Into violence? Into a state of terror?

Does anybody else see the neighbor or coworker's bad behavior? If so, who? If not, why not?

List out the ways the neighbor or coworker's behavior gets worse and more dangerous over the course of the story.

List out the ways the protagonist's behavior gets more obsessive and more determined to prove he or she is right over the course of the story.

Compare these two lists and think of ways you can make each list grow to bigger extremes and how extreme behaviors on one list provokes even more extreme behaviors on the other list.

How will your protagonist learn each progressively more scary, more shocking, more dangerous piece of information about what the neighbor or coworker is up to? How does he or she react to each new revelation?

Who cracks first, the protagonist or neighbor/coworker and escalates the conflict into violence or criminal acts? Why? How?

At what point does the protagonist engineer some sort of surveillance or trap to catch the neighbor or coworker doing bad things? How does that go? Does the neighbor/coworker spot the trap? If so, how does he or she react? How does he or she lash out at or take revenge upon the protagonist?

What does the protagonist lose by refusing to give up this obsession with proving the neighbor/coworker is awful? Can you make that loss worse? Much worse? How can you ruin the protagonist's entire life? Can you make it still worse?

Who provokes the final confrontation—the protagonist or the neighbor/coworker? Why? How? What happens?

Does anyone else come to join the fight to help one side or the other? Does anyone else witness the big fight? Does law enforcement or the boss get involved at some point in the climactic confrontation? If so, how? Why?

Who wins and how?

Who loses and how?

What is the evidence or proof that finally comes to light that shows the protagonist was right all along and the neighbor or coworker has been doing awful things all along? How does that evidence come to light? Who finds it? How?

Can you make this evidence shocking? More shocking? Much more shocking?

How do the family, friends, loved ones, other neighbors or other coworkers react to the revelation that the protagonist was right all along in his or her accusations?

Does the protagonist forgive these people for not believing him or her or not? Why or why not?

What happens to the neighbor or coworker? How is he or she permanently removed from the protagonist's life? How does the protagonist feel about this?

What does a return to normal life look like for the protagonist? Does he or she go back to exactly the life he or she had before, or have things changed in some way for the protagonist? If so, how have they changed?

What lesson(s) has the protagonist learned from this experience? How will he or she apply any new lessons to his or her life and what does that look like?

TROPE TRAPS

The neighbor or coworker is so likable that the audience roots for him or her throughout this story.

The protagonist is so obsessive about rules without you explaining why that the audience dislikes him or her.

You fail to explain why the protagonist is so stubborn about pursuing proving the neighbor or coworker is up to no good.

The thing the neighbor or coworker is doing is annoying but not deserving of the protagonist's extreme reaction.

The protagonist comes across as a snitch or tattletale and your audience dislikes him or her intensely.

Failing to justify why the neighbor or coworker is doing any of the awful things they're doing, even if that justification is that they just enjoy causing chaos and getting a rise out of people.

The protagonist is such a jerk that the neighbor or coworker appears to have good justification to harass him or her, and the audience thinks there is nothing wrong with the things the neighbor/coworker does to the protagonist.

The thing the neighbor or coworker is doing is so bad the protagonist is wildly in over his or her head trying to investigate it on his or her own.

The protagonist magically develops investigation skills, surveillance skills, and/or technical expertise to operate advanced equipment and to set up hides that he or she has zero reason to know how to do nor spends any time learning in your story.

The behavior(s) the protagonist witnesses and first reports to the police or the boss is concerning enough that any reasonable cop or boss would be alarmed and take the information very seriously.

The police or boss come across as stupid for assuming that, because the neighbor or coworker behaves normally in the police's or boss's quick spot check, they always behave normally and can't possibly be doing anything wrong.

The protagonist comes across as lame, old-fashioned, and totally implausible for not just whipping out his or her cell phone and filming the neighbor or coworker any time he or she does something bad that the protagonist witnesses.

The protagonist becomes unheroic to your audience if and when he or she retaliates against the neighbor/coworker and looks petty, vengeful, and nearly or fully as mean as the neighbor or coworker.

The police or boss come across as implausible for not believing the cell phone video evidence the protagonist can surely provide to them and fails to look into it further.

The story comes across as implausible when no other neighbors or coworkers also notice the weird things the protagonist is seeing, particularly after the protagonist asks them about it.

If the neighbor or coworker was really doing the terrible thing they're doing, they'd be smart enough to hide it better, particularly after they know the protagonist is watching them.

If the neighbor or coworker is psychotic enough, why wouldn't he or she just take out the protagonist and kill him or her or do something to scare the protagonist so badly he or she leaves them alone?

Why, after the protagonist realizes just how scary the neighbor or coworker is and the very real threat this person poses, does the protagonist still continue to doggedly pursue this very dangerous person? Which is to say the audience doesn't buy the protagonist continuing to tangle with someone who could seriously or fatally harm him or her and his or her family, property, or career.

The police or boss wait ridiculously, implausibly long to get involved as the situation escalates and your audience doesn't buy it.

The story has too many comic, silly, ridiculous, or absurd elements, events, or behaviors by the protagonist and the neighbor or coworker from hell for the audience to experience this as a thriller story and to feel tension, suspense, or fear. Instead, they laugh at it. (Which is okay as long as it's marketed as a comedy but isn't great if it's marketed as a thriller and will tick off people who paid to get a thriller story.)

The protagonist learns nothing from the experience and goes back to being exactly the way he or she was before—which may not, in fact, be a particularly appealing character.

NEIGHBOR FROM HELL TROPE IN ACTION
Movies:

- Pacific Heights
- The Hand That Rocks the Cradle
- Disturbia
- Lakeview Terrace
- Swimming With Sharks
- Disclosure

. . .

Books:

- The Family Upstairs by Lisa Jewell
- Behind Closed Doors by B.A Paris
- The Firm by John Grisham
- The Breach by Patrick Lee
- The Neighbor by Lisa Gardner
- The Killer Next Door by Alex Marwood

26

OLD ENEMY RETURNS

DEFINITION

This trope is the classic case of, "I thought I was safe, but..."

The protagonist in this story has an old enemy whom he or she has fled or who, for some reason, left town a while ago and has now come back. The protagonist's life has moved on in the interim, and he or she has established a normal life. But that life's about to be upended as an old enemy comes back to pick up where he or she left off.

The protagonist may have been a bad guy himself or herself in the past, or the protagonist may have been a good guy—someone who investigated, prosecuted, and/or imprisoned bad guys. In either case, the protagonist made an enemy (or perhaps many enemies) in the past.

And now one or more of those enemies is back...and presumably looking for revenge. This old enemy's return upends whatever's going on in the protagonist's current life. Your choice of life the protagonist is living now will set much of the tone of the story. Has he or she moved on to a career where the return of an old enemy would cause comic chaos, or does the protagonist live a life surrounded by people whom he or she loves and for whose safety the protagonist is terrified?

Of course the other tone setter for this book is going to be the old enemy. His or her prior relationship to the protagonist and what the old enemy now wants will drive much of the plot of your story.

This is another one of those tropes where it's important to remember that the goodness of your good guy is determined by the badness of your bad guy. A corollary to that maxim is the smartness of your good guy is determined by the smartness of your bad guy.

At its core, this is a traditional good guy versus bad guy story, good versus evil. An old enemy returns and poses a threat, and the protagonist protects himself or herself and loved ones from that threat.

ADJACENT TROPES
    -- Loved One in Danger
    -- Past Catches Up
    -- Deadly Pact Comes Due
    -- Mess With My Family and Find Out
    -- Victim Seeks Revenge

WHY READERS/VIEWERS LOVE THIS TROPE
    -- it's a relatable fear that the stuff we think we've left behind in our past could come back to haunt us
    -- this story speaks to our desire for revenge, redemption, and closure. We may like to imagine showing up in our old enemies' lives to finally settle an old score
    -- the trope also calls to unresolved (and potentially unresolvable) conflicts that still bother us and to our fear of those conflicts resurfacing
    -- someone stronger got the better of us before and forced us to flee or retreat, but we like to think we can take them on now and would love to get a second shot at them.

. . .

OBLIGATORY SCENES
THE BEGINNING:

This is a story in which you might actually want to take a minute to establish the normal world your protagonist lives in now. You might consider introducing loved ones, friends, and coworkers who are going to end up in danger later in your story and establishing how close the protagonist is to them and maybe how protective he or she feels about them.

Into this idyllic normalcy the old enemy returns, a nasty shock to the protagonist. The old enemy(ies) may directly approach the protagonist to let him or her know he or she is back or may simply open with an attempt to harm or kill the protagonist. More traditionally, the protagonist may glimpse a familiar face that then disappears and not even be sure he or she saw the old enemy.

The choice of how the protagonist finds out about the return of the enemy will depend on the kind of tension you plan to write about and whether it's a slow-roll build of tension or an abrupt explosion of tension and subsequent action.

Likewise, the old enemy may initially "just want to talk" with the protagonist, or the enemy may immediately launch an effort to harm or kill the protagonist.

SIDE NOTE: My personal opinion is that any reasonably smart bad guy whose only goal is to kill the protagonist won't bother to announce himself or herself and indulge in bad guy monologuing. This enemy will just go for the kill.

For the return of the old enemy to sustain an entire story arc, you're probably going to find that the enemy needs to want something more from the protagonist than just his or her life. Whatever that is will be established in Act One so your audience and protagonist understand the stakes going forward.

The old enemy will usually contact the protagonist to ask for or demand information, an object, a favor, or help with some nefarious endeavor. The protagonist, pretty much without exception, will turn the enemy down. This leads to a threat by the enemy against the protagonist, a loved one, or some important aspect of the protagonist's life.

The beginning typically ends with the enemy's first direct action to force the protagonist to do what the enemy wants. A loved one might be injured or kidnapped (if you want to throw in another often-paired trope with this one). The protagonist's home or business might be broken into or burned down. The protagonist is blackmailed (another often-paired trope with this one) and the proof the enemy has against the protagonist of past mistakes is revealed to the protagonist.

THE MIDDLE:

This story usually goes one of two directions in the middle. First, the protagonist may enter into direct conflict with the old enemy. They pick up where they left off in attempting to harm or kill each other. In this scenario, the protagonist leaves behind or evacuates his or her loved ones to clear the field for a fight.

The protagonist and old enemy hunt each other, the danger intense and staying intense through the whole middle of the story. As they each become more and more desperate, the stakes rise, the violence rises, the creativity of efforts to find and kill each other rise, and they may wreak destruction all around them.

Second, the protagonist may give in to the old enemy's coercion at the end of Act One and agree to do something with or for the old enemy. This, then, shifts into an Enemies Allied in Danger story as the pair work together—uncomfortably—to accomplish their goal.

What's different about this trope from the Enemies Allied in Danger trope is these two remain firm enemies all the way through the story. The protagonist probably spends the entire story watching for an opening in which to take out the old enemy and won't hesitate to incapacitate or kill the old enemy if he or she gets a chance.

The old enemy obviously needs the protagonist alive to do something or else the old enemy wouldn't have approached him or her in the first place. But the protagonist generally has no such vested interest in doing the thing the old enemy has coerced him or her into doing.

The only reason the protagonist is willing to go along with the old enemy is typically because of a looming threat to his or her loved ones if he or she does not cooperate. (You can, of course, come up with some other reason why the protagonist feels compelled to cooperate with the old enemy.)

In the first scenario, the middle of the story ends with a direct confrontation between the old enemy and the protagonist in which the protagonist loses. He or she generally launches an attack to ambush or kill the old enemy. In the second scenario, the protagonist typically tries to foil the enemy's plan. If he or he is trying to rob a bank, the protagonist my try to set off an alarm or catch the attention of the police. If he or she is trying to kill someone, the protagonist may try to warn the target. You get the idea.

BLACK MOMENT:

The protagonist's carefully planned and executed best shot at killing the enemy or spoiling the enemy's plans fails. The enemy might have been waiting for such an ambush and is prepared for it. The protagonist may mess up something or make a mistake. Something doesn't go as planned.

In the first scenario, the enemy now has the upper hand in their direct conflict. The protagonist is forced to flee or retreat in defeat the same way he or she did the last time he or she and the old enemy locked horns in the past. History has repeated itself in the worst possible way. Except now, the protagonist has loved ones who were counting on him or her, and he or she has let them down.

In the second scenario, the protagonist has broken the terms of the deal with the enemy, and the enemy may now attack the protagonist's family or turn his or her goons loose to attack the protagonist's loved ones.

The protagonist has not only failed to protect his or her loved ones, but now he or she is going to be the direct cause of harm or death to them.

THE END:

In the first scenario, the protagonist, now in hiding, has to make a decision. Is he or she going to live like this for the rest of his or her life, always looking over a shoulder, always worried that his or her family will be harmed or killed, running forever from this enemy he or she fears? Or is the protagonist going to take a deep breath, get his or her act together, and confront the enemy one last time? Live or die, it ends here and now.

In the second scenario, the protagonist races back to be with loved ones to protect them from the coming attack. The protagonist and his or her loved ones marshal their resources, frantically prepare for the attack, and a climactic fight ensues. Before this fight happens, the protagonist may attempt to evacuate his or her loved ones, but the enemy catches up with them and the climactic fight happens anyway.

With or without loved ones involved, the protagonist once and for all confronts the enemy with the full understanding that only one of them is walking away from this fight alive. This fight almost without exception ends in a direct, physical, hand-to-hand fight between the enemy and protagonist as they fight out their conflict up close and personal.

The enemy appears poised to win when the protagonist gathers himself or herself one last time and finally gets the upper hand. The protagonist subdues or kills the enemy in a profoundly cathartic moment.

Bloodied, bruised, and battered, the protagonist returns to his or her loved ones who are finally and permanently safe. The protagonist's past is laid to rest, and he or she can proceed with his or her normal life without fear this time.

KEY SCENES

-- the protagonist dismisses having glimpsed the old enemy as a hallucination...but a sick feeling remains in his or her gut

-- the protagonist confesses to a loved one who the old enemy is, what unfinished business the protagonist and old enemy have, and why this person may be back in town

-- the old enemy threatens the protagonist's loved ones

-- a loved one begs the protagonist to flee or retreat again, but he or she refuses

-- the enemy does something violent to prove how serious he or she is

-- the protagonist faces down his or her old insecurities, inadequacies, and fear...and doubts he or she can defeat the enemy

-- history repeats itself

-- the protagonist changes something about the repeating sequence of events that empowers him or her to win this time

THINGS TO THINK ABOUT WHEN WRITING THIS TROPE

Who's your protagonist? What's his or her past? How is that past radically different from his or her current life?

What does the protagonist's normal life look like now? Who are his or her loved ones? What else about his or her life is important to the protagonist? Who will the protagonist die now to protect?

Who's the old enemy? What did he or she do in the past when the protagonist knew him or her before? What does the old enemy do now? What has the enemy been doing in the interim since he/she and the protagonist last saw each other?

What's the old enemy's past relationship with the protagonist? Does the protagonist perceive that relationship in the same way or not? If not, how does the protagonist's perception of their shared past and past relationship differ?

How did the old enemy make the protagonist feel in the past?

Did they like each other at some point or were they always enemies?

Did the protagonist flee or retreat from the old enemy or did the old enemy go away? Why? How?

Why is the old enemy back now? What does he or she want from the protagonist?

Why is the protagonist completely uninterested in doing what the old enemy wants? What are the stakes to the protagonist for doing what the enemy wants?

Why is the old enemy determined to make the protagonist do what he or she wants? What are the stakes to the enemy if the protagonist does it? If the protagonist doesn't do it?

How will the enemy force the protagonist to do what he or she wants? Threats (and if so, what threats)? Blackmail (and if so, over what and what does the enemy threaten to expose)? Holding a loved one captive? Something else?

If the protagonist ultimately refuses to help the enemy or the enemy went straight to trying to harm or kill the protagonist, where will they hunt each other? Will they stay in the protagonist's home area or hometown? Move the fight into a rural or unoccupied area? Chase each other cross country?

Why doesn't or can't the protagonist involve law enforcement in dealing with the old enemy?

What do the protagonist's loved ones think of what's happening? Do they try to talk the protagonist into responding or not responding in any particular way? If so, what?

At what point does the protagonist confess the details of his or her old relationship with the enemy to loved ones? What do the loved ones think of that?

Will the enemy and/or the protagonist enlist help in their hunt for the other one or in the endeavor the protagonist has been forced into?

If the enemy is coercing the protagonist into doing something, what are the steps in that plan, and how do they become increasingly risky or dangerous for the protagonist?

How does the protagonist quietly try to sabotage the enemy's plan...or does he or she not dare try (and if not, why not)?

How does the protagonist try to take out the enemy either by overt hunting or by covert means if they're working together?

What old feelings, memories, failures, humiliations, and more are dredged up by the enemy's return and this new round of interaction with the old enemy?

How does history repeat itself in the protagonist and enemy's interactions now? Can you make this more pronounced?

How does the enemy anticipate the protagonist's moves and thwart the protagonist's efforts to sabotage the plan or to take out/kill the enemy?

How does the protagonist feel when he or she fails to stop or kill the enemy in the black moment? Can you make these feelings deeper, more painful, and more devastating?

What threat does the protagonist trigger the enemy to act upon when the protagonist tries to foil the enemy's plan or take out/kill the enemy outright? How much time does the protagonist have to stop this terrible thing from happening?

What idea, lesson learned, revelation, emotion, feeling, or interaction with the loved one causes the protagonist to emerge from his or her dark night of the soul (wallowing in having failed to defeat the enemy again and having provoked impending harm or death for loved ones)?

What does the protagonist change about himself or herself, the situation, or the preparations for a fight that makes the final confrontation with the enemy NOT exactly follow past history? How is the protagonist going to break the repeating cycle of events?

Does the protagonist attempt to remove loved ones from danger before the final fight? Do the loved ones refuse to go and insist on fighting with the protagonist or not?

Where does the final fight with the enemy happen? Is a fight here going to attract the attention of law enforcement eventually or not?

NOTE: If so, the arrival of police acts as a time lock on how long the fight can last. Once someone hears gunshots or sees the carnage, the authorities will be summoned and sirens will wail, forcing an end to the fight.

How does the protagonist feel going into the final fight? (It's okay for these feelings to be complicated and conflicting.)

What thought, image, or feeling in the midst of the fight, when the protagonist is on the verge of losing, motivates the protagonist to the final great effort that subdues, defeats, or kills the enemy?

What does the emotional catharsis for the protagonist look like when it finally hits him or her that the enemy is, once and for all, finished?

What does the protagonist's reunion after the fight with loved ones look like?

How is the protagonist changed by this experience? What has he or she learned?

Will you show the protagonist taking these lessons back into his or her normal life or not?

Will you give your audience a glimpse of the protagonist and loved ones having returned to their normal lives at the end or not? If so, what does that look like? Is it exactly the same as at the beginning of the story, or is it changed in some way?

TROPE TRAPS

The protagonist comes across as weak, wimpy, or cowardly for fleeing, retreating, or hiding from the old enemy.

The protagonist is so average now that your audience doesn't believe he or she has such a badass, criminal, or dangerous past.

The protagonist's shift from average family person to past badass persona is so abrupt the audience doesn't buy it.

The protagonist's loved ones seriously have no clue about his or her past, past actions, past associates, or past skills? How blind or stupid are they?

The old enemy could just as easily or more easily get someone else to do his or her dirty work or could do it himself or herself. It's not plausible that the enemy would go to all this trouble to find the protagonist, coerce him or her into cooperating, and then force the protagonist to do the thing.

The enemy isn't diabolical enough to be as scary as the protagonist is acting about him or her and the protagonist's fear feels fake.

You never explain why the old enemy represents the protagonist's own personal bogeyman, and if you do explain it, the explanation isn't plausible to your audience.

The stakes to the protagonist aren't high enough to force him or her to get into a life-or-death hunt or to do the bad thing the enemy wants him or her to do.

The stakes to the enemy aren't high enough to make him or her so determined to get what he or she wants from the protagonist.

The protagonist and enemy get along too well once they're working together to be plausible.

The protagonist and enemy fight too continuously once they're working together to be plausible.

The enemy trusts the protagonist too much once they're working together, or the protagonist trusts the enemy too much once they're working together to be plausible.

Law enforcement magically doesn't get involved in or catch wind of these two people running around trying to kill each other or running around plotting some crime.

The protagonist's loved ones don't recognize that they're in danger at all and generally act too stupid to live, causing your audience to not care if they're safe or to hope they die.

The danger and tension stay at one steady temperature through your story and don't go up and down...but mostly up.

The protagonist has no emotional landscape and never recalls past humiliation/defeat, never worries about how this will turn out, never doubts himself/herself, never considers fleeing again and feels like a cardboard character to your audience.

The final fight between the protagonist and enemy isn't staged in a way that makes it feel personal. If they stand off a half-mile apart and fire a couple of sniper shots at each other, where's the rage, hate, vengeance, and retribution in that?

The protagonist isn't changed at all by his or her experience, which is wildly unbelievable after finally confronting his or her personal bogeyman.

OLD ENEMY RETURNS TROPE IN ACTION
Movies:

- Cape Fear
- Skyfall
- Die Hard With a Vengeance
- Inception
- Memento
- Gone in 60 Seconds
- A History of Violence

Books:

- The Chain by Adrian McKinty
- Six Years by Harlan Coben
- The Godfather by Mario Puzo
- Layer Cake by J. J. Connolly
- The Gray Man by Mark Greaney

- The Lock Artist by Steve Hamilton
- The Lincoln Lawyer by Michael Connelly
- The Ghostman by Roger Hobbs
- The Drop by Dennis LeHane

27

ONE CRIME/MYSTERY HIDES MUCH LARGER ONE

DEFINITION

In this trope, the story starts with the main character(s) discovering and/or investigating what appears to be a fairly mundane or straightforward crime or mystery. But as the protagonist digs deeper, he or she realizes he or she initially only saw the tip of the iceberg. Something much larger, much more dangerous, and with much higher stakes is hidden behind the original crime or mystery.

What started as a single bad check leads to a cabal of billionaires trying to crash the Internet. When investigating a house robbery, a police officer finds a series of graves in the basement that hold human remains. A car accident turns out to be the murder of a high-level spy whose death sparks a shadow war.

This trope is unique in that it describes the structure of the plot exclusively and doesn't describe the protagonist or the villain of the story at all. Because of that, this trope is almost always paired with other tropes that define the flavor of good and evil represented by the protagonist and villain in your story.

While this is an extremely general story structure, without fail it combines two completely unrelated crimes, mysteries, conspiracies, or evil plots. The first, minor crime or mystery is only notable enough that it sparks an investigation of some kind. The second, larger crime or mystery is high-concept—an over-the-top, save-the-world or destroy-the-world crime or mystery—the bigger the better. It's the contrast between the inciting crime/mystery and the ultimate one that make this trope exciting to audiences.

Another required characteristic of this trope is that the second, much larger crime or mystery is either ongoing or hasn't happened yet. If the second, larger crime is a fait accompli, this story becomes little more than a forensic investigation of who should be charged for the crime or how a mystery really happened.

Yes, it's possible that a criminal doesn't want to be caught for a past crime and tries to derail or kill the protagonist(s)—which forms the backbone of your story. And yes, it's possible this story could be written in such a way as to hold an audience's rapt attention through an entire story. But in general, to rise to the level of a thriller, some serious current or future threat/evil must exist that has to be stopped.

At any rate, a junior cop, an amateur sleuth, or some other low-level investigator is typically the initial person on the scene of the first, minor crime or mystery. Although young or inexperienced, he or she is smart enough to spot some tiny anomaly, some dangling thread that he or she pulls on, something that catches his or her attention enough to cause him or her to dig further.

As the larger crime or mystery starts to be revealed, other experts may be brought in to help or take over the case. The protagonist(s) peels the layers of the plot onion until the larger crime or mystery is uncovered and solved or stopped.

NOTE: For ease in writing up the rest of this trope entry, I'm going to refer to the good guys and bad guys in the plural, with the understanding that this story could easily be told with a single protagonist and/or a single villain working against each other.

ADJACENT TROPES
-- Accidentally Find Dangerous Object/Information

-- Only Cop with Different Theory
-- Suicide's Actually Murder
-- More to Case Than Meets the Eye
-- Seemingly Random Events Connect
-- Small Event Leads to Crisis

WHY READERS/VIEWERS LOVE THIS TROPE

-- using a smaller, relatable starting point allows us to be drawn into the larger crime or mystery that might not be as relatable initially

-- the David and Goliath aspect of a little guy uncovering a very large and very dangerous plot appeals to all of us who perceive ourselves as little guys (which is most people)

-- we enjoy the exponential escalation of tension in this type of story that sucks us in

-- we can all plausibly imagine finding a small mystery or crime ourselves and love the idea of what we do ending up making us the hero who saves the world

-- how cool would it be to see the things the experts miss and show that we're smarter or more clever than they are

OBLIGATORY SCENES
THE BEGINNING:

This trope starts with the discovery or reporting of a minor crime or mystery. It's big enough to force somebody to come have a look, but barely. It's nothing to write home about, nothing that sparks any alarm or consternation. The very average-ness of it is the only thing remarkable about it.

Typically a low-level investigator is sent to check out the crime or mystery. Or, if the investigator is experienced, he or she is extremely casual about it. This is just another day at the office for either of these investigators. The investigator's initial impression of the crime or mystery does nothing to change his or her opinion that this is no big deal.

But then the investigator spots something just slightly out of the ordinary. This can happen during the walk-through of the crime scene or site of the mystery, or it can even happen afterward when reviewing photographs, witness statements, or something in the case file.

This tiny anomaly sparks the investigator's interest, and he or she digs a little deeper, looks a little closer, or returns to the crime/mystery scene. The more he or she investigates, the more anomalies or clues he or she finds.

Before long, this investigator becomes convinced he or she is looking at a larger crime or mystery. He or she may still have no idea what it is or the true extent of it, but he or she knows there's more going on than meets the eye. The low-level investigator takes his or her suspicions or initial findings to his or her superiors. At this point:

- the initial investigator may be ignored, in which case, he or she continues the investigation alone and is your protagonist throughout the story.
- the initial investigator may have the entire case taken out of his or her hands and the protagonist of the story may take over the investigation at this point.
- the low-level investigator may acquire a partner in the investigation who has more experience in general or who has specific expertise in the larger crime or mystery, and this team will be your protagonists through the story.

The beginning often ends with the protagonists making the first big finding that hints at a really big crime or mystery.

OR

The beginning ends with the first big twist that takes the investigation in a whole new direction that has little or nothing to do with the initial crime/mystery and first points at the larger crime.

OR

The investigation sparks some sort of threatening or violent response that is the first proof the protagonists need to know that they're on to something big...and furthermore that it could be very dangerous to continue investigating it.

THE MIDDLE:

The protagonists continue following the evidence, clues, and leads to figure out what the much larger crime or mystery is, what threat it poses, and figure out how to stop it. The more they dig, the more dangerous the investigation becomes.

People and forces who don't want their activities uncovered start fighting back, and this is a common midpoint reversal point. The protagonist(s) go from hunter(s) of information to being hunted.

Now the protagonists must continue investigating while also trying to stay alive. More resources may be called in to help. Government agencies may get involved. But the protagonists are still the lead investigators and still the primary targets of the hornet's nest of bad guys that is now very stirred up.

With each new piece of information the protagonists learn, the larger crime or mystery twists and turns. It's probable the good guys' understanding of what the crime/mystery is, what its goal is, and who's behind it will change course several times in the middle of the story as you keep your audience guessing and off balance.

With every step closer to the truth the good guys take and the more they interfere with the bad guys' plan, the more dangerous the situation becomes. It becomes more and more pressing for the bad guys to stop the investigation before it foils the larger crime, conspiracy, or evil plan.

The protagonists figure out almost all of the larger crime or mystery, and it *has* to be stopped. The stakes are inconceivably bad if they don't. The protagonists take action to stop the bad guys and stop their evil plan. At the same time, the bad guys try to stop or kill the bad guys.

BLACK MOMENT:

The protagonists lose in the confrontation and fail to stop the bad guys and their evil plan. The bad guys get away and are in the wind with the protagonists having lost their trail in the course of losing the big confrontation.

While directly confronting the bad guys, the protagonists learn the last, awful bit of what the bad guys have planned. Not only have the good guys failed to stop the bad thing that's coming, but now the good guys finally understand fully how terrible it's going to be and exactly how high the stakes are.

If there has been any friction between your protagonists or between your protagonists and other agencies or support personnel during the story, now is when that friction erupts into open argument. The good guys are in disarray, pointing fingers at one another without a plan or focus on how to proceed next.

It's a total disaster.

THE END:

Into this chaos and despair, the protagonists get a lead, a clue, a revelation, an idea—something to spark the seeds of a plan to find and catch up with the bad guys and stop them and their evil plan once and for all.

The protagonists gather their resources and forces for one last, frantic effort to stop the looming catastrophe and race to the climactic confrontation with the bad guys.

The final battle happens. It may go badly at first for the good guys, but the protagonists do something heroic to turn the tide and snatch victory from the jaws of defeat.

The larger crime or evil plan is stopped and the good guys win.

The good guys are hailed as heroes. The little guy who spotted the first hint of the larger crime or mystery is a hero and has saved the day. Even if that initial investigator was not part of the major investigation and confrontation that stopped the larger evil plan, he or she is also celebrated as a hero at the end of the story.

KEY SCENES

-- the initial investigator doesn't believe at first that he or she has seen something strange and questions his or her suspicion or intuition

-- the initial investigator's colleague or superior doesn't take him or her seriously at first

-- the initial investigator fights to stay on the investigation as it starts to blow up

-- the initial investigator's family, friends, or coworkers tell him or her he or she is in over their heads and don't think he or she is up to handling this growing investigation

-- the initial investigator doubts his or her ability to handle what this case is turning into

-- the larger crime or mystery is given a human face of the person(s) behind it

-- the protagonists were wrong about what the larger crime or mystery is—it's so much worse than they imagined

THINGS TO THINK ABOUT WHEN WRITING THIS TROPE

What's the minor crime or mystery that's investigated first? How is it found? How and to whom is it reported? How seriously is the report taken? Who responds to the report?

Who's the initial investigator? How experienced is he or she? Is he or she respected by peers? Why was he or she sent to investigate this minor crime or mystery and not someone else?

What does the initial investigator see that makes the crime or mystery seem completely run of the mill?

What's the anomaly, weird thing, piece of evidence, or something "off" that catches the initial investigator's attention? When does he or she notice it? What's his or her first reaction to it?

Does the initial investigator discount the thing he or she noticed at first or does he or she know immediately that something's not right?

What does the initial investigator do next? Does he or she investigate more or go straight to a colleague or boss with what he or she has noticed?

Do others take the initial investigator seriously right away, or does he or she have to get more evidence before being taken seriously?

Does anyone step in to help the initial investigator to take the case from him or her entirely?

Who is or are the ultimate protagonist(s) of your story?

What do the protagonists initially think the larger crime or mystery might be? Can you make them more wrong? Completely off base?

Have you made the initial crime or mystery and the larger crime or mystery completely unrelated and bearing no resemblance to each other, or does the first one logically lead to the second one?

If the larger crime/mystery flows logically from the first one you currently have planned, are you giving up an opportunity to create surprise, excitement, or interest from your audience? Is there a way to add another more mundane crime or mystery to the front end of your story and let the minor crime that's connected to the larger, end-game crime be the first step of the investigation into the larger crime/mystery?

Make a list of new information the protagonists uncover over the course of your story, building in twists, turns, and completely new directions that will keep your protagonists and your audience off balance. How hard can you mislead everyone using plausible logic based on the information available at that moment in your story?

How can you give your protagonists a personal stake in stopping the evil plan? Can you make the stakes more personal? Much more?

What's the bad guys' plan? What are the steps they have to do to plan, prepare, and execute their plan?

At what point do the bad guys become aware of the protagonists' investigation? What tips them off? How do the bad guys react?

How do the bad guys ratchet up their reaction to the good guys the closer the good guys get to the truth and to stopping them and their plan?

Who else helps the good guys—government agencies, experts, allies, friends, or others? How do these people help? How do these people hinder the protagonists or get in their way?

When, why, where, and how do the good guys try to confront or stop the bad guys to end Act Two? Why does the attempt fail? Is anyone on the good guys' side partially or wholly at fault? If so, who, how, and why?

What's the last big reveal of information about the bad guys' evil plan that surprises or shocks your audience and exponentially ups the stakes as the good guys fail to find a way to stop the bad guys? When is the best moment in your story to drop this bombshell?

What new piece of information or inspiration do the good guys get that allows them to make one last attempt to stop the bad guys before the evil plan is executed and a lot of people are harmed?

What does the climactic confrontation look like? Where does it take place? Who all participates in it? Who gets hurt or killed?

How do the good guys pull off winning the fight this time? What changes from the last fight where the good guys lost?

If the initial investigator isn't your main protagonist, how can you pull him or her back into the end of the story to get the recognition he or she deserves for finding the first clue that led to stopping the great evil?

TROPE TRAPS

The initial investigator is a super sleuth who sees something nobody could reasonably be expected to observe and it comes across as hokey.

Nobody, but nobody, will listen to the initial investigator, even though he or she has a valid suspicion or observation, and your audience doesn't buy it...or worse, thinks the authorities are too stupid to live and starts rooting for the bad guys.

The initial investigator is super likable, your audience connects with them, and then you sweep him or her aside to bring in someone else as the protagonist for the remainder of your story, ticking off your audience in the process.

The larger crime or mystery is a logical extension of the smaller crime or mystery. There's no surprise, no suspense, no questions in your audience's mind about where all of this is going after the first few scenes of your story...and your audience turns out to be exactly right.

You rely on inter-agency friction, competition, or territorial disputes as the main source of character conflict as the story progresses.

Failing to put a human face (or personality) on the larger crime or mystery. It's not exciting or engaging to track down computer algorithms, surveillance programs, or inanimate monsters/machines with no personalities, feelings, emotions, motivations, pet peeves, flaws, and other human qualities.

Failing to make the stakes personal for the protagonists in stopping the bad guys and their evil plan.

Revealing the full gist of the larger crime or mystery right away or very early in your story and leaving nothing more to reveal.

Boring your audience with a predictable and linear progression of information revealed about the larger crime or mystery.

The larger crime or mystery has no serious consequences if it's not stopped.

The good guys don't suffer losses serious enough to make your audience worry about whether they'll succeed or not when it's time for the final confrontation.

The bad guys don't suffer consequences appropriate to the evil they planned and tried to execute.

ONE CRIME/MYSTERY HIDES MUCH LARGER ONE TROPE IN ACTION

Movies:

- Chinatown
- A Simple Plan
- The Nice Guys
- Blue Velvet
- Fargo
- L. A. Confidential
- The Usual Suspects
- A Scanner Darkly

Books:

- The Gold Coast by Nelson DeMille
- The Girl on the Train by Paula Hawkins
- The Snowman by Jo Nesbø
- One False Move by Harlan Coben

- The Monkey's Raincoat by Robert Crais
- The Surgeon by Tess Gerritsen
- The Last Child by John Hart

28

PAST CATCHES UP

DEFINITION

In this trope, people or events from the protagonist's past—good, bad, indifferent, or criminal—reappear in his or her life long after the fact to cause problems for him or her. It's the protagonist's own experiences, actions, or mistakes that are the root of the problem that explodes back into his or her life.

In the Old Enemy Returns trope, the person who returns from the protagonist's past is specifically an enemy who returns to make trouble for the protagonist. While this trope may seem almost identical, in fact, the protagonist's emotional journey is wildly different in this version of the past coming back to haunt him or her.

The emotions the protagonist must deal with make all the difference in this trope. In the Old Enemies Return trope, the predominant emotional arc of the protagonist is one of anger, indignation, and perhaps fear. The protagonist blames the old enemy for some or all of the past actions, events, or mistakes that are bringing the enemy to the protagonist's doorstep now.

Furthermore, the protagonist holds the old enemy responsible for some or all of the negative feelings the protagonist has now. The protagonist had already put the past to rest, but then an old enemy shows up to stir the pot and stir up trouble and ugly old feelings.

In the Past Catches Up trope, the protagonist's dominant emotions are guilt, shame, regret, and remorse, with an eventual burst of anger after the protagonist first deals with the other emotions. In this trope, the protagonist feels personally responsible for the experiences, actions, or mistakes that are coming back to bite him or her now. The protagonist may not be responsible for the past traumas *at all*, but that hasn't prevented him or her from feeling responsible in some way.

It's possible the past catching up with the protagonist is having been the victim of a crime, abuse, neglect, or trauma. Some reminder or remnant of that past event surfaces to force the protagonist to deal with the unresolved trauma.

A variation on this scenario is a similar, mirroring trauma to the past one(s) happens in the current day to the protagonist or to someone close to him or her. This new trauma triggers all the old feelings and pain from the original trauma, and now both traumas have to be dealt with.

It's worth noting that it's easier to write this type of story if you put a human face on the past trauma. If you don't, you may actually be writing a Haunted By the Past trope or a Repressed Memories trope. In those, the protagonist has to deal with old, traumatic memories. But in this trope, the past itself, physically, tangibly comes back to interact with the protagonist.

The fact that the protagonist didn't deal with and put to rest the traumatic or terrible events of his or her past a long time ago is the responsibility of the protagonist. Of course, he or she may have had an excellent reason for not dealing with past events in the past. But the fact remains that these events and their aftermath were left hanging in such a way that they can come back to cause problems now...and they do.

.   .   .

ADJACENT TROPES
-- Old Enemy Returns
-- Diary/Old Letter/File Discovered
-- Repressed Memories
-- Haunted By Past Mistake
-- Deadly Pact Comes Due
-- Cold Case
-- Time Loop Terror
-- Ancient Prophecy Comes True

WHY READERS/VIEWERS LOVE THIS TROPE
-- many of us carry around memories of past mistakes and have regrets that influence the present

-- my boring, mundane life would be a lot cooler (to me and to potential romantic interests) if I had a mysterious, exciting, or hidden past

-- many of us wish for a chance to revisit our pasts and redo parts of it or finish unfinished business in a different way

-- the horror of thinking some past trauma or past mistake is gone and forgotten but having it pop back up is entirely relatable to most of us

-- we're different, wiser, stronger people than we were when we made past mistakes or experienced past trauma. We would like to think that, if the same situation occurred today, we would handle it immeasurably better this time around

-- if enough time passes, we're capable of looking back at past trauma, tragedy, pain, and mistakes and finally making peace with them

OBLIGATORY SCENES
THE BEGINNING:

We typically meet the protagonist and see a tiny slice of his or her life in the present. This gives us a picture of the protagonist's current (presumably better-than-before, reasonably stable, relatively happy) life to compare to the mess coming later in the story.

A person, memory, item, or reminder of the protagonist's past shows up and shocks the protagonist to his or her core. Quickly it becomes clear that this person or thing from the protagonist's past is going to have to be dealt with. The person might need something from the protagonist, or the thing might require a response. For example, a secret child may show up asking to move in. An abusive relative may arrive and announce that he or she is moving to this town. And old pal who just got out of jail for the crime they both committed comes to town to ask for help restarting his or her life.

If the arrival, discovery of, or exposure of an object is the inciting incident in your story, it is probably going to lead fairly quickly to a person or people who the protagonist must deal with if he or she is to put the past to rest and get back to his or her normal life.

For example, if an old arrest warrant arrives in the mail that was never resolved, the protagonist is going to have to deal with police, perhaps with an accuser who lied about what happened, or find a witness who can exonerate him or her.

The protagonist is probably overwhelmed by old emotions that come flooding back unexpectedly. He or she is off-balance and frankly, freaked out. It's in this agitated and upset frame of mind that the first confrontation with a person from the protagonist's past happens, and which forms the mini-crisis that marks the end of the beginning.

The person from the past might threaten the protagonist. He or she might push an emotional button and make the protagonist feel like a helpless child again. This person might ask something of the protagonist that he or she *really* doesn't want to do but feels shamed or guilted into doing. The person from the past may lay down an ultimatum, make a threat, or insist the protagonist do something for him or her. While this sounds a lot like the Old Enemy Returning, this person relies on guilt, shame, pain, and emotional vulnerability to manipulate the protagonist into doing something for him or her.

THE MIDDLE:

The confrontation with the protagonist's past (in the form of the person associated with it) and the demands this person makes re-traumatize the protagonist and upset him or her terribly. This event is a call to action the protagonist cannot ignore. He or she must deal with the past and deal with this person from the past now, like it or not.

The middle of this story is taken up with the protagonist taking action to deal with the past. This may involve going back to a hometown, getting in touch with other people from that past, looking for people who've moved away, searching for information or evidence about what happened.

Some or all of these people may not want to be found, and once found, they may not want to talk about past events any more than the protagonist wants to. But there's a compelling reason the protagonist must deal with this problem now.

After the protagonist is in touch with the past and has dredged up all the old memories and old information, he or she must form a plan to do what should have been done long ago. Once the protagonist has a plan, he or she goes ahead with starting to execute it. Often, this shift from information gathering to action marks the midpoint of the story. It also marks the point at which the person(s) from the past starts to push back against the protagonist.

The protagonist isn't doing what was demanded of him or her, and the person from the past isn't having it with this defiance. The person from the past tries to maneuver, manipulate, shame, or guilt the protagonist into getting back to the task he or she was given. This is when the head games against the protagonist get really bad and when the protagonist must wrestle with all of the worst of the old feelings of remorse, regret, shame, and guilt.

Crippled by his or her emotions, the protagonist struggles to confront the issues from his or her past, and the person from the past leans in hard on this show of weakness from the protagonist.

The person from the past may push the protagonist to the breaking point, and a complete melt down or explosion from the protagonist may result, marking the end of Act Two. It's also possible the protagonist finally loses control and lashes out against the person from the past in an explosion of long overdue rage.

BLACK MOMENT:

Either way, this emotional outburst, typically directed at the person from the past, may feel good to the protagonist and the audience, but it fails to resolve the situation. Indeed, the person from the past takes advantage of the protagonist's guilt and regret after losing his or her temper to manipulate the protagonist even more mercilessly.

The protagonist is even more in the grip of his or her past trauma and has failed to break free of it.

NOTE: While I'm mostly discussing the emotional journey of this character, the events of the plot will mirror these emotional beats and illuminate them for your audience.

For example, the protagonist's sexual abuser has moved to town and promptly starts stalking a child here, triggering the heck out of your protagonist. The protagonist spends the middle of the book following the person from the past and watching in horror as the same pattern of grooming and stalking unfolds...but is just subtle enough that law enforcement won't step in. Perhaps adults responsible for the child turn a blind eye the same way adults did to the protagonist's own abuse.

The protagonist spirals more and more into his or her past memories, pain, and trauma as the current events unfold. Eventually, the protagonist physically assaults the person from the past and gets arrested for it.

The person from the past taunts the protagonist—now that the protagonist is in jail, the person from the past can do whatever he or she wants. The protagonist is devastated and has failed the current child the same way he or she failed his or her past child self.

The protagonist is forced to face the darkest, worst, most painful parts of his or her past.

THE END:

The protagonist realizes that he or she is not the past version of himself or herself anymore. No matter how bad the events of the past were or how bad the mistakes he or she made, the protagonist is older, wiser, stronger, more knowledgeable than back then. He or she has loved ones now who support and believe in him or her. The protagonist does have the tools now to deal with what he or she couldn't deal with in the past or to correct past mistakes, now.

Strengthened by this revelation and by the love of family, loved ones, and friends, the protagonist gathers himself or herself to confront the person from the past one last time.

The protagonist finds the final piece of evidence, remembers the last piece of a missing puzzle, convinces a witness to tell the truth, or may choose to confront the person from the past and force him or her to admit what happened (with authorities listening in and swooping to make an arrest the moment the person from the past finally confesses).

Your protagonist may have to do something altogether different from these examples, but the point is, the protagonist directly confronts his or her past and defeats it. Defeating the past can mean dealing out long overdue justice, be it getting someone arrested or killing someone deeply in need of killing. Defeating the past can mean accepting responsibility for a past mistake and paying restitution...or it can mean letting go of responsibility for some past mistake and letting go of the guilt or shame over it.

The final confrontation in this trope can be a violent one, or it can be an emotional one. Either one works as long as it's dramatic, cathartic, and deeply satisfying to your audience.

In the aftermath, the protagonist realizes he or she is no longer afraid, guilty, or ashamed. He or she is free at last. The protagonist is profoundly changed by this experience and returns to his or her normal life, a new person. He or she joyfully reunites with loved ones.

On the subject of forgiveness, your personal beliefs will dictate whether or not you choose to have your protagonist forgive the person from the past for his or her transgressions. There is no wrong answer to this one. It's fine for your protagonist to forgive and move on with his or her life, and it's perfectly fine for your protagonist to decide some things are unforgivable or undeserving of forgiveness and move on with his or her life.

The key to a satisfying outcome for your protagonist is that he or she has dealt with the emotional baggage from the past, made peace with it in whatever way works for him or her, and is no longer letting the past harm him or her or interfere with his or her emotionally stable and healthy, if scarred, future.

KEY SCENES

-- the protagonist doesn't believe his or her first glimpse of the person or thing from his or her past

-- the protagonist confesses to a loved one about the past experience, action, mistake, or trauma. Or, if the protagonist has previously talked about it to some degree, he or she tells the full, terrible story this time

-- someone else who was there for the past events denies them having happened or having happened the way the protagonist remembers them

-- the protagonist learns what the current-day consequences will be if he or she doesn't deal with this piece of the past catching up with him or her

-- current-day events eerily mirror the events that happened in the past

-- the protagonist questions his or her own mental health or sanity and struggles to function

-- the protagonist pushes away loved ones who want to help

-- the protagonist tries to stand up to the person from the past but emotionally crumples

-- the person from the past taunts or terrorizes the protagonist and pushes his or her most vulnerable emotional buttons

-- the protagonist shifts over into outrage or just rage

-- after defeating the person from the past, the protagonist realizes how small that person from the past really is—the monster's teeth are pulled and the monster can no longer harm the protagonist

-- the protagonist's reunion with loved ones in his or her changed, emotionally freed state

THINGS TO THINK ABOUT WHEN WRITING THIS TROPE

What's your protagonist's backstory? You may need to flesh this out in detail for yourself so you understand how and why the past events, actions, traumas, or mistakes happened, why the protagonist made the decisions or reacted the way he or she did, and why the past events weren't fully dealt with at the time they happened.

What is your protagonist's life like now? How is it different from his or her life back then? How is it the same? What lingering aftereffects of the protagonist's past still show up in his or her current life? What do they look like when they do show up?

What thing from the protagonist's past is going to catch up with him or her in your story? How will you attach a person or people to that event to act as the personification of the past in your story?

What does the person from the past want from the protagonist? Does the person want something specific, or is his or her goal simply to terrorize the protagonist?

How does the protagonist feel when the past catches up with him or her? How does the protagonist feel when he or she first sees a person associated with the past? How about when the protagonist first interacts with this person from his or her past?

What are your protagonist's predominant feelings over the course of your story? How do those feelings evolve, change, and become more intense? What events provoke these changes and shifts in emotions?

How do the events in the current day mirror the events that happened in the past? Can you make these events mirror the past more closely?

What plan does the protagonist form to deal with the problem that has emerged as a result of his or her past? What goes wrong with this plan as the protagonist starts to execute it? What complications arise?

What will the consequences be if the protagonist refuses to or fails to deal with the problem from his or her past? Can you make these worse? Much worse? Can these consequences grow into these worse and much worse versions over the course of your story?

Why does the person from the past show up to interact with the protagonist? Why now? What does the person from the past overtly want? What does he or she really want?

When the protagonist starts to go off course and not do what the person from the past wants, how does that person react? What does he or she do? How does he or she try to make the protagonist feel?

How does the person from the past know what the protagonist's emotional buttons are? How does he or she push these buttons? For what purpose? Does the person from the past enjoy pushing the protagonist's buttons?

Who does the protagonist get back in touch with from his or her past? Who refuses to help the protagonist with his or her current problem? Why?

Who lies to the protagonist or to others about the past? Why? To whom? What do they say?

Can you structure the traumatic past events like an onion where you peel away layers of factual information in a way that gradually reveals the full scale or horror of what happened? (I use the word horror because you're writing a thriller and the events need to be dangerous, exciting, suspenseful, or scary.)

How will you peel this onion in your story? What order is most effective in revealing the details of the past?

Have you built in revelations that surprise your audience and throw your audience off balance? Can you build in revelations that take the truth about the past in an unexpected direction or that take a hard turn away from what seems obvious or predictable?

What provokes the protagonist to crack emotionally?

What provokes the confrontation at the end of the middle? Who starts it? What happens? How does the protagonist lose or at least fall apart in this confrontation?

What lesson does the protagonist learn, what personal revelation does he or she have, what evidence comes to light that changes what the protagonist believes about himself or herself or that puts past events in a whole new light?

How does this final, climactic revelation or new information convince (or force) the protagonist to confront the person from the past one last time and end this thing once and for all?

What does the final confrontation look like? Where does it happen? Who starts it? Does the protagonist lure the person from the past into it or vice versa? Does the protagonist take along law enforcement or a witness, or does he or she go alone?

What does the protagonist ultimately do to the person from the past, realizing this person from the past is a symbol, a personification, of the protagonist's own trauma? Is what the protagonist does symbolic in some way, or can you add a symbolic element to the final confrontation?

How does the protagonist feel when he or she defeats the person from the past and symbolically defeats the monsters from his or her past?

What lessons has the protagonist learned? How has he or she changed?

What does a reunion between the protagonist and loved ones look like? What's said?

Will you show the protagonist returning to his or her normal life, a changed person?

TROPE TRAPS

The protagonist's normal life to start the story is still so wounded or abnormal the audience can't relate to him or her.

The protagonist isn't sympathetic and likable right away.

When the protagonist's past trauma is revealed to the audience, it fails to evoke sympathy in the audience and they don't root for the protagonist to succeed in dealing with it.

You reveal the full extent of the past trauma right at the beginning and leave nothing to the imagination of your audience and blow an opportunity to build suspense as they anticipate learning what really happened.

Loved ones of the protagonist are overly perfect and supportive, or they're overly jerks and unsupportive and your audience disbelieves or dislikes them.

The person from the past is a cardboard character with no emotional range, depth, or dimension.

The person from the past is only and always a monster and has no redeeming qualities to give your audience any pause in just wanting them dead.

The current day events between the protagonist and person from the past have no connection to the events from the past and feel disjointed.

The person from the past is so likable the audience roots for him or her instead of the protagonist.

The protagonist never deals with his or her painful emotions, never makes mistakes because of them, and never breaks down or loses control.

The confrontations with the person from the past don't have any emotional element to them and are just shootouts.

What the protagonist does to the person from the past is not commensurate with the harm the person from the past has caused to the protagonist.

Your audience is mad something worse didn't happen to the person from the past.

You fail to show the catharsis the protagonist experiences and the audience never sees him or her feeling better or freed from his or her pain.

The protagonist isn't a changed person by the end of the story.

PAST CATCHES UP TROPE IN ACTION
Movies:

- A History of Violence
- Shutter Island
- The Bourne Identity
- Cape Fear
- Memento
- The Machinist
- Oldboy

Books:

- The Girl With the Dragon Tattoo by Stieg Larsson
- Gone by Mo Hayder
- The Truth About the Harry Quebert Affair by Joel Dicker
- Sharp Objects by Gillian Flynn
- The Midnight Line by Lee Child
- I Let You Go by Clare Mackintosh
- The Silent Patient by Alex Michaelides

29

PITTED AGAINST EACH OTHER

DEFINITION

In this trope, two people are pitted against each other—voluntarily or involuntarily, against a stranger or loved one—in some sort of life-or-death competition. I did debate calling this trope Gladiatorial Combat, Hunger Games™, or even Squid Games™.

NOTE: Trope names evolve to reflect current culture. When a story is so popular, so well known, and so iconic in its arc that it's recognized and known by absolutely everyone who hears its title, it's not uncommon for an entire trope to get renamed. Before Italian author, Giambattista Basile, wrote down the already well-known oral folk tale of Cinderella in 1634, other stories about children in tragic circumstances living off the charity of others had existed for at least two millennia. They just weren't called Cinderella stories. But when the Grimm brothers published their book of fairy tales in 1812 and widely popularized the story, the Cinderella trope got its name.

That's a long way of saying if you'd prefer to think of this trope as the Hunger Games™ or Squid Games™ trope, be my guest. I'm just not going to infringe on active trademarks by doing so.

. . .

In the creepiest case, a madman captures loved ones and forces them to fight to the death or else some even more terrible thing will happen. In a less horrific example, private investigators who've never met are hired to work a case and whoever solves it first gets the only paycheck. There are countless other variations on this theme of high-stakes competition or gladiatorial blood sport.

The common elements of all versions of this trope are:

- People are placed in competition against each other with something big, dangerous, or ominous on the line.
- The competitors may be random strangers, or they may be literal family members.
- They may be bribed, coerced, forced outright to race toward some goal or fight each other in some way, possibly to the death.
- This competition is heartless at best and cruel at worst.
- The villain is the person who pitted these people against each other.
- At some point in the story, the competitors turn together against the villain.

In most cases, the competitors refuse to engage in some element of the race or fight that constitutes a bridge too far for them. This balking at following through with the competition triggers a demonstration of the villain's seriousness that's horrifying or terrifying enough that competitors continue on.

Ultimately, the competitors work together to defeat the villain and subvert the race or fight. They probably have to do this in secret while appearing to prepare for/continue the fight or engage in the race.

The stakes are astronomical for the competitors. They spend most of this story in a state of terror. They're usually under close surveillance and must exercise the utmost of caution, stealth, and careful planning if they're to survive, let alone find and stop the villain.

By the end of this story, these terrorized competitors are in a state of mind where they're absolutely ready to kill the villain and may think it's an appropriate punishment for what they've been put through. It would be unusual for the competitors not to physically attack the villain when they finally find and defeat him or her.

For ease in writing this analysis, I'm going to speak of only two competitors. But it's entirely possible for there to be dozens, hundreds, or thousands, of competitors in some deadly competition or fight that has been arranged by the villain. All the same questions, things to think about, and traps apply if there are multiple competitors.

You might consider choosing to focus on just a few of the overall competitors as you develop your story to keep your cast of characters down to a manageable level.

ADJACENT TROPES
-- Loved One in Danger
-- Isolated Together and Dying
-- Dying One by One
-- Lethal Lottery/Life Auction
-- The Deadly Game

WHY READERS/VIEWERS LOVE THIS TROPE
-- while this probably isn't a trope readers want to participate in directly, unless they secretly fantasize about taking out a spouse, loved one, or close friend, they may enjoy the vicarious thrill of such a high-stakes situation

-- we all can enjoy exploring a subject or story idea that's taboo in our regular, mundane lives and learn survival or life lessons without having to experience something so terrible in real life

-- we all like to think we could function well under the most extreme pressure and would figure out a way to outsmart the most diabolical of bad guys

-- it's a fascinating thought exercise to strip down complex relationships to their simplest possible equations of life and death

OBLIGATORY SCENES
THE BEGINNING:

This story typically begins with two people whose lives may or may not connect in any way. We may meet them separately, we may see their paths cross by chance, or we may see them brought together by the villain.

One or both of the competitors may have an acute problem that makes one or both of them need an immediate solution to a crisis in their lives. Often, they both have money problems and the promise of a huge sum of quick cash is dangled before them if they'll participate in a "little game." In a case like this, they enter into the game voluntarily. They know the stakes, they know the risks, but they believe they have no other choice.

The competitors may be tricked, lured, or kidnapped outright into participating in the game. In this case, they're forced into it involuntarily and are more likely to resist playing along. The rules of the competition may not initially be spelled out and the stakes for them/loved one and consequences of refusing to play along may not initially be made clear. For these characters, much of Act One is taken up with them learning by painful trial and error what a mess they've been dragged into.

They may or may not even know who forced them into this situation. They may find out as part of Act One (which would be a reasonable way to end Act One), or they may not find out exactly who the villain is until sometime in Act Two.

If the set-up for the competition is elaborate or the villain's plan to ensnare the competitors is elaborate, the competition itself may not begin until the end of Act One and constitutes the crisis that ends the beginning of your story.

If your story dives into the competition itself very quickly and some of Act One involves the early portions of the competition, then Act One probably ends with the first death or other devastating outcome for a competitor, if there's a large group of competitors. If it's just two competitors, one of them suffers an injury, picks up a serious handicap going forward, or someone they love outside the competition has something terrible happen to him or her.

Act One may even end with one or both competitors refusing to engage in this competition. In this case, the act ends with the villain giving the competitors a demonstration of what will happen if they both don't go along with the competition. The demonstration is something shocking to the competitors and to your audience.

THE MIDDLE:

Now that the competitors understand what's at stake, they're forced to enter into or continue on with the competition whether they like it or not. If they didn't know their competitor well before, they get to know that person now, as they commence the race or fight. Even people who know each other extremely well may see a different side of their spouse, family member, loved one, or friend than they've ever seen before.

The competition heats up, becoming ever more dangerous. Likewise, the stakes continue to rise for the competitors as they learn just how diabolical the villain is and just how much danger they and those they love are in.

As the competition progresses, the stakes are stripped down to their essence—live or die, kill or be killed, do whatever it takes to survive no matter the difficulty or cost.

Any time the villain thinks the competitors aren't doing their best to win, he or she gives the competitors a chilling reminder of why they must fight no holds barred. These reminders should shock and surprise your competitors and your audience and increase the pressure on your competitors every time.

The competitors' stress should grow throughout the middle to a nearly unbearable pitch. They may suffer mini-breakdowns, major breakdowns, and personal crises.

Likewise, societal norms break down over the course of the competition. Polite behavior goes out the window. Kindness, compassion, and mercy fall by the wayside. Wanton violence and barbarism may become the norm.

Into the maelstrom, the competitors start plotting together in secret to get out of this horrible competition. They learn all they can about the villain and secretly compare notes, cover for each other, gather resources, and begin to form a plan to take out the villain.

The middle of your story may end with the main competitors being forced into direct conflict with each other or into deadly direct conflict. One of them is about to live and the other is about to die.

BLACK MOMENT:

If you have a single primary point of view character or protagonist, he or she may finally have to kill the other competitor (or another competitor) after having avoided doing so for the competition so far.

If killing has been the norm through the middle, he or she may have to maim or kill a loved one, now.

The competitor(s) may lose the big fight at the end of Act Two, and now a loved one dies, or something equally devastating happens that was the promised result of their defeat.

In a gentler version, your protagonist(s) may witness the death of someone they've considered to be an ally throughout the competition, or some terrible thing happens to another competitor/competitor's loved one because that competitor was defeated in the big fight at the end of Act Two.

Another possibility is the black moment is precipitated by the competitor(s) trying to subvert the competition or to attack the villain. But it goes badly and the plan fails. The villain has anticipated them or outsmarts the competitor(s), and someone pays a terrible price for the competitors' failure.

The black moment is when your competitor(s) fall apart emotionally. They've held it together more or less so far, but this moment breaks them. They may give up in this moment and literally or metaphorically sit down and wait to die. The devastation is complete. The competitor(s) are done. They have no more action or emotion left to give. Worst of all, they know their complete failure is now going to result—or is already resulting—in horrific consequences in their real life. The people they love are paying a horrendous price for the competitor's failure, and there's nothing he or she can do about it but suffer and grieve.

THE END:

The competitor's suffering and grief transforms to rage, a need for vengeance, and very likely an expectation of and acceptance of the inevitability of dying soon.

In this new, focused, and enraged state of mind, the competitor(s) gather themselves, their resources, everything they've learned about the villain, and everything they know about the competition, and form a plan to end this competition once and for all. And while they're at it, they plan to find the villain and take out him or her.

Act Three may show some of the planning and preparation process for this final fight, but most of the act is probably taken up with the climactic fight itself. The competitor(s) may need to eliminate other remaining competitors who stand between him or her and the villain. The protagonist may need to "win" the competition to get access to the villain, and if that's the case, the protagonist, using his or her new focus and resolve, makes short work of the other competitors.

This story frequently has a double action climax—the first one being the conclusion of the competition itself, and the second one being the protagonist's confrontation with the villain. The emotional climax of the story is not until the protagonist finally confronts and defeats the villain.

There is almost always a denouement to this story where we see the competitor(s) return home to the loved ones he or she has fought so hard to protect or save. Your audience is going to be as wrung out by this story as your competitors. They all deserve a moment of relief and return to the normal world after the nightmare they've all just lived through.

NOTE: For ease, I'm going to talk in terms of one protagonist for the Key Scenes, Things to Think About, and Trope Traps as if there's only one main point of view character for your story. But this can just as easily be an ensemble project with several main points of view. In this case, you'll need to answer all the questions I pose for a single protagonist for each one of your main characters.

KEY SCENES

-- the rules of the competition are explained to the protagonist

-- the protagonist forms alliances and makes enemies with other competitors. If there are only two competitors, they become temporary allies to deal with some portion of the competition but become enemies as they both declare their intent to survive and win

-- the protagonist breaks the first moral taboo to him or her

-- the protagonist loses some portion of the competition or disobeys, and something really awful happens that the villain threatened to do in response to loss or disobedience

-- the protagonist has a quiet moment of truce with a competitor

-- the protagonist convinces the competitor (or vice versa) to work with him or her in secret to take out the villain

-- we find out why the villain is doing this horrendous thing and how she or she feels about it

THINGS TO THINK ABOUT WHEN WRITING THIS TROPE

What is the competition going to be and what are the rules, if any, it will run under? **NOTE**: A number of really creative and really extreme Pitted Against Each Other stories have been portrayed in books, film, and TV in recent years, so you're going to have to really stretch your imagination to come up with something fresh and exciting.

Who plans, sets up, and runs the competition? How will the competition be monitored and observed?

Who's going to watch the competition? Is this just for the villain's entertainment, or will others be watching it, too? If others will see it, how do they feel about it? Are they horrified at being forced to watch loved ones do this or are they entertained by it? (And yes, there can be some of both.)

Has a competition like this happened before? If so, when? How often? Why?

Is the competition legal or illegal? Why is this legal carnage okay, or why hasn't this illegal carnage been discovered and stopped?

What does the villain want from putting on this competition (what's his or her goal)? What's his or her motivation for wanting this? Is there another unconscious or unspoken goal for doing this (a need the villain doesn't know he or she has)?

Finally, we can start thinking about our protagonist. Who is he or she? Why does this person get drawn into this competition?

Does the protagonist volunteer or is he or she chosen by the villain? Is the choice of this protagonist random or intentional? If intentional, what about him or her made the villain choose him or her?

What carrot will the villain dangle in front of the voluntary competitor to get him or her to agree to compete? What sword will the villain hold over the head of the involuntary competitor to force him or her to compete?

Can you give the villain a sword (a threat) to hold over the voluntary competitor, or a carrot to dangle in front of the involuntary competitor as well?

What initially motivates your protagonist—the sword or the carrot? Why?

At this point I know it sounds like a dumb question, but can you raise the stakes for the protagonist of not winning? Can you raise them more? Much more?

Can you give all the other competitors stakes fully as high as the protagonist's for not winning? How will you show these other competitor's stakes in your story?

How will you ensure your audience roots for your protagonist instead of some other competitor? What makes your protagonist the most relatable competitor?

Who will the protagonist team up/ally with during the competition? Is this temporary or will it last until they're the last two competitors standing? If it's temporary, why do they join forces? Why and when do they break up their alliance?

How much does the protagonist know about the rules of the competition when it starts? When does he or she learn any other rules?

How much does the protagonist know about the consequences or penalties of the competition when it starts? When does he or she learn any other consequences or penalties?

How much does the protagonist know about the stakes to himself or herself or to a loved one when the competition starts? When does he or she learn about any other stakes?

How much does the protagonist know about the villain when the competition starts? When and what more does he or she learn about the villain during the course of the competition?

Will the protagonist and other competitor(s) try to break the game? Subvert the entire competition? Take out the villain? If yes to any of these, what do they try? How does it go? How does the villain respond?

How does the villain maintain control of the game? How does the villain take back control if the competitor(s) get out of his or her control?

How does the competition get steadily more difficult, more harrowing, more dangerous? What are the levels of it, the layers of it, the progressive parts of it?

Have you built any levels, layers, or parts of the competition that are unexpected, surprising, shocking, or a creative twist that will keep your competitors (and audience) off balance?

Is the villain a person of his or her word or not? If the villain says the winner will be set free or paid a fortune, does he or she plan to follow through on this? Does the protagonist believe the villain will do what he or she promised or not? Is the protagonist right or wrong?

What event triggers the protagonist's black moment? Is it black enough to justify the depth of despair the protagonist experiences as a result?

Can you make the protagonist's emotional breakdown darker? Deeper? More complete? More devastating?

How will the protagonist pull himself or herself out of the black moment to carry on? Does something or someone outside the protagonist help him or her refocus? Does someone say something? Does the protagonist think of someone or something? Does some tiny object, event, or action trigger a memory that helps the protagonist gather himself or herself for one last effort? Does something happen within the competition that shifts the protagonist's despair to rage?

What does the protagonist plan going into the climactic fight of the competition to ensure he or she wins? What new object does he or she obtain, what new idea does he or she have, what new fact does he or she learn—something to tip the balance in his or her favor in the crucial moment of the fight?

When the protagonist finally wins, what does he or she feel? (Realizing this is not his or her final catharsis...but it may be a moment of profound emotion.)

Is your protagonist taken to the villain after winning or does he or she have to search out or go hunting for the villain...and if so, how does the protagonist find and reach the villain?

What does the protagonist do when he or she finally is face-to-face with the villain? What does the villain do in this moment?

What does the protagonist do to or say to the villain?

Are there any consequences to the villain (if he or she is still alive)? If so, what?

Are there consequences to the protagonist for what he or she did to the villain? If so, what?

What does the protagonist's reunion with loved ones look like? Where and when does it take place?

TROPE TRAPS

The competition is predictable and boring.

The competition is derivative of existing, well-known movie, TV, and book franchises and your audience is annoyed by it.

The competition isn't high-concept enough (meaning larger than life and exciting but with a clear, easy-to-understand premise).

The villain doesn't have a good reason for going to all the trouble of setting up this competition and torturing the competitors like this.

Your competition is allegedly secret, but it's so big, so bloody, so visible, and so many people know about it that no way would it plausibly remain secret.

Failing to create a plausible means by which the villain monitors and watches the competition.

Failing to create a plausible means by which the villain controls the competitors themselves. He or she has no leverage to force the competitors to obey or continue competing.

The stakes to the competitors aren't high enough to make them continue on as the competition gets worse and worse.

The conditions of the competition and the consequences for losing aren't terrible enough to break down the societal rules of good/lawful/acceptable behavior.

No characters are forced to cross personal boundaries or break personal taboos.

Your story isn't harrowing enough to hold your (jaded by other stories of this type) audience's attention.

The stakes and consequences don't grow in scale as the story progresses.

Your protagonist isn't likable or relatable enough for your audience to care what happens to him or her.

If you allow your audience to stray to rooting for a competitor besides the protagonist, they're going to be upset when their favorite fails or dies.

The protagonist's black moment isn't dark enough or isn't believable when he or she breaks down because you've failed to build the protagonist's stress to a breaking point beforehand.

Failing to let things go very badly for your competitors.

Failing to have the villain do terrible things, particularly terrible things he or she has threatened to do.

Failing to let characters your audience likes die.

Failing to set a clear condition that constitutes victory in the competition.

Failing to give the protagonist a shot at revenge against the villain.

Failing to show the protagonist's reunion with loved ones.

Failing to show at least a glimpse of the protagonist back in his or her normal world, where he or she is safe once more.

PITTED AGAINST EACH OTHER TROPE IN ACTION

.   .   .

Movies:

- Hunger Games
- Squid Games (TV series)
- Divergent
- Battle Royale
- Death Race
- The Running Man
- Gladiator
- Bloodsport
- Ready Player One
- Gamer
- The Tournament

Books:

- Ender's Game by Orson Scott Card
- The Long Walk by Richard Bachman (Stephen King)
- The Maze Runner by James Dashner
- Caraval by Stephanie Garber
- The Cabin At the End of the World by Paul Tremblay
- Endgame by James Frey and Nils Johnson-Shelton
- The Forbidden Game by L.J. Smith

POSTHUMOUS MESSAGE

DEFINITION

In this trope, someone has died recently but left behind or sent a message that reaches its intended receiver after his or her death. The classic version of this story begins with a note saying, "If you're reading this, I'm dead."

There are many variations on this message and variations upon how it's delivered or found. To name a few, the message can be left as a voicemail, email, video, social media post, suicide note, or a letter/document/file sent through the mail soon before the sender's death.

The message itself may have nothing to do with personal danger but might be a piece of important intelligence the sender has just discovered, a scientific breakthrough he or she has just made, a dangerous secret he or she knows, or some other piece of information the sender deems too important to risk having lost in the event of his or her death.

Because we're writing thriller novels here, the information in the message always leads to danger of some kind. It may describe a danger outright, or it might be a thread that, when pulled, reveals a grave danger that must be stopped. The danger this message leads to is often another trope in its own right that your protagonist must navigate over the course of the story. A terrorist plot must be stopped, a criminal caught before he or she murders again, an alien, monster, or disease found and destroyed before it destroys everyone.

The sender may have reason to believe he or she is in danger and might die. Hence, he or she records the important information to make sure knowledge of it doesn't die with him or her.

Conversely, the sender may have no reason to believe he or she is in danger. He or she may have simply recorded the information and sent it to someone whom he or she trusted or who would understand the significance of the information. Then, without warning, the sender died accidentally or by foul play.

It's also possible the sender recorded the important information and set up some sort of dead man's switch where, in the event of his or her death, the information was delivered to someone whom he or she trusted or who understands the significance of the information.

Whew. After all those possible inciting incidents, we finally come to the protagonist and the actual story arc. In this story, the protagonist is almost always the recipient of the posthumous message. He or she may know the now deceased sender or may have never heard of him or her before. But, for some reason, the sender chose the protagonist to receive the posthumous message.

Generally, the protagonist has the expertise required to do what's needed with the information. He or she is a cop if a crime has been revealed. He or she is a soldier or spy if a threat to the world's safety is revealed. He or she is a scientist of the right flavor if critical or dangerous scientific information is revealed. You get the idea.

Sometimes, the protagonist has no expertise at all to deal with the information in the posthumous message. In this case, he or she must obtain help or bumble along as an amateur to deal with the problem the deceased sender has dumped in his or her lap. This protagonist may have been someone the deceased believed could find a way to deal with the information or the protagonist might simply have been the only person the deceased had time to or opportunity to send the message to.

With the arrival of this posthumous message comes an implied or overt responsibility for the recipient (the protagonist) to act upon the information in the message. If the sender claims to have been murdered, the protagonist is obliged to investigate that claim. If explosive intelligence is contained in the message, the protagonist is obliged to get it to the right people and/or to act on the intelligence to stop a disaster from happening.

The story, then, is about the protagonist/recipient's journey to respond to the information in the posthumous message and stop the terrible thing the message warned about (or led to the protagonist learning about) from happening by the end of the story.

ADJACENT TROPES
-- Deathbed Confession
-- Mystery in Personal Effects
-- Diary/Old Letter/Old File Discovered
-- Accidentally Find Dangerous Object of Information
-- Crime Predicted by Mundane Means
-- Crime Predicted by Paranormal Means

WHY READERS/VIEWERS LOVE THIS TROPE
-- we like to believe that, if someone we loved sent us a message posthumously that asked us to do something, we would step up to the task and do what he or she asked of us.

-- we like to believe that, if we sent someone we love a message posthumously that asked them to do something, they would love us enough to do what we asked of them

-- getting a message like this would add excitement, adventure, and mystery to our otherwise mundane and boring lives.

-- we're intrigued by the idea of discovering secrets about our loved ones or finding out about hidden parts of their lives

-- people who know me believe I'm smart enough and capable enough to do something challenging or solve a mystery and one of them chose me to do this difficult thing for them

-- in our grief over losing a loved one, it would be nice to be able to do something to show them how much we loved them and to honor their memory

OBLIGATORY SCENES
THE BEGINNING:

You may start your story with a scene of the (alive) sender preparing and sending the message. If this person is or isn't in immediate danger, this scene will demonstrate that. It will also tell your audience whether this person knew he or she might die or how much haste in which he or she sent the message. It may even show your audience how the sender disappears or dies.

If the message was set up as a dead man's switch, this typically takes a fair bit of planning and the sender probably hasn't done it as a last-minute thing. In this case, you probably won't show the sender arranging for the delivery in case of his or her demise or disappearance.

The beginning of this story always shows the protagonist receiving the message. He or she may or may not know the sender is dead or disappeared when the message arrives. If the protagonist isn't aware of the sender's disappearance or death, the arrival of the message undoubtedly spurs him or her to reach out to the sender, only to get no response, or to find out the sender is missing or dead. Either way, the protagonist figures out very soon what has happened to the sender.

The protagonist feels a responsibility to the sender and decides what to do about the message. He or she may initially plan to hand off the information to someone else. But, for some reason, the protagonist can't or chooses not to turn over the response to the information in the message and to do it himself or herself.

The protagonist embarks on his or her investigation or response to the information, and the beginning typically ends with the protagonist learning just how dangerous this information is. Someone may try to steal the message, silence or stop the protagonist, or the protagonist may find evidence of foul play in the sender's disappearance/death.

THE MIDDLE:

Aware now that he or she is in danger, the protagonist presses on with the investigation or response to the sender's information. The protagonist may doubt his or her ability to stop the danger, but the sender trusted the protagonist enough to give this information to him or her. Obviously, the sender believed the protagonist was capable of dealing with the threat (and may have explicitly said so). Out of love or respect for the sender, the protagonist is willing to keep going, even if it's getting dangerous.

Over the middle of the story the protagonist follows the trail of movement or clues the sender engaged in before his or her disappearance/demise. The protagonist may find or learn things the sender never did. The protagonist also intentionally or accidentally draws the same attention from the same bad guy(s) that the sender did.

A common midpoint reversal for this story is the moment when the protagonist shifts from investigator/tracker/searcher to being actively hunted by the bad guys and going on the run or going into hiding. Once the bad guys are actively trying to stop or kill the protagonist, the danger increases exponentially.

As the story unfolds, the protagonist learns the full extent of what the information in the message only hinted at or only partially revealed. The full stakes of stopping the threat the protagonist is now chasing also are revealed in the middle of the story. The more he or she learns, the worse the situation is.

Act Two ends with a mini-crisis when the bad guys nearly succeed at snatching or killing the protagonist. He or she gets away, but only by the skin of his or her teeth. Or worse, he or she is captured by the bad guys. Another possible crisis to end the middle of the story is someone more powerful or more official than the protagonist shuts down his or her investigation. Even though the protagonist tries desperately to convince this person of the looming danger, the protagonist is ignored.

BLACK MOMENT:

The protagonist has failed to stop the imminent (or in progress) catastrophe the sender asked him or her to deal with in his or her stead. The thing the sender feared and the thing the protagonist now also fears is going to happen or is starting.

The protagonist has failed himself or herself, has failed the sender, and has failed all the people who are going to be hurt or killed by the coming disaster.

No one will listen, no one will help, and no one understands what's about to happen. All appears lost in this moment.

THE END:

The protagonist learns something, finds some clue or information, puts together some piece of the puzzle that eluded him or her before, or gets outside help from someone else at the last minute that gives the protagonist one last shot at stopping the disaster.

He or she races to the climactic confrontation and gets there at the last possible moment to confront the bad guy(s). A big fight ensues, and the protagonist prevails by the skin of his or her teeth and just in the nick of time.

Often, as the protagonist is on the verge of losing, memory of the deceased sender, of something the sender once said or of a moment the two of them shared, inspires the protagonist or gives the protagonist an idea that helps turn the tide of the battle.

A fun twist on the big ending is for the sender who disappeared to show up at the critical moment in the fight, when the protagonist is on the verge of losing, to fight beside the protagonist. Together, the two of them defeat the bad guy(s) and stop the disaster from happening.

The disaster has been averted. The protagonist has honored the memory of the sender and fulfilled the sender's final request.

Now, in the aftermath, the protagonist can pay his or her last respects to the memory of the sender and grieve in peace.

KEY SCENES

-- the protagonist considers ignoring the posthumous message because he or she doesn't initially understand its significance or because he or she doesn't believe he or she is capable of dealing with the problem described in it

-- the protagonist learns something about the task at hand that makes him or her sure he or she can't do it

--more knowledgeable or more expert people tell the protagonist he or she isn't up to succeeding at the task he or she is trying to do

-- the protagonist actually does get in over his or her head and gets in very serious trouble or danger...and may have to ask someone else for help or a rescue

-- the protagonist gets really angry with the sender for getting him or her into this mess and this danger

-- the bad guy(s) taunt the protagonist over what they did to the sender

-- the protagonist makes peace with dying to finish this task, which has become a personal quest for him or her

-- after the protagonist has won, the naysayers from before are impressed that he or she succeeded...and lived

. . .

THINGS TO THINK ABOUT WHEN WRITING THIS TROPE

Who's the person sending the message?

What does the message say?

What danger does the message spell out, hint at, or give a thread to that will lead to the danger?

Who does the sender send the message to? Does he or she know the protagonist? Why this person as the recipient and not someone else?

When the protagonist receives the message, does he or she know what has happened to the sender? If not, how does he or she find out?

Does the protagonist understand the message immediately or have to decipher it as the story progresses?

Does the protagonist understand the extent of the danger the message describes, or does that understanding grow as the story unfolds?

Is the protagonist an expert at something that suits him or her to respond to the message? If so, how?

What is the investigation or journey the protagonist is launched on? Where does he or she go? What does he or she have to find, learn, or prove?

Make a list of the layers of information the protagonist will discover over the course of the story? Can you add unexpected twists and turns? Can you make left turns and send the protagonist in directions he or she and your audience didn't see coming?

Can you make the ultimate danger much bigger than the message indicated or that the sender even knew?

What happens to the sender? Is he or she dead or alive?

Does the protagonist know for sure what happened to the sender or not? If not, how and when does the protagonist find out?

What do the bad guy(s) try to do to the protagonist to stop him or her?

How dangerous are the bad guy(s)? Can you make them more dangerous? Much more dangerous?

In what way is the protagonist in over his or her head and totally unprepared for what happens when things get really bad in the story? How will he or she get out of this situation?

What provokes the protagonist's black moment?

How does the protagonist feel in the black moment? What does he or she decide to do or not do in that moment?

What pulls the protagonist out of the black moment?

What does the protagonist learn that makes him or her willing to try one more time to stop the bad guys?

What does the final confrontation look like? When and where does it take place?

Has the bad guy(s) evil plan started to happen by the time the protagonist arrives, or does he or she have to stop it just before it starts?

What does it look like when the protagonist is on the verge of losing the big fight?

What changes in that moment to give the protagonist the boost he or she needs to finally prevail in the fight and stop the bad guy(s)?

Who rewards or congratulates the protagonist after he or she has averted disaster?

How does the protagonist honor the sender, grieve him or her, and make peace with the sender for having sent him or her on such an arduous journey?

TROPE TRAPS

The message is not one the sender would have plausibly sent if in the situation in which he or she sent it. (Someone running for his or her life doesn't stop in the middle of fleeing with a bad guy on his or her heels and record a detailed video.)

The sender chose to send the message to someone wildly unqualified to act upon his or her message and had no good reason for sending it to the protagonist.

Any reasonable person would not try to do the thing the protagonist decides to do, particularly if he or she has no qualifications to do it.

The message spells out so much information you fail to leave major information for the protagonist to discover.

The information about the dangerous thing unfolds predictably in a linear, logical fashion that never surprises your audience.

The ultimate danger that the sender warned of in the message is exactly the same. There's no changes or developments in what's really at stake that the sender wasn't aware of.

The sender leaves too complete a road map for the protagonist and the protagonist isn't required to exercise any ingenuity, intelligence, or creativity to proceed through the story.

The bad guy(s) are smart enough, diabolical enough, or vicious enough to make your audience worry about the protagonist's safety.

The sender is really alive but has no compelling reason for having disappeared and dumping this whole mess in the underserving protagonist's lap.

The event that triggers the protagonist's black moment of doubt and failure isn't a devastating enough failure to plausibly make him or her feel all that angst.

The amateur protagonist manages to bumble all the way through the story without ever dying...and he or she surely should have if the bad guys had two brain cells to rub together.

The protagonist isn't smart or clever enough heading into the final confrontation with a bigger, badder, better armed bad guy and should be dead within seconds. When he survives the initial confrontation, the audience doesn't buy that he or she is still standing.

The thing or moment that turns the tide and spurs on the protagonist to snatch victory from the jaws of defeat is hokey, cliché, or feels like a *deus ex machina*—an act of God that swoops in to save the day.

POSTHUMOUS MESSAGE TROPE IN ACTION

Movies:

- The DaVinci Code
- Don't Say a Word
- Eagle Eye
- The Game
- National Treasure
- Serenity
- Stay Alive

Books:

- Digital Fortress by Dan Brown
- The Apocalypse Watch by Robert Ludlum
- The Thirteenth Tale" by Diane Setterfield
- The Shadow of the Wind" by Carlos Ruiz Zafón
- The Historian" by Elizabeth Kostova
- The Last Templar" by Raymond Khoury
- The Atlantis Gene" by A.G. Riddle

.

31

RESCUE MISSION

DEFINITION

This is a broad trope that's often paired with other more specific tropes or with mainly character-driven tropes. Nonetheless it's a classic thriller story that remains perennially popular.

In this trope, the protagonist is officially assigned to rescue someone from danger or captivity, or the protagonist unofficially goes on a personal mission to rescue someone in harm's way.

If officially assigned to perform a rescue mission, the protagonist necessarily has the skills, training, and expertise to perform such a mission. In this case, you can go to town with how bad, how scary, how powerful, and how skilled the bad guys are in this story.

If unofficially on a personal mission to rescue a loved one, the protagonist may not be nearly as skilled. It would be highly unusual for a completely unskilled civilian to embark on such a dangerous mission, but it's not impossible.

In this case, however, you'll need to give careful consideration to how your civilian rescuer is going to pull off the rescue in a plausible and believable way.

The person being rescued is, in effect, a MacGuffin in this story if he or she does little or nothing to affect the course of the rescue.

If, however, your hostage, prisoner, kidnapping victim is actively doing things to change the course of the rescue mission, then he or she may end up being an important character and possibly get his or her own point of view.

> NOTE: I'm going to call the hostage, prisoner, or kidnapping victim the "prisoner", going forward. Although there's nuance to the situation of a hostage versus a prisoner versus a kidnapping victim, I'm sure you can make the correct substitutions in label in your head, if necessary.

It's not uncommon for stories of this type to do "check in" scenes on the prisoner to remind the audience of how terrible his or her situation is, how quickly his or her situation is deteriorating, and to instill a sense of urgency in the audience that the protagonist needs to hurry up and rescue this poor prisoner.

It's up to you how graphic you choose to make the scenes describing the plight of the prisoner. There is such a thing as showing too much for a given audience and turning your story into pain porn. Hence, you'll need to consider your audience and how much detailed violence against a helpless person they can tolerate.

Most importantly, be sure your marketing materials accurately reflect how gory, disturbing, or violent your story is. You might also consider including a trigger warning up front, if one is appropriate.

The climactic confrontation of this story is typically the rescue itself. If, however, there's going to be a protracted egress away from the site where the prisoner was rescued from, then the rescue itself may come as early as the midpoint of your story, and the remainder of the story is, in effect, the "getting out" portion of the rescue.

The story typically ends with the protagonist delivering the prisoner to safety. I have seen this trope turned on its head a few times, where the protagonist dies rescuing the prisoner successfully or takes the prisoner's place in captivity while the prisoner goes free and returns home.

NOTE: For ease of writing up this trope, I'm also going to talk in terms of only one prisoner being rescued. But it's entirely plausible to have multiple prisoners in need of rescue. In this case, you'll probably need to send in an entire team of rescuers. You'll probably choose one or a few of the rescuers' points of views to tell the story from in this scenario.

ADJACENT TROPES
   -- Buried Alive
   -- Missing Person
   -- Solving a Kidnapping
   -- Help Someone Defect
   -- Mercenaries Save the Day
   -- Off-the-Books Op
   -- Retired Operator Saves the Day
   -- Veteran (with PTSD) Saves the Day
   -- Mess With My Family and Find Out

WHY READERS/VIEWERS LOVE THIS TROPE
   -- if a loved one of ours disappeared, we would want the most badass possible person to go save them...or we would be frantic enough to do it ourselves
   -- there's a definite wish-fulfillment fantasy of imagining ourselves to be as smart, skilled, strong, and indomitable as the protagonists that are typical in these types of stories
   -- if I were ever kidnapped or taken hostage, I NEED to believe my government or my family would send in totally badass people who would, without fail, save me
   -- we all need to believe that if we ever disappeared, our loved ones (or at least our government) would never give up on us and would keep searching until they found us

.   .   .

OBLIGATORY SCENES
THE BEGINNING:

You may begin your story with the kidnapping or hostage taking itself. We get to meet the person(s) in need of rescue and form a connection with them. This establishes sympathy for them and urgency for someone to rescue them.

You may also begin your story with the protagonist being tasked to go find and rescue a missing person, known hostage, prisoner, or kidnapping victim. In this version of the opening, your audience will get to know the person he or she is rescuing more gradually, along with the protagonist. The protagonist knows nothing about the prisoner prior to receiving the mission in-brief.

As the search/investigation/mission progresses, the protagonist may trace the last known path of the missing person. He or she may talk to associates of the missing person or interview witnesses to the kidnapping/hostage taking/arrest. The missing person might have left a trail of breadcrumbs for potential rescuers or the kidnappers may have moved the hostage and left a trail the protagonist follows. All of this tells the protagonist (and your audience) a great deal about who the missing person is.

You may choose to insert vignettes told from the point of view of the prisoner that give us a glimpse of what he or she is experiencing. This is an excellent way to show your audience the bad guys, also. We learn how many there are, how smart, skilled, and organized they are, how well-armed they are, and what kind of support system they have. The more your audience learns about the bad guys, the better idea the audience has of how hard this mission is going to be to succeed at.

These vignettes are also a good way to spell out the stakes of failing to rescue the prisoner. Your audience may understand well before your protagonist just how critical it is to stop these bad guys and why getting the prisoner out of there is really, *really* important.

NOTE: Your audience is likely to enjoy being more informed than your protagonist—who's already super smart and super informed—even if it's only temporary. We all like getting one up on someone whose already so perfect they make us feel inferior and can border on being annoying.

The beginning of this story ends with a mini-crisis of some kind. This crisis ups the stakes of succeeding in this rescue mission. A few possibilities include:

- The rescuer finds where the prisoner is being held...and it's an impenetrable fortress or completely unassailable in some way.
- In a missing person's case, the rescuers get proof that the person has, in fact, been kidnapped or taken hostage.
- The loved ones and/or rescuers get communication from the kidnapper that shows the missing person alive, but in duress and terrified.
- A ransom demand is received.
- The bad guys propose a completely unacceptable trade.
- The rescuer finds out the prisoner knows something that, if the bad guys extract it from him or her, is going to be devastating and get a lot of people hurt or killed.
- The rescuer finds out there's some sort of deadline or ticking clock that, if it runs out, marks the moment when the prisoner will be killed.
- The protagonist finds out he or she knows the person he or she is being sent to rescue, and it's a loved one or close friend.

THE MIDDLE:

This is where the protagonist tracks the missing person or tracks the bad guys thought to have the missing person. It may involve travel, talking to sources or informants, collecting intelligence, or coercing unwilling people to give up information. The protagonist may physically track a trail on the ground. He or she may track the bad guys electronically or through the Internet, banking information, or other computer means.

This is also where the protagonist encounters resistance. He or she may be operating in a hostile place—a foreign country, inhospitable climate/terrain, unfriendly locals, or a neighborhood where he or she is not welcome. These characters (and the setting can act as a character in this context) may actively try to hinder or kill the protagonist.

And then, of course, the protagonist encounters the bad guys. If the bad guys are part of a large organization—a terror network, a gang, a corporation, an army, or a government, the protagonist runs into the outer rings of defense of this bunch and must commence penetrating deeper into the organization.

If the kidnapper is a lone wolf, the protagonist encounters the defenses and warning systems this person has put into place. The lone wolf may take his or her prisoner and go on the run. Or the lone wolf may leave the prisoner somewhere safe and sally forth to mislead, attack, or try to kill the protagonist.

The middle is likely to include more vignettes of the prisoner, showing his or her situation getting worse. The clock on his or her life is ticking down. With every passing hour, it's more urgent to find and rescue him or her.

Once the protagonist knows where the prisoner is, the mission shifts into a planning phase. How exactly is the protagonist going to get to the prisoner, sidestep or take out guards and kidnappers, and extract the prisoner?

The protagonist often engages in surveillance. He or she gathers equipment, disguises, additional support personnel, and any other resources necessary to execute his or her plan.

Act Two ends with a dramatic development that's a crisis:

- The rescue itself may happen, particularly if there's going to be a protracted escape from the site of the rescue that involves being chased by the kidnappers. In this scenario, the protagonist hoped to get away undetected but fails. The protagonist now has the prisoner with him or her but also has a bunch of pissed off kidnappers on their heels.
- The prisoner attempts an escape the protagonist doesn't expect. It aborts or messes up the protagonist's rescue plan—which may actually be in progress or on the verge of launching when the prisoner makes his or her failed escape that also puts the bad guys on full alert.
- Something changes in the prisoner's situation that forces the rescue plan to move forward drastically. Usually, the bad guys have decided to kill the prisoner. The protagonist, who's not yet ready and doesn't have all of his or her resources in place, has to launch the rescue now, anyways.
- The protagonist executes his big rescue plan only to arrive at where the prisoner is supposed to be and to find out the prisoner isn't there. The prisoner has been moved...or this is all an elaborate trap he or she has just walked into.

BLACK MOMENT:

The protagonist has failed. He or she has tried to rescue the prisoner or lost the prisoner, and now the bad guys are going to kill the prisoner. If the prisoner is a tool in a larger evil plan, that plan launches now.

The protagonist may also find himself or herself in grave danger, on the run, outgunned and outmanned. Not only is he or she not going to save the prisoner, but now he or she is likely going to die, as well. The protagonist's failure is complete.

. . .

THE END:

The climactic confrontation between the protagonist and bad guys happens. Each of the black moments I suggested has its own, slightly different version of this final battle, but they all involve the protagonist making one last attempt to rescue the prisoner or to have a direct confrontation with the bad guys chasing him/her (and possibly the rescued prisoner).

The protagonist is at the end of his or her resources, at the limit of his or her skills, exhausted, possibly afraid, frustrated, or simply done trying to play by the rules. Having reached the breaking point...and having broken in the black moment...this character may emerge from the black moment with a fatalistic attitude, possibly enraged, and be ready to do the suicidal, guaranteed to be dumb, grand thing to end this rescue mission once and for all.

One last time, the protagonist gathers himself or herself, collects all of his or her remaining resources, and plans one last, Herculean effort to rescue the prisoner or to escape the pursuing bad guys.

Something usually changes going into this final fight:

- The protagonist gets a new piece of information or a last-minute resource that will help him or her succeed this time, whereas he or she failed before.
- The protagonist has a different attitude after failing before and is now staring down his or her own death, as well.
- The protagonist learns something—it may be a lesson about himself or herself, it may be about the bad guys or about the prisoner, it may be something having to do with the mission itself or the place the final fight will occur.

Whatever changes, it gives the protagonist at least a tiny chance at succeeding, and that sliver of hope is all he or she needs at this point to proceed.

The final confrontation occurs, and the protagonist emerges triumphant. The bad guys are defeated or killed. If they have an additional evil plan, it's stopped. The prisoner is rescued and returned to safety.

We may see the bad guys punished. We may see the protagonist thanked or congratulated. We usually do see the prisoner reunited with loved ones. These three things establish for your audience that all is right with the world again and that good has triumphed over evil once more.

KEY SCENES

-- the protagonist learns there's a wrinkle to this rescue mission. It's not just another simple, straightforward, case of find prisoner, free prisoner, bring prisoner home. This mission is going to be special or has a special challenge

-- the protagonist figures out his or her superiors or officials dealing with him or her haven't told him or her everything. They've kept secrets or kept information to themselves

-- bureaucracy or politics gets in the way of the protagonist's mission and hinders it

-- the protagonist breaks the rules, goes off script, or does something he or she isn't supposed to that's going to infuriate his or her superiors or officials involved with the case

-- the protagonist sees where the prisoner is being held and it's much more heavily defended or much more dangerous than he or she was told to expect

-- the prisoner does something that makes his or her situation a lot worse and makes a rescue a lot harder or shortens the amount of time the protagonist has to rescue him or her

-- the protagonist has an encounter with the kidnapper and barely gets away without being seen, caught, recognized, or cover blown

-- the kidnapper may engineer an encounter of his or her own with the protagonist, either to play games with the protagonist or to size up the protagonist, to find out how the search for the prisoner is going. Or the protagonist and kidnapper may cross paths purely by chance

-- the protagonist reaches the prisoner and frees him or her

-- the bad guys nearly catch or kill the protagonist and prisoner making their escape

-- something goes wrong in the rescue plan and the protagonist has to wing it to continue the rescue...in greatly increased danger

-- the extraction and/or egress don't go to plan and are a LOT more dangerous than anticipated

-- the protagonist fights with the kidnapper

THINGS TO THINK ABOUT WHEN WRITING THIS TROPE

Who's the missing person, hostage, prisoner, or kidnapping victim? How is he or she captured? Is he or she a random victim or a targeted victim?

If the prisoner was specifically targeted for capture, why? Why him or her?

What does the kidnapper want from the prisoner?

Is the prisoner leverage to get someone else to do something the kidnapper wants? If so, who is the leverage being applied against? What does the kidnapper demand?

Who figures out the prisoner has been captured? Who does this person tell? What authorities are contacted? What authorities respond?

Who is the protagonist?

Does the protagonist know the prisoner or not? If so, how do they know each other and how close are they?

Is your protagonist an expert called in to do the rescue, or is your protagonist a loved one of the prisoner who's going to attempt the rescue on his or her own?

If the protagonist is going after a loved one without official sanction, what skills does he or she bring to the table? Who will he or she call on for help? Will he or she stay in touch with the authorities or not? Is so, who? If not, why not?

If the authorities officially assigned your protagonist to do the rescue mission, why is this protagonist specifically chosen to do the rescue mission? What's his or her skill set and qualification to do this mission?

What does the in-brief for the rescue mission look like? What's known about the prisoner and his or her situation? Is his or her location known? Is the identity of the kidnapper known? Are the details of the capture known?

What's unknown during the in-brief?

Will your story be a search followed by a rescue, or is your story only a rescue?

If the location of the prisoner is unknown to begin with, how will your protagonist find him or her? What steps does he or she take over the course of the story to find the prisoner?

What are the false leads, dead ends, important clues, hindrances, and obstacles along the way in the search that the protagonist must deal with?

At what point in the story does the protagonist identify the kidnapper? How?

Is the kidnapper part of an organization of some kind or not? If yes, what organization? How powerful is it? What are its goals?

What layers of defenses stand between the protagonist and the prisoner? How will the protagonist find them and get through each one?

What does the kidnapper (and any associates) do to hinder, mislead, scare off, attack, or kill the protagonist?

What happens that increases the urgency of finding the prisoner and rescuing him or her? Does the protagonist learn something about the prisoner that makes him or her special? Does the prisoner know something dangerous that the kidnappers must not find out? Is there something about the prisoner that, if the kidnappers learn, will put the prisoner in even more jeopardy?

If you plan to show vignettes of the prisoner's situation, what are they? What do they look like? How is he or she being treated or mistreated? What does a snapshot of his or her surroundings, confinement, and restraints look like?

Is the prisoner being put under duress or tortured in some way? If so, how, why, and for what purpose?

How little or much of the prisoner's situation will you show your audience?

How will you garner sympathy in your audience for the prisoner?

Does the prisoner do anything to try to improve his or her situation, for example talk to the kidnapper or plan an escape?

Does the prisoner do anything to make his or her situation worse, for example resisting interrogation, attacking the kidnapper, or trying to escape?

If the prisoner is a tool in a larger evil plan, what is that plan? How does the prisoner fit into it? How will the protagonist learn of this plan and learn its details?

What changes or what new information comes to light over the course of the story that raises the stakes a LOT for making this rescue critically important to succeed at?

What changes in the course of the story sharply changes what the protagonist has to do, how he or she has to do it, or how dangerous this mission is?

What revelation in your story will surprise your audience? Shock your audience? Throw your audience off balance? Will these events have a similar effect on your protagonist or not? Why?

Can you make your bad guy smarter, more diabolical, more merciless, more fanatical—something to really put your audience on edge and fear for the prisoner?

What's the protagonist's rescue plan? What resources will he or she need?

What goes wrong, mid-rescue? How does the protagonist overcome it?

How hairy is the extraction and egress? Who's chasing the protagonist and prisoner? How close a call is it to get away from the bad guys? How many bad guys give chase and why is it uncertain that the protagonist and prisoner will get away from them?

Is there one last piece of an evil plan that the protagonist and prisoner have to stop? If so, what is it? How will they stop it? How does the prisoner help the protagonist in some key way?

NOTE: It's possible this could constitute a large section of your story. In that case, most of the same questions that applied to the protagonist's search for the prisoner apply to this section of the story. The protagonist must gather information, locate the spot where the plan is launching from or where it can be stopped, get through the bad guy's defenses of this spot, and then stop the evil plan.

How do the protagonist and prisoner ultimately get away from the bad guys? Do they turn around and fight off the bad guys? Does help arrive, and if so, who?

What happens to the bad guys in the end? Is it appropriate to whatever they did to the prisoner while he or she was in captivity? Will your audience be satisfied with what happened to the bad guys?

To whom does the protagonist turn over the rescued prisoner once they're out of danger?

Do we see the prisoner's reunion with loved ones?

Do we see the protagonist get thanked or congratulated for completing the rescue?

TROPE TRAPS

The person who was kidnapped should have fought back or was

really dumb by putting himself or herself in a situation that allowed the kidnapper to snatch him or her, and your audience dislikes the prisoner and doesn't care what happens to him or her.

The protagonist is so badass it almost doesn't seem fair to the bad guy to turn the protagonist loose on him or her.

The protagonist is a frantic loved one with NO skills to track down or rescue his or her loved one and your audience doesn't buy this person as a plausible protagonist.

There are no clues at all to go on, and yet the protagonist manages to find the prisoner...as if by magic, ESP, or by implausibly lucky chance.

The kidnapper doesn't have a good reason or any motive for kidnapping the prisoner.

The kidnapper is a cardboard cut-out of a one each sociopath, sex predator, or pedophile who acts predictably, does totally predictable things to the prisoner, and never surprises your audience.

Why, if the protagonist has the resources of an entire government at his or her fingertips, can't he or she find the prisoner sooner and more easily, or bring better technology to bear in locating the prisoner?

The amount of violence or the graphic representation of it that you show happening to your prisoner upsets your audience so much they stop reading or watching your story.

The prisoner never does anything to try to rescue himself or herself, to improve his or her situation, or to take care of himself or herself in any way, and the audience finds him or her unlikeable and weak.

The protagonist manages to get past defenses over and over again that no mere mortal could get past and the whole rescue feels unbelievable, let alone a civilian protagonist who's going after a loved one and isn't fully trained in overcoming these sorts of defenses.

There's always a random guard who just happens to be in the wrong place at the wrong time (because of a smoke break, snack, or potty break) who sends up an alarm. Be more creative than that in how the rescue plan goes wrong.

The protagonist's extraction and egress plan isn't as thoroughly planned and thought out as getting to the prisoner to free him or her, and the protagonist comes across as stupid or half-assed.

The prisoner isn't suitably injured, incapacitated, or traumatized by what has happened to him or her over the course of the story.

The prisoner, after days or weeks of starvation, deprivation, or torture pops to his or her feet and sprints like a champion athlete beside the protagonist on their way out to freedom. Adrenaline's only good for so much, kids.

The protagonist takes no hits, no falls, no injuries, and no wounds in a bloody battle against a dangerous, violent bad guy, and your audience doesn't buy it.

RESCUE MISSION TROPE IN ACTION
Movies:

- Taken
- Die Hard
- Rambo
- Saving Private Ryan
- Argo
- Gone
- The Disappearance of Alice Creed
- The Frozen Ground

Books:

- The Searcher by Tana French
- Hostage by Robert Crais

- The Hard Way by Lee Child
- The Kill Artist by Daniel Silva
- Orphan X by Gregg Hurwitz
- Hostage Zero by John Gilstrap
- Consent to Kill by Vince Flynn
- Along Came A Spider by James Patterson

32

SECRET/FALSE IDENTITY

DEFINITION

In this story the protagonist has a secret identity or is living under a false identity. I hear you yelling at me, "But according to your definition of a trope, that's not one!" And, yes, you would be correct in some cases.

While the fact of a character living a secret or false identity is, in and of itself, merely a character element that describes some important aspect of a character, **it rises to the level of a trope when it causes a serious problem that the protagonist must overcome**. For example:

- Someone may learn of the protagonist's real identity, which poses a serious threat to the protagonist, and he or she has to find a way to stop his or her true identity from being revealed.
- The protagonist's true identity and secret or false identity each experience a crisis. These clashing crises, both of which demand the protagonist's full attention, force the protagonist to find a way to fix the crises in both of the sides of his or her identity without destroying the other.

- The protagonist lives a separate life in each of the
  identities, and the two grow harder and harder to sustain.
  A crisis in one or both forces him or her to give up one
  identity and just live in the other identity.

There are any number of additional variations upon this idea. What
they all have in common and that define this trope are:

- The protagonist has a secret or false identity that he or
  she lives under part or all of the time.
- The protagonist also has a real identity. He or she may
  not live under it often, but his or her real life does exist.
- The secret/false identity must remain secret for some
  important reason.
- Something happens to threaten its secrecy.
- The protagonist must fix the problem or stop the
  uncovering of the secret/false identity...or must face the
  fallout of the secret/false identity being uncovered.

The first things that come to most people's minds when they hear
this trope's name are a superhero who must keep his or her identity
secret and an undercover cop living a double life.

There are many other reasons someone might assume a false
identity, however, or might need or want to keep his or her real identity secret.

A woman might be hiding from a violent ex. A witness against a
dangerous criminal has been given a new identity. A spy is working
under an assumed identity. A person is leaving behind a traumatic,
troubled, or criminal past and changes his or her name.

Have fun coming up with your own reason why someone has a
secret or false identity and the problems caused when this identity
collides with a big problem.

. . .

ADJACENT TROPES
-- Big Secret
-- Past Catches Up
-- Stolen Identity/Stolen Life
-- Split Personality
-- Burned Spy
-- Secret Powers

WHY READERS/VIEWERS LOVE THIS TROPE
-- many readers/viewers love the idea of escaping their current life and reinventing themselves as someone else, particularly someone with an exciting, adventurous life

-- getting two protagonists for the price of one, as it were. Characters with dual identities are more complex and interesting than other characters

-- who doesn't relate to some poor soul who's overworked, stretched thin, and trying to juggle all the hassles of life? Even worse, this poor soul is juggling the hassles of TWO lives at the same time.

-- your audience loves being in on the secret that nobody else in the story knows. It makes them feel smart and like insiders to a special world

-- we can all relate to having to make choices between the competing priorities in our lives and how difficult those choices can be

OBLIGATORY SCENES
THE BEGINNING:
We meet the protagonist in one of his or her identities—going about his or her real life or going about his or her secret/false life. You may choose the identity he or she spends the most time in now, but

honestly, whichever one makes the most sense for your story or gives you the best opening is fine.

It's normal to have an incident happen fairly early on in the story that forces the protagonist out of his or her real identity and into the secret/false identity (or vice versa), either physically or metaphorically. It may not be that he or she completely shifts over to living in the other identity, but the protagonist is forced to deal with it in some way.

For example, a letter addressed to the protagonist's previous name arrives at his or her house. He or she must hastily hide the letter and prevent anyone else from seeing it. Plus, he or she is highly alarmed that someone obviously knows his or her old name and knows where he or she lives now. The protagonist never breaks out of his or her current identity, but surely tries to hide the old one from new friends and family and probably starts a secret investigation to find out who sent the letter.

In one or both of the identities, a serious problem crops up. This may the initial incident, or it may be another incident shortly after your audience is introduced to the second identity. This is a big problem, one that threatens the safety of the protagonist. As listed before, any number of problems could arise that put the protagonist at serious risk of discovery in one or both of the lives.

The protagonist may try to go on with his or her current daily life as if nothing ever happened, but now he or she is on edge, looking over his/her shoulder, and frantically trying to figure out how he/she was discovered or outed.

Into this tension, a mini-crisis occurs to end the beginning of your story. Somebody recognizes the protagonist from his or her other life. Someone from the other life threatens him or her. Someone threatens to reveal his or her other identity. Something dangerous happens to the protagonist in one identity that threatens to upend, expose, or harm his or her other identity.

. . .

THE MIDDLE:

The stakes are spiraling out of control in both of the protagonist's identities as he or she tries to maintain one and juggle the other. Threats come at the protagonist thick and fast as he or she tries to keep up the false identity and not let the real or original identity come back to bite him or her in the worst possible way.

If the protagonist has a new family, loved ones, and friends in his or her new identity, they're threatened by whatever specter from the protagonist's past life or secret/false identity is coming after him or her.

At some point, the protagonist may have to confess to loved ones about his or her previous identity or his or her current secret/false identity. It's possible a few loved ones know about it, but they don't know the full extent of it and they learn that in the middle of your story. They may react supportively, or they may react with horror, depending on that character's past or secret/false identity holds.

Threats are now coming at the protagonist from every direction, and he or she scrambles to contain the damage. The protagonist tries to maintain the secret/false identity, manage the problems happening in his or her real identity, and solve a huge problem that's rapidly getting out of control.

Whatever the main plot problem in your story is, it undoubtedly begins to affect both of the protagonist's identities in negative and potentially deadly ways until it explodes into a full-blown crisis.

BLACK MOMENT:

The frazzled protagonist, stretched thin between two incompatible and competing identities is distracted or paralyzed by having to make an impossible choice between the two halves of his or her life. When the crisis explodes, he or she doesn't react soon enough or well enough and fails to stop the big bad thing from happening.

Worse, the protagonist typically blows his or her cover in one of the identities and is unmasked as having a secret or false identity for all the world to see. All his or her hard work to build a new life or hide a secret/false identity has been for naught.

Very bad things are happening around the protagonist now, and potentially his or her loved ones are in the middle of the bad happenings. And it's all his or her fault. The protagonist had a great chance to stop this mess but didn't have his or her act together sufficiently.

Had the protagonist gone all in on one identity or the other, perhaps he or she might have stood a chance of winning. But by waffling between his or her identities, he or she didn't stand a chance of winning.

Worse, he or she has no cover from either of his or her identities now and is exposed, vulnerable, and visible to anyone out to harm him or her.

THE END:

Typically, in the ending of this trope, a bad guy who's out to get the protagonist comes after him or her. The bad guy knows who the protagonist really is now and knows where to find him or her. The protagonist has no chance to run, hide, or create another new identity. His or her only option is to stand and fight.

Like it or not, the protagonist finds himself or herself entering into a climactic confrontation with the big bad guy. It may not be a fight the protagonist wanted, but now that it's here, he or she is determined to win. Using everything he or she knows from both of his or her identities, the protagonist battles the bad guy.

It's an evenly matched fight, but at the crucial moment, something from the protagonist's other identity often turns the tide of the combat and tips the fight in the protagonist's favor.

The bad guy from a past life, the bad guy threatening the protagonist's new life, the bad guy out to kill the protagonist's alter ego is defeated and frequently killed.

This bad guy went to a lot of time and trouble to expose the protagonist's false/secret identity, and if the bad guy lives to cause mayhem another day, it's very likely he or she will come back for round two. Therefore, it's most common to see this bad guy killed at the end of this story.

The protagonist may have succeeded in keeping the whole world from finding out about his or her secret/false identity (or about his or her previous identity), but the loved ones closest to him or her know now who he or she really is...in both personas.

At long last, the protagonist gets a chance to be both sides of himself or herself openly and honestly around his or her loved ones. In turn, they get to know both sides of this complex person whom they know and love all the sides of, now.

KEY SCENES

-- the protagonist realizes someone has recognized him or her, and there's no way he or she can refute who he/she really is to this person

-- the protagonist gets stuck in one identity or the other and for some reason *really* needs to shift over into the other identity but can't

-- a loved one nearly catches the protagonist doing something in the other identity the loved one isn't familiar with

-- the brewing crisis in one of the protagonist's identities bubbles over into his or her other identity and causes big trouble

-- the protagonist does something to fix or contain the crisis in one identity but accidentally makes things a lot worse in his or her other identity

-- the protagonist is desperately needed simultaneously to handle something in each of his or her identities, but he or she can't be both places at once. No matter who the protagonist chooses to be, he or she is going to let someone down in the big way in his or her other identity

-- as the protagonist's worlds collide more and more, even the protagonist gets confused sometimes about who he or she is supposed to be

-- a loved one confesses that he or she has known for a while about the secret/false identity and has been waiting for the protagonist to tell him or her about it.

THINGS TO THINK ABOUT WHEN WRITING THIS TROPE

Who's your protagonist? What's his or her original backstory?

Why and how has he or she assumed a secret/false identity? What is this secret or false identity? What's its story?

What's the purpose of the secret/false identity?

In what identity does the protagonist spend most of his or her time these days—the original one or the secret/false one?

Does anybody from his or her real or original life know about his or her secret/false identity now? Does anybody from the protagonist's secret/false life know about his or her real or original life? How did this person find out? How does the protagonist feel about them knowing? Why does this person keep the protagonist's secret for him or her?

Which identity does the protagonist consider his or her "real" life? Has he or she completely abandoned his or her original identity to live full-time in a new one? Or does the protagonist temporarily assume a secret/false identity part-time to do something that has nothing to do with his or her real life?

What does the protagonist do while living in his or her secret/false identity?

Who, if anybody, knows about the protagonist's secret/false identity? How does this person(s) know? Does the protagonist know they know?

What big problem arises that threatens one or both of the protagonist's identities?

What is the human face of this problem, meaning who's the bad guy? How does he or she know the protagonist, and in which identity?

How does it cross over to threaten the other identity?

Does it threaten loved ones from one or both of the protagonist's identities? If so, who and how?

How will this problem grow until it threatens to destroy one of the protagonist's identities? How will it grow to threaten to destroy both identities? How will it threaten to kill the protagonist and/or loved ones of the protagonist?

At what point does the protagonist confess to loved ones about his or her real or secret/false identity (the one the loved ones don't know about or only know a little about)?

What does the protagonist tell his or her loved ones in this confession? Does he or she tell them the whole truth? If not, what does he or she omit and why?

How do the loved ones react to finding out the truth?

Do the loved ones help the protagonist with his or her crisis going forward, or do they get out of the way, flee to safety, watch from the sidelines?

What does the protagonist do to try to stop the crisis? How and why does he or she fail?

What changes happen that make it possible for the protagonist to win the next time he or she tangles with the big bad guy?

At what point, how, and why is the protagonist's secret/false identity (or real identity) unmasked? How many people find out about it? Who are they? Will they keep the secret after this story ends or not?

What does the climactic fight with the big bad guy look like? What's different about it from the last time these two fought? How does the protagonist win? Does he or she have any help?

What happens to the bad guy? Does he or she live? Flee? Go to jail?

When the protagonist reunites with his or her loved ones at the end of the story, what does life look like for all of them, now that they know the full truth about the protagonist? Is he or she relieved? Worried about how loved ones are going to keep the secret? Or delighted to finally be able to be himself or herself all the time and to stop lying and obfuscating to loved ones?

How do the loved ones feel about knowing both sides of the protagonist now?

TROPE TRAPS

The protagonist doesn't have a compelling reason for having assumed a secret or false identity.

The protagonist's two identities are so similar as to be nearly indistinguishable to your audience and are confusing.

The bad guy in your story doesn't know the protagonist in one of his or her identities, meaning he or she is just some random bad guy who wanders into your story and happens to cause trouble for the protagonist.

The big problem the bad guy causes only ever affects one of the protagonist's identities. There's never any overlap...which is thematically weak and will disappoint your audience.

The protagonist has no friends within the secret/false identity and lives an entire life and never develops any friendships or at least acquaintances?

The protagonist's loved ones in the identity he or she considers to be his or her current real life know everything about the secret/false identity to begin your story, and you give away a huge potential source of stress, tension, and conflict for your story by choosing this.

The big plot problem in your story has no personal stakes for the protagonist—he or she isn't in direct danger nor is a loved one of the protagonist in serious danger.

When the big problem finally explodes into a big crisis, it's so big the protagonist by himself or herself isn't able to stop it, and he or she fails recognize this or fails to call for help from the appropriate people quickly enough, thereby looking stupid, slow, or inattentive.

Nothing changes between the big fight at the end of the middle and the bigger fight to end the story that would help the protagonist win the second time around.

The bad guy's fate at the end of the story isn't commensurate with the bad things he or she did and your audience is dissatisfied.

The protagonist's relationship with loved ones isn't changed in any way by them now knowing everything about both of the protagonist's identities and finally seeing him or her as one integrated, whole person who contains both identities.

SECRET/FALSE IDENTITY TROPE IN ACTION

Movies:

- Face Off
- Donnie Brasco
- V for Vendetta
- Deep Cover
- The Punisher
- The Insider
- White Heat
- Enough

Books:

- The Day of the Jackal by Frederick Forsyth
- You by Caroline Kepnes
- The Cartel by Don Winslow
- Tell No One by Harlan Coben
- The Passenger by Lisa Lutz

- The Choirboys by Joseph Wambaugh
- In the Woods by Tana French
- The Hunter by Richard Stark
- The Repairman Jack by F. Paul Wilson
- The Camel Club by David Baldacci

33

SECRET TWIN/DOPPELGANGER

DEFINITION

Before we jump into this trope, it's worth noting there are dozens of twin tropes—evil twin, separated at birth, twin powers, twins switch places, always identical, and twin telepathy, to name a few. In this trope, however, we're going to focus on only the secret twin. The world doesn't know that a character has a twin, or the character himself/herself doesn't know he or she has a twin.

In the first scenario, the character uses the twin to his or her advantage to be in two places at once. The character may do this to give himself or herself an alibi while one of the twins commits a crime. The secret twin could be produced when the first twin wants to take a break from his or her life for some reason. Having a secret twin allows one of the characters to live a dual life as the other twin holds his or her place in an alternate life as he or she comes and goes from it.

In the second scenario, where the character doesn't know he or she has a twin, the secret twin could be used to steal the character's life, to challenge an inheritance the character has received, to frame a character for a crime the twin committed, or simply to mess with the character's mind (or some other character's mind when they seem the same person in two places so close together as to be impossible).

The protagonist in this story could be either the twin or somebody else altogether, for example, someone who's trying to unravel a mystery, solve a crime, or do something dangerous that requires twins to pull it off. The twins can be the main focus of the story, or they can be the big reveal that explains the events that have been happening in the story...which is to say secret twins can be the main trope of your story, or they can be a secondary trope that explains some strange happening within your story.

The German word, Doppelgänger, means "double walker." Tradition has it that everybody has one and that seeing yours means you'll die soon. Perhaps this is because he or she has come to kill you and take over your life.

It's generally assumed that most people have never met their own doppelganger. Thus, when an exact look-alike either shows up in your life or removes you from your life and takes it over, it's a nasty surprise. In this story, the protagonist is almost always the person who doesn't know he or she has a doppelganger, and then an exact look like enters his or her life to cause havoc.

In a variant on the traditional doppelganger trope, a very rich, very powerful villain creates their own doppelganger using plastic surgery to make an exact look-alike. He or she may want a body double for security reasons, to commit a crime, or for the same reasons people would employ a secret twin to their own advantage. In this variant, the protagonist is almost always the person trying to catch the villain.

So, in both the secret twin and doppelganger tropes, the protagonist has a lookalike whom nobody or a very few people know about and whom he or she uses to solve a mystery, stop a crime, run an espionage or sting operation, go undercover, or do something else creative with being able to be in two places at once to stop evil and save the day.

Or, if the villain is the one with a secret twin or doppelganger, then the protagonist spends the entire story trying to figure out how the bad guy is managing to do the things he or she is and eventually figures out the villain is using a look-alike to pull off his or her evil plans. In this case, the protagonist must stop the villain and stop the secret twin or doppelganger.

ADJACENT TROPES
-- Stolen Identity
-- Impostor In Our Midst
-- Mistaken Identity
-- Split Personality
-- Stealing My Life
-- Shapeshfiter/Skinwalker
-- Cloned/Cloned Goes Bad

WHY READERS/VIEWERS LOVE THIS TROPE
-- how great would it be to let someone else step into our lives for a little while and take over all of our responsibilities and boring duties while we go off and do something fun and exciting or relaxing and exotic for a while

-- we wonder what it would be like to live a completely different life than the one we currently have, to reinvent ourselves into someone radically different than who we are

-- it would be great to have someone just like us who truly understands us

-- we wonder what we would be like if we had grown up in completely different circumstances than the ones we did

OBLIGATORY SCENES
THE BEGINNING:
This story usually needs to begin with introducing the protago-

nist. It's going to be confusing enough already keeping the twins or doppelgangers straight, particularly if your story is told in a visual medium where the two characters look exactly the same. We also don't want to confuse the audience over who the good guy is.

After that, you have the choice of introducing the villain next and giving a first peek into what dastardly thing he or she is planning or of introducing the protagonist to his or her secret twin or doppelganger.

Once both of these introductions have been made, and regardless of whether the protagonist already knew about his or her look-alike, he or she quickly sees an opportunity to use the secret twin or doppelganger to help catch the bad guy or to stop a brewing crisis.

The protagonist recruits the secret twin or doppelganger to help him or her, and the pair commence planning how they're going to work together to save the day.

OR

We meet the protagonist first, just like in the previous version to avoid confusing the heck out of our audience. Then we meet the villain and get a glimpse into his or her evil plans.

In this scenario, you probably won't introduce the secret twin or doppelganger immediately. Instead, you'll probably want to confuse your protagonist and your audience for a while with wondering how on earth the villain is managing to be in two places at once or is pulling off the impossible stunts he or she is.

You can, of course, let your audience in on the secret that there's an exact look-alike of the villain who works for the villain and not let your protagonist in on that secret.

This has the advantage of making your audience feel smart and of not asking them to pretend this explanation doesn't exist, particularly if it's fairly obvious in your story. It has the disadvantage of dissolving the audience's curiosity about how the villain is managing to do the things he or she is doing, and of making the audience think the protagonist isn't very smart because he or she doesn't see the obvious answer that there's a look-alike.

The beginning of this type of story usually ends with the secret twin or doppelganger doing something major—committing a crime or making an important public appearance for the first time while pretending to be the protagonist or villain. The look-alike is almost caught but slips away in the nick of time or recovers from his or her major flub before the protagonist spots him or her or before the bad guys spot him or her.

THE MIDDLE:

The plan to do something bad or to catch someone doing something bad is in full swing in the middle of your story. The protagonist is tracking down the villain, trying to figure out what he or she is up to, and trying to find a way to stop the villain's evil plans and save the day. The secret twin/doppelganger is hard at work helping the protagonist or villain in his or her endeavors.

This is when we see friction develop between the secret twins or doppelgangers. They may begin to resent the other one or feel threatened by the other one. Paranoia may set in—they may worry their look-alike is considering killing them and taking over their life.

Conversely, this may be when the secret twins/doppelgangers compare their upbringings, their different life experiences, and explore the could-have-beens if they'd grown up somewhere else as someone else. They may find commonalities and shared experiences that draw them closer together. They may even trade places in their day-to-day lives for a short time to experience life in the other person's skin.

As the danger increases, it becomes harder and harder to keep the secret of the existence of the secret twin or doppelganger. The look-alikes have to be more careful not to be seen together, and the secret twin/doppelganger is put into higher and higher risk situations where it's ever harder not to slip up and give away that he or she isn't the protagonist or villain whom the look-alike is impersonating.

The secret twin or doppelganger may get sick and tired of taking all the risks for the protagonist or villain and try to back out of their deal or may intentionally flub an appearance or disobey his or her instructions, throwing the protagonist or villain into a crisis.

Just as the relationship between the protagonist or villain and their look-alike is reaching the breaking point, the big arrest or the big crime is set to happen. The protagonist or villain talks the look-alike into doing this one, last thing for him or her, and the secret twin or doppelganger reluctantly agrees.

The crime, the arrest, the assassination, or the culmination of an evil plan finally goes down...

In the scenario of the protagonist's secret twin or doppelganger, he or she messes up. The look-alike is recognized as not being the protagonist, and the whole plan to stop the big bad thing or bad person falls apart.

In the scenario of the villain using a look-alike, the protagonist finally figures out the villain has been using a secret twin or doppelganger all along, but the protagonist figures it out too late and isn't in time to stop the villain from pulling off some or all of his or her evil plan.

BLACK MOMENT:

The protagonist's secret twin or doppelganger is devastated. He or she has let down the protagonist, and something bad has happened that's all the look-alike's fault. The protagonist is also devastated but because he or she put too much pressure or expectation on the look-alike and should have figured out another way to stop the bad guy or just done it by himself or herself. The protagonist believes the failure to stop the bad thing or bad person is all his or her fault.

OR

The protagonist is chagrined and angry with himself or herself for not figuring out sooner that the villain has a look-alike. The protagonist's failure to realize this is why the bad guy has succeeded in doing a terrible thing, and the protagonist blames himself or herself for everything going wrong.

THE END:

The secret twin or doppelganger may be the one to talk the protagonist out of his or her guilt, self-blame, and devastation and convince the protagonist that, if they work together or they execute their plan better this time, they can stop the villain.

Vice versa, it may be the protagonist who gives the secret twin or doppelganger a pep talk to convince him or her that they can stop the villain if they work together.

Working together, they form a plan. Using the lessons they learned from their failure or defeat the last time, their new plan has a better shot at success this time around. Now that the bad guy knows there are two protagonists, they may find a clever way to use this knowledge against the villain.

OR

Now that the protagonist knows the villain has a secret twin or doppelganger, a fact the villain may or may not be aware of, the protagonist can plan differently and strategize to take down both the villain and the villain's look-alike this time.

The protagonist, villain, and secret twin or doppelganger come together for a final, climactic confrontation. This is a traditional final battle with the bad guys arrayed against the good guys in a straight-up, winner-take-all combat of good versus evil. The bad guys are going to pull some nasty tricks, the good guys are going to take some hits, but in the end, the good guys win and the bad guys go down to defeat.

I make that sound casual, but your job is to keep your audience members on the edge of their seats until the very last moment as they frantically race to the end of your story to find out if the good guys win and how they pull it off.

The villain is pretty much guaranteed to get what he or she deserves. It can be a little trickier to know what do to with the secret twin or doppelganger at the end of the story, however.

The protagonist's secret twin or doppelganger may return to his or her old life, or he or she may stick around and get to know the protagonist more. They may become friends, family, or coworkers going forward. The villain's secret twin may get a lesser punishment in the end, which may simply mean he or she lives. It's really up to you to decide what you think is an appropriate ending for this person and what would satisfy your audience.

KEY SCENES

-- if the protagonist or villain doesn't know about the secret twin or doppelganger, he or she glimpses this person and thinks he or she has seen an illusion

-- the look-alikes are in the same room together, and someone else walks in who doesn't know about the secret twin or doppelganger

-- the look-alikes learn something fascinating about each other when they trade places that they use for good or for bad against their look-alike later in the story

-- the look-alikes share an intimate moment together

-- the look-alikes rub each other the wrong way

-- one of the look-alikes mimics something about the other look-alike that really bugs, irritates, or offends the person being imitated.

-- the look-alike makes a huge blunder that puts him or her in serious danger, and the protagonist or villain has to do something fast to save them

. . .

THINGS TO THINK ABOUT WHEN WRITING THIS TROPE

Who has a secret twin or doppelganger in this story, the protagonist or the villain? Does the protagonist know this secret twin or doppelganger exists before your story begins? If not, how do the secret twin/doppelganger and the protagonist or villain first meet?

What's the big problem or plan that the protagonist or villain recruits the secret twin or doppelganger to help him or her with? How will the secret twin or doppelganger be used in this plan?

Why does the secret twin or doppelganger agree to participate in this plan? What's in it for him or her? Is it compelling enough that when things get dangerous, he or she is willing to continue on with the plan and being in danger anyways?

Describe the relationship between the protagonist/villain and his or her look-alike? What's the power dynamic like? Who calls the shots? Do they like or dislike each other? Trust or distrust each other?

How do the protagonist's/villain's upbringing and the secret twin or doppelganger's upbringing differ? How are they the same? How have their differing backgrounds turned them into different people?

In what ways are the protagonist/villain and his or her look-alike the same?

In what ways are the protagonist/villain and his or her look-alike different?

How do these similarities and differences help or hinder the plan the look-alike is helping with?

What preparations does the look-alike make before appearing in public for the first time as the protagonist or villain? How does that appearance go? What slip-ups does the look-alike make and how does he or she cover for them or recover from them?

What do family, friends, coworkers, or the protagonist/villain who know about the look-alike think of him or her?

What are the steps of the evil plan that unfold over the course of your story? Do they increase in risk as the plan progresses? Is the secret twin/doppelganger in ever-increasing danger? What does the protagonist do to discover what the evil plan is and to try to foil the evil plan?

At what point does the protagonist or villain who does NOT have the secret twin or doppelganger find out the other one does have a secret twin or doppelganger? How is this discovery made? What's the protagonist's or villain's reaction to the discovery?

How does the protagonist's plan to stop the bad guy change from the end of the middle of the story to the climactic confrontation? Why does it change?

In the final battle, what happens to harm or hinder the protagonist? Does the bad guy pull any dirty tricks? If so, what?

What turns the tide in the final battle and finally gives the win to the protagonist?

What happens to the bad guy?

When the dust of the final battle has settled, what happens to the secret twin or doppelganger?

If both of the look-alikes are alive at the end of the story, what's their relationship like now? What is it going to look like going forward, and is there a way to show your audience a glimpse of that?

TROPE TRAPS

The look-alike is so identical in every way to the protagonist or villain from the moment he or she shows up in the story as to be totally implausible.

The look-alike has none of his or her own mannerisms, ways of moving or speaking, has the same taste in clothes, music, and food as the protagonist or villain.

The look-alike goes along with whatever the protagonist or villain wants him or her to do, never questioning the right or wrong of it, never questioning the danger, and never having any compelling reason to play along with the protagonist's or villain's plan.

There's never any friction between the protagonist/villain and the look-alike.

The secret twin or doppelganger magically comes to the story with all the specialized skills, training, or knowledge he or she needs to step into a dangerous role and not only play the part but do dangerous things like a pro.

The secret twin or doppelganger never has to practice impersonating the protagonist/villain. He or she is a natural, talented mimic and actor...just like magic!

The protagonist or villain seems stupid or a bit slow for not catching on sooner that the other one has a secret twin or doppelganger.

You let the audience in on the secret of the twin/doppelganger's existence too soon and all the suspense goes out of your story.

The protagonist and villain aren't evenly enough matched. One is a whole lot more powerful, more heavily armed, and has a lot more people and resources than the other one, and your audience doesn't believe there's a plausible way the underdog in this fight has a chance to succeed...and moreover, you fail to show your audience a plausible path to victory for the underdog.

The fights between the protagonist and villain are cliché and predictable.

The secret twin/doppelganger is used in entirely predictable ways that never surprise your audience.

The protagonist or villain comes across as a big coward for putting the secret twin/doppelganger in danger and staying out of danger himself or herself.

The look-alike pair never explores their differing upbringings, differing lives, or what it would have been like to grow up in the other's shoes. It's never explained why one twin was kept secret, or it's not explained how the doppelganger found his or her look-alike, or the protagonist/villain found his or her look-alike.

The look-alike meets a fate he or she doesn't deserve and it upsets your audience.

You never let your audience know what the secret twin or doppelganger does after the final battle.

. . .

SECRET TWIN/DOPPELGANGER TROPE IN ACTION
Movies:

- Dead Ringers
- The Prestige
- Black Swan
- Enemy
- The Double
- Face Off

Books:

- The Thirteenth Tale by Diane Setterfield
- The Scapegoat by Daphne du Maurier
- The Dark Half by Stephen King
- The Third Twin by Ken Follett
- The Double by José Saramago
- The Reversal by Michael Connelly
- Sister by Rosamund Lupton

34

SEEKING VENGEANCE

DEFINITION

The protagonist of this story is a dark one, a grieving person living to get revenge for some heinous wrong done against him or her or against a loved one.

Indeed, the wrong done was terrible enough to deeply traumatize your protagonist and send him or her on an all-consuming journey of seeking vengeance against the wrongdoer.

Your protagonist may embark on this journey because his or her emotional pain is so severe that nothing else will assuage it.

Another motivator for the protagonist personally seeking vengeance is that the wrongdoer was never caught or once caught, managed to evade prosecution or consequences commensurate with his or her crime.

Typically, the protagonist or the protagonist's loved one has been the victim of horrific violence. Often the loved one has been killed by the wrongdoer.

The protagonist may not know initially who committed the crime and if not, his or her first step is to identify his or her target. Next, the protagonist must hunt and find the target. Lastly, the protagonist must take his or her revenge.

NOTE: this revenge may not be pretty. The protagonist has thought long and hard about what he or she wants to do to the wrongdoer and may have come up with something creatively gruesome that he or she believes to be an appropriate punishment for the protagonist.

If the protagonist ends up merely killing the wrongdoer quickly, the protagonist (and probably your audience) will perceive it to be a merciful end for the wrongdoer.

The protagonist may expect to die when this quest ends, and indeed, the protagonist may want to die along with the wrongdoer. This protagonist is in the grip of unrelenting grief so severe it drives him or her to take the most extreme possible action and commit a crime of the same scale as the one his or her target committed.

It's entirely possible to end your story at the moment when the protagonist finally achieves his or her vengeance. But it's also possible your story will continue on and deal with the aftermath of the protagonist's vengeance.

The protagonist may face severe legal consequences for what he or she has done, but this protagonist is usually willing to face whatever consequences may come.

If there's more than one wrongdoer to be hunted down, the protagonist may become a fugitive after the first act of vengeance and continue hunting down additional wrongdoers while also evading the authorities.

Once the vengeance is accomplished, you have a number of choices in how the protagonist responds emotionally. He or she may find that:

- Revenge is sweet.
- Revenge is empty.
- Vengeance doesn't change anything.

- The loved one who has now been avenged wouldn't have approved of what the protagonist did.
- He or she is now no better than the person he or she took vengeance upon.

And of course, the protagonist's act of vengeance could spark a cycle of revenge where loved ones of the original wrongdoer now come after the protagonist to seek their own vengeance for what he or she did.

ADJACENT TROPES

-- Obsessed

-- Mess With My Family and Find Out

-- Stop Vigilante Justice

-- Only One Willing to Solve a Crime

-- Fugitive Hero

-- Vengeful Ghost

WHY READERS/VIEWERS LOVE THIS TROPE

-- for everyone who's ever been wronged, it's likely they've spent at least a moment relishing the idea of getting back at the person who wronged them. This is that moment on steroids

-- if something terrible happened to someone we love, we would feel the same way this protagonist does and we loved imagining being able to do what this protagonist does to the person who wronged us or a loved one

-- our sense of justice being served is satisfied

-- when the system fails us, we can (and should) go outside of it and take matters into our own hands

OBLIGATORY SCENES

THE BEGINNING:

You may start your story showing the crime that launches the protagonist's journey of vengeance, or you may choose to leave this event a mystery initially and instead reveal it in bits and pieces as the story progresses.

If there was a miscarriage of justice that launches your protagonist's quest, you may choose to start the story there.

All that's really necessary, though, is to introduce your audience to a protagonist in profound emotional pain. All of us relate to that immediately and powerfully.

As soon as the protagonist is introduced, you can feel free to launch into his or her quest for vengeance. There's no need for preamble, explanation, or extended backstory. You can catch up your audience on all of that later, once the action of the story is well under way and the audience is fully invested in seeing the protagonist get his or her target.

Occasionally, this story is told in a dual timeline or dual storyline sequence, where one thread follows the protagonist's quest for vengeance in current time and the other thread follows the unfolding of the crime or terrible events that have led to the protagonist's current journey of seeking vengeance.

In this case, the other timeline or story line is also introduced, and we see the set-up of the terrible events to come.

The beginning often ends with the protagonist's first big milestone in his or her quest:

- The protagonist may find out the identity of the wrongdoer.
- The protagonist may find the wrongdoer's whereabouts.
- The protagonist may have a confrontation with officials (law enforcement or government) who tell him or her in no uncertain terms to leave it alone and not to seek vengeance.

. . .

THE MIDDLE:

As it turns out, criminals tend not to take being the target vengeance passively. They tend to fight back. In the middle of this story, the protagonist fully hunts the villain...but the villain commences hunting the protagonist as well.

The protagonist plans in gory detail everything he or she plans to do to the bad guy when he or she catches up with the bad guy.

But the bad guy is doing the exact same thing. While this villain may be motivated by self-preservation, he or she may also be excited at the prospect of doing the same thing or worse to the protagonist that was done to the protagonist's loved one. The combatants are locked together, engaged in a dance of being both hunter and hunted.

Initially, the bad guy may try to get away from the protagonist. But at some point, he or she tires of running and lashes out, turning the tables and actively going on the hunt for the protagonist.

It's also possible government or law enforcement authorities are hunting the protagonist through the middle of the story. The protagonist may be interfering with their own investigation or is breaking the law to pursue the bad guy, and the authorities are out to stop him or her.

In this trope, it's fairly common for the authorities to have cynical and self-serving reasons for trying to prevent the protagonist from pursuing his or her course of revenge. Their reasons are rarely as straightforward as stopping the protagonist from doing something morally grey or morally wrong.

The middle of the story builds to and culminates with a direct confrontation between the protagonist and the bad guy. At last, the protagonist is face-to-face with the person who wronged him or her or wronged the protagonist's loved one.

OR

The protagonist may actually succeed at taking his or her vengeance at the end of Act Two. He or she punishes the bad guy in whatever way he or she has imagined.

The protagonist may or may not kill the bad guy, although in most cases, a protagonist in this much emotional pain is going to kill the wrongdoer before he or she is finished.

Use this version of ending the middle of your story if you plan to spend significant time dealing with the aftermath of the vengeance—in the form of legal consequences for the protagonist or a vengeful response by the associate or loved one of the now damaged or dead wrongdoer.

BLACK MOMENT:

In this overwhelmingly emotional moment of confrontation, the protagonist has underestimated the bad guy, or may have overestimated his or her own skills or his or her own ability to commit violence. The moment to take his or her revenge is finally here, and for some reason, the protagonist fails.

He or she may simply lose the fight with the protagonist. Or the protagonist may find himself or herself captured by the bad guy and subjected to the same thing that happened before to him or her or that happened to the protagonist's loved one.

The bad guy may slip away from the protagonist and flee, leaving the protagonist with no vengeance and back at square one.

OR

If the protagonist achieved his or her revenge at the end of the middle, the protagonist experiences the emotional aftermath of having achieved vengeance.

He or she may realize he or she doesn't know what comes next. The protagonist may be relieved or may be completely empty. He or she may be surprised to still be alive and have no plan for how to proceed with life after this moment.

And someone is coming after him or her, now. It could be government or law enforcement officials, or it could be associate or loved ones of the wrongdoer. In either case, payment has come due for the protagonist's rash decision to pursue personal revenge.

THE END:

If the protagonist failed to kill the wrongdoer at the end of the middle, he or she gathers all of his or her remaining energy, will, and resources to make one last try to take revenge upon the bad guy. Using the power of his or her emotions, the protagonist finally defeats the protagonist and usually kills him or her.

OR

If the protagonist has fallen victim to the wrongdoer, he or she finds a way to break free. But, instead of running, he or she lies in wait, or goes hunting one last time, for the bad guy to kill him or her.

OR

If the protagonist is on the run from the authorities or vengeful friend of the wrongdoer's, the protagonist stops fleeing, turns, stands, and fights. The protagonist may engineer this final confrontation to suit him or her, or he or she may be cornered and forced into the confrontation.

In a climactic battle, the protagonist faces those who would now take retribution against him or her. If he or she faces the associate or loved one of the bad guy, the protagonist may kill this person outright.

OR

The protagonist may defeat the associate/loved one, but this time he or she shows mercy. After all, the protagonist *was* this person only a short time ago.

It's up to you whether the authorities lose the fight and the protagonist gets away, or the authorities kill the protagonist, capture him or her and bring the protagonist in to face justice, or they ultimately decide to let him or her go.

It's not an unreasonable ending either way if the protagonist lives or dies at the end of his or her journey of vengeance.

If your protagonist lives, no matter how you ended the plot of your story, this person is going to face an emotional reckoning, which you may or may not choose to hint at or show your audience a glimpse of at the end of your story.

KEY SCENES

-- the crime the protagonist is reacting to is revealed to your audience. This may happen in direct description or in backstory

-- a loved one, friend, or colleague of the protagonist tries to talk him or her out of this determination to seek vengeance

-- an official person—a government agent, law enforcement official, or lawyer—tries to convince or threaten the protagonist into not pursuing or continuing his or her course of vengeance

-- the protagonist questions his or her course of action

-- the protagonist comes face-to-face with the wrongdoer for the first time

-- the protagonist tells the wrongdoer what he or she has been waiting to say to him or her—a good guy monologue, as it were

-- the protagonist treads close to the line of acting like a bad guy but stops short of doing something your audience would perceive as evil

-- the bad guy gets exactly what he or she deserves

. . .

THINGS TO THINK ABOUT WHEN WRITING THIS TROPE

What act is your protagonist seeking vengeance for? Who did it happen to? Is that person alive or dead?

Is the thing that happened terrible or traumatic enough to justify your protagonist's self-destructive obsession with seeking vengeance?

What skills does your protagonist have to use to track down and deliver vengeance to the wrongdoer? Did he or she already have these skills or has he or she had to develop them recently as part of seeking vengeance?

How will you introduce your character to your audience? Is this opening guaranteed to make your audience sympathize with the protagonist? Will they like and relate strongly enough to him or her to root for him or her even as he or she pursues doing something terrible?

How will you reveal to your audience the details of what happened? In what order will you reveal the various details? How will you make each new piece of information more shocking than the last?

Who did the terrible thing, which is to say, who's the target of your protagonist's wish for vengeance?

Why did the bad guy do what he or she did? Did he or she have a good reason in his or her own mind for doing it? If so, what was that reason?

Did this bad guy ever get caught? If not, how did he or she get away? If so, why isn't he or she in jail or dead now?

Are the authorities still seeking the bad guy? If not, why not? If so, why isn't the protagonist willing to leave the manhunt to them? Who are these authorities? What agency do they work for, and who are the specific characters that represent the agency?

What do the authorities think of the protagonist's plan to seek vengeance? What do they say to the protagonist about it? How does the protagonist react?

Who else tries to talk the protagonist out of going on his or her journey of vengeance?

Where is the bad guy now? What's he or she doing these days?

How will the protagonist find the bad guy?

How will the bad guy find out the protagonist is coming for him or her? What does the bad guy do in response?

Does the bad guy initially try to flee from the protagonist, or does the bad guy immediately confront the protagonist?

How do they hunt each other? Who does what? What are the mechanics of their near misses and near confrontations?

Is anyone from the government or law enforcement chasing the protagonist to stop him or her? If so, who? How is the protagonist evading this person? How does this person complicate the protagonist's hunt for the wrongdoer?

How does the protagonist feel over the course of this hunt? How will you show your audience the protagonist's state of mind?

How do the interactions between the protagonist and wrongdoer grow in danger, suspense, and intensity as your story progresses?

At what point does the wrongdoer start hunting the protagonist? What does that look like?

Does the protagonist hope to live or hope to die when he or she finally gets vengeance?

What happens in the big confrontation at the end of Act Two? Who wins? Who loses? Who lives or dies?

How does the protagonist feel after this confrontation?

Who participates in the final, climactic fight of your story? How do they get to that place and that moment? Who lives and dies in this fight?

After the wrongdoer is captured, damaged, or killed, does anyone who cares about him or her come after the protagonist? If so, who? How?

If your protagonist lives, how does he or she feel afterward? What happens to him or her? Does he or she get to return home or not? How does he or she plan to go on with his or her life, now?

What's the emotional aftermath for the protagonist of getting vengeance? How does he or she feel? Did he or she expect to feel this way?

Will you show your audience the protagonist's life going forward at the very end of your story or not? If so, what glimpse of his or her life will you show your audience?

TROPE TRAPS

The protagonist isn't skilled enough to take off with the intent to hunt down and harm or kill a dangerous criminal and your audience doesn't buy the entire premise of your story.

The bad thing that happened isn't traumatic enough to justify the protagonist's extreme reaction.

Your portrayal of the bad thing that happened is so graphic your audience walks away and doesn't finish your story.

The people who try to talk the protagonist out of pursuing vengeance have really compelling reasons for him or her not to do it... and the protagonist ignores them, making him or her seem selfish, stubborn, or stupid.

The protagonist never gives the authorities a chance to catch the wrongdoer and administer justice, and he or she comes across like an overzealous, trigger-happy vigilante.

The wrongdoer had a decent justification for doing the thing he or she did to the protagonist or to the protagonist's loved one—and your audience thinks the protagonist is in the wrong for seeking vengeance.

The protagonist never questions his or her course of action and never has any doubts, which makes him or her seem inhuman and unrelatable.

The bad guy could easily evade the protagonist but doesn't do so, and seems dumb or implausible.

If government or law enforcement officials chase the protagonist, he or she has an implausibly easy time evading them, and furthermore, this pursuit doesn't impact the protagonist's own hunt enough to be believable.

The protagonist is so vicious in his or her single-minded hunt that your audience is put off by him or her.

What the protagonist does to the bad guy is way worse than what the bad guy ever did, and your audience is upset by it and dislikes your protagonist.

The protagonist never has any sort of emotional reaction to having just done something violent and awful to someone else.

The protagonist never has any sort of emotional letdown or reaction after finally getting the vengeance that has driven his or her every action for the whole story.

The wrongdoer doesn't suffer consequences severe enough to be commensurate with what he or she did.

The protagonist doesn't suffer the consequences he or she should for what he or she did.

SEEKING VENGEANCE TROPE IN ACTION

Movies:

- John Wick
- Oldboy
- Kill Bill: Vol. 1
- Memento
- Taken
- Law Abiding Citizen
- I Saw the Devil
- Death Wish
- The Revenant
- The Brave One

. . .

Books:

- Gone Girl by Gillian Flynn
- The Girl with the Dragon Tattoo by Stieg Larsson
- First Blood by David Morrell
- Eye for an Eye by Jeffrey Archer
- The Executioner series by Don Pendleton
- The Punisher: Year One by Dan Abnett

35

STOLEN IDENTITY

DEFINITION

This is perhaps one of the most universally relatable tropes in the thriller genre because everyday people are all subject to suffering some form of identity theft in their lifetime. While most thriller tropes deal with high concept crimes and save the world heroics performed by nearly superhuman characters, this crime is suffered by millions of people from every walk of society, every year.

Additionally, our identity is deeply personal. It's something we build with intent and take care of assiduously. It feels like an immense violation to have a stranger break into our life and steal our money, job, friends, identity, or even our name.

Traditional identity theft occurs when a criminal steal a victim's personal information to commit criminal acts. Using this stolen information, a criminal takes over the victim's identity and conducts a range of fraudulent activities in their name.

Whereas the Impostor In Our Midst trope describes someone who physically impersonates the protagonist, in this trope the villain electronically or remotely impersonates the protagonist, stealing the physically intangible aspects of the protagonist's life.

The identity theft may be confined to credit card fraud or

emptying the protagonist's bank account, or it may be bigger than that. The bad guy may impersonate the protagonist with the intent to take over their entire online life, perhaps stealing work contracts, clients, credit ratings, resumés, or hijacking social interactions, for example.

In some ways, technology makes stealing identities much easier, but technology can also make discovering attempts to steal one's identity much easier.

In this story, someone tries to steal the protagonist's identity and partially or completely succeeds. The authorities are unable to reverse the damage or are being very slow in reversing the damage, and the protagonist tires of waiting for them. Instead, the protagonist embarks on a journey of finding and catching the identity thief and stopping or punishing this person.

While this is generally not a violent story arc in and of itself, it certainly can become violent if conflict between the protagonist and the identity thief escalates sufficiently.

In the end, the protagonist recovers his or her identity and puts his or her own life back together once more.

ADJACENT TROPES
-- Impostor In Our Midst
-- Stealing My Life
-- Amateur Sleuth
-- Civilian Becomes Spy
-- Clear My Name
-- Stranger With No Identity

WHY READERS/VIEWERS LOVE THIS TROPE
-- many of your audience members have experience identity theft to at least some degree and will relate strongly with a protagonist who goes after the person who stole his or hers. We've all had that impulse

-- we hate feeling powerless against this type of crime and love the idea of being able to strike back against those who do it

-- this type of crime feels intensely personal and we all fear being stripped of our identity or of having all our secrets exposed in this way

-- the little guy gets to hit back against the big bad guy

OBLIGATORY SCENES
THE BEGINNING:

The protagonist's first indication that someone has stolen a piece of their identity is often an email notification, a phone call, or standing at our bank and realizing someone has emptied our account. It's a sickening moment that most of your audience members will relate to strongly from personal experience.

The protagonist initially tries to go through official channels to deal with the identity theft, but gets nowhere, or the official response is painfully slow.

Your protagonist may have a compelling reason for needing the problem sorted out quickly, and the slowness of the response is unacceptable to him or her, hence he or she takes action personally to fix the problem. Or your protagonist is so offended by the stolen identity that he or she decides to take action to remedy the situation himself or herself. It's possible that the information stolen from the protagonist is embarrassing, deeply private, or confidential for some reason... and the protagonist feels an urgent need to recover the information personally. Indeed, in this case, the protagonist may not go to the authorities at all for help.

If the protagonist turns to a hacker or computer expert for help, we meet that person in the beginning of the story, and he or she begins helping the protagonist track down the bad guy.

It's not uncommon that this trope leads into a bigger crime or conspiracy that constitutes a second full trope within your story. If this is the case, the beginning usually ends with the first big clue as to what that larger crime or evil plan is.

The beginning often ends with the authorities failing to catch the bad guy or being unable to reverse the damage caused by the identity theft, which forces the protagonist to proceed with fixing the problem for himself or herself.

THE MIDDLE:

This is where the protagonist and anyone who is helping him or her tracks the bad guy. They learn the identity of the bad guy, where to find the bad guy, and may commence some sort of plan to take back whatever was stolen from the protagonist.

It's possible the bad guy stole something very private or very consequential to the protagonist which, if not recovered, will have big negative consequences that reach well beyond the protagonist. If this is the case, as the clock ticks and the stolen information continues not to be recovered, the risks from potential exposure climb exponentially.

If the protagonist happens to be a computer expert or is working with one, he or she may attempt to steal back the protagonist's money, get back a confidential file or document that was stolen, and he or she may decide to get a little payback while he or she is at it and steal something of the bad guy's.

If the identity theft in this story leads to a larger crime, the middle is where the protagonist discovers this and finds himself or herself mired in something much more dangerous than he or she anticipated.

The protagonist's stolen identity may be used in the commission of a larger crime, and the middle of this story is where that usually happens. Indeed, this is a frequent midpoint reversal. The protagonist spends the first half of this story tracking down the identity thief, a large crime is committed in the protagonist's name, and the last half of the story is spent with the protagonist running from people trying to catch him or her for the crime he or she allegedly committed, or the last half of the story is spent with the protagonist scrambling to clear his or her name.

The middle of the story culminates with the protagonist confronting the bad guy directly for the first time, or with the protagonist confronting the people chasing him or her directly for the first time. If there's a larger crime or evil plot unfolding in your story, the end of the middle is the protagonist's best chance to stop it before it happens. He or she makes a run at stopping the bad guy but fails.

BLACK MOMENT:

The protagonist has failed to catch or even just to stop the bad guy. The protagonist's name is not cleared. Indeed, he or she is in even worse trouble and in a bigger mess now than before when he or she set out to regain his or her stolen identity. He or she has no means of stopping the larger crime or evil plot, and the protagonist has no path forward for regaining what was stolen from his or her.

If something sensitive was stolen from the protagonist that really needed not to become public, it does so now.

If the protagonist was framed for a crime, he or she is apprehended by the authorities. Now that he or she is in custody, he or she has no chance to recover his or her stolen identity and prove he or she is innocent of whatever he or she has been accused of.

In every way the protagonist can possibly fail, he or she has done so.

The protagonist's reputation is in ruins, and potentially his or her career, family, and life are also in ruins. Other people have now been harmed as well as a result of the protagonist's rash behavior in coming after the identity thief or as a result of failing to recover his or her stolen identity.

THE END:

If the bad guy got away in the black moment, the protagonist gets a clue that leads him or her to the location of the bad guy. The protagonist has one last chance to get back what was taken from him or her. He or she races to confront the bad guy.

If a larger crime or evil plot is about to happen, the protagonist learns something about it that gives him or her one last chance to stop it from happening. He or she may find out when and where it's going to happen, may find a clue online that leads him or her to the bad guy, or something else that puts the protagonist in a position to stop disaster. The protagonist races to confront the bad guy and stop the evil plot.

If the protagonist has been framed for a crime he or she did not commit and has been arrested, he or she is released on bail and can race after the bad guy. Or someone official finds evidence that the protagonist is telling the truth and was framed and the protagonist is released, allowing him or her to race to confront the bad guy.

Regardless of the path taken to the end, this story climaxes with the protagonist directly confronting the bad guy. This may not be a lethal fight given the relatively non-lethal nature of the crimes that set up this confrontation.

But, if a larger crime or evil plot is launching, then this ending might turn into a large-scale shootout with plenty of blood and violence.

The protagonist stops the bad guy in the nick of time before the larger crime or evil plot can harm a bunch of other people. By defeating the bad guy, the protagonist now can also force the bad guy to admit he or she framed the protagonist, force the bad guy to give back what was stolen, and the protagonist's reputation can be restored.

While not all the damage of the identity theft may be reversible, enough of it is that the protagonist can resume his or her life. He or she may be poorer and wiser, and now know how important it is to protect one's important personal information, but at least the protagonist has his or her reputation back and can rebuild a new, safer life.

It's not uncommon for the protagonist or his computer expert-ally to have secretly hacked the bad guy and stolen a bunch of money in the chaos of the climax of the story. If this is the case, it's typically not revealed until the police are gone, the dust has settled, and the protagonist is finally alone or alone with the computer expert friend. Only then is it revealed to the audience what they've done. It's a nifty little bit of revenge that gives the protagonist the wherewithal to not only replace his or her old life but to build a new and better one.

KEY SCENES

-- the protagonist realizes the identity theft is even worse than he or she first realized

-- your audience finds out why the protagonist can't wait for the authorities to deal with the identity theft or can't go to the authorities at all and must handle it himself or herself

-- the protagonist discovers what else the bad guy is up to and how the bad guy is using the protagonist's stolen identity

-- the protagonist is accused of doing something he or she didn't do but all the evidence is actually his or hers

-- the protagonist almost catches the bad guy, but the bad guy slips away at the last moment

-- the larger, worse consequences of whatever the bad guy took from the protagonist happen

-- somebody finally listens to the protagonist and realizes he or she isn't guilty or that the bad guy really is up to something bigger and more dangerous

THINGS TO THINK ABOUT WHEN WRITING THIS TROPE

What is stolen from your protagonist? Money, files, photos, a computer program, clients, a social media profile, something else?

How is what was stole from your protagonist damaging to him or her? How is it damaging to someone else? Can you make the damage worse? Much worse? Catastrophic?

Who stole the identity or information from the protagonist? Why? Was it random or targeted?

How much of the protagonist's identity was stolen? Was it just credit card numbers? Just some work files or just a social media profile? Or was it a lot more? All of it?

Did the protagonist make a mistake that allowed the identity to be stolen?

What about the information that was stolen is the protagonist frantic to recover? Why? Can you make the consequences of not recovering it worse? Much worse?

Does the protagonist go to the authorities or not? If not, why not?

What do the authorities do or not do to help recover the stolen identity? Why isn't what they're doing fast enough or thorough enough?

What compelling reason does the protagonist have for taking this investigation into his or her own hands?

Who tries to talk the protagonist out of going after the identity thief on his or her own? Why doesn't the protagonist listen?

How does the protagonist proceed with the investigation?

Does the protagonist have any computer expertise or other expertise useful to this mission of his or hers?

Does the protagonist get help with his or her investigation? If so, from whom? What expertise does this person bring to the hunt?

What's the bad guy really up to? How is the identity theft part of something bigger?

How will the protagonist uncover this larger crime or evil plot?

How does this story take a dangerous turn? Is the bad guy more than just an identity thief? Is the bad guy up to something worse? Much worse?

Does the bad guy commit some other crime using the protagonist's stolen identity? If so, what crime? How?

Do the authorities come after the bad guy for this crime? Does the protagonist run or try to convince the authorities he or she didn't do the crime?

How does the protagonist catch up with the bad guy?

What does a confrontation with the bad guy look like?

How does the protagonist finally convince the authorities that he or she was the victim of a crime and isn't a bad guy, personally?

What does the protagonist learn that allows him or her to catch up with the bad guy for a climactic confrontation and ultimately for the protagonist to win that fight?

Is it a cyber confrontation or a physical one?

How violent is the bad guy and how violent does the confrontation with the bad guy become?

What happens to the bad guy after the protagonist defeats him or her?

Does the protagonist get back whatever was taken from him or her?

Does the protagonist take something extra from the bad guy while he or she is at it by way of compensation? If so, what is it? How valuable is it?

TROPE TRAPS

The protagonist seems excessively vengeful after experiencing a crime many of us are victims of.

The protagonist has no particular expertise that would allow him or her to find and capture the bad guy, and it makes no sense for him or her to personally go after the bad guy.

The bad guy stole something readily replaceable, like a social media profile or a client list, but the protagonist is acting as if the nuclear codes were stolen.

There's no compelling reason for the protagonist not to go to the authorities or for the protagonist not to just wait for the authorities to investigate and catch the bad guy.

The protagonist suddenly turns into a super hacker.

The protagonist suddenly turns into a skilled tracker and surveillance expert.

The bad guy isn't bad enough to be scary to your audience.

The bad guy isn't doing any larger crime and is boring when the protagonist finally catches up with him or her.

The protagonist is never put in any personal danger and your story bores your audience.

The authorities flatly refuse to consider that your protagonist might be telling the truth and come across as unreasonable and unrealistic. Conversely, the authorities accept the protagonist's story far too easily when all the evidence points at him or her having committed a crime.

The climactic confrontation doesn't have anything super suspenseful riding on its outcome, and there's no sense of a ticking bomb about to go off to add tension.

The climactic confrontation is non-violent, but you fail to replace the action and excitement of violence with something else equally exciting to your audience.

What happens to the bad guy at the end doesn't seem appropriate in comparison to his or her actions and it ticks off your audience.

The protagonist suffers no ill effects whatsoever from having had his or her identity stolen.

The protagonist suffers no ill effects whatsoever from running off to chase the bad guy after explicitly being told not to by the authorities.

STOLEN IDENTITY TROPE IN ACTION
Movies:

- The Net
- Untraceable
- Open Windows

- Black Hat
- Disconnect
- Who Am I
- Cam

Books:

- Takedown by Brad Thor
- The Net by Irwin Winkler
- Identity Crisis by Debbi Mack
- The Outsider by Stephen King
- Hacked by Ray Daniel
- You Are Not You by Michelle Davidson Argyle

36

TICKING BOMB/TICKING CLOCK

DEFINITION

Many, many tropes rely on a ticking clock to add tension to the story. A person who is buried alive is running out of air. A kidnapped victim is running out of time before the kidnapper kills him or her. A rescue mission must reach a prisoner before he or she dies from torture. In these, the ticking clock is a plot element to add tension, but not the core of the story itself.

In the Ticking Bomb or Ticking Clock trope, the deadline itself is the problem. Given enough time, the protagonist could carefully, and methodically find the bad guy, track down where the bad guy has put the bomb, and disarm it. But in this story, the protagonist is thrown into a frantic race against time. He or she must do everything at a breakneck pace to figure out the details of what's about to happen, figure out how to stop it, and then get there in time to stop the very bad thing from happening.

This is a classic thriller trope where the protagonist is told or finds out for himself or herself that something bad is going to happen. He or she races to find the bad guys and to find the literal or metaphorical bomb. Then, at the last possible moment before cata-strophe, the protagonist manages to stop the bomb from exploding with only seconds to spare.

The bomb usually includes blinking lights and countdown timers so the audience can sweat right along with the protagonist as he or she races to uncover the red wire or the blue wire and decide which one to snip.

SIDE NOTE: In reality, very few bombs ever display an actual timer on their face. And in today's technological world, most bombs are built without timers at all. Instead they rely on some sort of remote detonator or detonate via a cell phone. However, the timer and blinking lights are effective visual ways to increase audience stress.

At any rate, this core of this story is a race against time to stop something very bad from happening.

The protagonist is pretty much always an expert at finding bad guys or at defusing bombs. It's more common to have the bad guy find the bomb but then have to talk to a bomb expert by phone or some other remote means—again, to increase the drama for the audience.

The "bomb" may be a literal bomb, or it may be something else catastrophic—a release of poison gas, a guillotine will drop on a char-acter's neck—the possibilities are endless.

Likewise, the protagonist may not have to stop a literal timer on a literal weapon. He or she could have to solve a puzzle, open a lock, solve a mystery, or find someone before something terrible happens. But in every case, the protagonist and the audience are acutely aware that there's a finite amount of time to solve a problem before some-thing bad happens and the seconds are slipping away.

The protagonist had better get there in time, or else...

ADJACENT TROPES
-- Buried Alive
-- Locked Room

-- Dying One by One
-- Race to Find Evidence Before Trial
-- Natural Disaster Threatens
-- Stop Weapon of Mass Destruction
-- Crash Imminent
-- Crime that Repeats
-- Future Crime Predicted

WHY READERS/VIEWERS LOVE THIS TROPE

-- there's a special kind of tension in watching a clock tick down to zero. We all do it during sporting events, even on New Year's Eve, and are familiar with the excitement and suspense of those last few seconds ticking off the clock

-- we need to believe that if a disaster is looming, someone who knows what to do will get there in time and stop it from happening

-- we love to imagine ourselves being heroic and saving the day and we live vicariously through the hero/heroine of this story

OBLIGATORY SCENES
THE BEGINNING:

Somebody finds out that something bad is being planned. It may be an intelligence report someone receives, it may be a tip from someone, or it may be the protagonist himself or herself who discovers that something very bad is about to happen.

If someone else learns of this brewing crisis, the protagonist is an expert who is called in, briefed on the situation, and tasked with finding the bad guy, figuring what the bad guy is up to, and stopping it.

The protagonist may or may not know initially that there's a ticking clock on stopping the literal or metaphorical bomb. The act of him or her poking around and alarming the bad guy may be what gets the countdown clock started in the first place. Or it may be later in the story that the bad guy sets the actual deadline.

The bad guy may set a deadline based on the protagonist having to do something by a certain time or else something bad will happen. Conversely, the deadline may have nothing at all to do with the protagonist, and it's simply up to the protagonist to get there before the bad thing happens and stop it.

The starting of the countdown clock is often the crisis that ends the beginning of this type of story. Now we know the stakes, and we know how much time the protagonist has to stop it. The race is on...

THE MIDDLE:

The entire middle of this story is a frantic race to find the bad guy, learn what he or she is doing specifically, find where the bad guy's doing it, and get there in time to stop the big bad thing from happening.

For his or her part, the bad guy is throwing up roadblocks and obstacles to slow down the protagonist, each one more frustrating than the last as it costs the protagonist precious time to deal with it, go around it, solve it, or recognize it for the distraction that it is.

In addition, the bad guy may be racing against the protagonist as the bad guy tries to finish preparing his or her evil plot and launching it. It's not uncommon to show your audience vignettes of the bad guy rushing to finish his or her plans as a way of further increasing your audience's tension.

The middle of the story ends with some sort of deadline that the protagonist must meet or else something bad is going to happen that's part of the larger bad thing but not the ultimate "explosion" of the bomb. For example, a prisoner's fresh oxygen supply will run out if the protagonist doesn't turn over a ransom by a certain time. The prisoner won't die yet, but the final countdown will begin. Another example is the bomb will be armed if the protagonist can't get to the airport in time to stop the bomb designer from getting on a plane and flying to where the bomb has been assembled to finish arming it.

BLACK MOMENT:

The protagonist hurries for all he or she is worth but doesn't quite make it in time to meet the deadline and stop the bad thing from happening. Now, a chain of events has been set in motion that accelerates with every passing moment, and which the protagonist may not get another chance to interrupt.

He or she has failed to stop the clock. By not stopping it, the countdown will now continue and run out, and the very bad thing will happen as soon as the clock reaches zero.

An innocent person or a whole lot of innocent people are going to be harmed or die, now, and it's all the protagonist's fault.

The black moment may be the one moment in the entire story when the protagonist slows down for even a second. In this moment, he or she believes that there's nothing more he or she can do to stop the bomb from exploding; hence, there's nothing more to be done, no more deadline to race to meet.

In this moment of stillness, the importance of what he or she has failed to do is crushing.

THE END:

Some new information comes in, some hint, that sends the protagonist tearing off into a renewed race against the clock. And this time, there's very, very little time left and no time to spare. The protagonist must work at hyper speed to get to the bomb, fight through the bad guys standing between him or her and the bomb, and diffuse the bomb before it blows.

It's in this portion of the story that we get lots of glimpses of how much time is left, how fast it's ticking off the clock, and how many bad guys the protagonist still has to fight through.

Your audience is on the edge of its seats, breathless with panic, terrified the protagonist isn't going to get there in time. The red timer counts down, the lights blink ominously, and we have to wait till the very last second to find out if the protagonist stops the bomb from exploding or not.

SPOILER ALERT: In almost every situation, the protagonist does manage to screech under the wire and stop the bomb with a second or two to spare. Now and then, the protagonist only has time to push the bomb out of the plane or take it to some contained area where it can explode, but in a safe place where nobody gets hurts.

The protagonist often returns home to a hero's welcome and is congratulated for saving the day while your audience's heart rates slowly come back down to normal.

KEY SCENES

-- the protagonist finds what the exact nature of bad thing is going to happen if he or she fails and who's going to be hurt by it

-- the public finds out about the ticking bomb and panics

-- the stakes for the protagonist become personal in stopping the very bad thing

-- the protagonist has to make a terrible choice between protecting his or her loved ones or continuing to try to find and to stop the bomb

-- it looks as if the protagonist isn't going to have enough time to get to the bomb, but then something changes or the protagonist comes up with a solution that means he or she might make it in time, after all

THINGS TO THINK ABOUT WHEN WRITING THIS TROPE

What's the ticking bomb going to be in your story? Plot backward from that to what your bad guy does to start this story that catches the attention of the authorities or of the protagonist.

Who's the protagonist? Who does he or she work for? What's his or her expertise to handle this crisis? Why him or her and not someone else? Is he or she the first choice for this job or not? If not, why not?

What is the protagonist initially told about the problem? Is any information withheld from him or her? If so, what? Why? Who withholds it?

Who's in direct danger from the bad guy to begin with? How about by the end of the story?

Does the protagonist have any help? If so, who? What's their expertise? What kind of support team and resources does the protagonist have?

What does the protagonist do to go hunting for the bad guy?

At what point does the bad guy realize the protagonist is coming for him or her?

At what point does the protagonist realize there's a deadline on this search and destroy mission? Is that briefed up front or not?

Is there more than one deadline in the story? Does the protagonist meet all of them, or does he or she miss one or more of them? What's the consequence of missing a deadline?

How does the protagonist find the bad guy?

How does the protagonist figure out what the bad guy's ultimate plan is?

How does the protagonist find the bomb itself?

What does the bad guy do to slow down, hinder, or interfere with the protagonist's race?

Is the bad guy monitoring the protagonist's race against the clock? Is the bad guy enjoying it?

What new information does the protagonist learn over the course of the story that changes what he or she thinks the bad guy is planning to do, or that is shocking or a big twist?

What happens in the story—specifically, what does the protagonist mess up, do, or not do that causes the final countdown clock to be initiated?

What will happen when the final countdown reaches zero? Can you make it worse? Much worse?

What does the protagonist have to do to stop the final countdown? Does he or she have to accomplish some task or does he or she have to physically reach the bomb and stop the timer?

What is the ultimate "bomb"?

Who will be harmed or killed by it? Can you make that worse? Much worse?

How do the stakes for stopping the bomb become personal to the protagonist? How do these stakes interfere with his or her ability to do the mission?

Why does the protagonist fail to stop the final countdown from being initiated? What task did he or she fail to do or deadline did he or she fail to meet?

What does the final fight between the protagonist and the bad guy look like?

What happens in this fight that makes the audience certain the protagonist isn't going to get to the bomb in time to stop it? How does the protagonist ultimately get past this obstacle?

How does the protagonist disarm the bomb or make it detonate someplace harmless?

What happens to the bad guy? Does the protagonist kill him or her on the way to the bomb, does the protagonist do that afterward, or does something else happen to the bad guy? Is it appropriate to his or her crime?

What does the protagonist's reunion with loved ones look like after the crisis is over?

TROPE TRAPS

The protagonist is so badass initially that your audience fails to buy him or her failing along the way in this story.

The bad guy isn't bad enough to keep your audience worried.

The authorities and/or protagonist know the whole bad guy plan up front and there are no shocking twists or new revelations along the way in this story.

If there's a hostage or victim involved from the beginning, he or she makes no effort to escape, help his or her own situation, or foil the bad guy but is merely a passive, weak, cardboard character.

The protagonist never does anything to make the situation worse or speed up the clock and is too perfect to be relatable.

It seems so obvious or certain that the protagonist is going to get to the bomb in time to stop it.

The "bomb"—the very bad thing that's going to happen—isn't creative, interesting, original, or scary.

The bad guy isn't smart enough to anticipate what the protagonist is going to do and take countermeasures.

The bad guy fails to defend the approaches to his or her lair and to the bomb, itself.

The protagonist never misses a deadline along the way.

The protagonist is never distracted by or worried about loved ones who are in danger.

The authorities don't take appropriate measures to evacuate civilians around the bomb like any reasonable officials would.

The protagonist, who has no training in disarming bombs, magically is able to disarm a complex bomb simply because someone gives him or her some instructions over the phone.

The actual bomb expert can tell, without ever seeing the bomb, exactly how to disarm it.

There's two seconds left on the timer when it stops. It's always two seconds. Try stopping with one second, or three maybe.

TICKING BOMB/TICKING CLOCK TROPE IN ACTION
Movies:

• Speed

- The Dark Knight
- Mission Impossible
- The Rock
- Source Code
- Blown Away
- Armageddon
- Olympus Has Fallen

Books:

- The Andromeda Strain by Michael Crichton
- Rogue Lawyer by John Grisham
- The Cobra Event by Richard Preston
- Pandemic by Robin Cook
- The Last Minute by Jeff Abbott
- 24 Hours by Greg Iles
- 3 Minutes by Anders Roslund and Börge Hellström

37

UNRELIABLE NARRATOR/DECEPTIVE PROTAGONIST

DEFINITION

As fun a trope as this is, it's been used so heavily in recent years that readers and viewers go into most stories these days with a healthy dose of skepticism about the motives of the protagonist and automatically distrusting him or her initially.

That being the case, it's your job to convince your audience that the protagonist in this story is absolutely honest, trustworthy, and morally upright well before you reveal that he or she may not be as honest as he or she seems.

This trope is almost always paired with another trope that shapes the plot and main action of the story. The narrator faithfully retells the events of the story in his or her point of view and gives the audience no reason whatsoever to mistrust him or her.

But then, later in the story, it's common to switch points of view and retell the same story, making it clear that the first narrator's telling of the story isn't accurate or that it has been spun heavily in the first narrator's favor.

It's also common to have the narrator's point of view gradually shift or devolve as the narrator leads the audience down the gently sloping path of his or her decline into villainy.

It's also common for the plot itself to shift. The narrator's point of view never changes, but we realize at some point in the story that the narrator is actually preparing to do something heinously evil and we've been going along with him or her, cheering for the narrator to complete the tasks without ever realizing his or her tasks are setting up an evil plot that will harm innocents.

You may choose to stick with the narrator all the way through your story, even through the climactic battle where the real protagonists of your story attempt to defeat your narrator, who we all know now to be the villain.

Or you may choose to switch into the protagonist's point of view to tell the end of the story and the climactic conflict between good and evil, in which your first narrator is captured, harmed or killed.

One way to handle a point of view swap is to do steady point of view shifts all the way through your novel. Swapping back and forth from the narrator to a supposed villain, and then having them swap roles over the course of your story is an effective way to disguise the unreliability of your narrator but still give your audience someone to root for. It's just that who the audience roots for changes somewhere along the way in your story.

ADJACENT TROPES

-- Descent Into Madness
-- Gaslighting/Am I Losing My Mind?
-- The Lie
-- Client is Lying About Everything
-- Can Defector Be Trusted?
-- Can Trust Anyone
-- Loved One Controlled by Alien
-- Loved One Possessed

WHY READERS/VIEWERS LOVE THIS TROPE

-- readers enjoy getting a peek inside the head of a complex, nuanced, or twisted mind

-- a story like this forces readers to really engage in the story, pay attention, and get sucked all the way into it as they form their own opinions about who's telling the truth and what's really going on

-- we're fascinated by questions of the nature of truth, the nature of perception, and the nature of perspective

-- we're cynical and don't believe anyone tells the truth all the time—this story reinforces that perception as truth

-- by questioning and ultimately judging the narrator, your audience feels more powerful, smarter, and perceptive than the characters and may enjoy having a sense of control over the story that he or she wouldn't otherwise have

OBLIGATORY SCENES
THE BEGINNING:

Keeping in mind that this trope is almost always paired with another trope to provide the core plot structure, we typically see the story begin with the movement and action required by that other trope.

What we do see of this trope in the beginning, however, is the narrator and his or her voice. It's critical in the beginning of the story to establish your narrator as likable, empathetic, and trustworthy. Give your audience no reason at all initially to distrust this person.

It's common that this character makes lots of value judgments and critical observations of other characters that color the audience's initial opinions of all the other people in the story. The narrator needs to be subtle in expressing his or her opinions and efforts to color the audience's opinion of others in the story, however, or your audience will immediately suspect an unreliable narrator.

If you slip in the narrator's manipulations in and among the more interesting, exciting, or captivating elements of the action trope in your story, it's fully possible for your audience not to realize at all what your narrator is doing.

If you're going to use multiple points of view throughout your story, you'll introduce the other point of view character(s) and let us get to know this person as well. Don't do this so early that you confuse your audience as to who the main narrator is...unless your plan is to use two main characters equally and have them swap positions as the "reliable" one and the "unreliable" one/villain at some point.

The beginning ends with a mini-crisis whose action is probably related to the primary plot. However, this mini-crisis is often the first time we see a slip in the narrator's composure. He or she may become overly reactive or angry at what happens to end the first act of your story. He or she may underreact or perhaps not react entirely appropriately.

You can make it subtle or shout it loud, but this is probably the first time when your audience may start to feel a sense of disquiet or unease about the narrator.

If nothing else, the audience may start to sense that *something* is not as it seems in this story.

THE MIDDLE:

The main plot action of the story unfolds as dictated by the action trope your story revolves around. As the danger in this storyline ratchets up, the pressure on your narrator also increases, and we see more and larger slips of reason and calm...or larger slips away from total honesty.

If you're using multiple points of view, the second point of view may start to converge with the narrator's. We may see these two characters' journeys starting to head toward a point where they will converge, or where their paths will eventually cross.

We may see both point of view characters observing and

commenting on similar or identical events but starting to draw differing conclusions or observing them in differing ways.

As the story progresses, one of both point of view characters may be in danger and high stress. For a while, this might explain a certain irregularity in behavior or thought. But at some point, your audience should start to wonder if all is well with your narrator's mental health.

At the same time, we may see that the second point of view character, who started the story making wild claims or suggesting that something deeply implausible is happening may suddenly be starting to make more sense. It may be that he or she is speaking more calmly, or it may simply be that the reality of the story is heading closer and closer to the seemingly wild claims this character initially made.

If you've done the middle of your story well, your audience may have strong opinions about who they like and dislike or who they trust and distrust...but they're not sure. It's this uncertainty that keeps pulling them forward, racing toward the climax to find out who's telling the truth and who's lying.

BLACK MOMENT:

There are a bunch of fun possibilities for the black moment in this type of story:

- The narrator's reality shatters and he or she has some sort of break with reality.
- The truth may emerge and the audience may find out that the narrator has been lying all along.
- The dueling realities of each of your narrators may crash into each other headlong—in conflicting testimony, conflicting memory of how it happened, or in a tremendous argument.
- The audience loses faith in your narrator and suddenly

doesn't know who to believe in your story, making the audience feel untethered and at sea emotionally.

- A deep trauma to the narrator is revealed that explains why he or she has been remembering everything all wrong.

THE END:

In the final scenario of the above list, the one where the audience learns why the narrator was lying and being unreliable, you can still salvage sympathy for this character and hope in your audience that he or she will get treatment, support, or counseling and get well.

In the absence of information to exonerate or redeem your narrator, the roles of villain and narrator/protagonist swap. Your audience's sympathies are going to shift sharply, and it's normal that your portrayal of the narrator and villain-now-good guy switches sharply, as well. In the ending, you'll now show the narrator in all his or her delusional, arrogant, manipulative, lying, glory.

This portion of the story is also where you'll zing your audience with the narrator pointing out archly how everyone in the story (and your audience) bought his or her lies and manipulations. The narrator steps fully into his or her bad guy role, now. While the audience may understand why, that doesn't forgive the fact that this character is doing bad things to nice people and good people.

Vice versa, the second point of view character who's been maligned, doubted, and torn down throughout the story finally gets his or her moment of redemption as everyone in the story and your audience finally realize he or she has been telling the truth all along.

While the action plot of your story comes to its thrilling climax, it's typical that the two competing point of view characters will be part of the final conflict and will confront each other directly. This may be a violent combat scene or physical fight of some kind, or it might be dueling testimony in a court of law, competing answers in interrogations, or some other kind of confrontation.

By the end of this climactic confrontation, the truth usually comes out or is finally, clearly revealed to your audience. Audience members now know for sure who was lying and who was telling the truth all along.

Occasionally, writers choose to end the story still leaving the truth ambiguous and letting the competing version of the truth stand in conflict with each other. In this ending, the audience members can continue to debate and disagree over what really happened after the story has ended. While audiences enjoy this gimmick now and then, a steady diet of "nobody knows for sure what happened" endings quickly tire and annoy most audiences.

Likewise, a steady diet of unreliable narrators also annoys audiences. While you individually may be fine writing an unreliable narrator now and then, if every protagonist you write is unreliable, audiences will quickly memorize your name and expect every character you create to be delusional or a liar. Because this entire trope relies on surprising your audience, this *is* a problem. Your stories will lose all element of surprise (and appeal) if you come back to this trope too frequently in your body of work as a writer.

KEY SCENES

-- the protagonist first mentions the second point of view character and gives us some pithy or compelling insight about that person that may or may not be true

-- the second point of view character, if there is one, first mentions the narrator and gives us some pithy or compelling insight about that person that may or may not be true

-- something bad happens, and nobody's sure exactly what happened or who did it

-- the narrator's judgments, jabs, and attacks on the other characters become obvious enough that the audience actually is likely to notice them, now

-- as other information is revealed over the course of the story, the competing version of the truth to the narrator's seems implausible, then starts to sound possible, then seems about as likely as the narrator's explanation of events, then starts to seem more likely true than the narrator's version of events

-- we get the backstory between the narrator and second point of view character or the other character in the story who refutes the narrator's version of events

-- the protagonist reacts to the reveal of the information that makes it clear to the audience that the narrator is lying at a minimum and may be deeply disturbed or twisted at worst

-- the second point of view character says, "I told you so" to a character, but the remark is really aimed at your audience

-- the narrator and second point of view character speak to each other for the first time in this story

THINGS TO THINK ABOUT WHEN WRITING THIS TROPE

Who's your narrator? What's his or her backstory? How does he or she know the other point of view character or other main character who tells the truth and acts as a foil to the narrator's version of events?

Who's the person who will disagree with the narrator? How does this person function as a villain in the story until this person and the narrator/protagonist becomes the eventual villain?

How do the narrator and the second main character know each other? What's their shared history? Why are they at odds now?

What's the major event(s) that happens or happened that the narrator isn't being truthful about and that the other character is being truthful about?

Is either character being entirely truthful, or are both of them bending the truth or lying outright?

What is the truth about what happens or happened in your story? Will you ever reveal this to your audience in its entirety? If so, how?

How does the narrator alter, distort, or manipulate the truth about various characters and events in your story? You might want to make a chart of the truth versus the narrator's version of events and possibly add a column for the perceptions of the character who refutes the narrator's version of events...letting the truth lie somewhere in the middle between the two versions.

At what point will you reveal to your audience that the narrator isn't entirely truthful? At what point will you reveal the true extent of the narrator's lies and distortions?

Why is the narrator lying, distorting, and manipulating the truth?

Will you ever reveal why the narrator is lying, distorting, and manipulating the truth? If so, when? If not, why not?

Do you intend for your narrator to be the ultimate villain in your story or not? If not, how will you avoid your audience thinking that he or she is the villain? What redeeming quality or sympathetic reason will you give the narrator for lying?

Can you give the narrator at least a little of this redeeming or sympathetic quality anyway, even if you do intend for him or her to be the villain in your story?

What's the big confrontation at the climax of your story? How will the narrator and whoever is refuting his or her version of the truth be part of this confrontation?

How will the narrator and other point of view character or person refuting the narrator's version of events confront each other directly?

What happens when they do confront each other?

How does the big climax reveal the truth or as much of the truth as you plan to reveal to your audience?

Is the revelation of the truth shocking, surprising, or fascinating to your audience when they finally learn it? If not, can you make it that way? If so, can you make it more that way?

Will the ending be satisfying and enjoyable to your audience?

What happens to the narrator and to the other point of view character in the end? Is what happens to each of them going to seem appropriate to your audience?

TROPE TRAPS

The protagonist isn't likable up front and your audience never trusts him or her.

The protagonist's story of events doesn't hang together plausibly and the audience never buys that he or she is telling the truth.

The other point of view character or character who refutes the narrator's version of events is too likable as soon as we meet him or her and the audience immediately gets on board with this person being the one telling the truth.

The events of the story happening in real time are boring or don't engage the audience enough to care about them.

The protagonist isn't subtle about his or her attempts to manipulate what the audience believes about various characters, and the audience catches on to him or her very quickly.

You signal too early that something's off about the narrator and by the time you reveal that he or she is lying, the audience has known this for a long time and isn't the least bit surprised.

The point of view character who is telling the truth starts out with a perfectly plausible story that's very easy to believe. Nothing about it stretches the ability of your audience to believe it initially.

If the lies are being told about past events, the current day events don't have anything to do with those past events and the various storylines don't mesh together at all.

There are no consequences to somebody being untruthful about what happened or is happening in the story.

There's no reason for your audience to care who's lying and who's not—the story is nothing more than a he said-she said style argument with no stakes attached to who's right or wrong.

The stakes don't grow as the story progresses over who's lying and who's not.

The big climax doesn't reveal the key pieces of the truth or the whole truth that's unknown up until now. That revealed truth isn't a big twist on what the audience believed until now and it isn't surprising or shocking.

The only kind of narrator or protagonist you write is a deceptive or lying one and your sales drop dramatically after the first few stories you sell.

UNRELIABLE NARRATOR/DECEPTIVE PROTAGONIST TROPE IN ACTION

Movies:

- Fight Club
- The Usual Suspects
- Gone Girl
- Shutter Island
- The Machinist

Books:

- The Girl on the Train by Paula Hawkins
- American Psycho by Bret Easton Ellis
- We Were Liars by E. Lockhart
- The Murder of Roger Ackroyd by Agatha Christie
- Before I Go to Sleep by S.J. Watson
- The Woman in the Window by A.J. Finn
- In the Woods by Tana French

- The Dinner by Herman Koch
- You by Caroline Kepnes
- The Thirteenth Tale by Diane Setterfield
- The Collector by John Fowles

38

VICTIM SEEKS REVENGE

DEFINITION

In this story, someone who has been the victim of a crime—necessarily a serious and traumatic one—decides to go after his or her attacker and get revenge. To be clear, **vengeance is retribution or retaliation done on behalf of someone who has been wronged. Revenge is retribution or retaliation done by the same person who has suffered the wrong.**

So, in the Seeking Vengeance trope, we dealt with the psychology of a person whose loved one has died or been terribly harmed by a crime. In this trope, we deal with the psychology of the victim himself or herself.

When someone is the victim of the crime, he or she is likely to go through a wide range of emotions before it's all said and done. No two people respond the same way, so feel free to have your victim respond however makes sense to that character and to you.

That said, a typical serious crime victim will go through stages of anger along the lines of:

- Shock or numbness
- Denial and disbelief

- Anger
- Confusion
- Guilt
- Desire to "do something"

It's possible for your protagonist to decide to take action at any step along the way in this process. It's possible your victim will cycle through these emotions several or many times, and it's possible he or she will feel none of these things or all of them at once.

No matter how your victim-protagonist feels, for some reason, he or she decides it's a good idea to find his or her attacker and take revenge against that person(s). For the sake of ease, I'll talk in terms of there being only one attacker, but you could just as easily make your story about the protagonist tracking down and punishing multiple attackers.

At the end of the day, the protagonist gets his or her revenge...and then must deal with the fallout from that. Perhaps he or she feels closure or satisfaction. Or perhaps he or she realizes it doesn't help him or her feel batter at all. And perhaps the protagonist simply feels empty. Any reaction to this is acceptable as long as it makes sense for your character and his or her experience and psychology.

ADJACENT TROPES
-- Seeking Vengeance
--Obsessed
-- Civilian Becomes Soldier/Action Hero
-- Haunted By Visions of a Crime
-- Only Survivor and Things Get Weird
-- Vengeful Ghost

WHY READERS/VIEWERS LOVE THIS TROPE

-- if we've ever been wronged, we may relate to the victim's anger and need to take revenge against the person who wronged us

-- it makes us feel like the best possible kind of justice has been served by the person most deserving of serving it up

-- we want victims of great crimes to heal, and we want their attackers to suffer. This story meets that deep need for justice to be done

-- we want to know that victims of serious crimes do get better. We *need* to know this in case a loved one or we ourselves are ever the victims of a serious crime

OBLIGATORY SCENES
THE BEGINNING:

We meet the victim of the crime. We may experience the crime along with this person in real time.

If you'd rather not show the crime in real time or it happened sometime in the past, you may only want to show a brief snippet of the crime or simply acknowledge that it happened and tell your audience nothing about the crime itself initially.

We see the protagonist decide that he or she is going to find his or her attacker and take revenge. This is a really risky decision and threatens to make the protagonist a victim of this attacker a second time, so the victim has a darned compelling reason for making this momentous decision.

Everyone around the protagonist may try to talk him or her out of it. But the protagonist is not deterred.

We may see the protagonist doing some sort of training or learning skills before going on this mission. And we may see this mission to seek revenge becoming an obsession for this character.

The beginning typically ends with the victim departing on his or her quest to find the bad guy.

. . .

THE MIDDLE:

The victim hunts the bad guy. The audience gets bits and pieces of details about the crime and of the protagonist's experience of being its victim. Indeed, the protagonist may remember things he or she had forgotten as the investigation dredges up suppressed memories or triggers new recollections. You may show the audience dreams, flashbacks, or triggered memories as the protagonist closes in on the attacker.

Side Note: Not all of these memories may be accurate, so feel free to have the protagonist questions his or her own memory of events.

Meanwhile, the attacker gets wind of the fact that someone is hunting him or her. Eventually, the attacker figures out who it is. He or she may try to flee the protagonist, or the attacker may gleefully enter into a new game with his or her victim.

It's a common midpoint reversal that the protagonist goes from hunter to hunted as the attacker turns the tables and commences hunting the protagonist instead.

As the protagonist engages with the attacker or gets close enough to get the attacker's attention, the risks go up exponentially. The protagonist's target is already the perpetrator of one serious crime. There's no reason to believe he or she wouldn't do the same thing again or do something worse this time.

The protagonist may have doubts and fears but is determined to press ahead with this quest of his or hers.

The middle typically ends with the protagonist trying to confront the attacker directly for the first time. It's also possible that the protagonist ambushes or attacks the protagonist again. He or she may intentionally mirror the way the crime happened the last time just to upset and mess with the protagonist.

BLACK MOMENT:

The   protagonist   freezes   or   underestimates   the strength/skills/smarts of the attacker and is taken by surprise in some way. The fight with the attacker goes terribly. The protagonist may be the captive of the attacker once more or may have been the victim of a crime *again*.

Sometimes the victim gets completely lost in a flashback and fails to follow through with the attack, which the attacker simply walks away from.

The complete failure to achieve revenge breaks something inside the protagonist. All of the feelings he or she has been suppressing, trying and failing to deal with, or didn't even know he or she had come rushing out and overwhelm him or her.

The full weight of his or her folly in trying to get revenge on someone as dangerous and evil as the attacker slams into him or her. The protagonist was wrong to try to do this. But now the attacker is hunting him or her again, and the protagonist is going to die this time. In every way the protagonist could fail, he or she has.

THE END:

Like it or not, the protagonist has awakened the sleeping bear, and the attacker is coming for him or her. The difference is this time the protagonist is prepared for it, knows the attack is coming, and can take steps to defend himself or herself.

The protagonist gathers himself or herself emotionally and is determined that this time the attack won't go the same as it did the last time. Whatever mistakes the protagonist believes he or she made the first time, he or she won't be making those mistakes again.

Perhaps the biggest difference of all is the protagonist's mindset, now. He or she already knows what it's like to be a victim and knows he or she can survive and come out the other side. He or she isn't afraid this time—or at least is afraid in a way that he or she can still function and think through.

The attacker attacks, or possibly the protagonist surprises the attacker and attacks him or her first.

The final confrontation happens. It's a pitched fight and very close. The attacker seems to get the upper hand, but then, the protagonist gathers himself or herself for one last push. The preparation, planning, and training he or she has done for this moment pays off, and he or she manages to turn the tide and tip the fight in his or her own favor.

The protagonist wins and defeats the attacker. With the attacker subdued, the protagonist now can do all the awful things to the attacker that he or she has imagined for all this time...or not. The heroic protagonist may do something to the attacker, but it's not anywhere near as bad as what the attacker did to him or her.

Indeed, now that the protagonist sees the attacker cowed, afraid, begging for mercy or for his or her life, the protagonist may realize that the attacker isn't the scary monster he or she has always imagined the attacker to be. Instead, the attacker is a rather pathetic human being who's not worth going to jail over.

The protagonist may, instead, choose to call the authorities and hand over the attacker to them. If the attacker managed to walk free the last time he or she was prosecuted for attacking the protagonist, this time the protagonist finds evidence of other crimes, or the attacker can be prosecuted for new crimes against the protagonist.

The attacker has gotten what he or she deserves. The protagonist has exorcised his or her personal demons. The audience believes justice has been served, and everyone's happy...except, of course, for the attacker, who none of us want to end up happy anyway.

The protagonist has learned something about himself or herself and put his or her feelings and reactions to rest. He or she can return home, cleansed and changed by this experience.

KEY SCENES

-- the protagonist refuses to be talked out of going after the attacker to get revenge

-- the protagonist, after training intensely, decides he or she is ready to go after the attacker

-- the protagonist remembers some detail about the attacker that, when he or she finds the person he or she believes to be the attacker, identifies that person as the actual attacker

-- something the attacker does makes the protagonist have a sharp flashback to some moment during the attack

-- the protagonist remembers something about the attack he or she has never recalled until now

-- the protagonist sees the attacker for the first time and reacts

-- the attacker admits to the original crime to the protagonist

-- the protagonist debates what to do to the attacker once he or she has the attacker at their mercy

-- the protagonist returns home to loved ones and friends who notice how the protagonist has changed

THINGS TO THINK ABOUT WHEN WRITING THIS TROPE

Who's your protagonist? What crime did he or she experience? Can you make it worse? Much worse?

How did the protagonist survive the crime? What made this crime traumatic?

Does the protagonist have any lingering physical effects left over from the crime? If so, what? Any psychological leftovers? If so, what?

Why can't the protagonist move past the crime and his or her need for revenge? What keeps him or her hanging on to the idea of getting revenge?

Who's the attacker? Why did he or she do this crime?

Was the attacker ever caught? If not, why not? If so, what happened to him or her? Why isn't the attacker in custody now?

Has the attacker already served out a prison sentence? If so, why does the protagonist still feel a need for revenge?

What emotional response did the protagonist have to the attack?

What were its various stages? What stage is he or she in predominantly now?

What does the protagonist do to prepare to go after the attacker? Why these things?

What does the protagonist hope to do to the attacker?

How does the protagonist track, hunt, and ultimately find the attacker?

At what point does the attacker become aware of the protagonist hunting him or her?

How does the attacker respond to being hunted? Why does the attacker ultimately decide to hunt down the protagonist instead?

What does the attacker do to track and hunt the protagonist? What does the attacker plan to do to the protagonist when the attacker catches him or her?

What happens when the protagonist and attacker come face to face the first time? How do they both react?

What does the protagonist do to fail utterly in his or her quest to catch the attacker and get revenge? Does the protagonist get away from the attacker or does he or she get captured?

What triggers the protagonist's black moment? What does that black moment look like? What are the emotions and feelings the protagonist experiences in the black moment?

How will the protagonist confront the attacker one last time? What resources does he or she still have to work with? What is his or her plan for taking down the attacker?

How does that plan work out? What goes wrong with it? How does the protagonist freestyle part or all of the plan?

What kind of fight do the protagonist and attacker get into? Hand to hand? A gunfight? Something else?

What training does the protagonist call on now that he or she has acquired since the last time the protagonist and the attacker tangled?

How does the protagonist turn the tide in their fight and win?

What condition is the attacker in at the end of the fight?

Now that the protagonist has the attacker at his or her mercy, what's he or she going to do to the attacker?

Does the protagonist end up taking any revenge against the attacker? If so, what?

What has the protagonist imagined doing to the attacker that he or she doesn't do?

What does the protagonist do with the attacker after he or she is done with him or her? What will happen to the attacker next? How will the attacker be out of the protagonist's life for a long time or permanently?

What does the protagonist feel when he or she realizes it's all over?

What lesson(s) does the protagonist learn from having sought revenge like this?

How is he or she changed for the better? How is the protagonist change for the worse?

What does returning home look like for the protagonist? Who's waiting for him or her? What changes do they notice in the protagonist?

What will the protagonist do now? Will you show a slice of that next chapter to your audience? If so, how?

TROPE TRAPS

The protagonist no way has the skills to go after the attacker and hope to win.

The protagonist doesn't learn to do the things he or she needs to know how to do to track, hunt, and take down the attacker.

The crime the protagonist suffered doesn't seem traumatic enough to the audience to provoke this obsession with revenge that the protagonist has, now.

The attacker isn't clever or dangerous enough to make the protagonist's hunt scary or dangerous.

Nobody tries to talk this delusional protagonist out of doing something this dumb.

The protagonist magically turns into a ninja when he or she goes after the attacker.

How is the protagonist able to find the attacker when the authorities weren't?

You don't give the audience a plausible explanation for why the attacker is still running around free.

The protagonist remembers the whole crime all at once and you give the audience the entire information dump right at the beginning of the story and leave nothing to the audience's fearful imagination.

The bits of the original crime you reveal don't get worse as they get revealed, and there's nothing surprising or shocking revealed about the crime.

The attacker never turns the tables to hunt the protagonist and just seems like a coward...and hence, not very scary.

The protagonist way overreacts upon seeing the attacker or way underreacts.

The protagonist does something really stupid in the confrontation at the end of Act Two that ought to have gotten him or her killed.

The fact that the attacker doesn't kill the protagonist immediately upon the protagonist showing up makes him or her seem weak or dumb.

The thing that triggers the protagonist's black moment doesn't seem dark enough to throw him or her into that big of a tailspin.

The thing that brings the protagonist out of the black moment doesn't seem big enough to do that, either.

The protagonist really should just run away and forget the whole revenge thing when the going gets bad enough, but he or she doesn't... and you don't give the audience a compelling reason why the protagonist sticks around.

The attacker is so much stronger and better a fighter than the protagonist, there's no way the protagonist would plausibly survive a minute in the final fight against the attacker, and yet he or she goes toe to toe with the attacker successfully.

The protagonist never calls upon any training he or she did or any skills he or she learned before coming on this hunt.

Once the attacker has lost the fight, the protagonist unleashes too violently upon the attacker and grosses out the audience, or at least turns them off.

Or conversely, the protagonist doesn't give the attacker a swift kick in someplace painful on behalf of the audience, who's more than ready to see this jerk get what he or she deserves.

The protagonist doesn't turn the attacker over to the authorities but just walks away, presumably leaving the attacker alive and capable of coming back after the protagonist someday.

The protagonist doesn't learn any powerful lessons out of all this.

The protagonist still hasn't put his or her emotional demons to rest.

The protagonist's return home is all sweetness and light. Nobody's mad he or she put loved ones through hell while they waited to see if he or she came home alive or dead.

VICTIM SEEKS REVENGE TROPE IN ACTION
Movies:

- John Wick
- The Count of Monte Cristo
- Oldboy
- Gladiator
- Revenge
- Blue Ruin
- V for Vendetta

Books:

- The Girl with the Dragon Tattoo by Stieg Larsson
- Gone Girl by Gillian Flynn
- Carrie by Stephen King
- And Then There Were None by Agatha Christie
- Best Served Cold by Joe Abercrombie
- The Hunter by Richard Stark (Donald E. Westlake)
- First Blood by David Morrell
- The Power of the Dog by Don Winslow
- The Ghosts of Belfast by Stuart Neville

39

VOYEUR/BEING WATCHED

DEFINITION

This trope speaks to that sensation we've all had at one time or another in our lives...a feeling that someone is watching us. In this story someone is watching someone else. The protagonist is typically the person being watched, but from time to time, you'll see stories told from the point of view of the voyeur as protagonist. In this version the voyeur usually witnesses a crime of some kind and then has to convince people that he or she has seen something dangerous that should be acted upon.

The casual voyeur—the nosy neighbor who watches what everyone in the neighborhood is doing—isn't a criminal. The more intrusive voyeur who peers in your windows if you leave the curtains open, is creepy and can cross over into the realm of criminal. But the voyeur who invades your home to plant video devices or drills holes in walls to peer through is definitely a criminal.

In and of itself, being watched by a voyeur doesn't do any physical harm, although we can probably all agree that it's unsettling and can be very scary. One of the problems with voyeurism is it can be a gateway behavior to more direct criminal behavior and possibly violence.

In thriller novels, it's common to see a stalker start out by watching his or her victim. The voyeurism isn't a trope in this scenario, rather, it's a plot element the stalker or future kidnapper/murderer uses as his or her obsession is escalating.

The Voyeur can stand by itself as a story trope where the protagonist is a victim of voyeurism. If the protagonist reports it to the authorities, it's likely to result in the police getting involved at least a little. At a minimum, the report will be recorded by law enforcement so it can be used as evidence for issuing a restraining order, or eventually, for arresting the voyeur. If the voyeur's "watching" behavior never escalates, you may be left with a fairly dull thriller novel—boy watches girl. Girl is scared and tells police. After several incidents, the police arrest the boy. Boy stops watching girl—and this is why you'll rarely see this type of voyeurism stand alone as a trope.

The Voyeur rises to a more interesting trope when the person doing the watching witnesses a crime. Does he or she report it to the police, given that their voyeuristic behavior is sketchy at best and may have crossed over into criminal? Does the voyeur call in an anonymous tip? Or does the voyeur tell no one and wait for the police to come around asking questions before admitting to what he or she has seen? Even then, is the voyeur certain of what he or she has seen? Is the voyeur sure enough to testify to it under oath? Or maybe he or she should just keep his or her mouth shut.

Now, we have the stuff of an interesting story. The Voyeur as protagonist (or at least a major point of view character) witnesses a crime or what might be a crime. He or she debates whether or not to say anything to anyone. Maybe he or she witnesses a second crime, or clean-up behavior, or some other proof that he or she actually saw a crime occur. But, having delayed saying anything, now the voyeur doesn't feel right speaking up. Either the police don't believe the voyeur when he or she finally does come forward to speak out, or the criminal, whose crime the voyeur witnessed, finds out the voyeur saw him or her and decides to silence the voyeur.

Now the watcher is the watched, the hunter becomes the hunted as the voyeur scrambles to hide from the criminal and get someone in law enforcement to listen to him or her. Eventually, the voyeur and the criminal have a direct confrontation, and the voyeur subdues the criminal or helps the police catch the criminal.

The voyeur is vindicated and is safe once more.

It's this version of the trope I'll concentrate on for the purposes of the remainder of this write-up.

ADJACENT TROPES
-- Witness/Bystander Sucked Into Danger
-- Can't Report A Crime to Police
-- Stalked Online
-- Stalked by a Stranger
-- Stalked by a Loved One/Ex
-- Criminal Helps Cop
-- Reluctant Informant/Witness

WHY READERS/VIEWERS LOVE THIS TROPE
-- for everyone who's ever looked out of their window and casually noticed what the neighbors are doing, it's intriguing to imagine what we would do if we saw something sketchy or suspicious

-- if I witnessed a crime, I would call the police right away and be a hero for helping the authorities solve a crime

-- we find the moral ambiguity and ethical questions fascinating. What would I do if, in the course of committing a minor crime of being a peeping Tom, I witnessed another crime

-- this type of story plays to our concerns about surveillance technology and the notion of living in a surveillance state

-- this story also plays to our concerns about being alone, isolated, and without the support of law enforcement.

· · ·

OBLIGATORY SCENES
THE BEGINNING:

We meet the voyeur, doing his or her voyeur thing. Through this protagonist's eyes, we get to know the normal world around him or her, specifically, we get to know what the normal life is of the victim of the upcoming crime.

We witness the crime from the point of view of the voyeur, seeing exactly what he or she sees. If something is unclear or obscured to him or her, it's unclear or obscured to your audience as well. If it's alarming to the voyeur, it's alarming to your audience. In effect, your audience becomes the voyeur along with the protagonist.

If you want to add an extra degree of tension and terror to this scene, think about having the criminal look up and spot the voyeur looking back at him or her. Or the criminal might move to the window to close the curtains and spot the voyeur then. If nothing else, the criminal might take a long, hard look at the voyeur's home, clearly realizing that whoever lives there could have seen what he or she did.

The voyeur is thrown into a dilemma. He or she was committing a crime while witnessing another crime. Does he or she call the police or not? Typically, the voyeur makes an anonymous phone call, tipping off the police, who may or may not respond to the call.

If there's no police response, the protagonist's dilemma deepens. Perhaps he or she goes to the neighbor's home to check on him or her. This is a risky behavior, of course, given the chance of leaving behind DNA, hairs, fingerprints, or other evidence that might tie the voyeur to the crime.

If the voyeur doesn't check on the victim, he or she may call the police again. Or the voyeur might contact another neighbor and try to get them involved. Or the voyeur may just fret, stuck in his or her moral dilemma.

While I'm not personally a fan of portraying law enforcement as incompetent, they can get overloaded and stretched too thin at times to respond (quickly or at all) to a vague, anonymous tip. And it will help your story along if the initial police response is not robust.

The longer the voyeur waits to tell law enforcement what he or she witnessed, the more difficult it becomes to make that call since questions will arise over why he or she didn't call the police immediately. Hence, the worse the voyeur's dilemma becomes.

The beginning of this story typically ends with the crime scene finally being discovered. If, instead, you want the police to respond immediately to the crime earlier in your story, then the beginning usually ends with the police knocking on the voyeur's door to ask him or her what they might have seen.

THE MIDDLE:

If the police don't show up at the voyeur's door to end Act One, they surely will do so during Act Two. The voyeur has a clear line of sight to the crime scene and is a perfectly logical person to interview, after all.

The voyeur may or may not tell the truth at this point. This decision may depend on the kind of surveillance equipment he or she uses. Which is to say, just how criminal was the nature of his or her voyeurism?

This decision may also depend on the psychology of your voyeur. If he or she is painfully shy or withdrawn, has some sort of severe social anxiety, perhaps is terrified of having to leave his or her home— you may come up with a perfectly reasonable explanation of why your voyeur chooses not to tell the police what he or she witnessed.

At any rate, if the voyeur *does* tell law enforcement what he or she saw, that news could leak to the press, neighbors could find out the voyeur saw the crime, or you may come up with another way for the criminal to find out that there was a witness to his or her crime.

Even if the voyeur *does not* tell law enforcement about what he or she saw, the criminal may still realize (or know) that the voyeur saw him or her. And, as the investigation of the crime heats up, the criminal decides to come after the voyeur to silence him or her.

In a classic midpoint reversal, the watcher becomes watched, the stalker becomes the stalked, the voyeur becomes the criminal's next target.

In the absence of cover by the police, the voyeur is on his or her own to defend himself or herself from the criminal who's now coming after him or her. If the voyeur was scared before, he or she is terrified now. If you've done your job in the beginning of the story, your audience identifies strongly with this protagonist and is terrified right along with your hapless voyeur.

The latter portions of the middle of your story are usually taken up by the voyeur hiding from or running from the criminal who is out to silence him or her for good. The middle of the story climaxes with a crisis where the voyeur almost gets caught by the criminal and barely gets away alive. Alternately, if your criminal is the sort to capture a victim and toy with them for a while before killing them, the voyeur may be captured to end Act Two.

BLACK MOMENT:

The voyeur has no way of calling the police for help because of his or her earlier decision not to call the police. He or she is completely at the mercy of the criminal. The voyeur may be literally at the criminal's mercy if the voyeur has been taken captive, or the voyeur may be metaphorically at the criminal's mercy since the voyeur is no match for the smart, dangerous criminal. Having tangled with the criminal already, the voyeur knows he or she is lucky to be alive and won't trick, defeat, or outrun the criminal next time.

The voyeur has not only failed to help law enforcement, but because of his or her failure to provide aid, the criminal is still on the loose. It's the voyeur's own fault he or she is in this pickle now, and there's no way out. He or she is doomed to die.

It's in this moment of despair that the voyeur may finally accept responsibility for having done something wrong in not calling the police and for being a petty criminal himself or herself. But it's too late to make any amends because the criminal's coming for him or her and can't be stopped.

THE END:

Something happens to jolt the voyeur out of his or her despair. It can be a will to survive that kicks in and spurs him or her to fight for his or her life. This one applies particularly in the scenario where the voyeur has been taken captive by the criminal.

If the voyeur is not captive, someone—a friend or neighbor—may finally convince the voyeur to go to the authorities and tell all. In this scenario, the police may bait a trap for the criminal using the voyeur.

The voyeur may not go to the authorities, but a friend or neighbor might. It's not uncommon for the police to arrive at the last second before the criminal kills the voyeur to rescue the protagonist.

And it's also possible the voyeur uses his or her skills at surveillance to see the criminal coming and set some sort of trap for him or her. If nothing else, the voyeur may set up apparatus to film his or her own death so the authorities can finally catch the criminal. In this case, the voyeur will physically end up fighting for his or her life against the voyeur and having to find a way to win. It may be messy, it may be ugly, and it may involve sheer dumb luck, but the voyeur finds a way to stop the criminal and subdue or kill him or her.

The police are called this time. The voyeur confesses everything he or she has seen, and the criminal is hauled off, dead or alive. The voyeur has not only stopped a dangerous criminal but solved the original crime for the police. The protagonist has redeemed himself or herself thoroughly enough to be forgiven for his or her petty voyeurism...with the understanding that he or she won't do it anymore.

The voyeur's arc is complete. He or she has transformed from a mildly despicable person to a self-sacrificing hero.

KEY SCENES

-- the protagonist sees the criminal spot him or her

-- the protagonist watches the police investigate the crime scene

-- the protagonist spots the criminal returning to the scene of the crime

-- the protagonist tells a trusted loved one, friend, or neighbor that he or she might have witnessed a crime and asks for advice

-- the police question the voyeur a second time and press him or her harder about what he or she might have seen. (By then, the police may have a tip from someone else that the protagonist watches people.)

-- the protagonist sees the criminal coming for him or her and hides or flees

-- the protagonist returns home. Loved ones, friends, and neighbors may ask him or her to keep watching the neighborhood, turning his or her creepy habit/crime into a positive

THINGS TO THINK ABOUT WHEN WRITING THIS TROPE

What kind of person is the protagonist? What's his or her daily life like?

Why does the voyeur watch the neighbors? When does he or she watch them? What equipment or techniques does the voyeur employ to watch everything?

Does the voyeur record anything or take notes?

What do the neighbors think of the voyeur? Do they have any idea he or she is watching all of them? If so, what do they think of it?

If the voyeur has family or friends, do they know of his or her behavior and what do they think of it? If not, why don't they know about it?

Who is the neighbor who becomes the victim of the crime?

Why does the voyeur watch that neighbor? Is there a reason for watching that person in particular?

What crime does the voyeur witness? What time of day or night? What exactly does the voyeur see? What doesn't he or she see? **NOTE**: Be sure to target the degree of detail and graphic information to your target audience's sensibilities.

Did the voyeur record the crime in some way? If so, how? If not, why not?

Does the criminal spot the voyeur in the immediate aftermath of the crime? If so, how? If not, does the criminal take note of which windows face the crime scene and had a potential view of it?

Who is the criminal? How does he or she know the victim of the crime? Why does he or she commit the crime?

How is the crime committed, and the damage done to the victim serious enough that the victim can't tell the police himself or herself who did it?

Does the victim live or die? If he or she lives, how injured is he or she?

Why doesn't the voyeur call the police immediately and identify himself or herself? What prevents him or her from doing so?

Does the voyeur make an anonymous call to law enforcement to get help for the victim?

Does law enforcement respond right away? If not, why not?

Does the voyeur call the police again? Does the voyeur prompt another neighbor to check on the victim in an effort to get the crime discovered so help will be called?

Does the voyeur go to the victim's home to attempt to render aid to him or her? If so, what does the voyeur find when he or she gets there? Is the victim alive or dead? What does the voyeur do next?

When is the crime finally discovered and reported? By whom? How?

What kind of law enforcement response happens? Does the voyeur hide from the police or watch it all, or both?

When do the police interview the voyeur about what he or she might have seen? What does the voyeur tell and not tell the police?

At what point does the voyeur figure out that the criminal may still be nearby and may be looking for him or her?

When is the voyeur sure the criminal is coming after him or her? If the voyeur tries to tell someone about it, who does the voyeur tell, and does that person believe him or her? Why or why not?

How does the voyeur end up on his or her own to deal with a criminal now stalking him or her? Why doesn't the voyeur break down and go to the police for help? Or if the voyeur does go to the police, why don't they help?

How does the voyeur try to hide or flee from the criminal? How does the criminal hunt down the voyeur?

What does the criminal do once he or she has found the voyeur? Does he or she attack the voyeur? Invade the voyeur's home? Try to take the voyeur captive?

What happens? Does the voyeur escape or is the voyeur taken captive?

At what point does the voyeur realize all is lost, he or she is doomed to die, and the black moment hits him or her? What triggers this moment?

What happens to cause the voyeur to collect himself or herself for one last confrontation with the criminal?

What does that final confrontation look like?

What happens to help the voyeur win the fight, or who shows up to save the voyeur?

What happens to the criminal to end the fight?

What happens to the criminal (or his/her remains) after the fight?

When does the voyeur confess everything to the police? How do the police respond?

Are charges pressed against the voyeur, or is he or she forgiven because the voyeur caught the criminal who did the original crime and nearly died doing so?

What orders do the police give the voyeur regarding what's okay to do by way of watching the neighbors and what's not okay?

Does the voyeur seek any counseling or psychological help as a result of this whole trauma? Does he or she want to treat the underlying reason why he or she stays at home and watches the neighbors, perhaps he or she wants help with some other emotional or psychological disorder, or perhaps he or she has trauma from his or her own attack to work out?

How do loved ones, friends, and the neighbors respond to the voyeur after his or her return home? Is the reaction a hero's welcome, suspicious, or a mixture of both?

What lesson(s) has the voyeur learned from this experience? How is he or she changed?

Does the voyeur see his or her own transformation from petty criminal to hero? If not, does someone else point it out to him or her?

How does the voyeur plan to live going forward?

TROPE TRAPS

The voyeur is so gross or squicky that the audience dislikes him or her too much to root for him or her through the story.

Nobody around the voyeur has any idea he or she is a little off, and the audience doesn't buy it. **NOTE**: True or not, we all want to believe that people who spy on their neighbors would give away some hint of that.

Failing to show your audience the emotional or psychological drivers behind why your voyeur spies on other people so the audience can develop any sympathy for him or her.

The crime is described or shown so graphically, it turns off your audience.

The criminal is a complete idiot for doing a crime in front of an open window, and the audience doesn't believe he or she doesn't get caught right away.

The crime is done in such a way that the victim would see his or her attacker and then the victim survives in such a way that he or she can give the police all the information they need...hence the police have no good reason to speak to the voyeur nor for the voyeur to speak to them.

The criminal doesn't see the voyeur in the aftermath of the crime but magically knows the voyeur witnessed the crime without you ever giving your audience an explanation of how the criminal knew.

If any sane person would immediately report having witnessed such a serious crime, failing to explain plausibly why your voyeur doesn't do so.

The police are portrayed as merely incompetent for not responding if the voyeur calls in an anonymous tip about a serious crime because the police aren't given a reason why they don't come check out the report.

The voyeur lies to police when they first interview the voyeur about what he or she might have seen, the cops have no clue the voyeur is lying or not telling them everything, and the audience doesn't buy it.

If the criminal does know the voyeur saw the crime, failing to explain why he or she waits to come silence the voyeur. Why not run over right after committing the crime to take out the witness, too?

The criminal doesn't just kill the voyeur when he or she finds the voyeur and comes across as an idiot for not doing so.

The voyeur doesn't have a good reason for sticking around home once he or she knows the criminal is hunting him or her.

The way the voyeur gets away from the criminal when the criminal comes for him or her is wildly out of character for the voyeur, or the voyeur magically turns into a ninja or MMA fighter.

The voyeur's black moment doesn't include him or her taking responsibility for having made mistakes—a necessary story beat in any kind of redemption arc.

In the final confrontation between the voyeur and criminal, the voyeur wins purely because he or she has decided to fight to live. Will to survive isn't nearly enough against a bigger, stronger, more experienced fighter. It just means you might die slower.

The voyeur is passive going into the final fight and does nothing to save himself or herself in the end but is instead rescued by someone else taking positive action to save him or her—the voyeur being proactive is another necessary beat in a redemption arc.

Once the criminal is subdued or killed and the police have arrived, the voyeur fails to confess everything—yet another necessary story beat in a redemption arc.

The authorities don't forgive the voyeur and throw the book at him or her, an act guaranteed to severely tick off your audience if they like your protagonist and particularly if they feel he or she has paid enough already for his or her mistakes.

The voyeur doesn't learn a life-changing lesson or two out of this whole ordeal.

The voyeur is exactly the same person at the end of the story as he or she was at the beginning of it.

VOYEUR/BEING WATCHED TROPE IN ACTION
Movies:

- Rear Window
- Disturbia
- Body Double
- Blow Up
- The Conversation
- The Girl On the Train
- Sliver

Books:

- The Woman in the Window by A.J. Finn
- The Watcher by Ross Armstrong
- The Safe House by Nicci French
- Someone is Watching by Joy Fielding
- The Neighbor by Lisa Gardner
- The House Across the Lake by Riley Sager

40

WITNESS/BYSTANDER SUCKED INTO DANGER

DEFINITION

Whereas the voyeur was intentionally watching someone one and happened to see a crime, in this trope, someone going about his or her own life happens, purely by accident, to witness a crime or some very dangerous event.

The witness of the crime is the protagonist of this trope, and you can choose anyone—any kind of person, with any background, any past, any race, culture, or religion, any skills or knowledge, any age, any gender—you name it. Sky's the limit on who you choose to be your protagonist in this story.

Indeed, you can make the witness's story its own trope altogether, covering the thing he or she were on their way to do when they were so rudely interrupted by a crime happening right in front of them and messing up their arriving on time to do the thing their trope required of them.

For example, they were on their way to get married and were so late to their own wedding that the bride or groom leaves. They were involved in a tightly planned heist that goes wrong because they weren't where they needed to be to do their part in the robbery. They were on their way to file for divorce, to whistle blow on their employer, defect to another country, and their plan gets scuttled by the interruption.

The beauty of this trope is literally anyone can be the protagonist in this tale, which opens up all kinds of fun story possibilities in addition to the protagonist being in danger because of what he or she witnessed.

The witness may or may not report the crime and may or may not admit to having witnessed the crime for a variety of reasons. But somebody had to have seen him or her at the crime scene or else you wouldn't have a story at all. The witness could walk away, never say a word of it to anyone, and nobody would be the wiser.

However, assuming someone did see your witness watch the crime happen, this witness has seen something that someone else really didn't want him or her to see that puts him or her into grave danger. This witness, whose only crime was being in the wrong place at the wrong time, is hunted by someone—usually the criminal, but not always—who wants to silence him or her.

Typically, it's the criminal who perpetrated a crime who's trying to silence the witness. But it could also be the victim of the crime who doesn't want a scandal trying to keep the witness silent. Or it could be an outsider who stands to be embarrassed by the crime who wants the witness to say nothing.

Yet another variation is that a witness has given an initial statement to law enforcement, and someone wants him or her to change the statement or not testify in court to what he or she saw. Someone may try to buy off this witness, intimidate or harass this witness, or attack loved ones of the witness to silence him or her.

The general structure of the trope, then, is that an innocent, random person sees something bad happen. Someone doesn't want him or her to tell others what they saw, and the story unfolds as the witness tries to avoid danger, culminating in some sort of climactic confrontation between the witness and those who would silence him or her. The witness ultimately does tell the truth or testify truthfully about what he or she saw, and the consequences of his or her testimony unfold as they rightfully should.

I can't dive any deeper into this trope without pointing out that witnesses are notoriously inaccurate in what they perceive when they witness a crime or shocking event. Also, human beings have a tendency to re-write their memories to make sense of things they've seen that their minds can't make sense of. Hence, what your witness saw and what really happened may diverge a little or a lot within your story.

ADJACENT TROPES
-- Voyeur/Being Watched
-- Can't Report a Crime to Police
-- Repressed Memories
-- False Memory
-- Someone Doesn't Want It Solved
-- Reluctant Informant/Witness
-- Sucked Into Someone Else's Problem
-- Haunted by Visions of a Crime

WHY READERS/VIEWERS LOVE THIS TROPE
-- this is one of the most relatable thriller protagonists there is. Some regular person just like you and me ends up in danger purely by accident and then has to deal with it

-- we get to see an average person grow into a hero the way we would like to believe we would if thrust into the same situation

-- this is often a David and Goliath story of an average person taking on someone stronger, smarter, more skilled, and more powerful

-- we'd love to be swept out of our boring, mundane life all of a sudden and find ourselves in the middle of an exciting, adventurous world like this protagonist had happen

• • •

OBLIGATORY SCENES
THE BEGINNING:

We meet the protagonist going about his or her normal life. Or alternately, we meet the protagonist launching into the action of another trope that will provide much of the plot movement in your story. Into the middle of that beginning, the protagonist witnesses something bad happen.

This event the protagonist witnesses can be anything—a car accident, a robbery, a murder, an argument between two people. But whatever it is the protagonist saw, it has the potential to be deeply damaging to someone.

That someone could be the criminal who committed the crime, the celebrity whose career will be ruined if he or she is seen in public with his or her illicit lover, the politician whose career will be ruined if he or she is revealed to have been driving drunk, or anything else you can cook up that might make someone want to hide what happened.

The witness may or may not call the police. The witness may or may not give a report to the police. Indeed, the witness may leave the scene immediately after the event. But someone sees the witness and knows there is a witness to what happened. And that's what sets in motion the remainder of your story.

After this big opening, the beginning may spend some time introducing various characters, showing us more of the witness's life that was just interrupted, and perhaps giving us a look at the victim's or perpetrator of the crime's life.

Someone typically catches up with the witness to ask what he or she saw. It may be law enforcement, a publicist for a celebrity, a government official looking to bury the incident. But the witness knows now that someone realizes he or she did, in fact, witness whatever happened.

The beginning usually ends with an event or interaction that makes it clear that the protagonist is in danger. Someone tries to run down the protagonist in a car and kill him or her. Something ominous happens like a lot of money appears in his or her bank account, or a threatening message is delivered to his or her home.

THE MIDDLE:

Your protagonist may or may not have the training and skills to deal with being the target of a dangerous campaign to silence him or her. The protagonist is rattled at best and terrified at worst to realize he or she is in real danger.

The protagonist may know exactly who's trying to silence him or her, or the protagonist may have no clue who it is.

If the protagonist doesn't have a compelling reason for avoiding the police, he or she surely goes to them for help, now. It's up to you how much you want to isolate your protagonist in your story. The police may be unwilling to help your protagonist for some reason—the police may be corrupt or under orders not to help the protagonist.

Someone very powerful may pull strings to frame the protagonist for some crime that prevents him or her from going to the police. How will the protagonist explain the million dollars that suddenly showed up in his or her secret checking account, or the kilo of cocaine that just showed up in his or her desk drawer?

With or without police protection of some kind, the danger to the protagonist continues to grow. The pressure grows on the protagonist to change his or her story, recant it altogether, decline to testify, or to disappear.

Meanwhile, if you're writing an additional trope into your story, the complications from it continue to tangle with the complications from this trope. While the protagonist is trying to dodge a bad guy from another trope or investigate/solve a problem from another trope, he or she is also having to dodge whoever is trying to pressure him or her into being silent or changing his or her story.

If you do mix multiple tropes and they just happen to overlap with this one, be careful. This is usually a *random* trope. But if it's somehow tied to another trope, it will strain the credibility of your audience if you ask them to believe in too big a coincidence. If this trope is, indeed, related to another one in your story, by the middle of your story, you should explain to your audience how and why the two plotlines overlap.

For example, what are the odds that a guy who's just decided to divorce his wife is going about his or her normal life and happens to witness the man she's having an affair with kill another person? Now, if the protagonist is leaving the hotel where he's just seen his wife in bed with another man, and that man happens to drive recklessly out of the hotel garage and run down a pedestrian, your audience might believe that.

The protagonist may hide and run for your entire story, or at some point, your protagonist may decide to fight back. He or she may go public with what he or she saw. He or she may avoid the publicity for whatever reason and instead lay a trap for the person trying to intimidate or harm him or her.

In retaliation, the person trying to silence the protagonist may attack loved ones, friends, or colleagues of the protagonist's. The villain may go after the protagonist's reputation or job, or in some other way ruin the protagonist's life—anything that puts additional pressure on him or her to play ball and change stories or stay quiet.

The middle of the story typically culminates in a crisis where the protagonist comes alarmingly close to dying. It's way too close a call for comfort, and that was the final warning given by the villain. The protagonist knows that next time he or she won't survive.

BLACK MOMENT:

The protagonist has an impossible choice to make. Does he or she do what's right and tell police what he or she saw, stand by his or her original statement, or testify truthfully in a trial...or does the protagonist protect loved ones and/or save his or her own life?

This is a dilemma the protagonist didn't ask for and feels unfairly put upon for having it forced upon him or her. But regardless of how the protagonist ended up in this pickle, he or she still has an impossible decision Do the right thing or harm himself/herself and loved ones?

Paralyzed by the impossibility of it, the protagonist may do nothing. He or she may decide to run away and avoid making a decision at all, or the protagonist may decide to acquiesce to the pressure and change his or her story.

The protagonist may even go so far as to contact the authorities and give a different statement. The pressure is off of the villain, but now the protagonist has to live with a guilty conscience and the knowledge that he or she caved and did something immoral and illegal. This, too, proves to be an impossible dilemma of living with guilt and shame or protecting self and loved ones.

THE END:

If the protagonist made no decision, something happens that makes the choice for him or her. The villain attacks the protagonist and makes a good faith effort to kill him or her this time (or Heaven forbid, tries to kill a loved one). It freaks out the protagonist and something inside the protagonist cracks open. He or she is sick and tired of being afraid, sick and tired of being manipulated and harassed, and sick and tired of being a victim himself or herself. The protagonist fights back, standing his or her ground literally by engaging in a climactic fight, or metaphorically by making a definitive (often public) statement of what he or she witnessed, telling everything and telling it truthfully.

If the protagonist made a false statement in the black moment, he or she recants it now, returning to the original statement and standing by it. Furthermore, he or she reveals all the shenanigans the villain has been engaging in to try to silence him or her. Law enforcement may use the protagonist as bait in a sting operation to catch the criminal/villain.

Alternately, the criminal/villain may attack the protagonist one last time in a final effort to stop the consequences of the event to the criminal or villain that the protagonist witnessed. The protagonist fights back and/or the police show up in the nick of time, and the criminal/villain is subdued, defeated, or killed. Now, the protagonist is free to tell the truth or testify without fear of recrimination and does so.

In any of these endings, the truth of the crime or event the protagonist witnessed finally comes out once and for all. The bad guy in that crime or event suffers the consequences for his or her role in that crime or event. If a scandal was being avoided by the bad guys, the scandal explodes and the fallout from it does all the damage and more that the bad guy(s) feared. Now, there's the additional scandal of the attempted cover-up and the way an innocent bystander was harassed, intimidated, threatened, and harmed by the bad guy(s).

The protagonist invokes legal protection for himself/herself and for his or her loved ones, if necessary. The protagonist has no more secrets to keep and everything he or she saw is now public record, so he or she can finally resume his or her normal life.

KEY SCENES

-- the protagonist doubts his or her own eyes—"Did I just see that?"—particularly if he or she saw something odd, strange, or unexpected for that type of event

-- the protagonist has somewhere else to be or really doesn't want to stick around and give a witness statement to police

-- the protagonist tells someone he or she trusts what he or she saw and gets advice from this confidante

-- something dangerous or bad happens to the protagonist and he or she realizes it's because of the event he or she witnessed

-- the protagonist tries to get protection from someone. It could be police or someone else entirely, but that person thinks the protagonist is overreacting

-- the protagonist or a loved one of the protagonist nearly dies in a suspicious "accident"

-- people around the protagonist—loved ones, friends, coworkers, believe the smear campaign tactics the bad guy uses to ruin him or her

-- the protagonist feels completely trapped and considers fleeing, tries to flee, or does flee

-- the protagonist is reprimanded for and/or apologizes for not coming forward sooner or for changing his or her story

-- the protagonist is forgiven for his or her mistakes because of the extraordinary pressure he or she was under from a bad guy

-- the scandal or trial happens and the bad guy gets what he or she deserves

-- the protagonist's life is restored to normal...or he or she makes a change he or she has been wanting to make for the better in his or her life

THINGS TO THINK ABOUT WHEN WRITING THIS TROPE

Who's your protagonist? What does his or her normal life look like? What is he or she doing as part of normal life when he or she witnesses the crime or incident?

What happens in the crime or incident? Who's the victim? Who's the perpetrator?

What does the protagonist see accurately? What does he or she NOT see accurately? What is he or she unsure of about what he or she saw? What's fuzzy or obscured from where the protagonist was?

Why would someone not want a witness to tell exactly what he or she saw? Is it the criminal who committed a crime? A celebrity who did something bad? Someone else who stands to be harmed by the truth being exposed?

Does the witness stay and speak with police? If so, what does he or she say? Does he or she tell the truth right then? If not, why not?

Does this witness have a compelling reason to stay out of the aftermath of the crime or incident besides just not wanting to get involved? If so, what is it?

Who sees the protagonist witness the crime or incident? Who does that person tell, if anyone?

Does the protagonist tell anyone else about seeing the crime or incident besides or in addition to the police?

How quickly does someone approach the protagonist and ask him or her to say nothing about what he or she might have seen? Who makes this approach? Where? When? What's the tone of the approach—friendly, intimidating, ominous?

What happens next that nearly harms the protagonist or is a near miss with disaster that the protagonist realizes is a threat from whoever wants him or her to stay silent?

What other bad things start happening to the protagonist and/or loved ones, friends, and coworkers?

Does the protagonist go to the police over these incidents? If so, what do the police say? Do they take the protagonist seriously or not? Do they offer any protection?

If the protagonist doesn't go to the authorities over these intimidation tactics, why not? Does the protagonist take any actions to protect loved ones or himself/herself? If so, what?

Is there some sort of hush campaign or cover-up of the crime or incident the protagonist witnessed? Has it gotten news coverage, are there rumors about it, or is there thunderous silence?

What does the bad guy threatening the protagonist want him or her to do? Why doesn't the protagonist want to do this?

How will you put the protagonist in a dilemma of choosing between telling the truth and safety for self and loved ones, taking the massive bribe, and/or ruination and possible death? Can you make this dilemma worse? Much worse? Can you make it absolutely excruciating?

Can you give the protagonist a compelling personal reason why it would be better for him or her to keep his or her mouth shut that has nothing to do with coercion and threats?

Can you give the protagonist a compelling personal reason why it would be better for him or her to tell the truth that has nothing to do with coercion and threats?

Does the protagonist ever change his or her story? Why? Is the new story a lie, or did he or she legitimately remember something new? How do the authorities react when he or she changes stories?

Does the protagonist recant his or her story? If so, why? How does he or she explain doing this?

Does the bad guy merely want to ruin and discredit the protagonist, or is the bad guy out to kill the protagonist, if necessary, to silence him or her?

Does the bad guy work for a bigger bad guy? Is the bad guy protecting someone famous or important? Or is the bad guy doing his own dirty work to shut up the protagonist?

At what point does the protagonist stand and fight back against the bad guy?

What form does this fight take? What skills does the protagonist bring to the fight that gives him or her a chance, even if slim, of winning?

How does the protagonist finally subdue, defeat, or kill the bad guy? Does someone else join the fight at some point to help the protagonist? Does law enforcement show up to help?

NOTE: this protagonist is an average person off the street...be cautious of having him or her kill the bad guy because he or she may face legal consequences for doing so. The exception to this is when the bad guy is SO bad, does such terrible things to the protagonist, and makes such a violent effort to kill the protagonist that the protagonist has no other choice.

How does the protagonist directly defeat the bad guy in part or in full, regardless of who else jumps in to help?

Is this a physical fight with weapons or fists? Or is this a metaphorical fight, for example, a hacking fight where the protagonist tries to save evidence while the bad guy tries to destroy it.

What happens to the bad guy at the end of the climactic fight? Is he or she arrested? Exposed to the media? Ruined?

What happens to the protagonist after the climactic fight? Does he or she have a reckoning with the authorities? If so, how does that go? Does he or she testify in a trial? Make a public statement?

How is the bad guy so ruined or incarcerated that there's no more threat to the protagonist and his or her loved ones?

How is the protagonist's good name restored?

What lesson(s) has the protagonist learned over the course of this whole mess? What changes will he or she make to his or her life as a result of these lessons learned?

Will you show your audience a glimpse of this new and improved life at the end of the story? If so, what does that look like?

TROPE TRAPS

The protagonist isn't a reliable witness for some reason (for example, a high drug addict or a very young child) and nobody would plausibly take him or her seriously no matter what they claim to have seen.

The protagonist doesn't see enough to make him or her worth ruining or killing to silence.

The crime witnessed is portrayed so graphically it upsets your audience.

The crime or event had many other witnesses and the statement of the protagonist isn't that important, making this whole story moot.

The witness has no compelling reason not to make a statement to police, but decides not to help out anyway, making him or her unlikable.

The person who's sure the protagonist's statement will ruin him or her is overreacting massively. Sure, there might be a brief news cycle or a fine to be paid, but nothing so grand and dramatic as their ruin is at stake.

Any sane criminal would flee the area and not stick around to track down and silence the protagonist, and you fail to explain why this criminal does stick around.

There's only one criminal who does the crime and tries to silence the witness, and your story never leads to anything bigger, more interesting, more complicated than that.

The protagonist magically happens to be a highly trained, highly skilled soldier, special operator, cop, or something else along these lines who just happens to have all the skills necessary to fight back when the bad guy comes looking for him or her.

The protagonist has no non-combat skills, expertise, or knowledge that he or she can use creatively to defend himself or herself from the bad guy. Everybody knows how to do *something* cool, interesting, or unique.

Failing to explain why law enforcement doesn't have this witness's back through the whole ordeal.

Failing to explain why the protagonist doesn't go to the police when things are getting really dangerous or damaging for him/her or loved ones.

Failing to make the choice the protagonist faces truly impossible.

Ticking off your audience when the protagonist doesn't make the obvious right choice.

Your audience doesn't buy that this protagonist has a ghost of a chance in a straight up fight against the bad guy and doesn't buy it when the protagonist manages to win.

Failing to give the protagonist some advantage, some element of surprise, or some hidden skill that allows him or her to get the best of the bad guy.

The bad guy doesn't get what he or she deserves for both the original crime/incident and the more recent harassment or threats against the protagonist.

The protagonist isn't cut a break by law enforcement after

changing his or her story, recanting it, or refusing to cooperate with them.

The protagonist learns nothing and his or her life goes back to exactly the way it was before all this started...total failure of the protagonist to make lemonade from lemons.

WITNESS/BYSTANDER SUCKED INTO DANGER TROPE IN ACTION

Movies:

- Witness
- The Net
- Enemy of the State
- Phone Booth
- North by Northwest
- Cellular
- Blue Velvet

Books:

- The Witness by Nora Roberts
- The Cuckoo's Calling by Robert Galbraith (J.K. Rowling)
- The Quiet American by Graham Greene
- The Accident by Linwood Barclay
- The Kind Worth Killing by Peter Swanson
- The Woman in Cabin 10 by Ruth Ware
- The Killer Next Door by Alex Marwood

<u>THE TROPOHOLIC'S GUIDES:</u>

<u>UNIVERSAL ROMANCE TROPES</u>

Volume 1, The Tropoholic's Guide to Internal Romance Tropes

Volume 2, The Tropoholic's Guide to External Romance Tropes

Volume 3, The Tropoholic's Guide to Backstory Romance Tropes

Volume 4, The Tropoholic's Guide to Hook Romance Tropes

NOTE: I've chosen not to make future volumes in this series available as pre-orders because I'm committed to getting each book right instead of hurrying to meet a deadline.

If you'd like to be notified when the next volume goes on sale, please visit www.cindydees.com/tropes and sign up for my (rather infrequent) tropes newsletter.

<u>FICTION</u>

Second Shot, A Helen Warwick Thriller

Double Tap, A Helen Warwick Thriller

The Medusa Project

The Medusa Game

The Medusa Prophecy

The Medusa Affair

The Medusa Seduction

Medusa's Master

The Medusa Proposition

I've received and heard your requests (with great delight, I might add) for more books covering the tropes of specific genres of fiction.

I'm currently developing lists of tropes for what I expect will amount to a lot more Tropoholic's Guides covering tropes in genres including but not limited to:

- The Tropes of Spicy Romance
- Historical and Paranormal Romance Tropes
- Sweet, Clean & Wholesome, and Inspirational Romance Tropes
- Cozy Mystery Tropes
- Noir Mystery Tropes
- Crime Fiction Tropes
- Thriller Trope Volumes on:
- Psychological Thriller Tropes
- Crime & Legal Thrillers
- Spy & Political Thrillers
- Military & Action Thrillers
- Mystery & Paranormal Thrillers
- Sci-Fi Thrillers
- Fantasy Thrillers
- Horror Tropes
- Science Fiction Tropes
- Fantasy Tropes
- Paranormal Tropes
- Action/Adventure Tropes
- Melodrama Tropes

If I've missed any genres you'd like to see books on, please feel free to contact me at www.cindydees.com and let me know!

ABOUT THE AUTHOR

New York Times and USA Today bestselling author of over a hundred books, Cindy Dees has sold over two million books worldwide. She writes in a variety of genres, including thrillers, military adventure, romantic suspense, romance, fantasy, and alternate history. Cindy is also the creator and executive producer of an upcoming Netflix television series based on her Helen Warwick thriller novel series about a woman assassin.

2-time RITA winner, five-time RITA finalist, and 2-time Holt Medallion winner, she's also a 2-time winner of Romantic Times' Romantic Suspense of the Year Award and a Career Lifetime Achievement Award nominee from Romantic Times.

A former U.S. Air Force pilot and part-time spy, she draws upon real-life experience to fuel her stories of life (and sometimes love) on the edge of danger. Her social media links are at www.cindydees.com and www.cynthiadees.com.

www.ingramcontent.com/pod-product-compliance
Lightning Source LLC
Chambersburg PA
CBHW052014030426
42335CB00026B/3139